AFTER SCHOOL NIGHTMARE

Story and Art by
SETONA MIZUSHIRO

③

go!comi

Translation – Christine Schilling
Adaptation – Mallory Reaves
Lettering & Retouch –Eva Han
Production Manager – James Dashiell
Editor – Brynne Chandler

A Go! Comi manga

Published by Go! Media Entertainment, LLC

Houkago Hokenshitsu Volume 3
© SETONA MIZUSHIRO 2005
Originally published in Japan in 2005 by Akita Publishing Co., Ltd., Tokyo.
English translation rights arranged with Akita Publishing Co., Ltd.
through TOHAN CORPORATION, Tokyo.

Visit us online at www.gocomi.com
e-mail: info@gocomi.com

ISBN 978-1-933617-24-4

First printed in April 2007

2   3   4   5   6   7   8   9

Manufactured in the United States of America.

Koukoku Senior High School

Table of contents

Our Story So Far

Mashiro Ichijo is a high school student whose body is half female, and half male. One day, he's called down to a secret infirmary to participate in a special "class" he needs to graduate. He learns from another student, Kureha, that each person takes on their true form in this class. When each person reaches their personal goal, their most heart-felt dream will come true. Mashiro decides to use this class to become a true male.

But, when another dreamer – a merciless knight -- exposes Mashiro's secret, and everyone witnesses Kureha's tragic past, Mashiro begins to hate these "classes" that so cruelly open the wounds in people's hearts, and vows that he'll protect the weaker students, like Kureha.

Who is the real person behind the character who exposed his body's secret? He is trying to identify the other dreamers, when suddenly a guy student he's never gotten along with tells him "You're a girl!" and forces a kiss on him! How does Sou know the secret behind Mashiro's body? Could it be that Sou is another dreamer?

The newest member of the "class" is a giraffe who can see through everyone's dream-form! The student behind the giraffe, Shinonome, suddenly confronts Mashiro in school. He promises to identify the true person behind the knight – for a price...

Sou Mizuhashi

Mashiro Ichijo

The form she takes in the class

Kureha Fujishima

Participants in the Class

If you get a hold of the key, you can graduate.

Every time your heart takes damage, a bead on the cord breaks. When all three break, you are eliminated from the dream.

The Same Person?

Shinonome

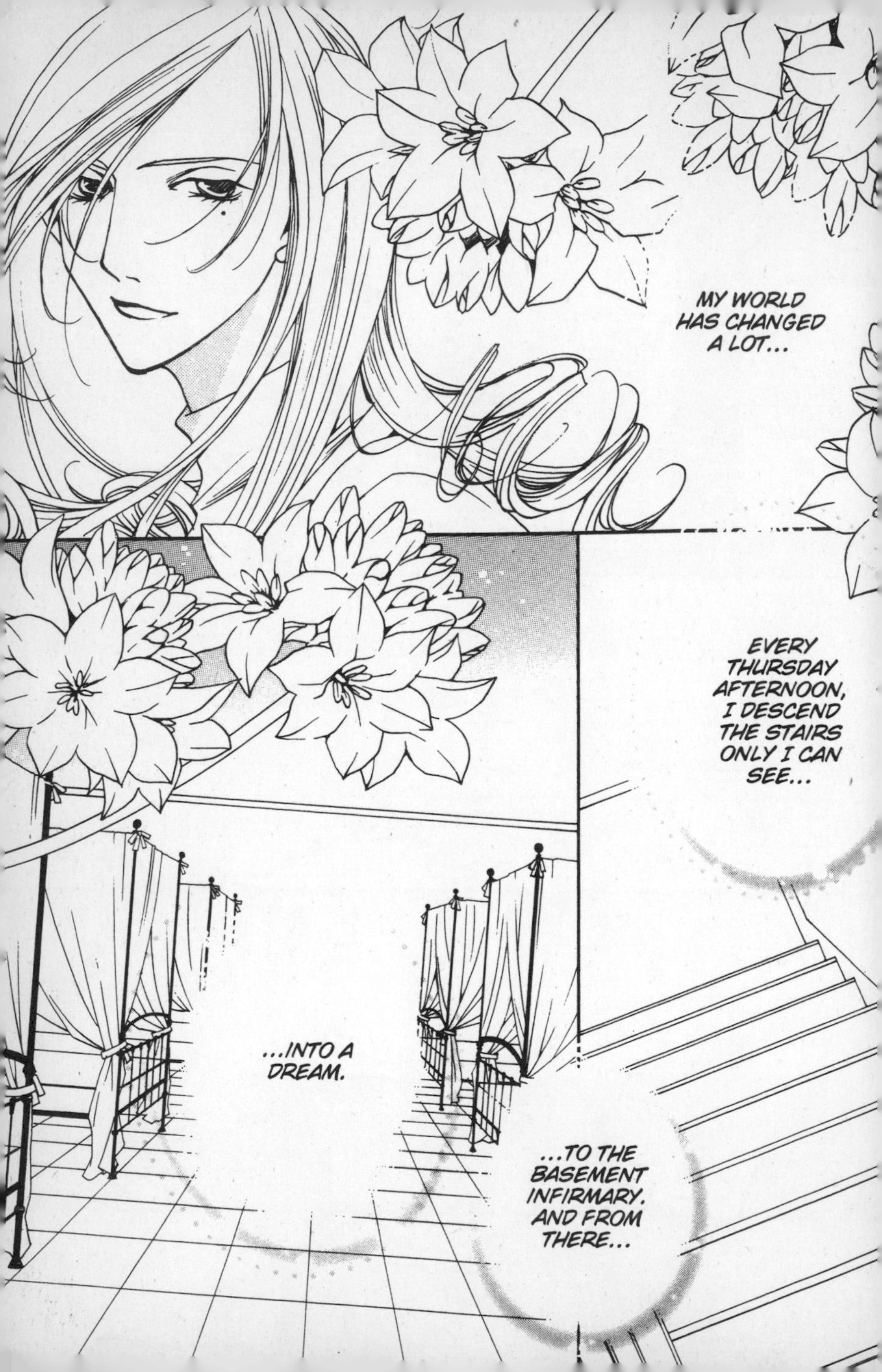
MY WORLD HAS CHANGED A LOT...
EVERY THURSDAY AFTERNOON, I DESCEND THE STAIRS ONLY I CAN SEE...
...TO THE BASEMENT INFIRMARY. AND FROM THERE...
...INTO A DREAM.

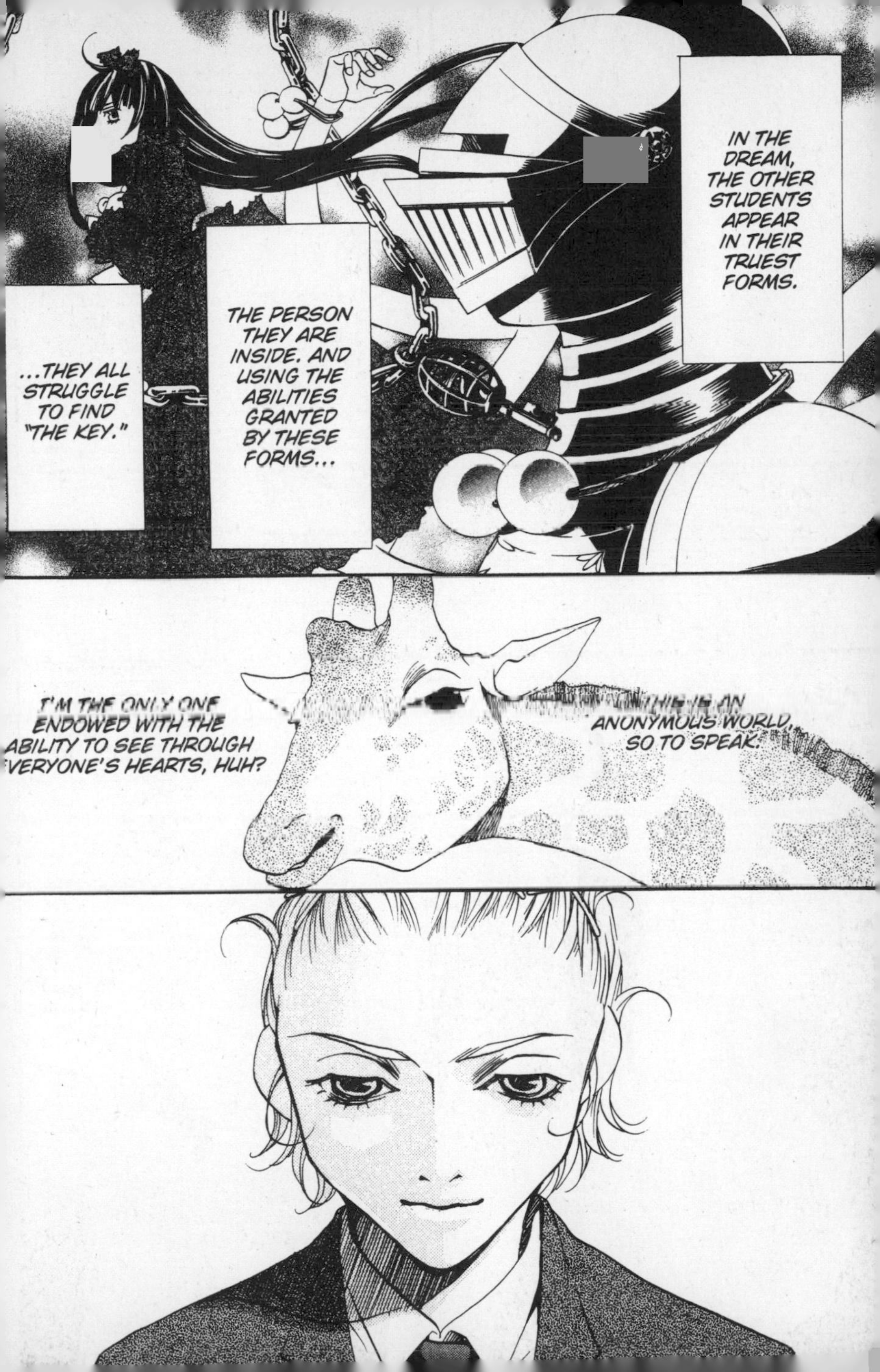
IN THE DREAM, THE OTHER STUDENTS APPEAR IN THEIR TRUEST FORMS.
THE PERSON THEY ARE INSIDE. AND USING THE ABILITIES GRANTED BY THESE FORMS...
...THEY ALL STRUGGLE TO FIND "THE KEY."
ANONYMOUS WORLD, SO TO SPEAK.
I'M THE ONLY ONE ENDOWED WITH THE ABILITY TO SEE THROUGH EVERYONE'S HEARTS, HUH?

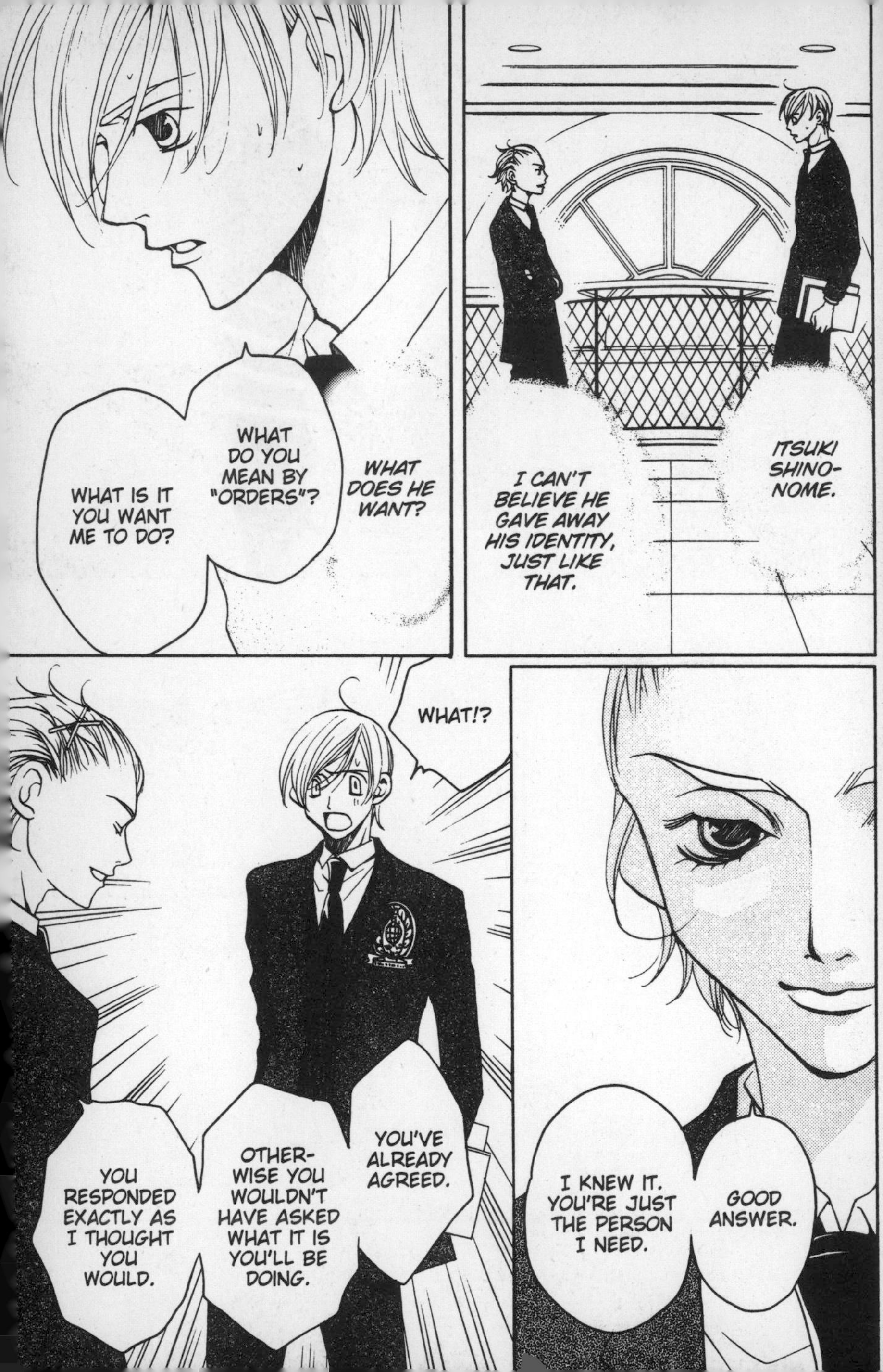
ITSUKI SHINONOME.
I CAN'T BELIEVE HE GAVE AWAY HIS IDENTITY, JUST LIKE THAT.
WHAT DOES HE WANT?
WHAT DO YOU MEAN BY "ORDERS"?
WHAT IS IT YOU WANT ME TO DO?
GOOD ANSWER.
I KNEW IT. YOU'RE JUST THE PERSON I NEED.
WHAT!?
YOU'VE ALREADY AGREED.
OTHERWISE YOU WOULDN'T HAVE ASKED WHAT IT IS YOU'LL BE DOING.
YOU RESPONDED EXACTLY AS I THOUGHT YOU WOULD.

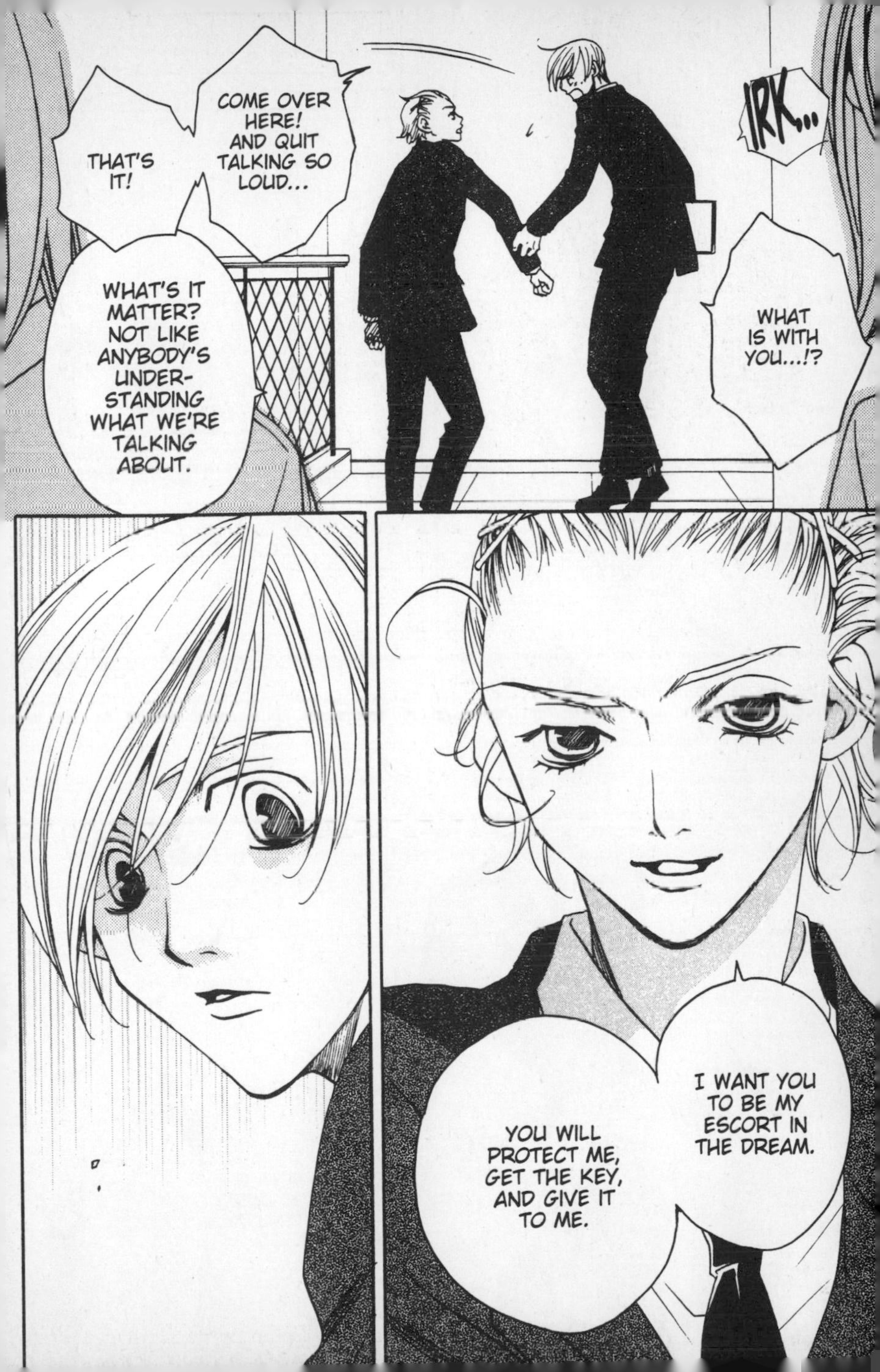
IRK...
COME OVER HERE! AND QUIT TALKING SO LOUD...
THAT'S IT!
WHAT IS WITH YOU...!?
WHAT'S IT MATTER? NOT LIKE ANYBODY'S UNDER-STANDING WHAT WE'RE TALKING ABOUT.
I WANT YOU TO BE MY ESCORT IN THE DREAM.
YOU WILL PROTECT ME, GET THE KEY, AND GIVE IT TO ME.

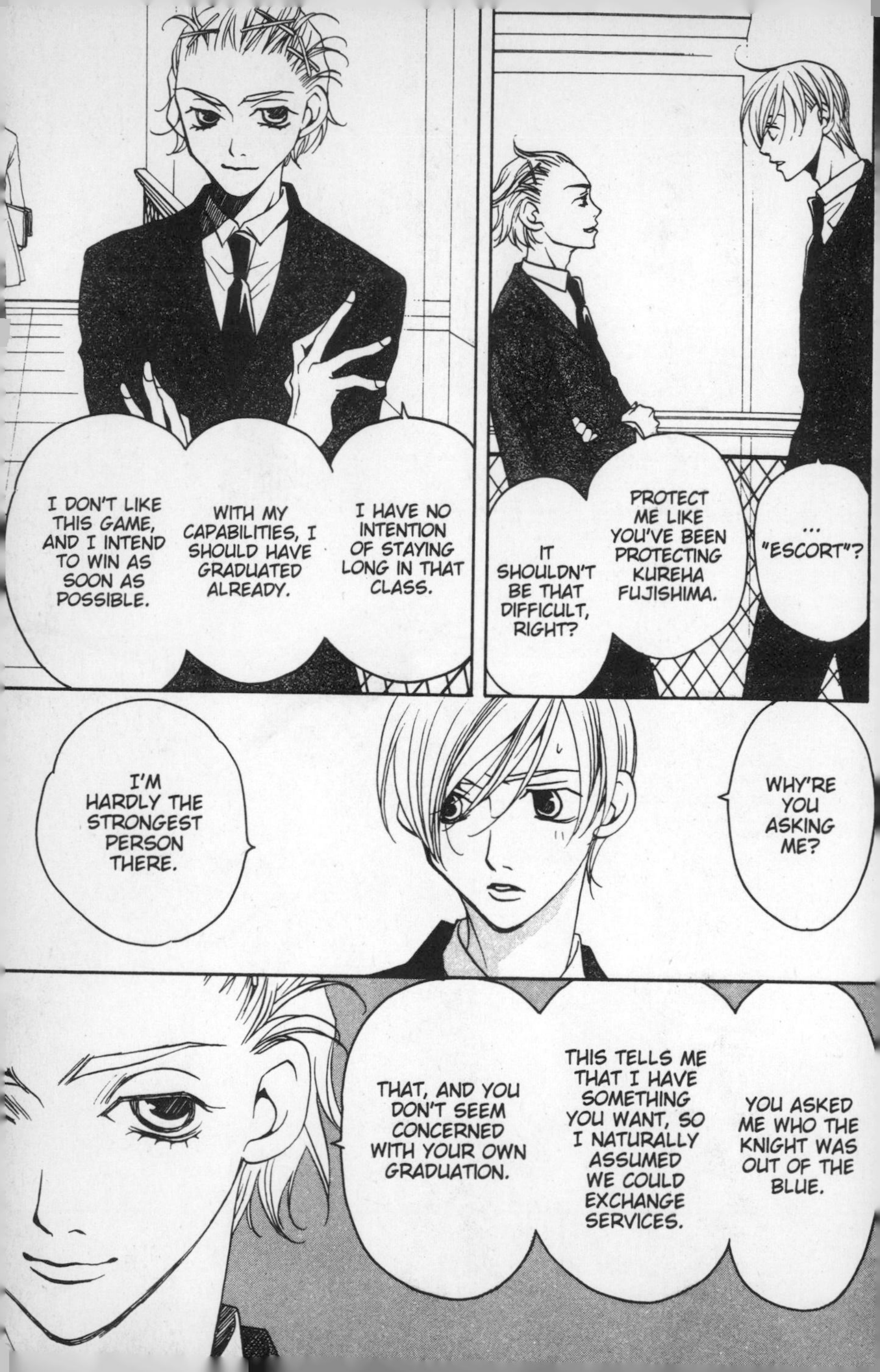

... "ESCORT"?
PROTECT ME LIKE YOU'VE BEEN PROTECTING KUREHA FUJISHIMA.
IT SHOULDN'T BE THAT DIFFICULT, RIGHT?
I HAVE NO INTENTION OF STAYING LONG IN THAT CLASS.
WITH MY CAPABILITIES, I SHOULD HAVE GRADUATED ALREADY.
I DON'T LIKE THIS GAME, AND I INTEND TO WIN AS SOON AS POSSIBLE.
WHY'RE YOU ASKING ME?
I'M HARDLY THE STRONGEST PERSON THERE.
YOU ASKED ME WHO THE KNIGHT WAS OUT OF THE BLUE.
THIS TELLS ME THAT I HAVE SOMETHING YOU WANT, SO I NATURALLY ASSUMED WE COULD EXCHANGE SERVICES.
THAT, AND YOU DON'T SEEM CONCERNED WITH YOUR OWN GRADUATION.

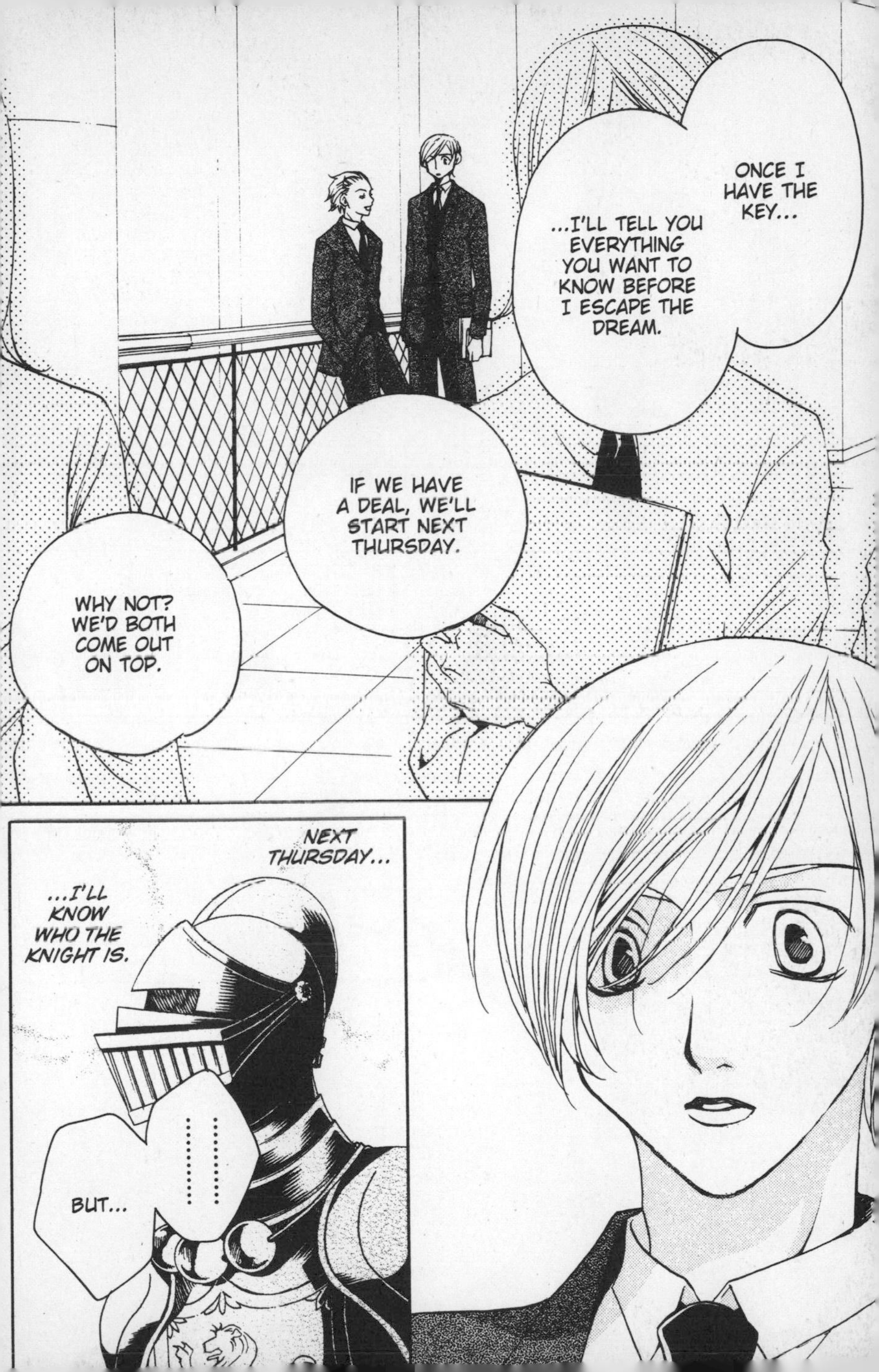
ONCE I HAVE THE KEY...
...I'LL TELL YOU EVERYTHING YOU WANT TO KNOW BEFORE I ESCAPE THE DREAM.
IF WE HAVE A DEAL, WE'LL START NEXT THURSDAY.
WHY NOT? WE'D BOTH COME OUT ON TOP.
NEXT THURSDAY...
...I'LL KNOW WHO THE KNIGHT IS.
......
BUT...

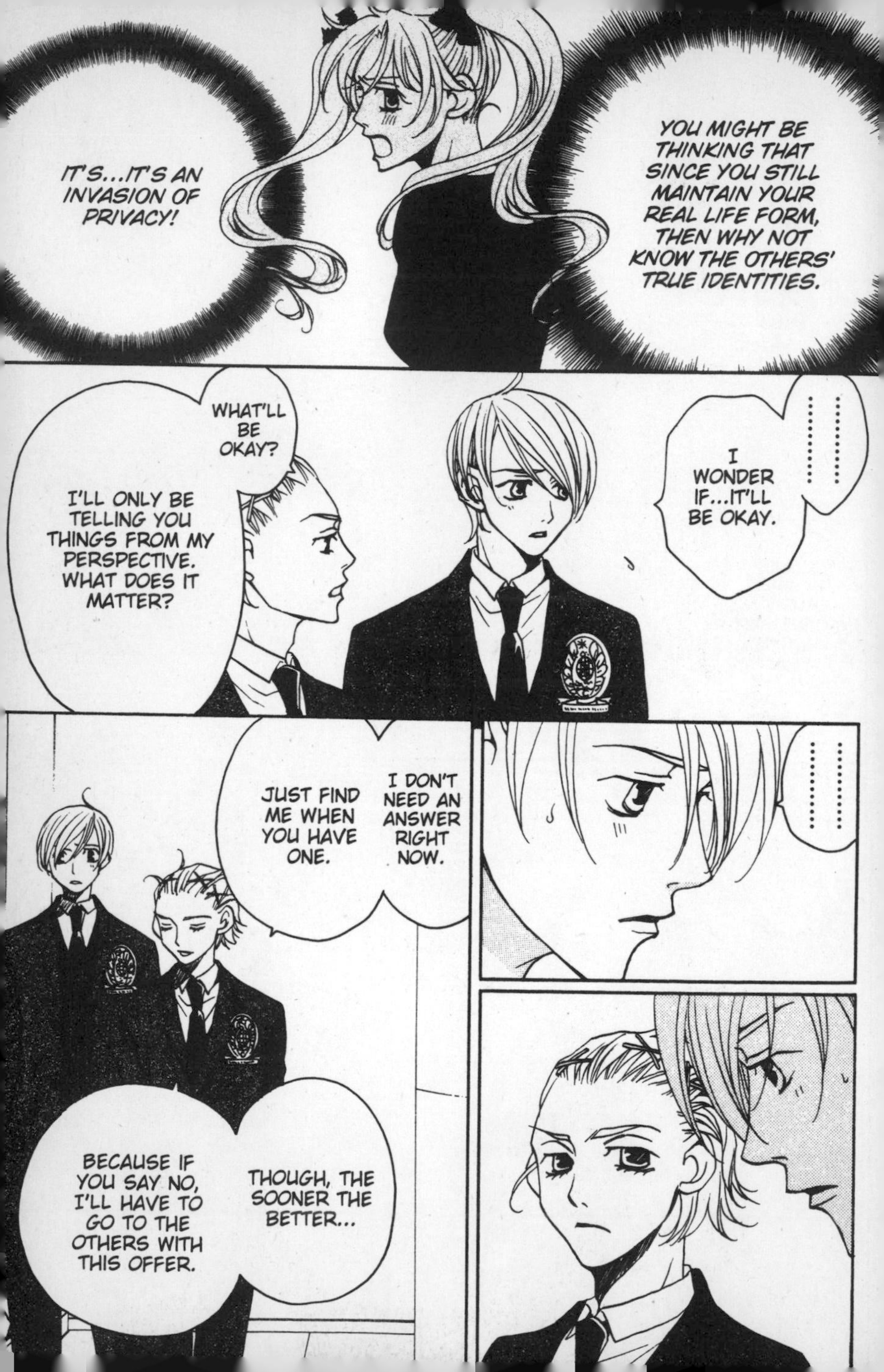
YOU MIGHT BE THINKING THAT SINCE YOU STILL MAINTAIN YOUR REAL LIFE FORM, THEN WHY NOT KNOW THE OTHERS' TRUE IDENTITIES.
IT'S...IT'S AN INVASION OF PRIVACY!
......
I WONDER IF...IT'LL BE OKAY.
WHAT'LL BE OKAY?
I'LL ONLY BE TELLING YOU THINGS FROM MY PERSPECTIVE. WHAT DOES IT MATTER?
......
I DON'T NEED AN ANSWER RIGHT NOW.
JUST FIND ME WHEN YOU HAVE ONE.
THOUGH, THE SOONER THE BETTER...
BECAUSE IF YOU SAY NO, I'LL HAVE TO GO TO THE OTHERS WITH THIS OFFER.

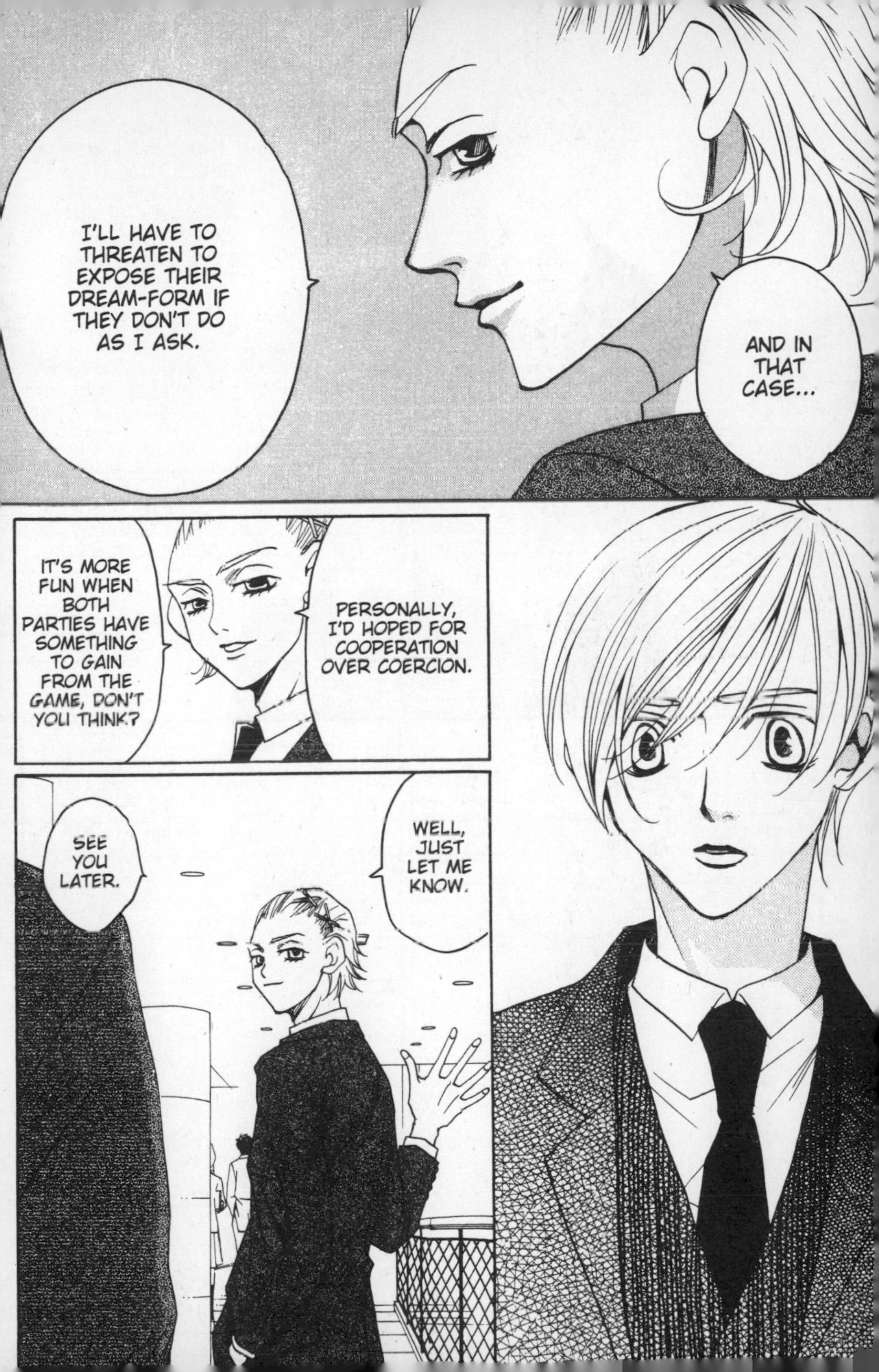
AND IN THAT CASE...
I'LL HAVE TO THREATEN TO EXPOSE THEIR DREAM-FORM IF THEY DON'T DO AS I ASK.
PERSONALLY, I'D HOPED FOR COOPERATION OVER COERCION.
IT'S MORE FUN WHEN BOTH PARTIES HAVE SOMETHING TO GAIN FROM THE GAME, DON'T YOU THINK?
WELL, JUST LET ME KNOW.
SEE YOU LATER.

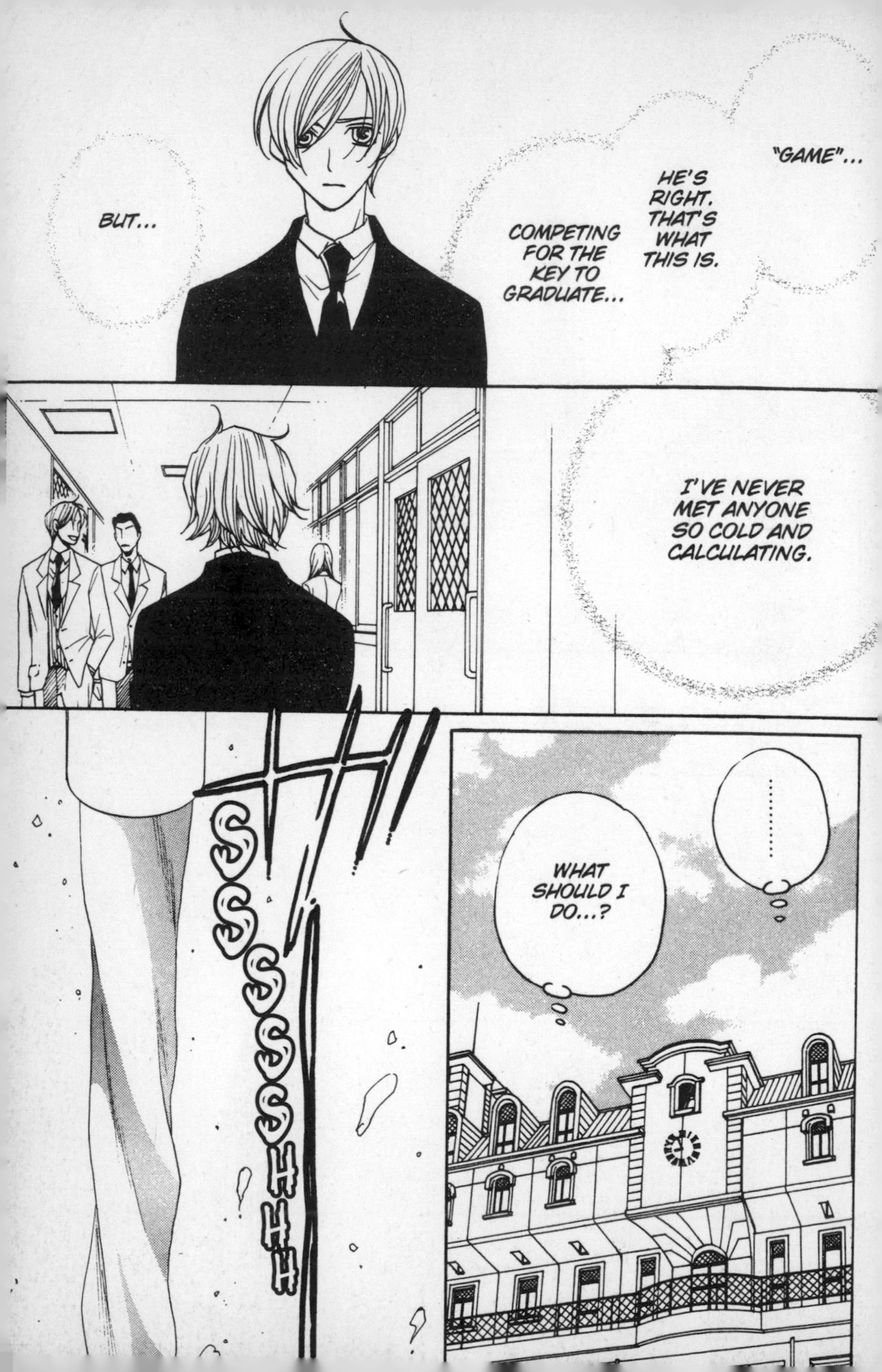
"GAME"...
HE'S RIGHT. THAT'S WHAT THIS IS.
COMPETING FOR THE KEY TO GRADUATE...
BUT...
I'VE NEVER MET ANYONE SO COLD AND CALCULATING.
......
WHAT SHOULD I DO...?
SSSSSHHH

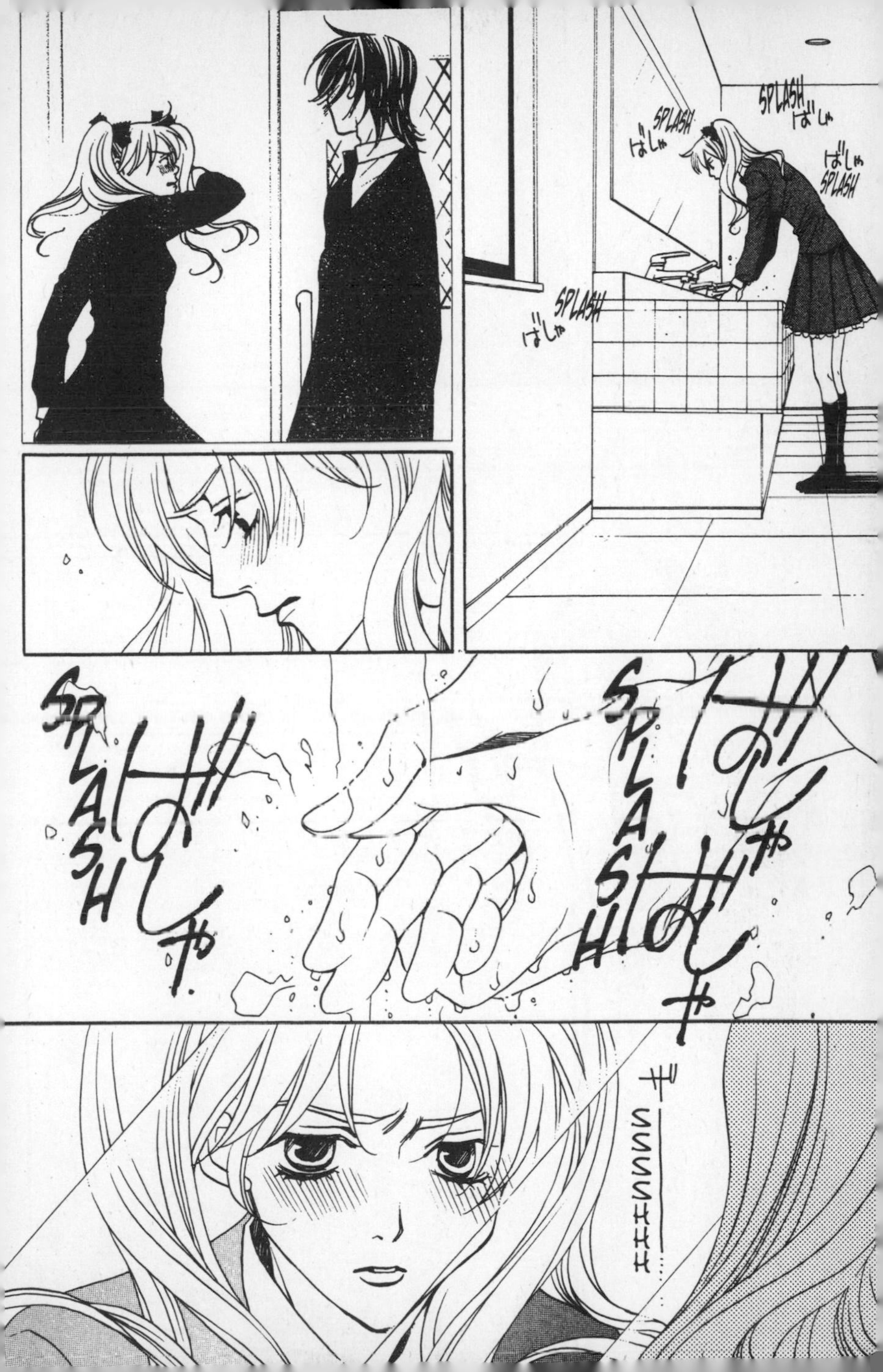
SPLASH
ばしゃ
SPLASH
ばしゃ
ばしゃ
SPLASH
SPLASH
ばしゃ
SPLASH
ばしゃ
SPLASH
ばしゃ
ギー

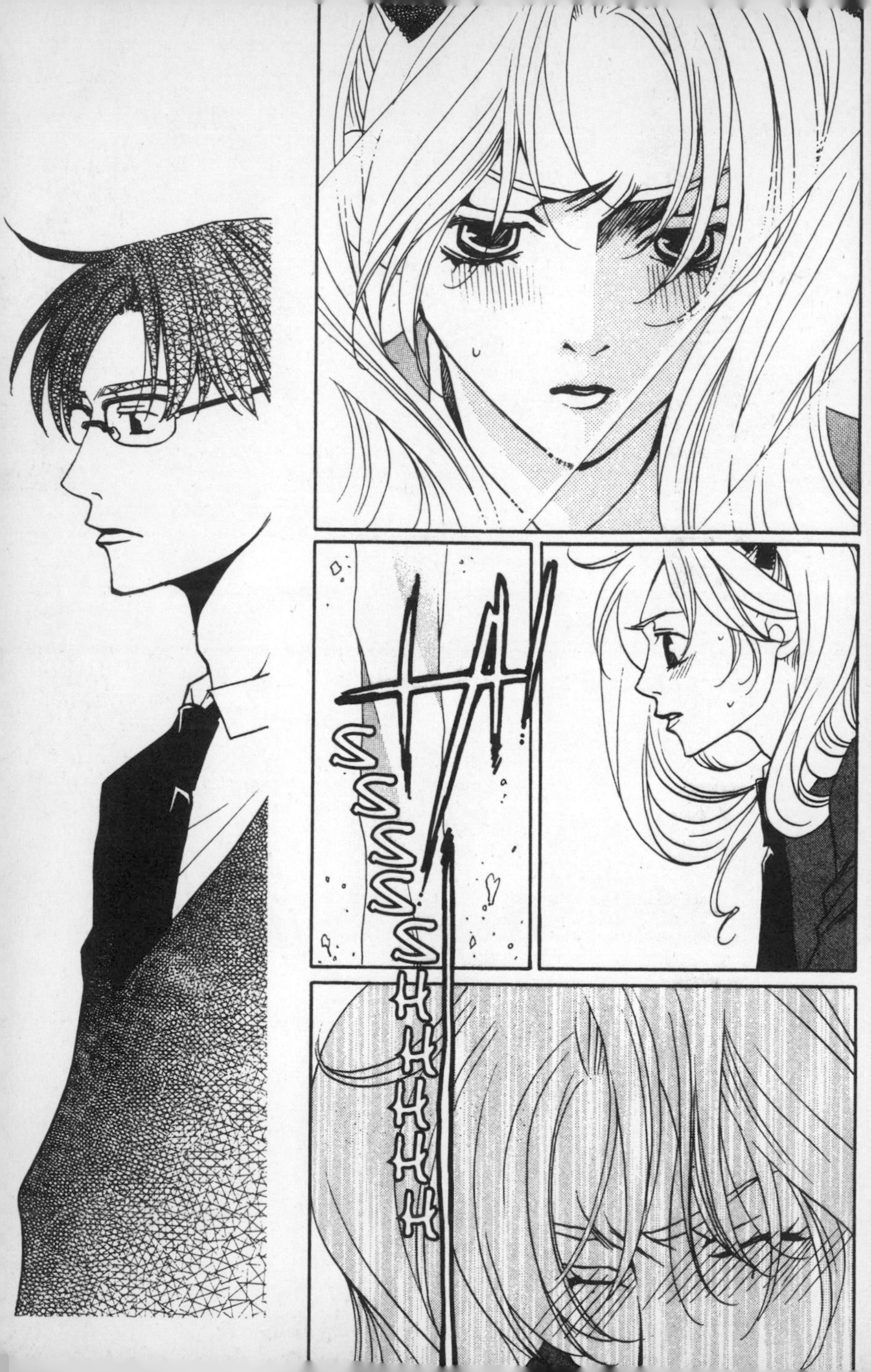
SSSSSHHHHH

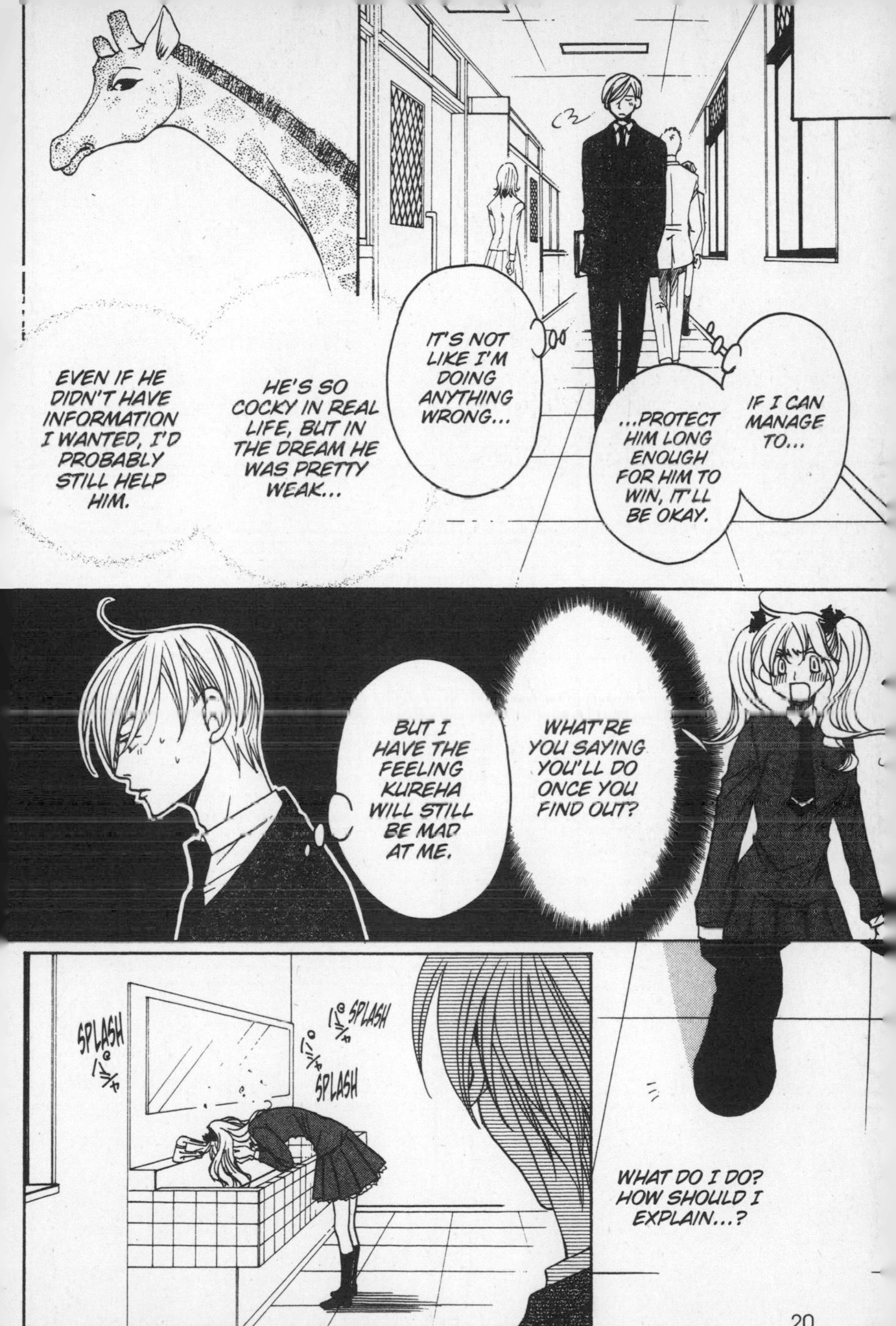
IF I CAN MANAGE TO...
...PROTECT HIM LONG ENOUGH FOR HIM TO WIN, IT'LL BE OKAY.
IT'S NOT LIKE I'M DOING ANYTHING WRONG...
HE'S SO COCKY IN REAL LIFE, BUT IN THE DREAM HE WAS PRETTY WEAK...
EVEN IF HE DIDN'T HAVE INFORMATION I WANTED, I'D PROBABLY STILL HELP HIM.
WHAT'RE YOU SAYING YOU'LL DO ONCE YOU FIND OUT?
BUT I HAVE THE FEELING KUREHA WILL STILL BE MAD AT ME.
WHAT DO I DO? HOW SHOULD I EXPLAIN...?
SPLASH
SPLASH
SPLASH

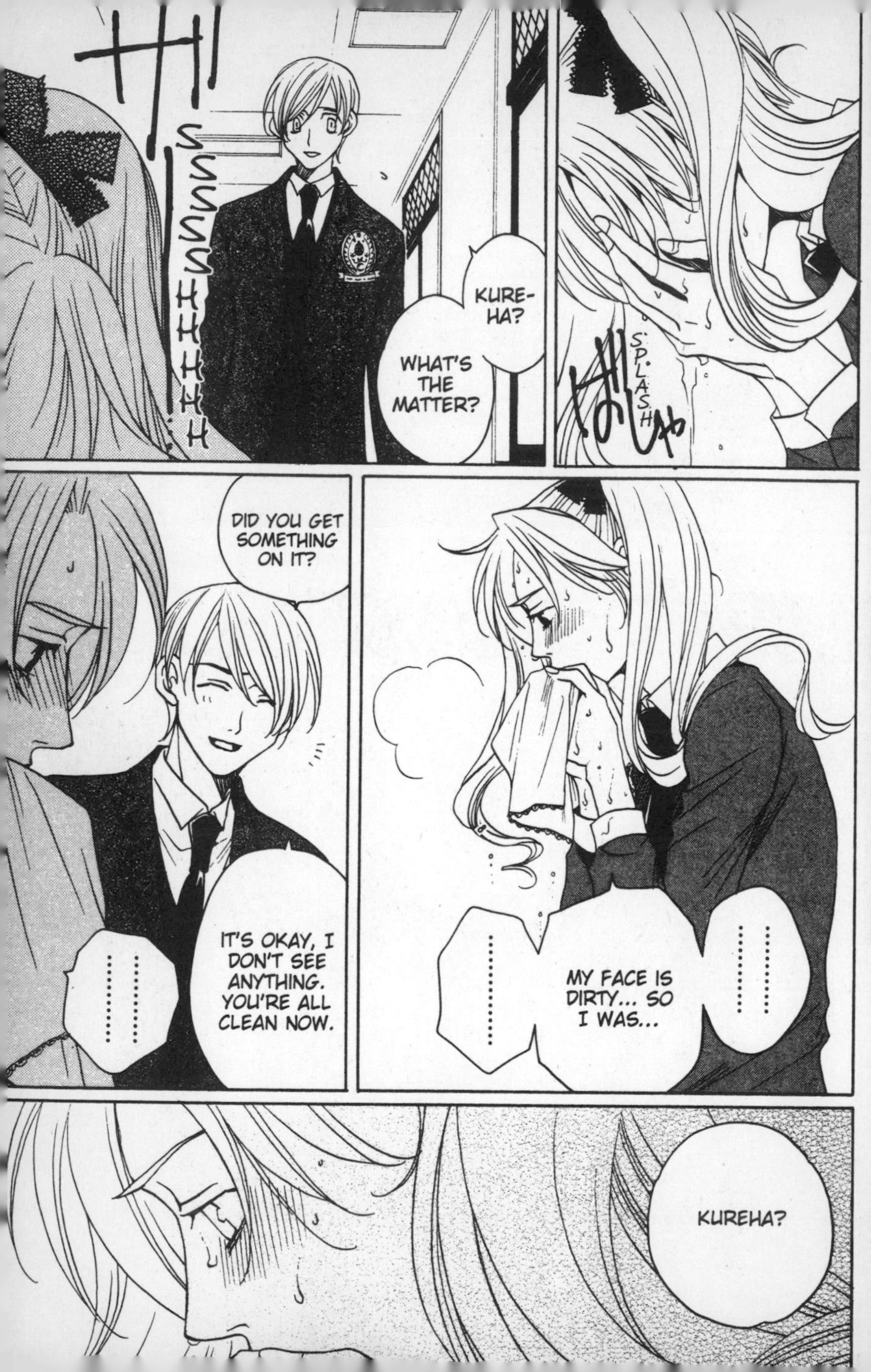
SPLASH
KURE-HA?
WHAT'S THE MATTER?
SSSSHHHHH
……
MY FACE IS DIRTY… SO I WAS…
……
DID YOU GET SOMETHING ON IT?
IT'S OKAY, I DON'T SEE ANYTHING. YOU'RE ALL CLEAN NOW.
……
KUREHA?

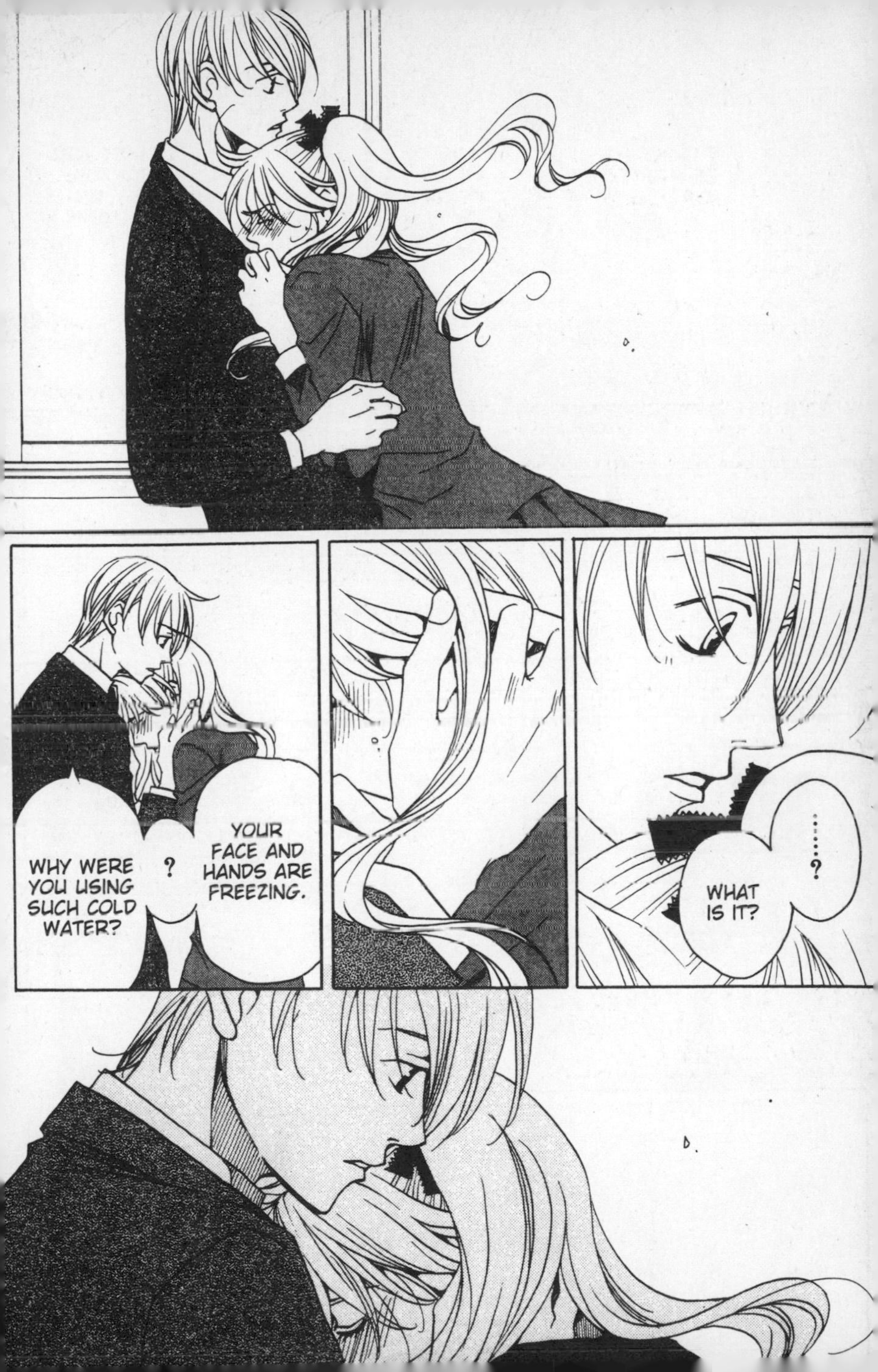

......?
WHAT IS IT?
YOUR FACE AND HANDS ARE FREEZING.
?
WHY WERE YOU USING SUCH COLD WATER?

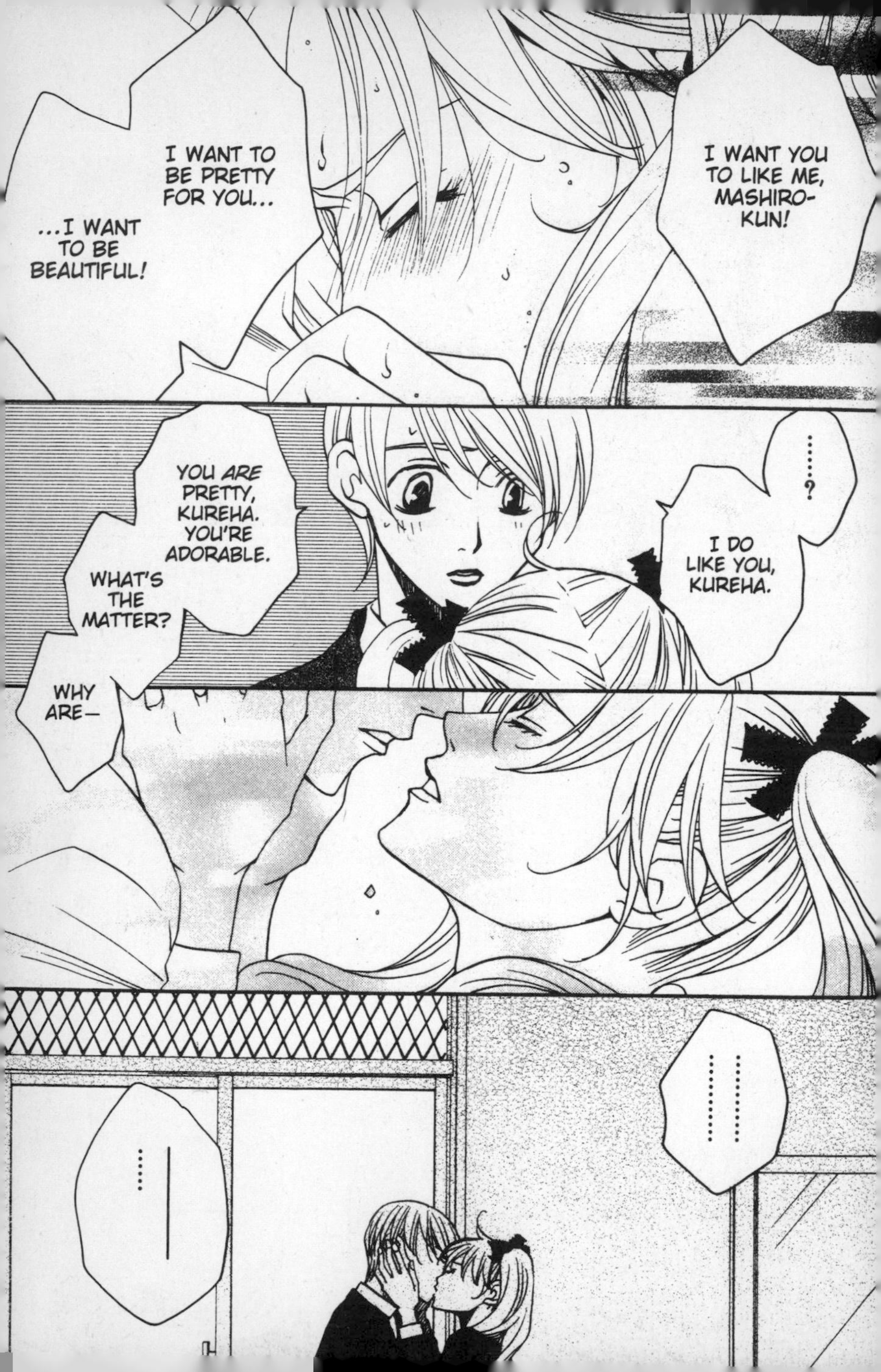
I WANT YOU TO LIKE ME, MASHIRO-KUN!
I WANT TO BE PRETTY FOR YOU...
...I WANT TO BE BEAUTIFUL!
......?
I DO LIKE YOU, KUREHA.
YOU ARE PRETTY, KUREHA. YOU'RE ADORABLE.
WHAT'S THE MATTER?
WHY ARE—
......!!
......!

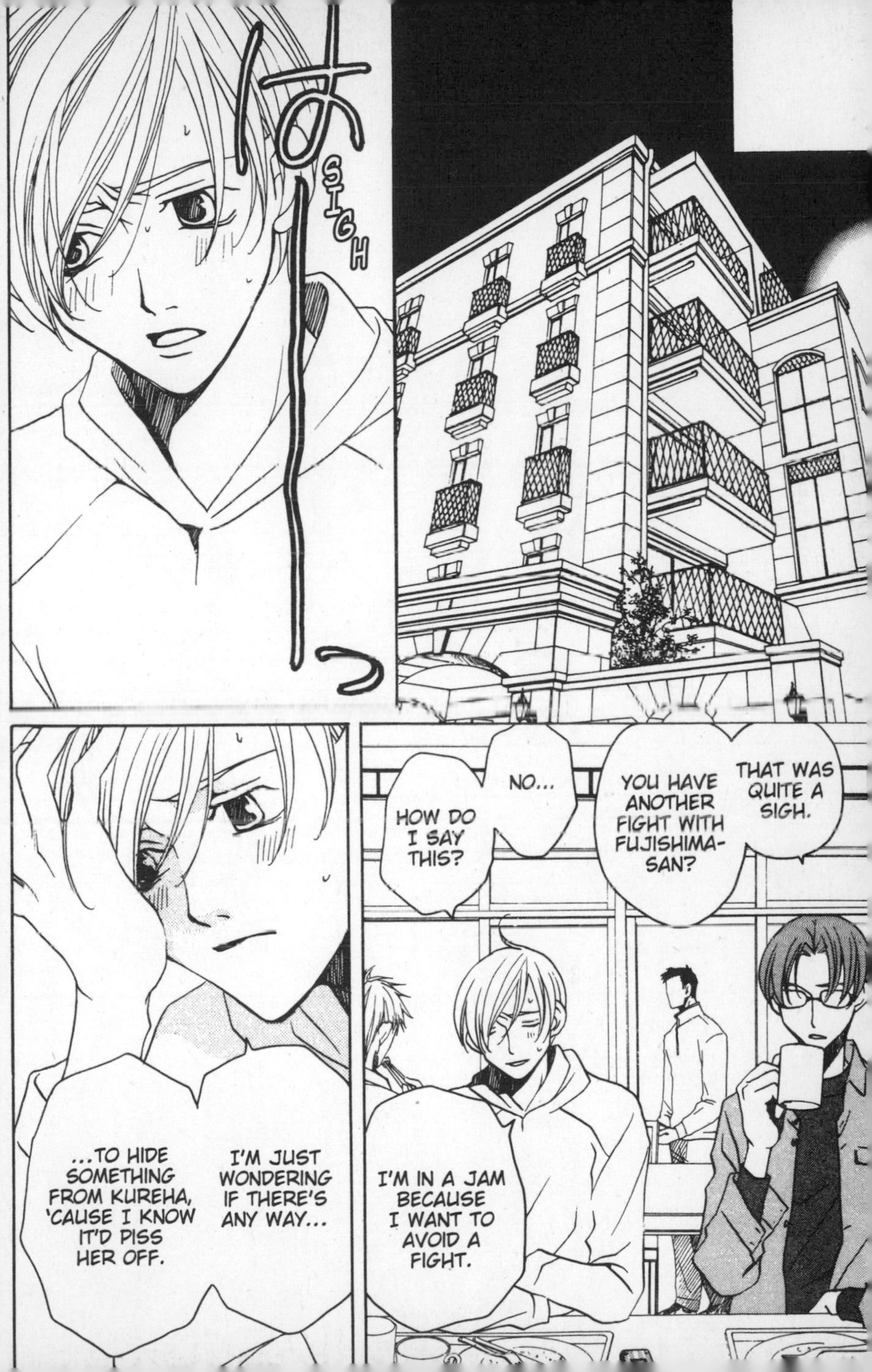
SIGH
THAT WAS QUITE A SIGH.
YOU HAVE ANOTHER FIGHT WITH FUJISHIMA-SAN?
NO...
HOW DO I SAY THIS?
I'M IN A JAM BECAUSE I WANT TO AVOID A FIGHT.
I'M JUST WONDERING IF THERE'S ANY WAY...
...TO HIDE SOMETHING FROM KUREHA, 'CAUSE I KNOW IT'D PISS HER OFF.

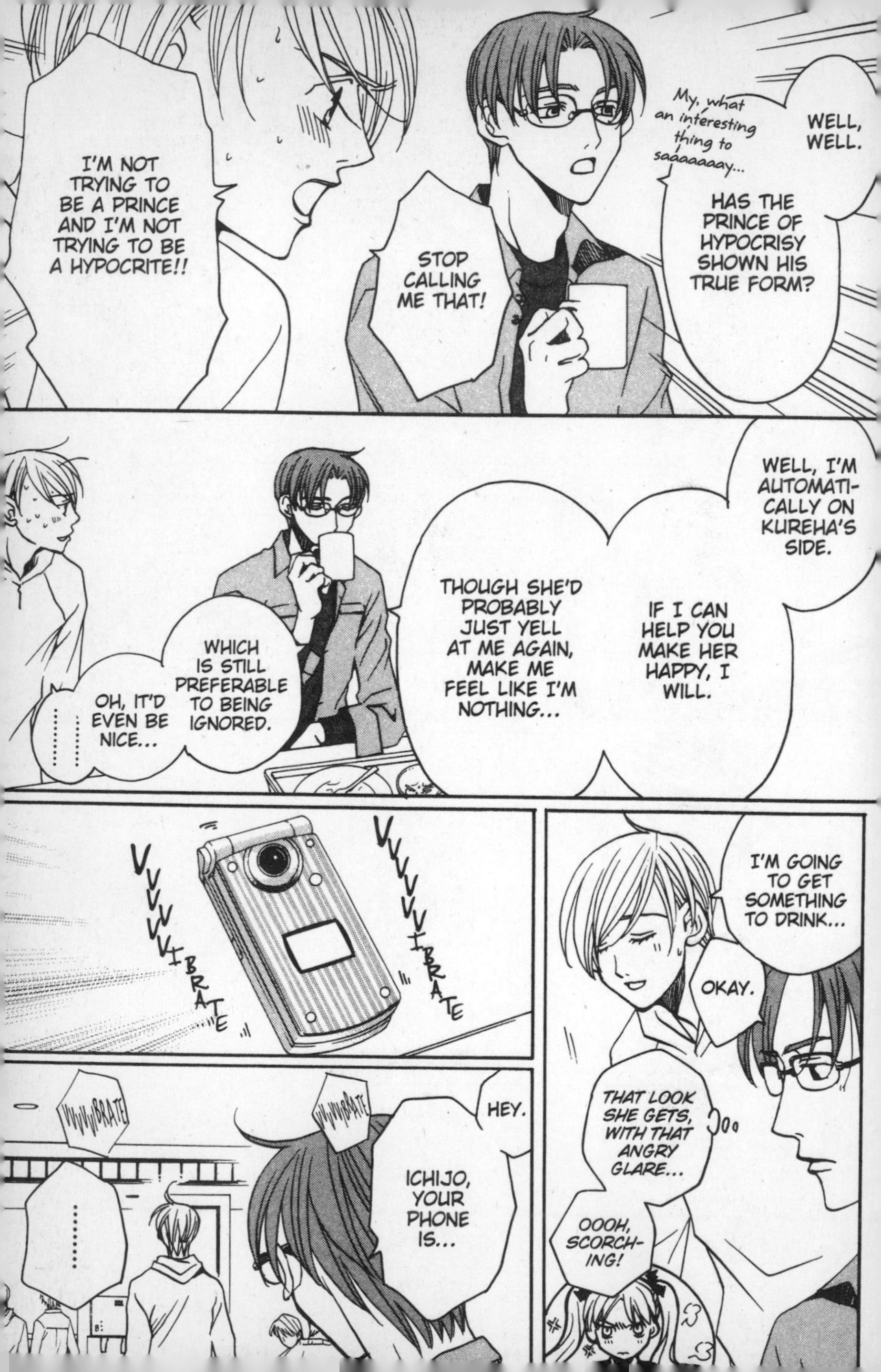
WELL, WELL.
My, what an interesting thing to saaaaaaay...
HAS THE PRINCE OF HYPOCRISY SHOWN HIS TRUE FORM?
STOP CALLING ME THAT!
I'M NOT TRYING TO BE A PRINCE AND I'M NOT TRYING TO BE A HYPOCRITE!!
WELL, I'M AUTOMATICALLY ON KUREHA'S SIDE.
IF I CAN HELP YOU MAKE HER HAPPY, I WILL.
THOUGH SHE'D PROBABLY JUST YELL AT ME AGAIN, MAKE ME FEEL LIKE I'M NOTHING...
WHICH IS STILL PREFERABLE TO BEING IGNORED.
OH, IT'D EVEN BE NICE...
......
I'M GOING TO GET SOMETHING TO DRINK...
OKAY.
THAT LOOK SHE GETS, WITH THAT ANGRY GLARE...
OOOH, SCORCHING!
VVVVVVVIBRATE
VVVVVIBRATE
VVVVVIBRATE
HEY.
ICHIJO, YOUR PHONE IS...
VVVVVIBRATE
......

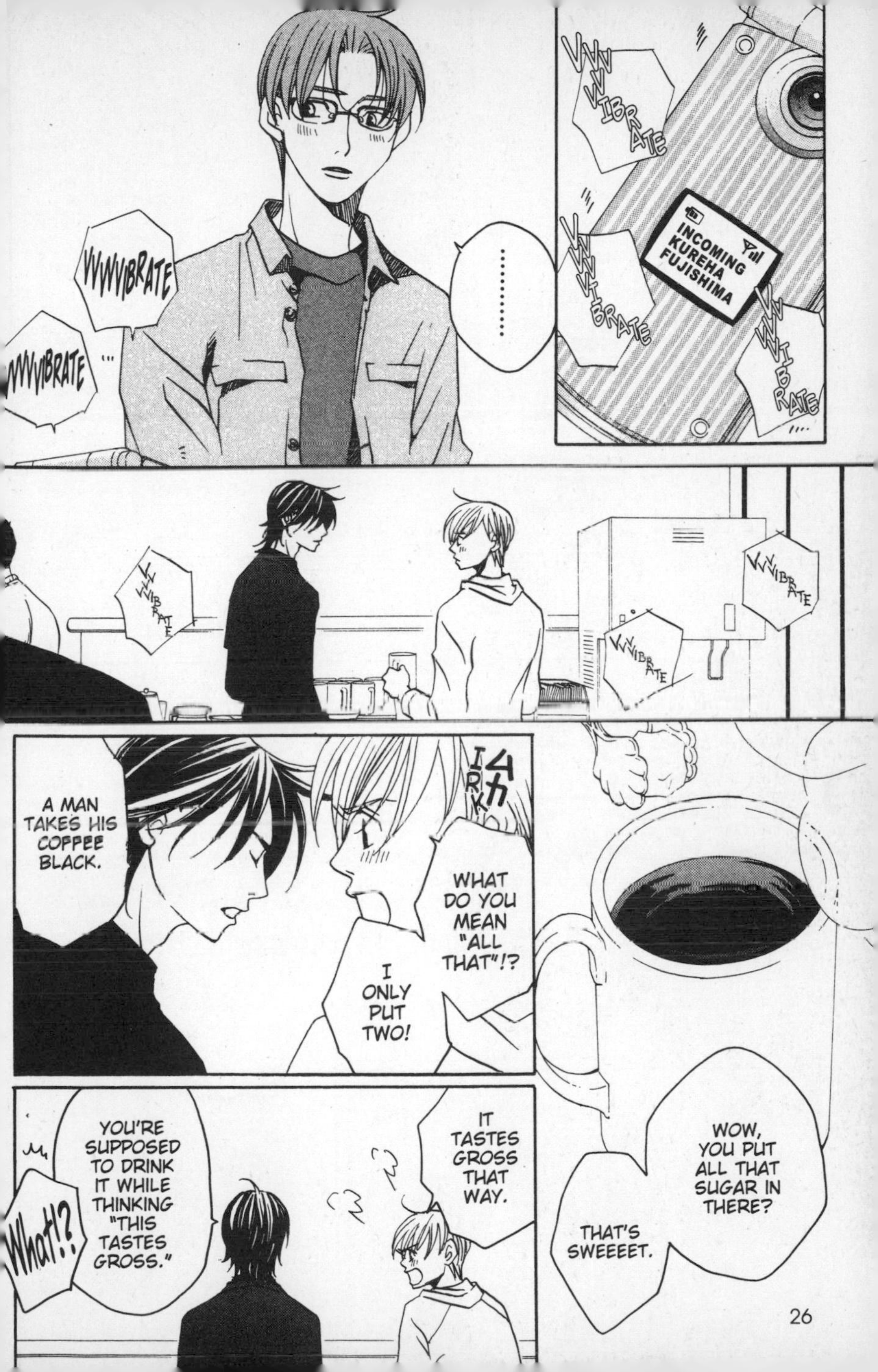
VVVVIBRATE
INCOMING KUREHA FUJISHIMA
VVVVIBRATE
VVVVIBRATE
......
VVVVIBRATE
VVVVIBRATE
VVVVIBRATE
VVVVIBRATE
VVVVIBRATE
WOW, YOU PUT ALL THAT SUGAR IN THERE?
THAT'S SWEEEET.
IRK
WHAT DO YOU MEAN "ALL THAT"!?
I ONLY PUT TWO!
A MAN TAKES HIS COFFEE BLACK.
IT TASTES GROSS THAT WAY.
YOU'RE SUPPOSED TO DRINK IT WHILE THINKING "THIS TASTES GROSS."
What!?

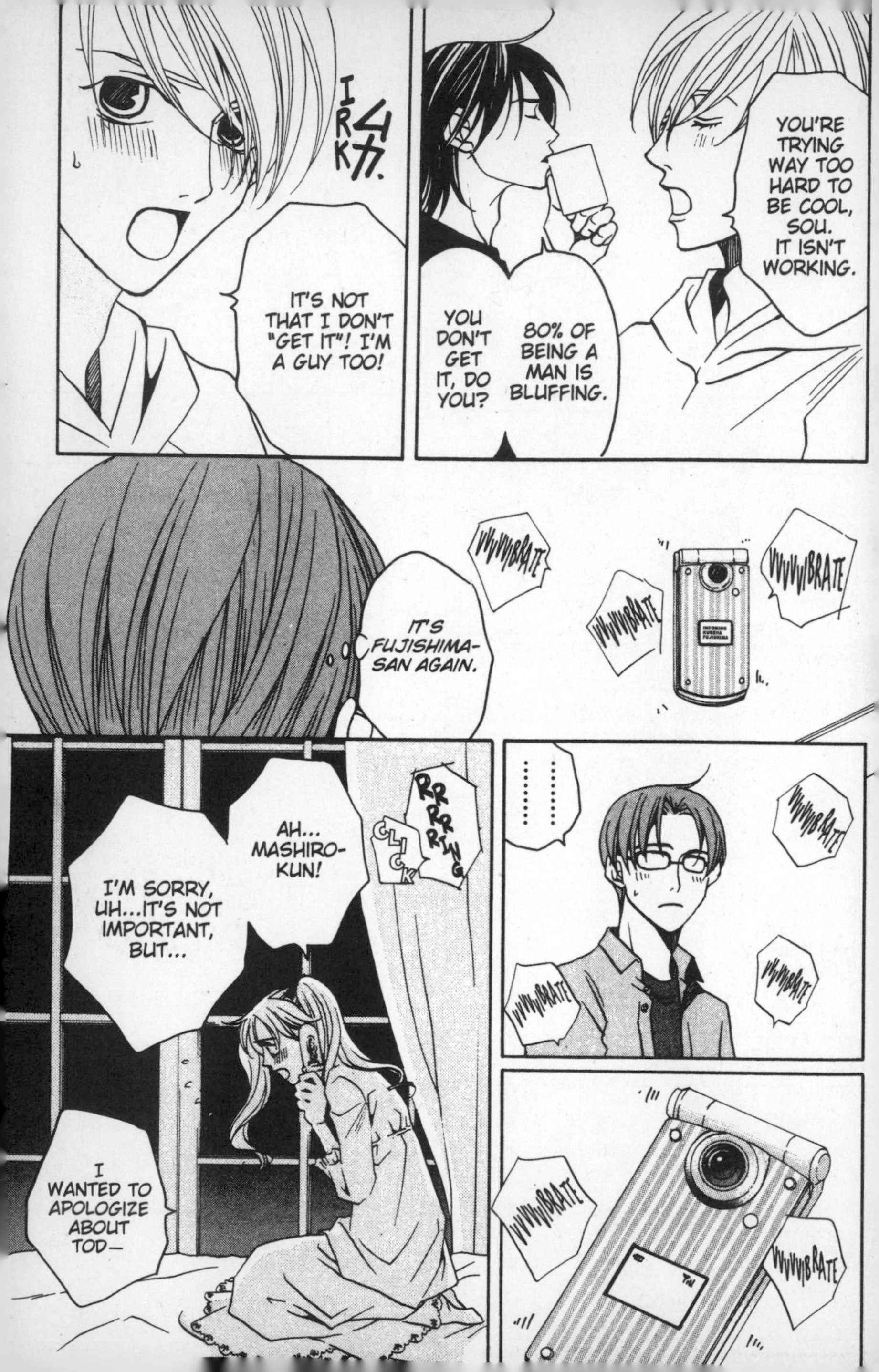
YOU'RE TRYING WAY TOO HARD TO BE COOL, SOU. IT ISN'T WORKING.
80% OF BEING A MAN IS BLUFFING.
YOU DON'T GET IT, DO YOU?
IRK
IT'S NOT THAT I DON'T "GET IT"! I'M A GUY TOO!
VVVVVIBRATE
VVVVVIBRATE
INCOMING KUREHA FUJISHIMA
VVVVVIBRATE
IT'S FUJISHIMA-SAN AGAIN.
......
VVVVVIBRATE
VVVVVIBRATE
VVVVVIBRATE
VVVVVIBRATE
VVVVVIBRATE
RRRRRRING
CLICK
AH... MASHIRO-KUN!
I'M SORRY, UH...IT'S NOT IMPORTANT, BUT...
I WANTED TO APOLOGIZE ABOUT TOD—

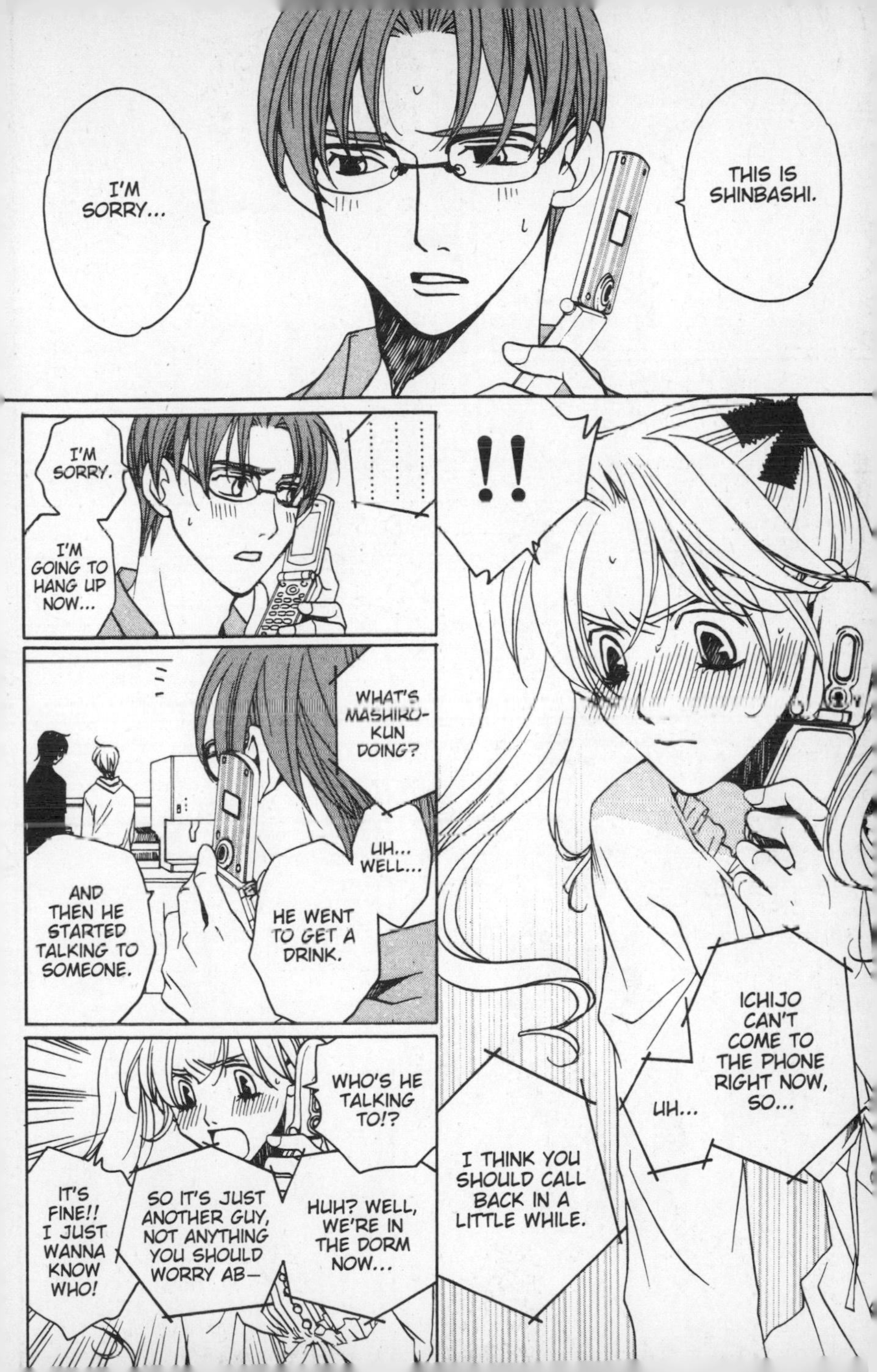
THIS IS SHINBASHI.
I'M SORRY...
!!
ICHIJO CAN'T COME TO THE PHONE RIGHT NOW, SO...
UH...
I THINK YOU SHOULD CALL BACK IN A LITTLE WHILE.
I'M SORRY.
I'M GOING TO HANG UP NOW...
WHAT'S MASHIRO-KUN DOING?
UH... WELL...
HE WENT TO GET A DRINK.
AND THEN HE STARTED TALKING TO SOMEONE.
WHO'S HE TALKING TO!?
HUH? WELL, WE'RE IN THE DORM NOW...
SO IT'S JUST ANOTHER GUY, NOT ANYTHING YOU SHOULD WORRY AB—
IT'S FINE!! I JUST WANNA KNOW WHO!

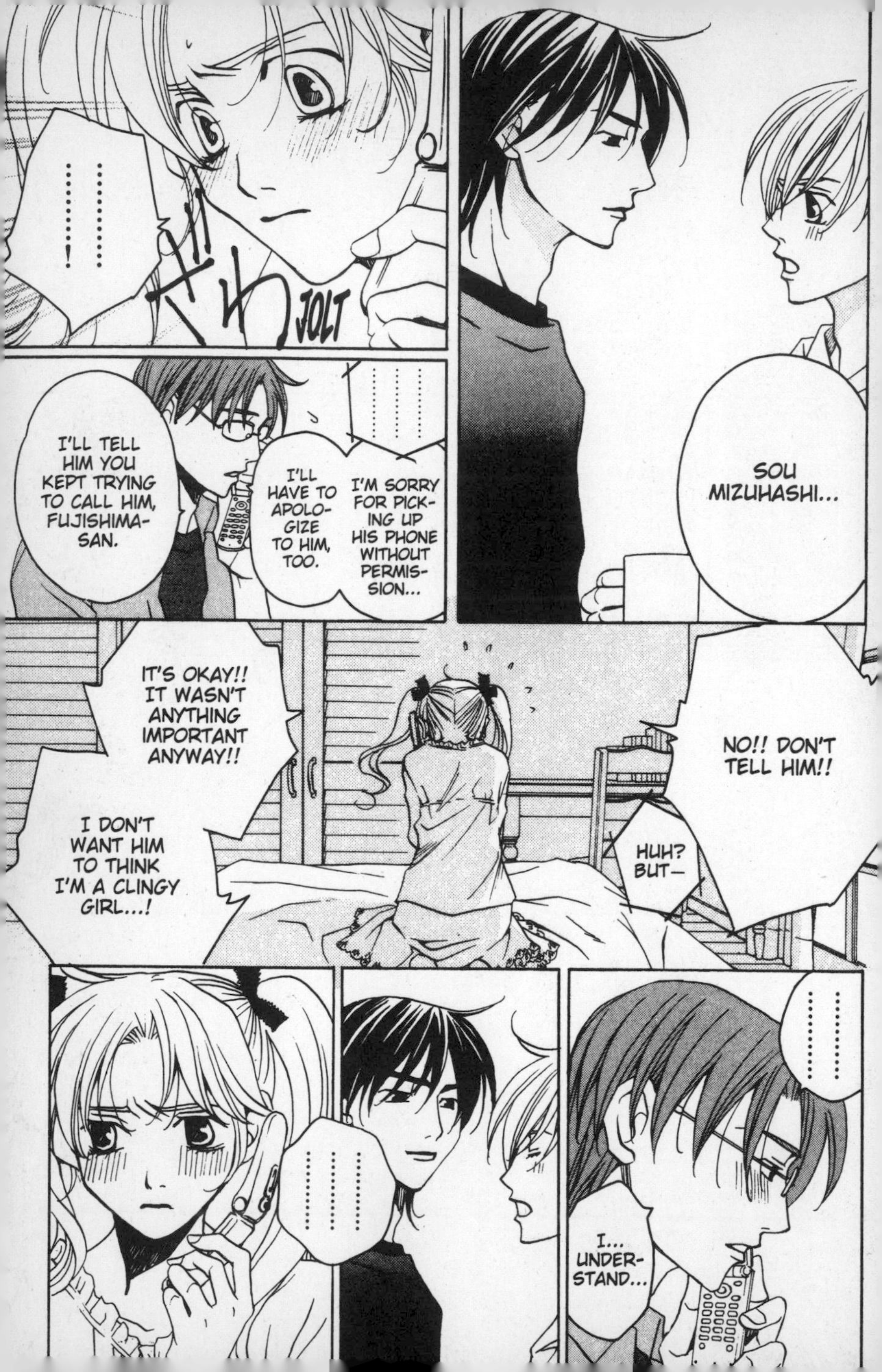
SOU MIZUHASHI...
......!
JOLT
......
I'M SORRY FOR PICKING UP HIS PHONE WITHOUT PERMISSION...
I'LL HAVE TO APOLOGIZE TO HIM, TOO.
I'LL TELL HIM YOU KEPT TRYING TO CALL HIM, FUJISHIMA-SAN.
NO!! DON'T TELL HIM!!
HUH? BUT—
IT'S OKAY!! IT WASN'T ANYTHING IMPORTANT ANYWAY!!
I DON'T WANT HIM TO THINK I'M A CLINGY GIRL...!
......
I... UNDERSTAND...
......

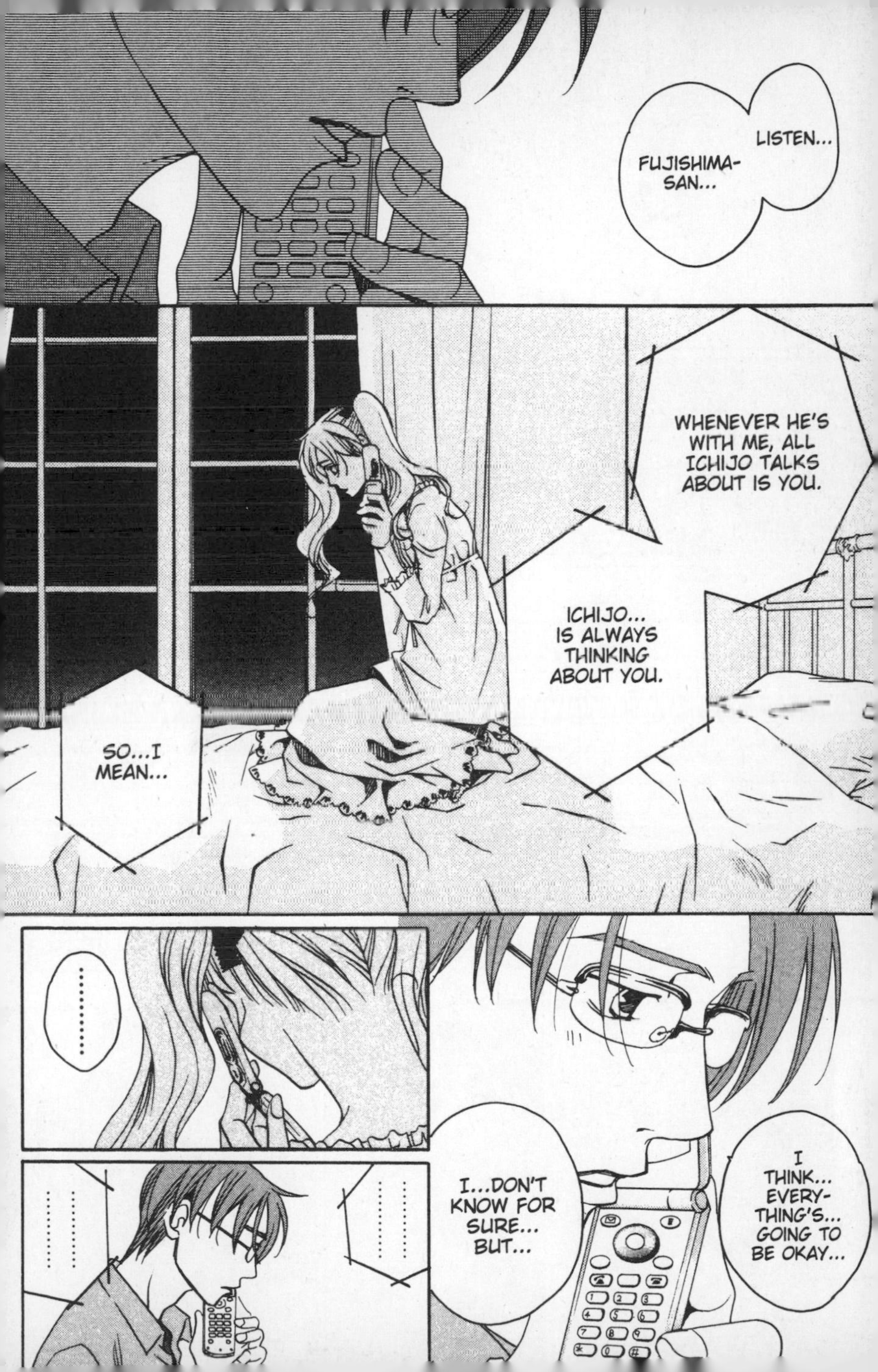
LISTEN...
FUJISHIMA-SAN...
WHENEVER HE'S WITH ME, ALL ICHIJO TALKS ABOUT IS YOU.
ICHIJO... IS ALWAYS THINKING ABOUT YOU.
SO...I MEAN...
I...DON'T KNOW FOR SURE... BUT...
I THINK... EVERY-THING'S... GOING TO BE OKAY...
......
......
......

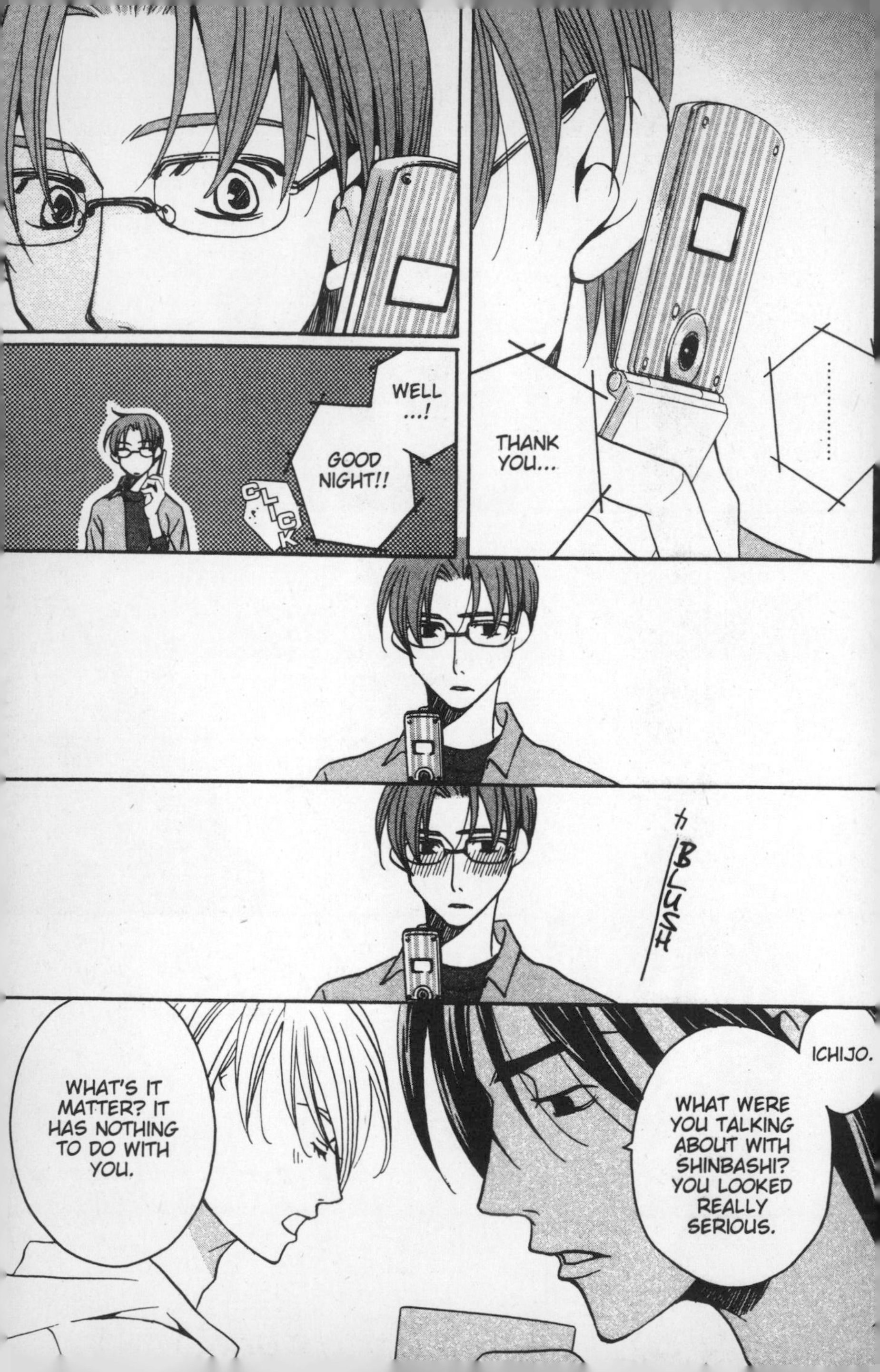
THANK YOU...
......
WELL ...!
GOOD NIGHT!!
CLICK
BLUSH
ICHIJO.
WHAT WERE YOU TALKING ABOUT WITH SHINBASHI? YOU LOOKED REALLY SERIOUS.
WHAT'S IT MATTER? IT HAS NOTHING TO DO WITH YOU.

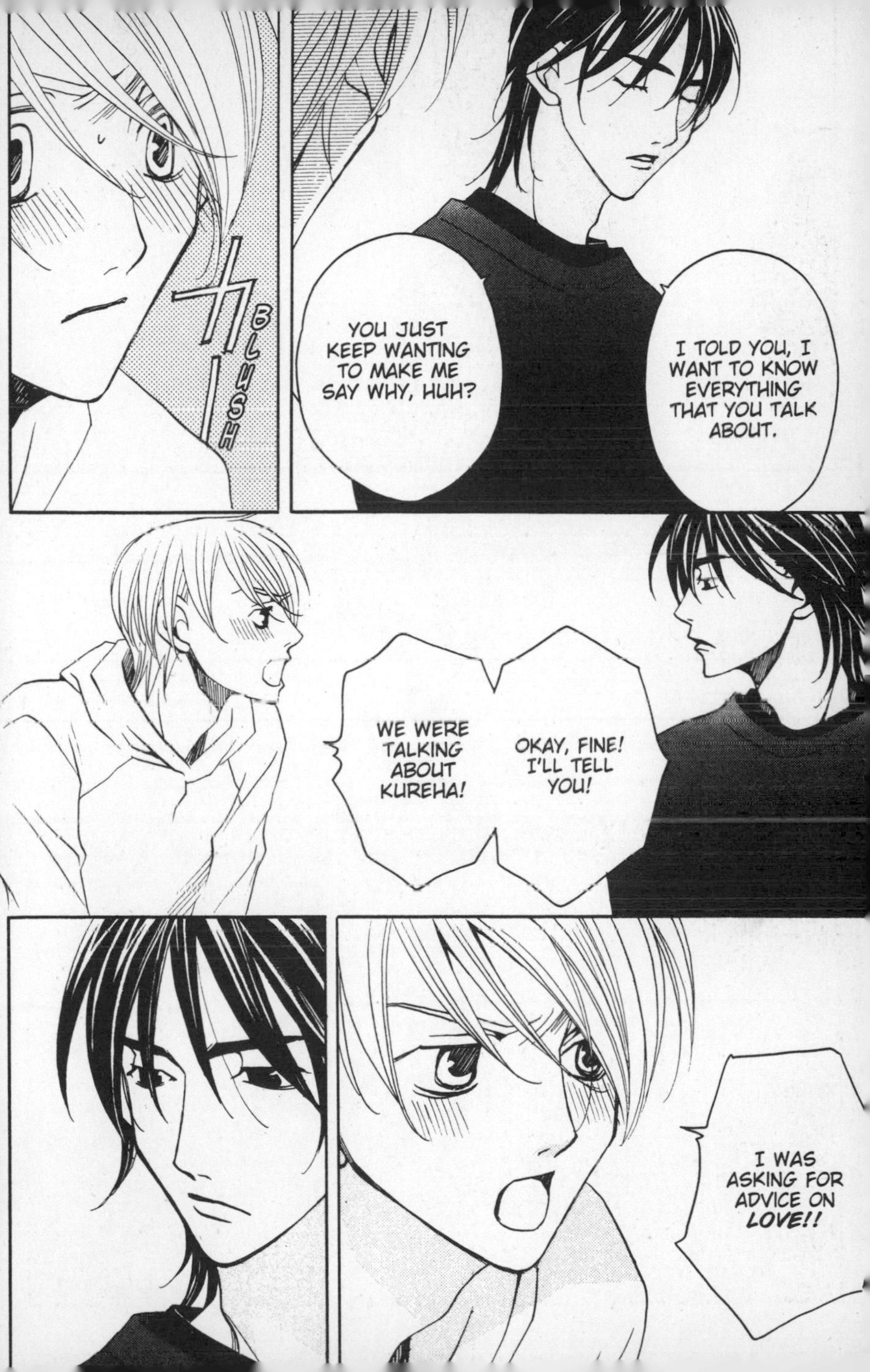
I TOLD YOU, I WANT TO KNOW EVERYTHING THAT YOU TALK ABOUT.
YOU JUST KEEP WANTING TO MAKE ME SAY WHY, HUH?
BLUSH
OKAY, FINE! I'LL TELL YOU!
WE WERE TALKING ABOUT KUREHA!
I WAS ASKING FOR ADVICE ON *LOVE!!*

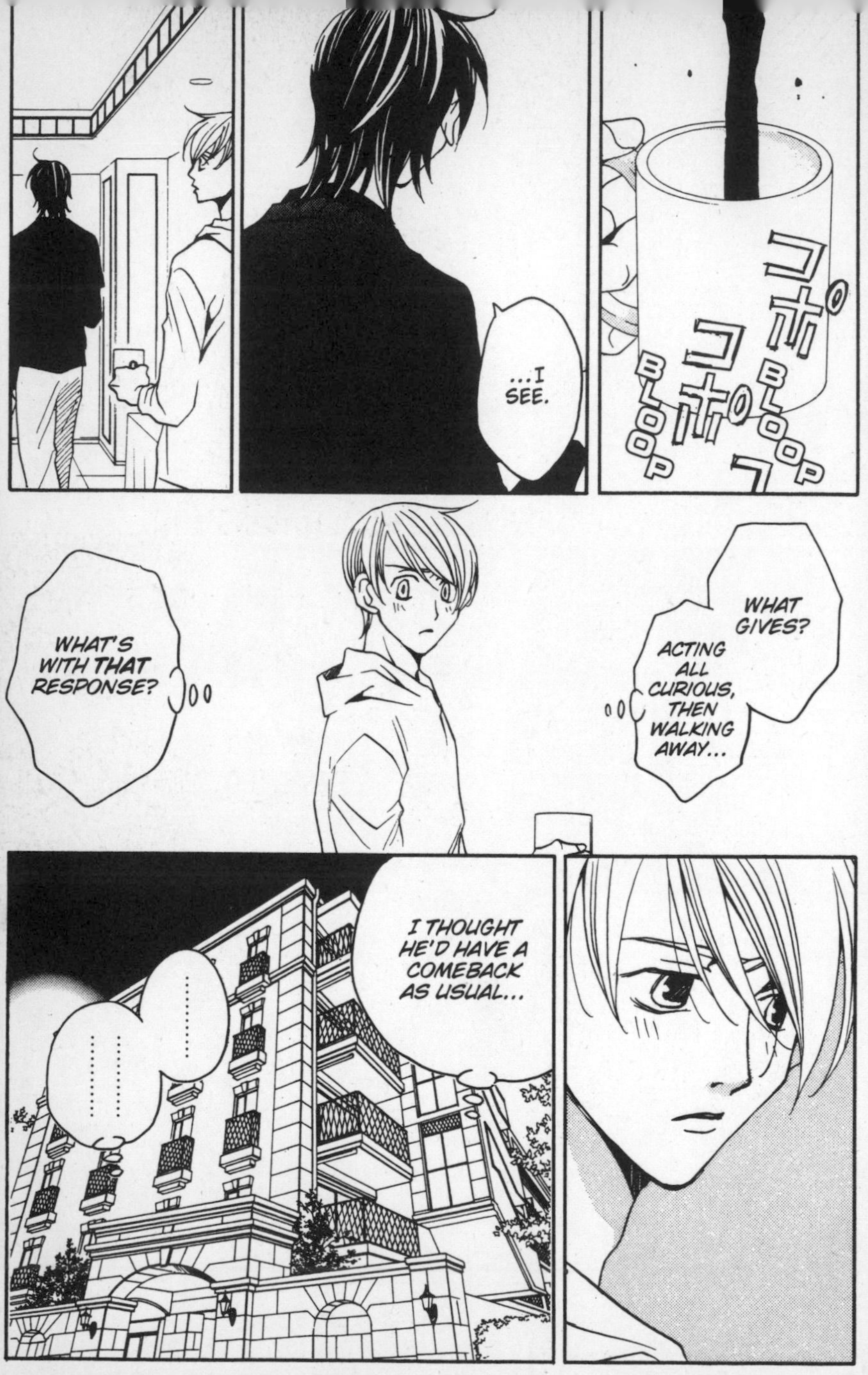
コポコポ
BLOOP BLOOP
...I SEE.
WHAT GIVES? ACTING ALL CURIOUS, THEN WALKING AWAY...
WHAT'S WITH THAT RESPONSE?
I THOUGHT HE'D HAVE A COMEBACK AS USUAL...
......

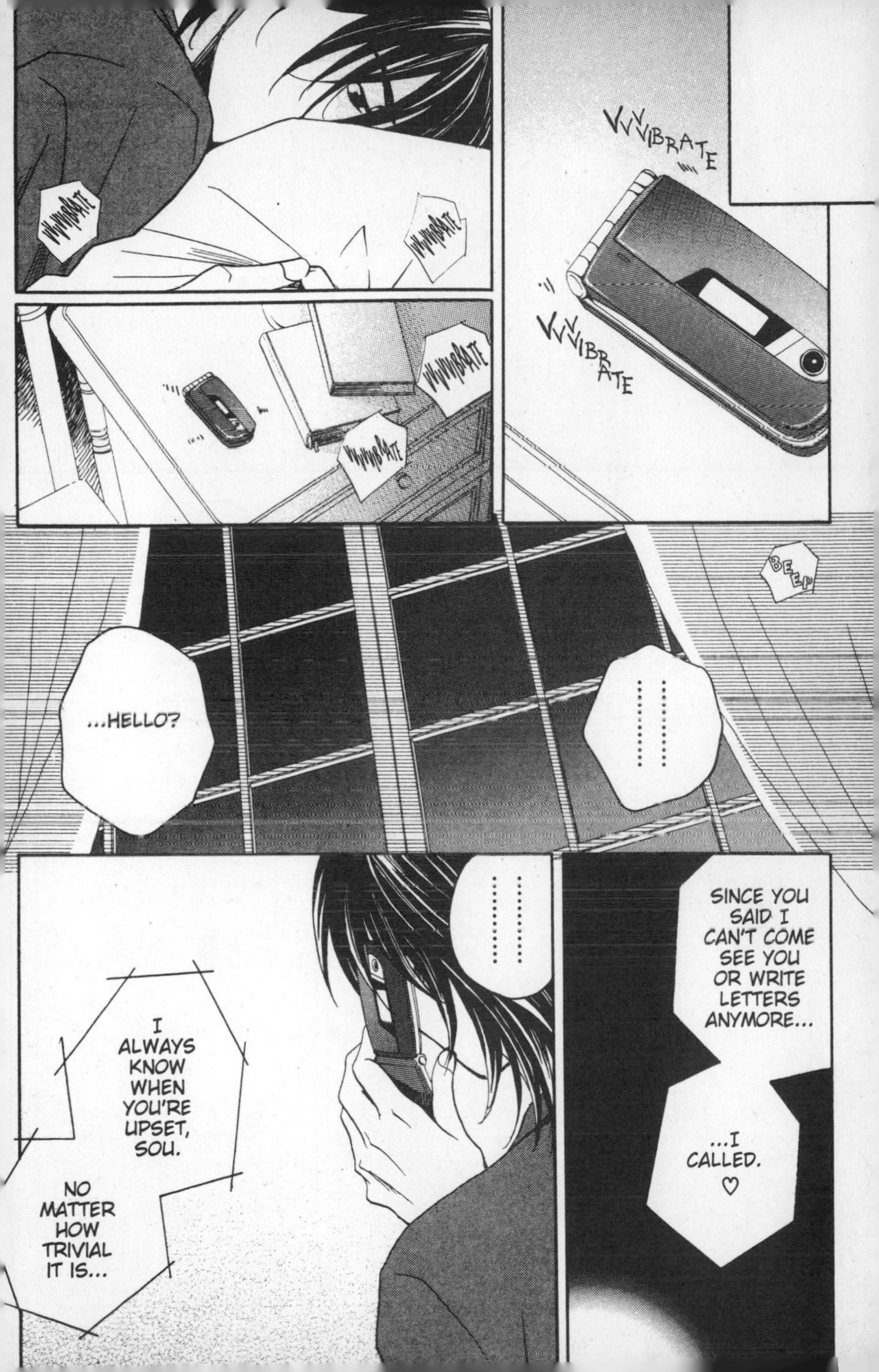
VVVIBRATE
VVVIBRATE
BEEP
......
...HELLO?
SINCE YOU SAID I CAN'T COME SEE YOU OR WRITE LETTERS ANYMORE...
...I CALLED. ♡
......
I ALWAYS KNOW WHEN YOU'RE UPSET, SOU.
NO MATTER HOW TRIVIAL IT IS...

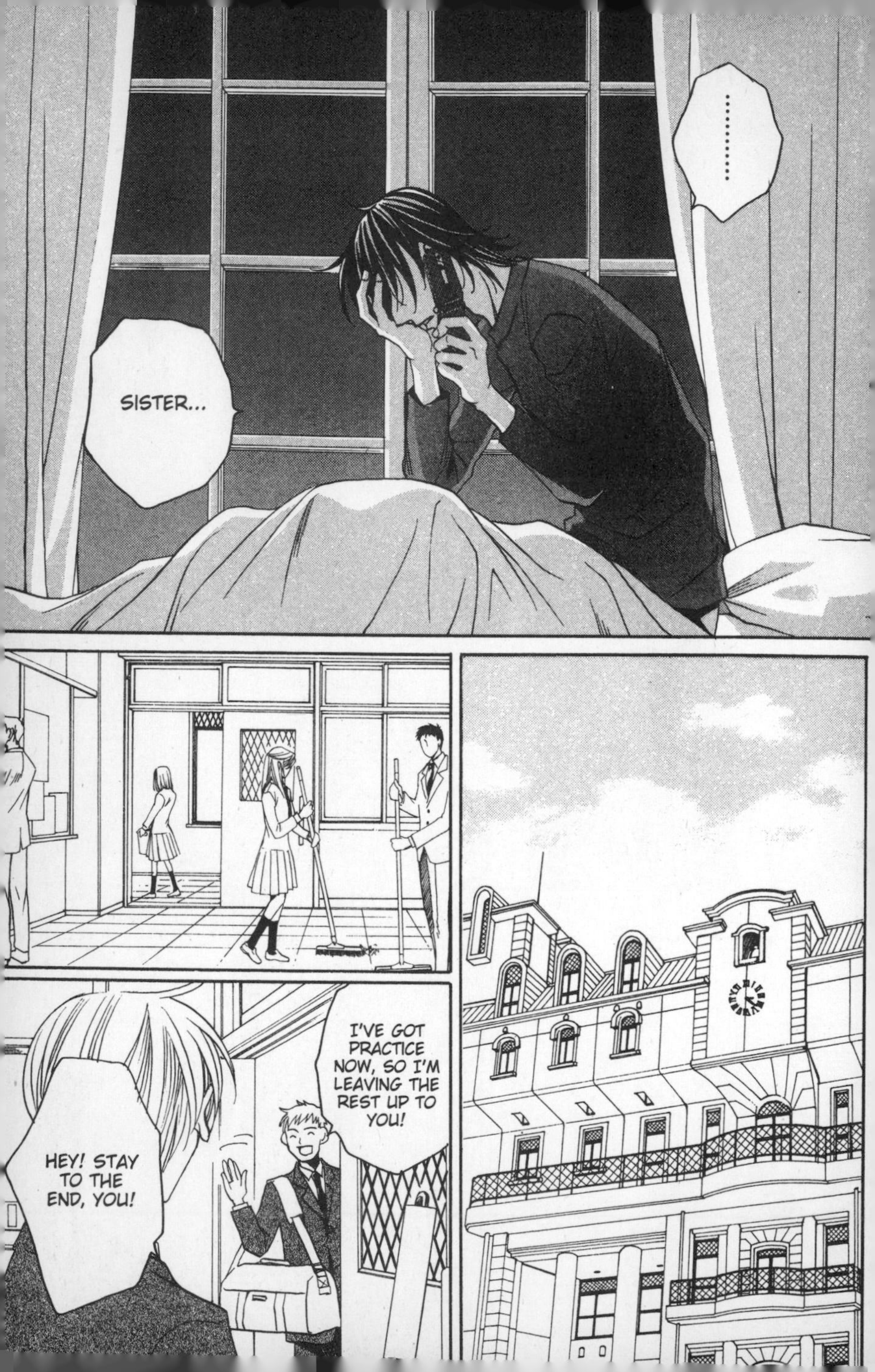
......
SISTER...
I'VE GOT PRACTICE NOW, SO I'M LEAVING THE REST UP TO YOU!
HEY! STAY TO THE END, YOU!

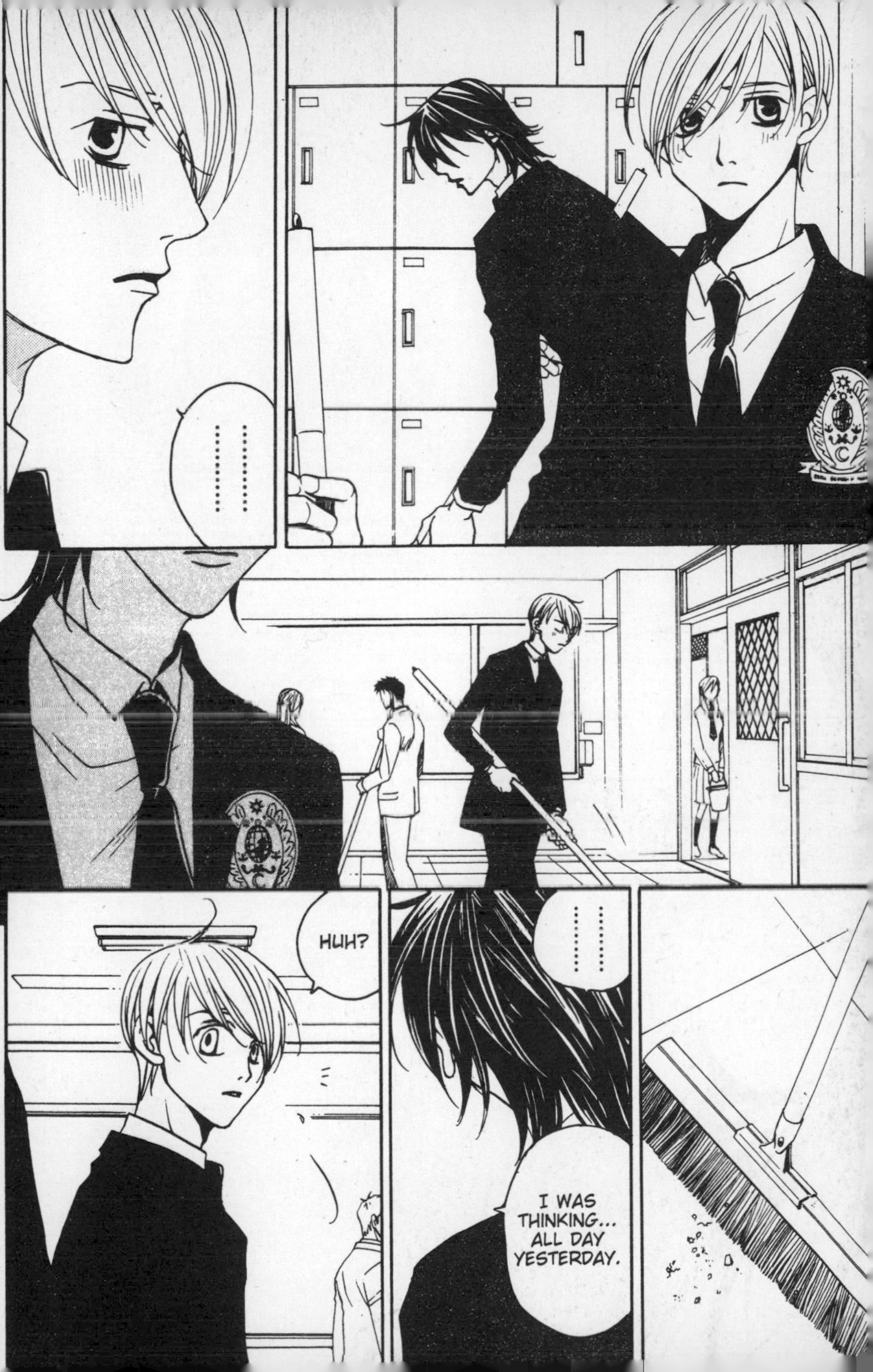
……
……
I WAS THINKING… ALL DAY YESTERDAY.
HUH?

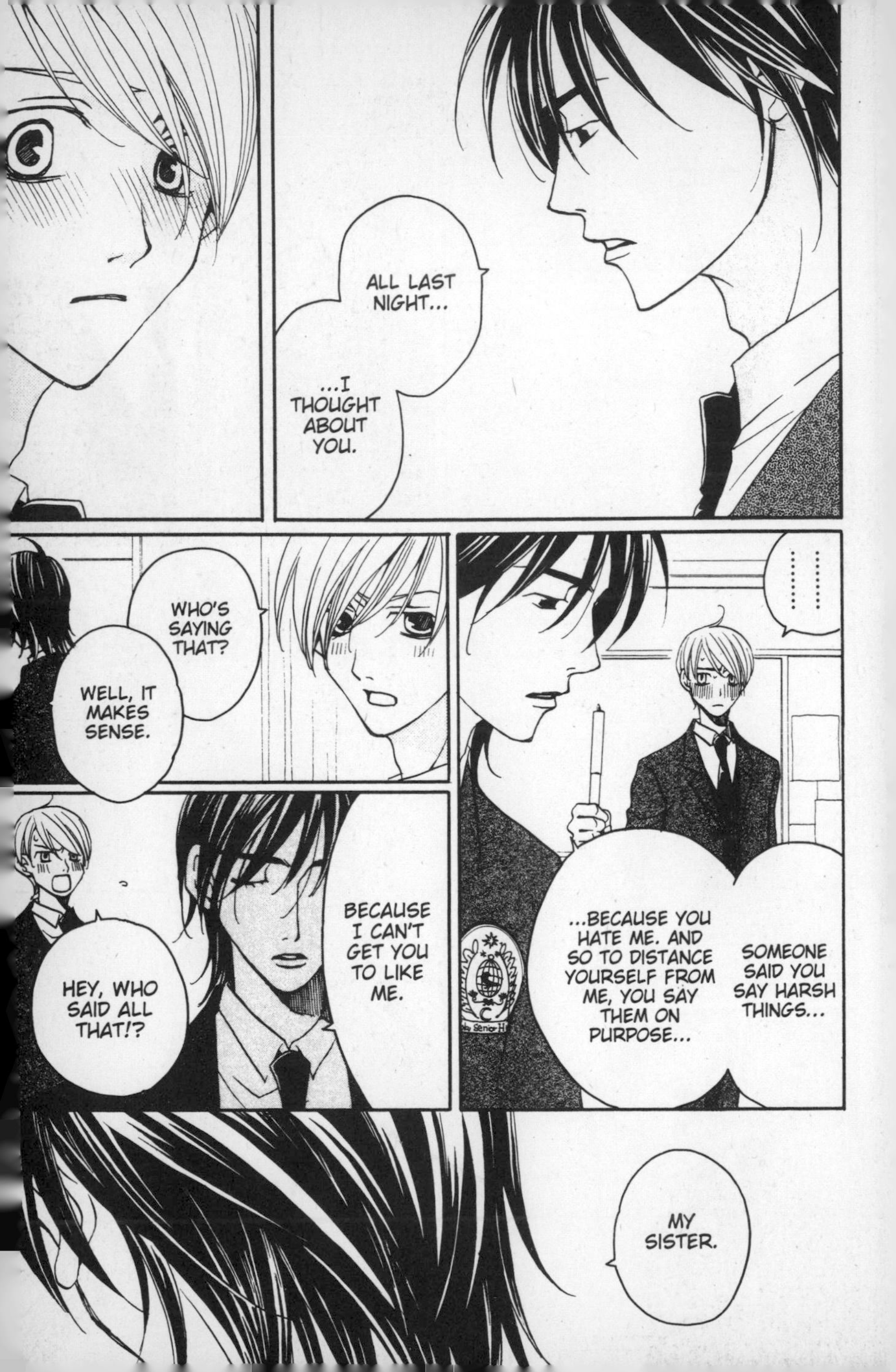
ALL LAST NIGHT...
...I THOUGHT ABOUT YOU.
......
SOMEONE SAID YOU SAY HARSH THINGS...
...BECAUSE YOU HATE ME. AND SO TO DISTANCE YOURSELF FROM ME, YOU SAY THEM ON PURPOSE...
WHO'S SAYING THAT?
WELL, IT MAKES SENSE.
BECAUSE I CAN'T GET YOU TO LIKE ME.
HEY, WHO SAID ALL THAT!?
MY SISTER.

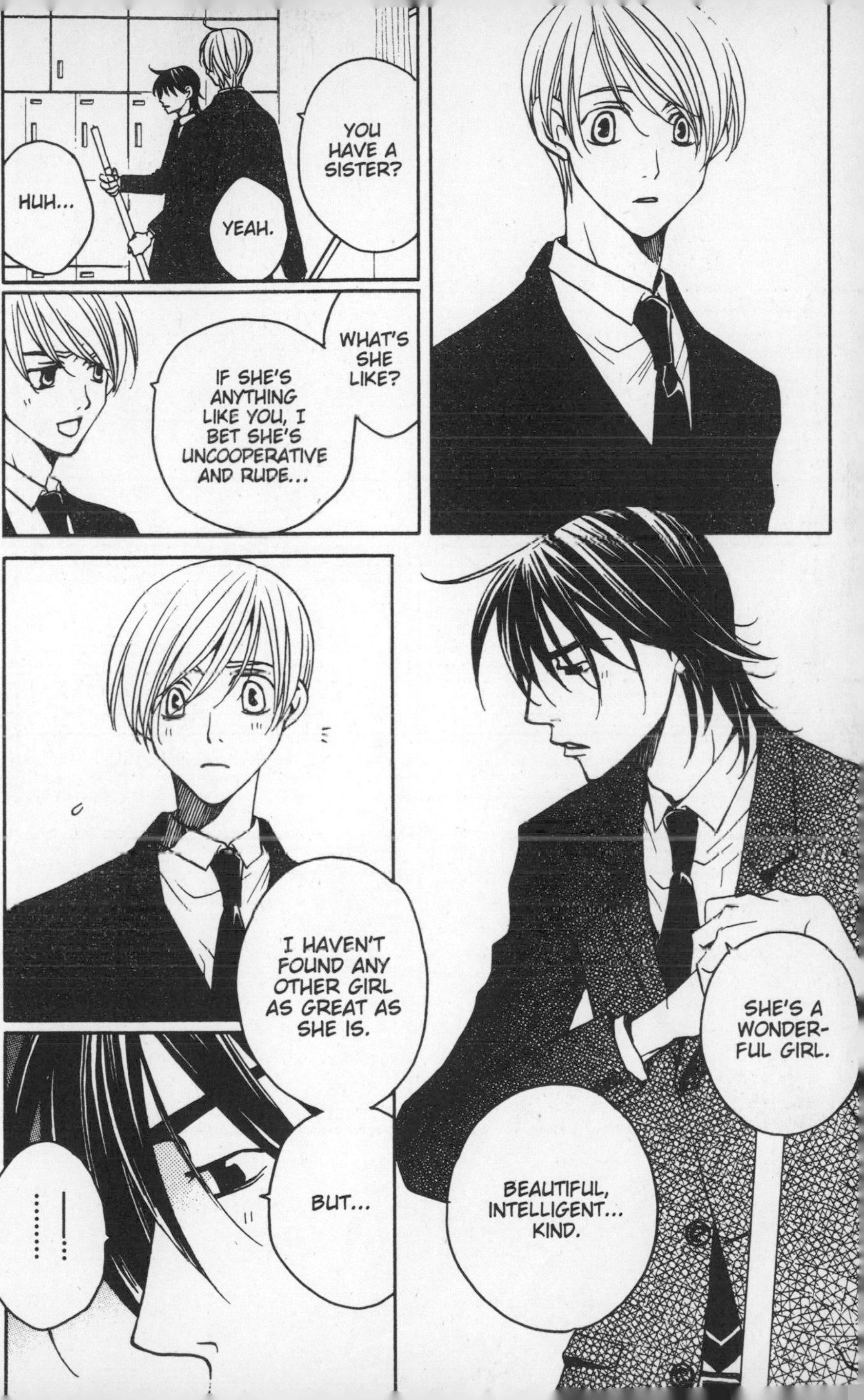
YOU HAVE A SISTER?
YEAH.
HUH...
WHAT'S SHE LIKE?
IF SHE'S ANYTHING LIKE YOU, I BET SHE'S UNCOOPERATIVE AND RUDE...
SHE'S A WONDER-FUL GIRL.
BEAUTIFUL, INTELLIGENT... KIND.
I HAVEN'T FOUND ANY OTHER GIRL AS GREAT AS SHE IS.
BUT...
......!

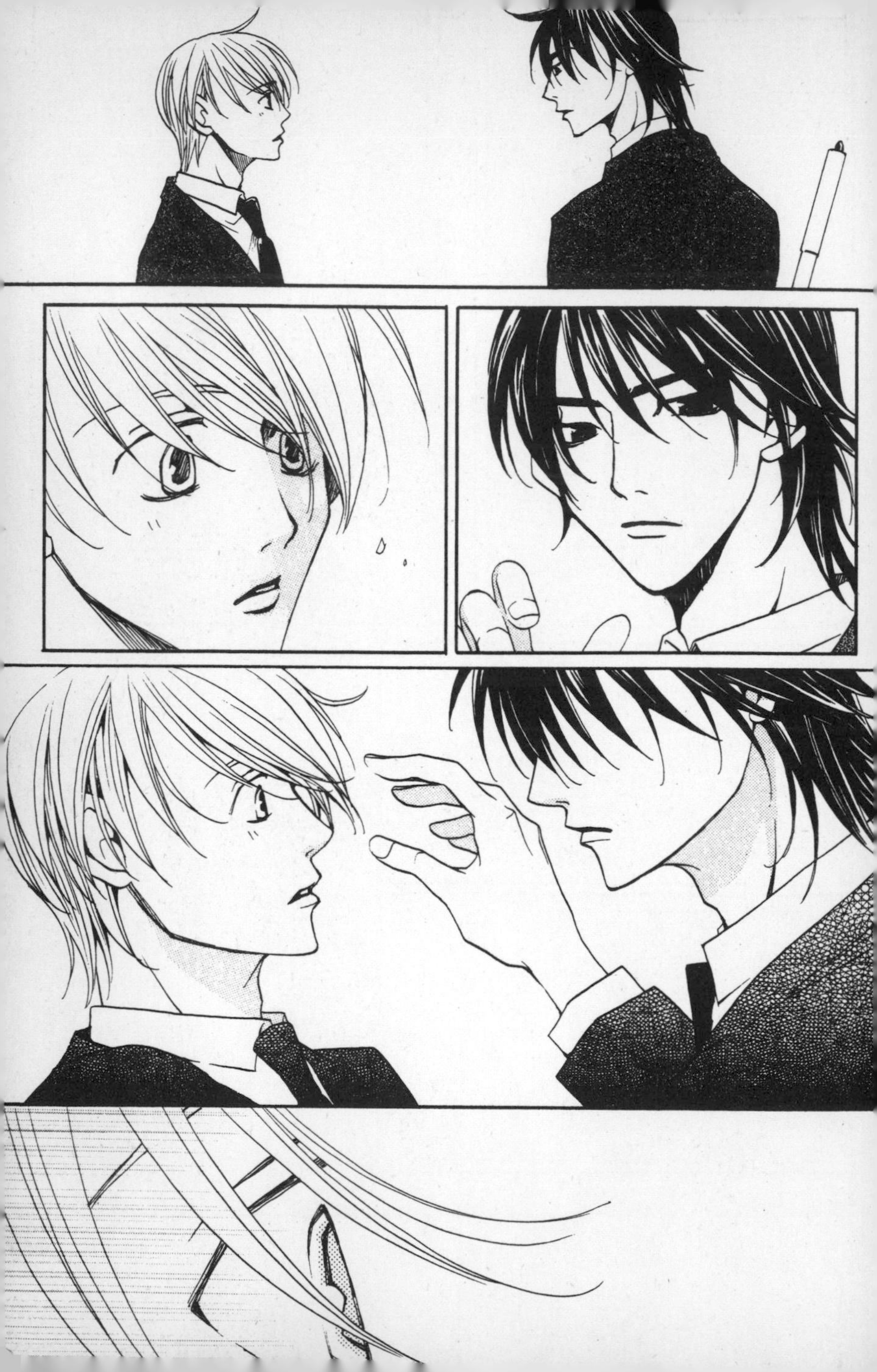

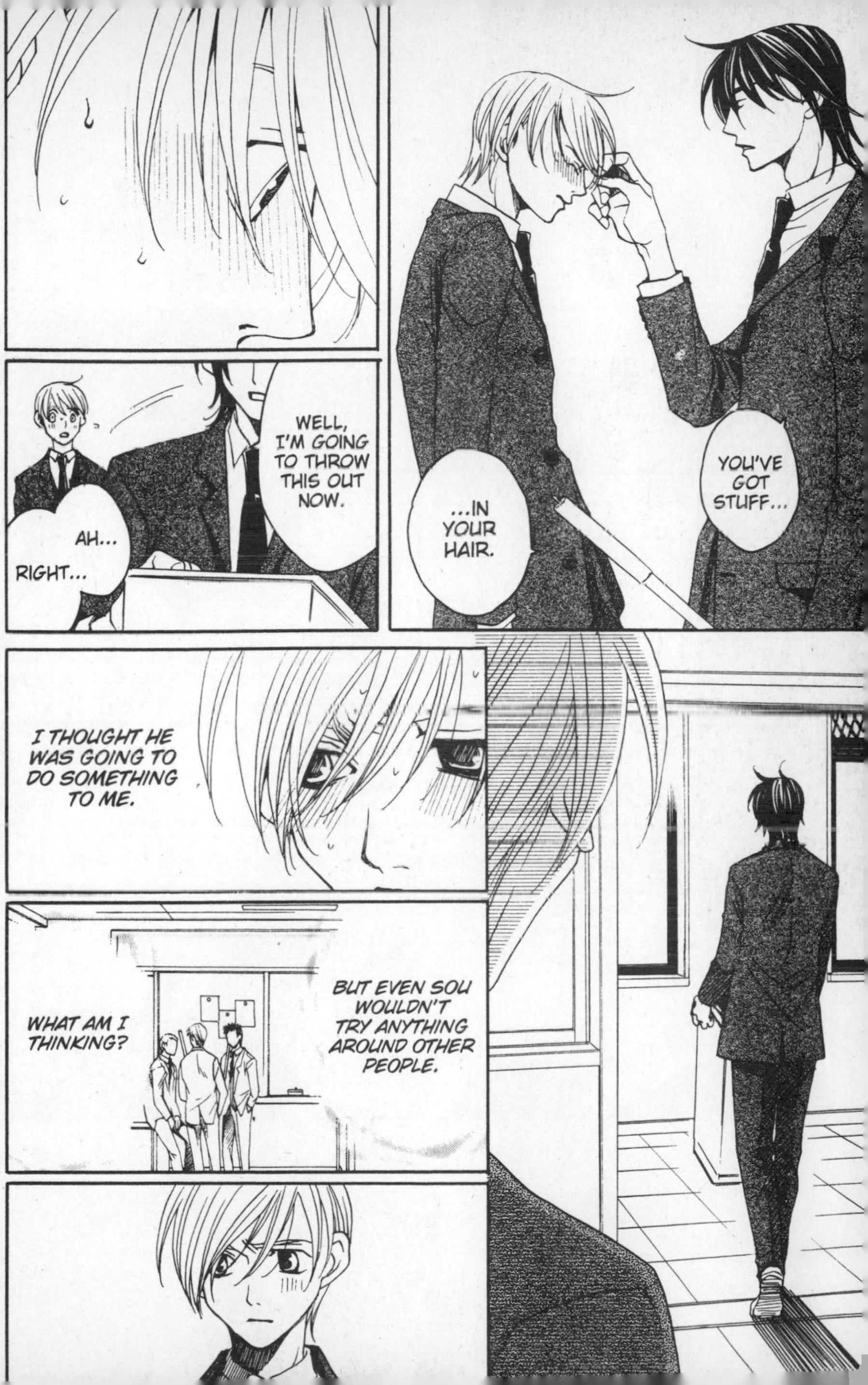
YOU'VE GOT STUFF...
...IN YOUR HAIR.
WELL, I'M GOING TO THROW THIS OUT NOW.
AH... RIGHT...
I THOUGHT HE WAS GOING TO DO SOMETHING TO ME.
BUT EVEN SOU WOULDN'T TRY ANYTHING AROUND OTHER PEOPLE.
WHAT AM I THINKING?

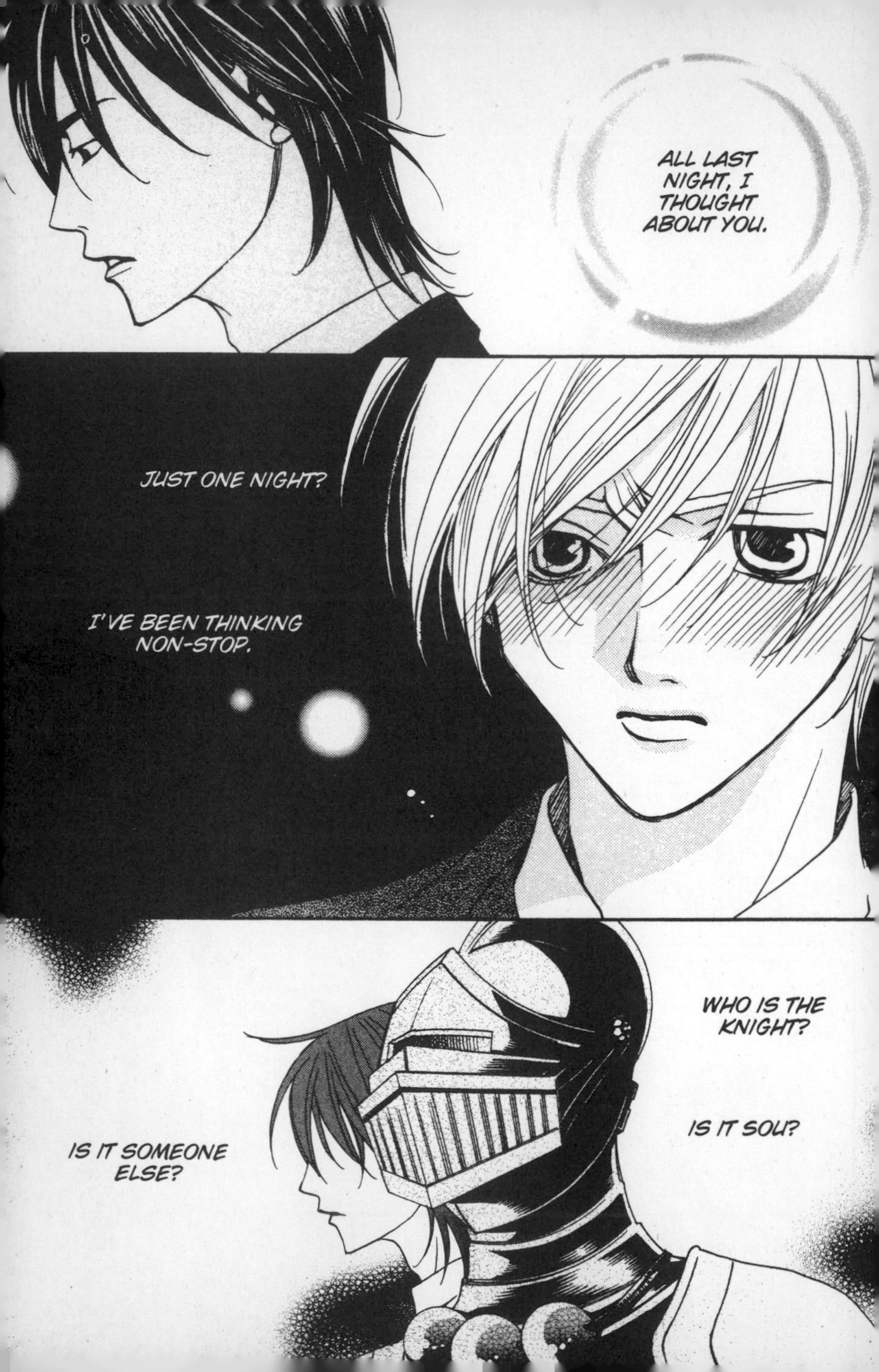
ALL LAST NIGHT, I THOUGHT ABOUT YOU.
JUST ONE NIGHT?
I'VE BEEN THINKING NON-STOP.
WHO IS THE KNIGHT?
IS IT SOU?
IS IT SOMEONE ELSE?

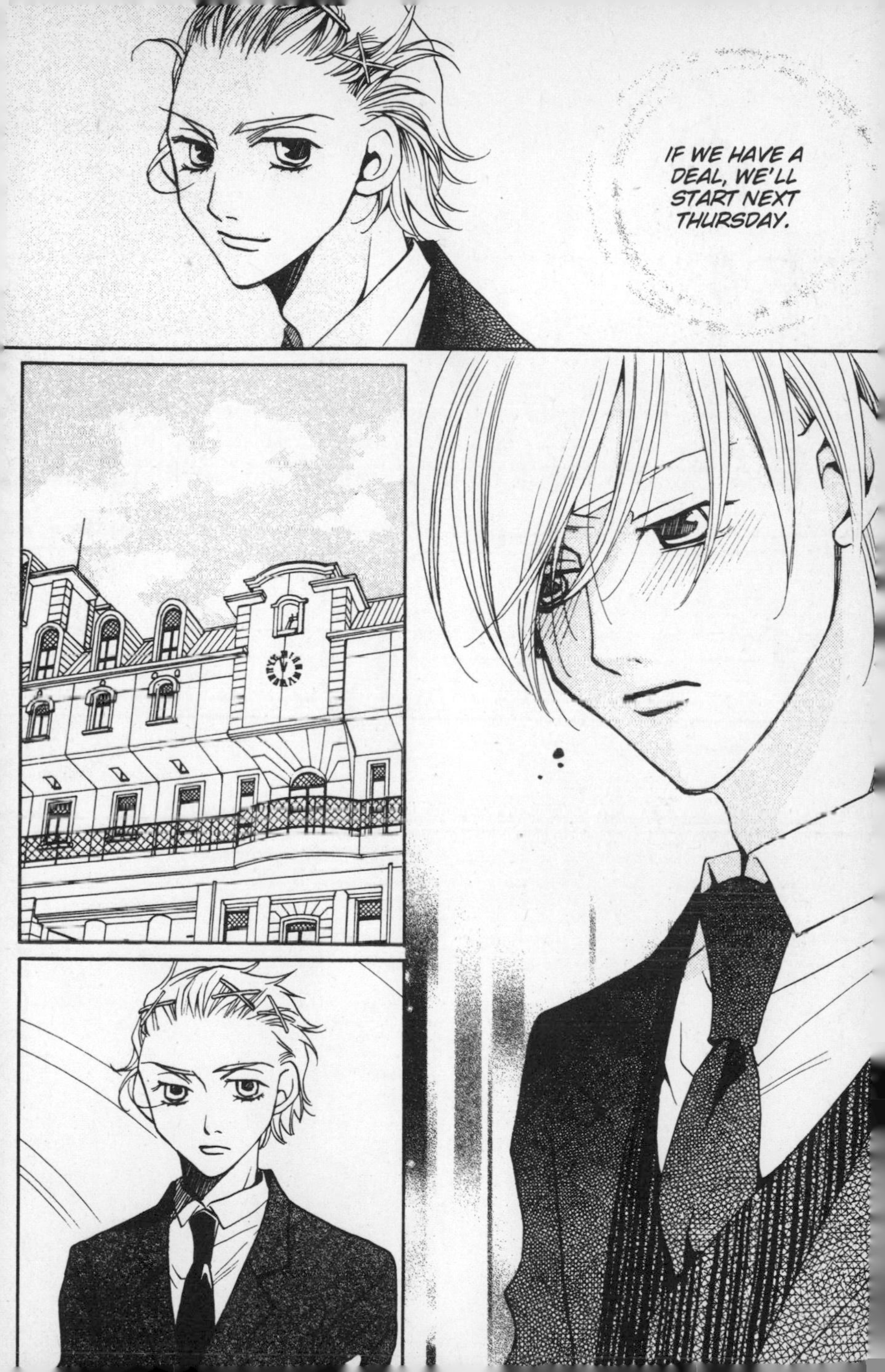
IF WE HAVE A DEAL, WE'LL START NEXT THURSDAY.

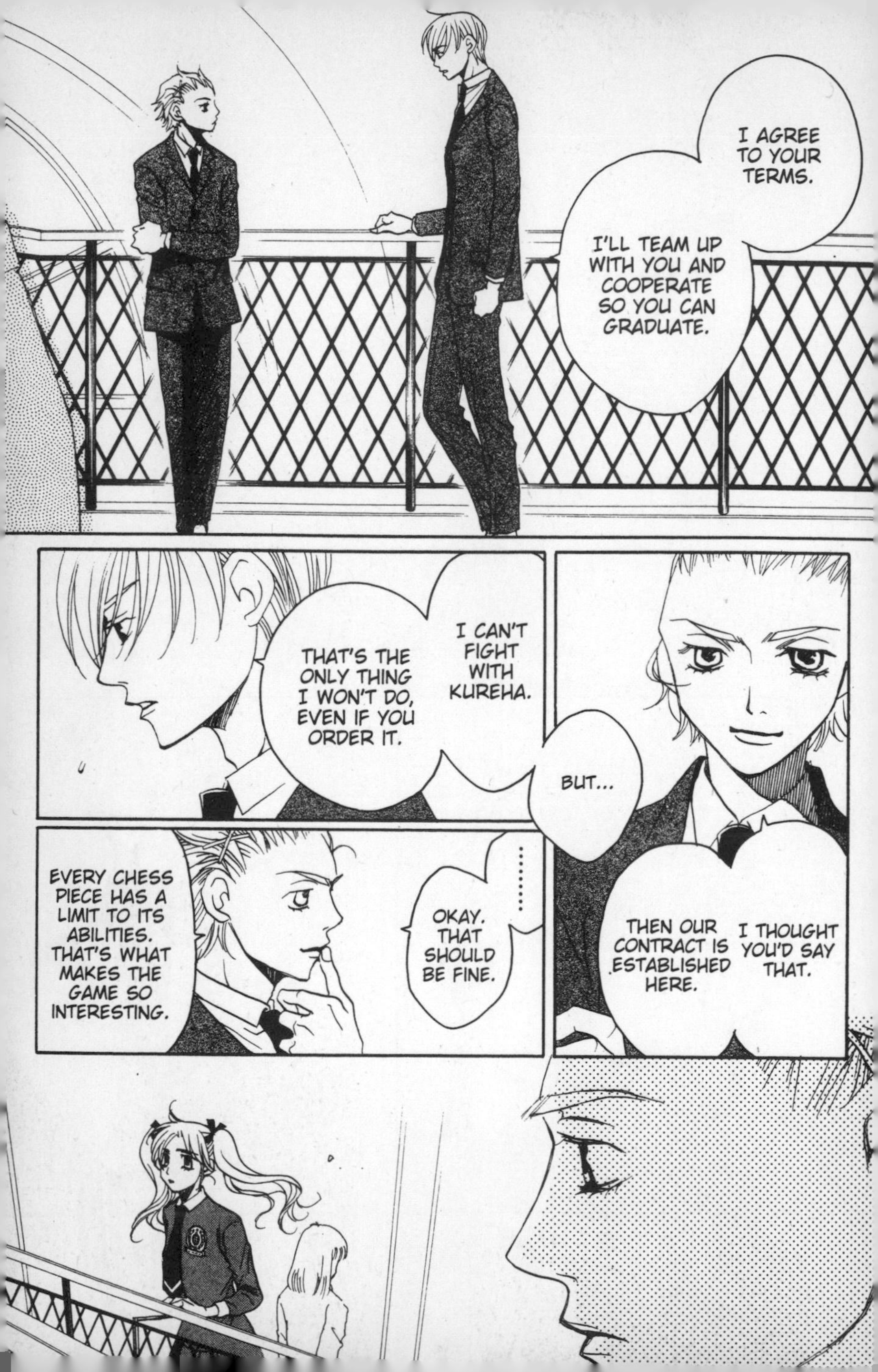
I AGREE TO YOUR TERMS.
I'LL TEAM UP WITH YOU AND COOPERATE SO YOU CAN GRADUATE.
I CAN'T FIGHT WITH KUREHA.
THAT'S THE ONLY THING I WON'T DO, EVEN IF YOU ORDER IT.
BUT...
I THOUGHT YOU'D SAY THAT.
THEN OUR CONTRACT IS ESTABLISHED HERE.
......
OKAY. THAT SHOULD BE FINE.
EVERY CHESS PIECE HAS A LIMIT TO ITS ABILITIES. THAT'S WHAT MAKES THE GAME SO INTERESTING.

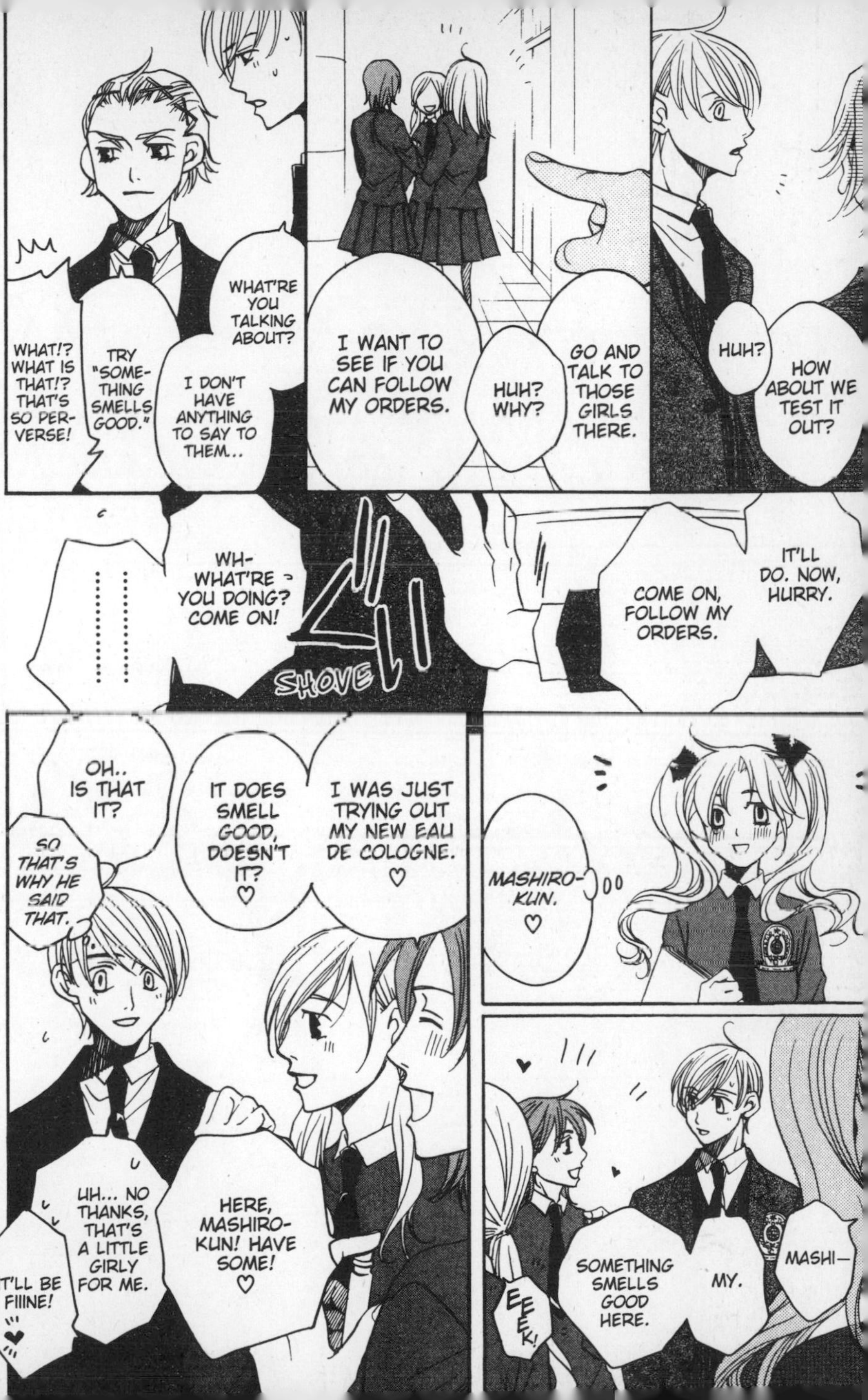
HOW ABOUT WE TEST IT OUT?
HUH?
GO AND TALK TO THOSE GIRLS THERE.
HUH? WHY?
I WANT TO SEE IF YOU CAN FOLLOW MY ORDERS.
WHAT'RE YOU TALKING ABOUT? I DON'T HAVE ANYTHING TO SAY TO THEM...
TRY "SOMETHING SMELLS GOOD."
WHAT!? WHAT IS THAT!? THAT'S SO PERVERSE!
IT'LL DO. NOW, HURRY.
COME ON, FOLLOW MY ORDERS.
SHOVE
WH- WHAT'RE YOU DOING? COME ON!
......
MASHIRO-KUN. ♡
MASHI—
MY.
SOMETHING SMELLS GOOD HERE.
EEEK!
I WAS JUST TRYING OUT MY NEW EAU DE COLOGNE. ♡
IT DOES SMELL GOOD, DOESN'T IT? ♡
OH.. IS THAT IT?
SO THAT'S WHY HE SAID THAT.
HERE, MASHIRO-KUN! HAVE SOME! ♡
UH... NO THANKS, THAT'S A LITTLE GIRLY FOR ME.
IT'LL BE FIIINE!

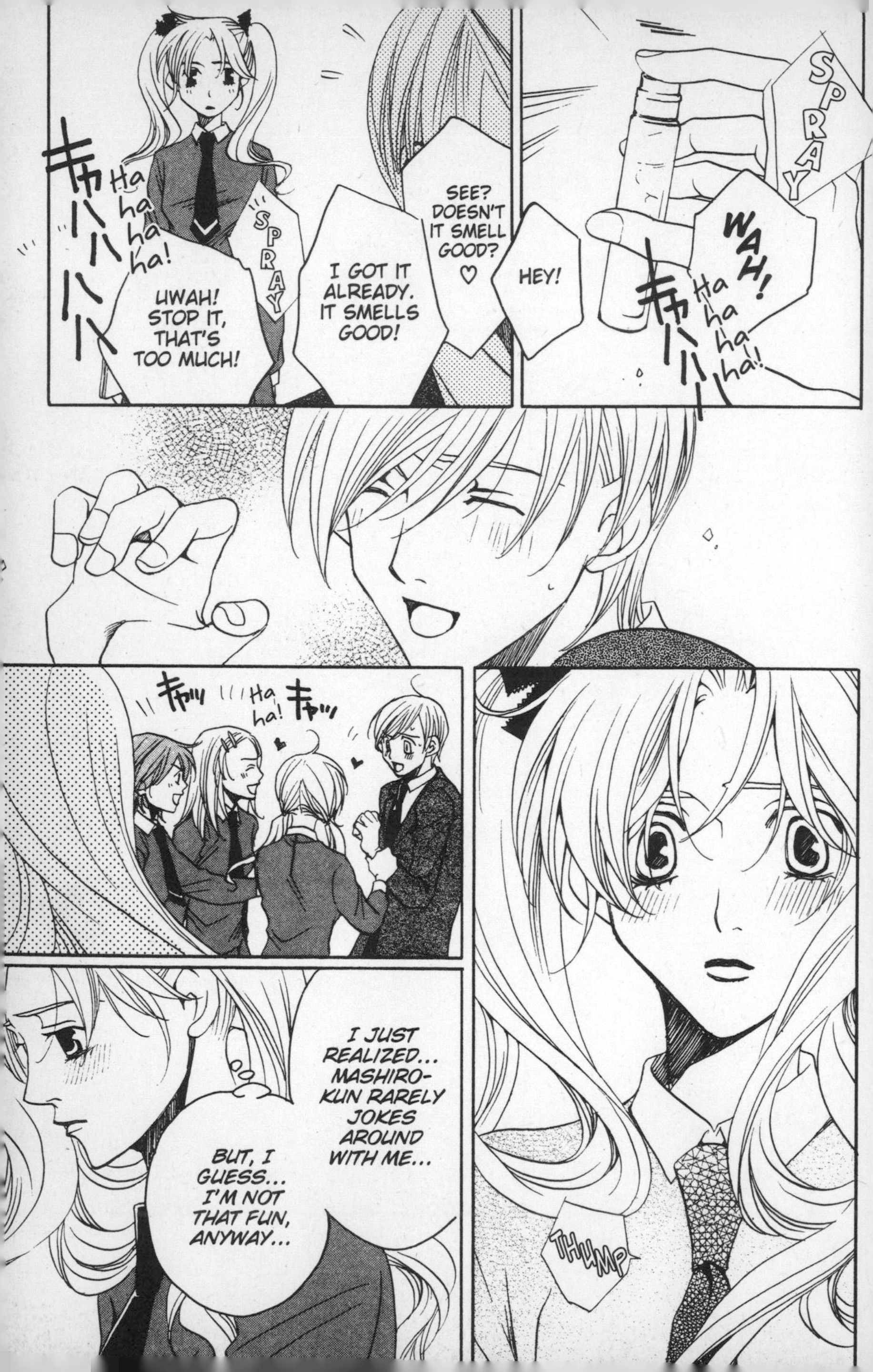
SPRAY
WAH!
Ha ha ha ha!
キャハハハ
HEY!
SEE? DOESN'T IT SMELL GOOD? ♡
I GOT IT ALREADY. IT SMELLS GOOD!
SPRAY
Ha ha ha ha!
キャハハハハ
UWAH! STOP IT, THAT'S TOO MUCH!
THUMP
キャッ
Ha ha!
キャッ
I JUST REALIZED... MASHIRO-KUN RARELY JOKES AROUND WITH ME...
BUT, I GUESS... I'M NOT THAT FUN, ANYWAY...

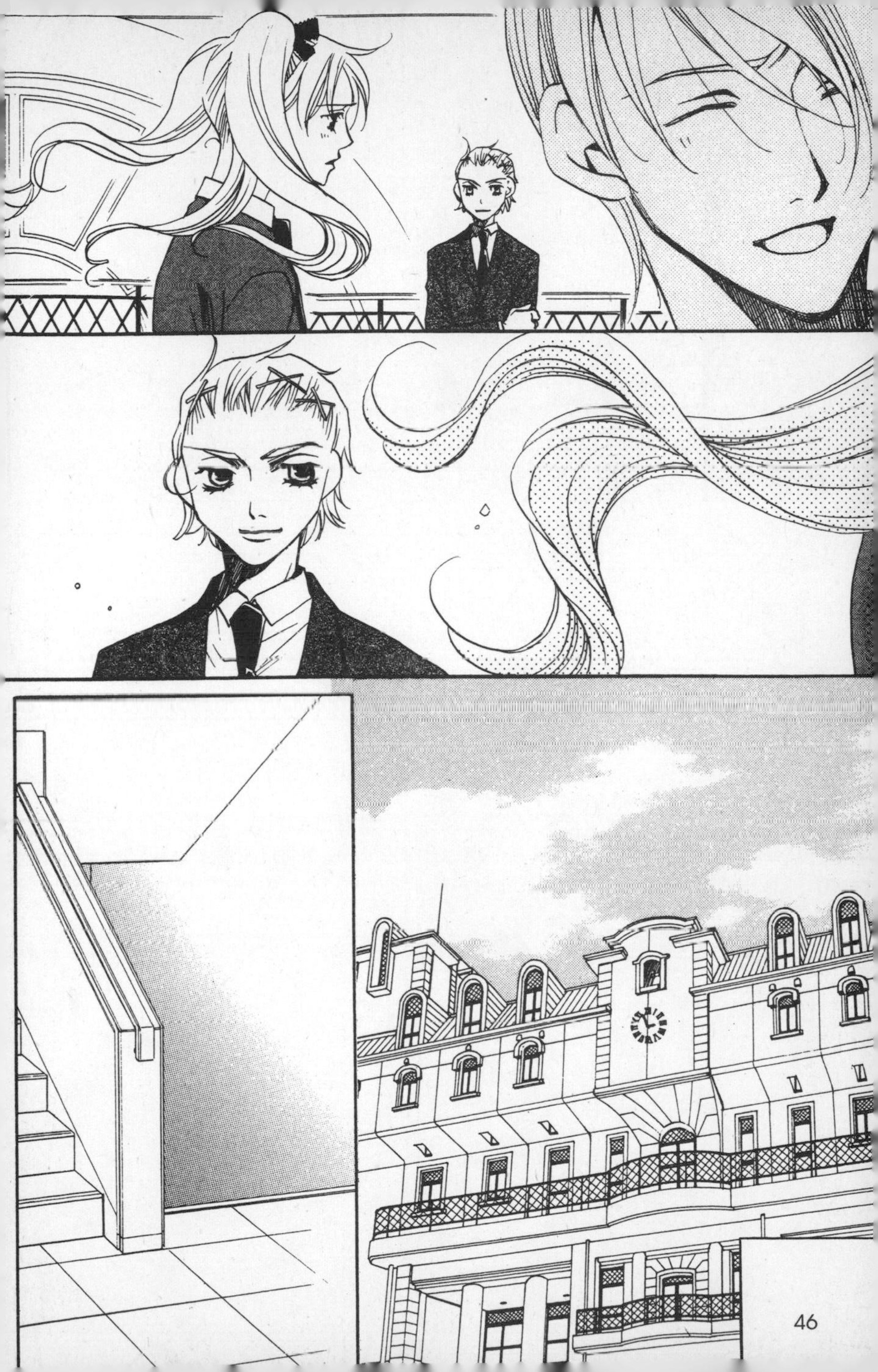

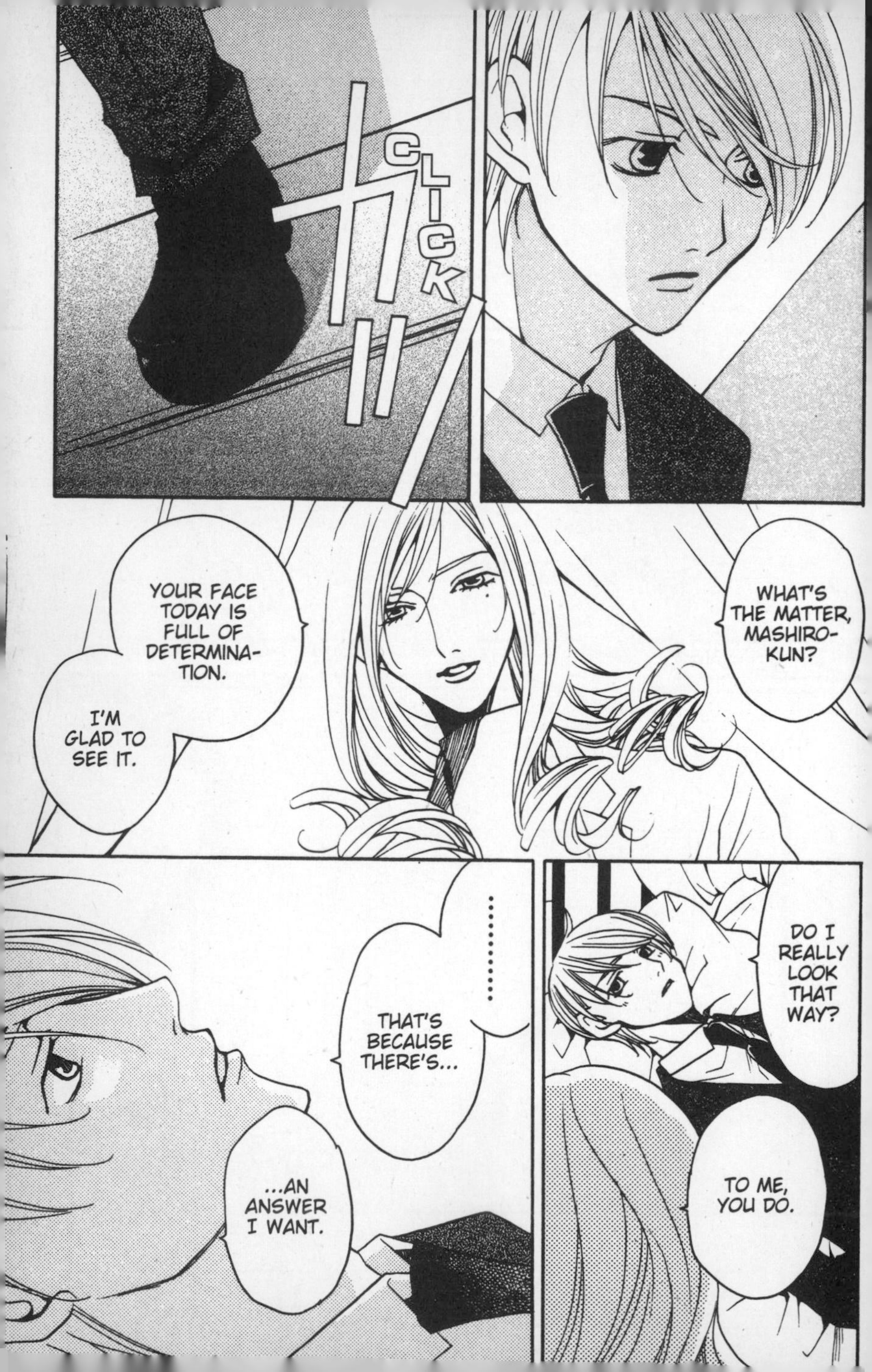
CLICK
WHAT'S THE MATTER, MASHIRO-KUN?
YOUR FACE TODAY IS FULL OF DETERMINATION.
I'M GLAD TO SEE IT.
DO I REALLY LOOK THAT WAY?
TO ME, YOU DO.
......
THAT'S BECAUSE THERE'S...
...AN ANSWER I WANT.

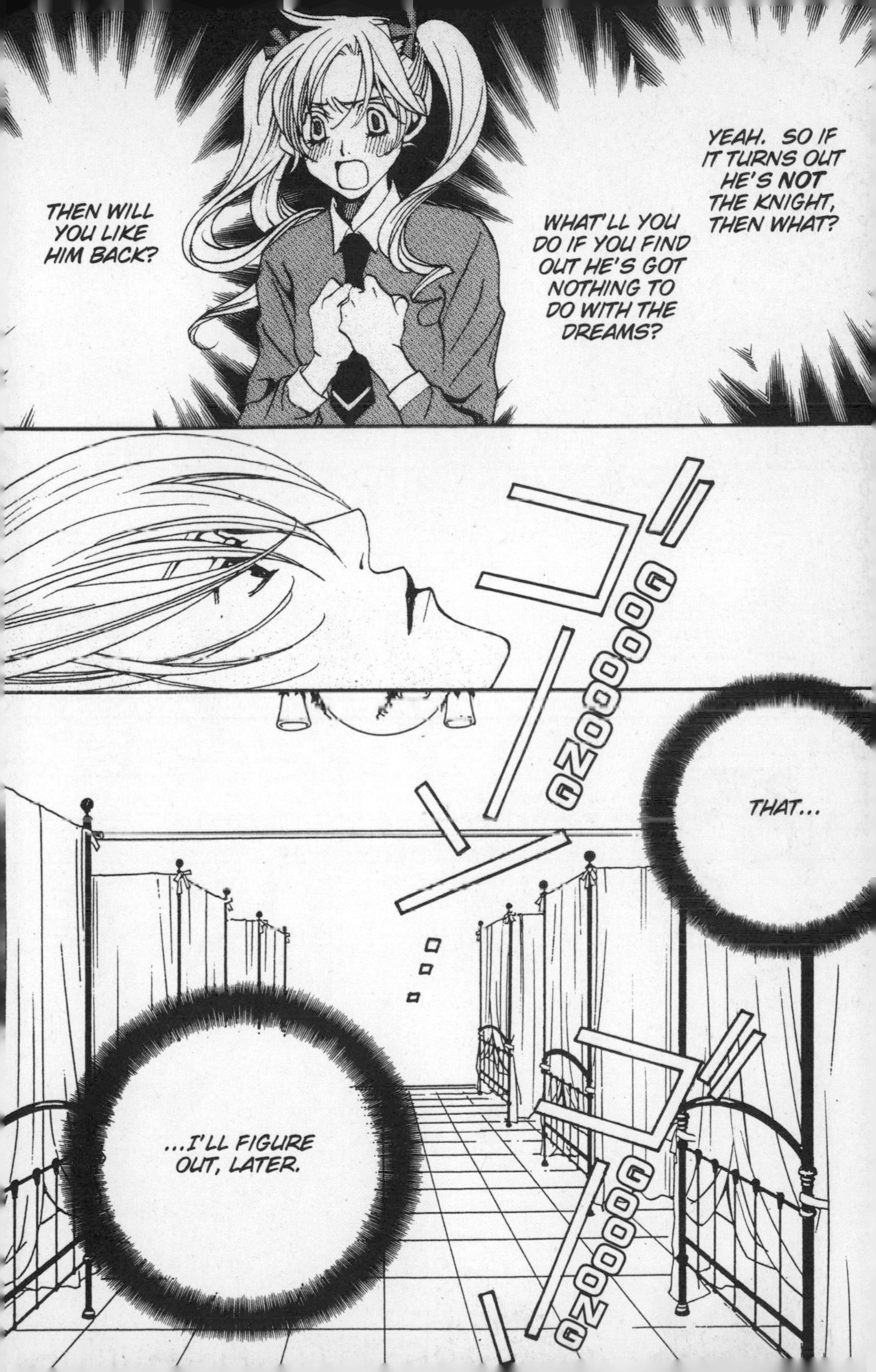
YEAH. SO IF IT TURNS OUT HE'S NOT THE KNIGHT, THEN WHAT?
WHAT'LL YOU DO IF YOU FIND OUT HE'S GOT NOTHING TO DO WITH THE DREAMS?
THEN WILL YOU LIKE HIM BACK?
GOOOOOONG
THAT...
GOOOOONG
...I'LL FIGURE OUT, LATER.

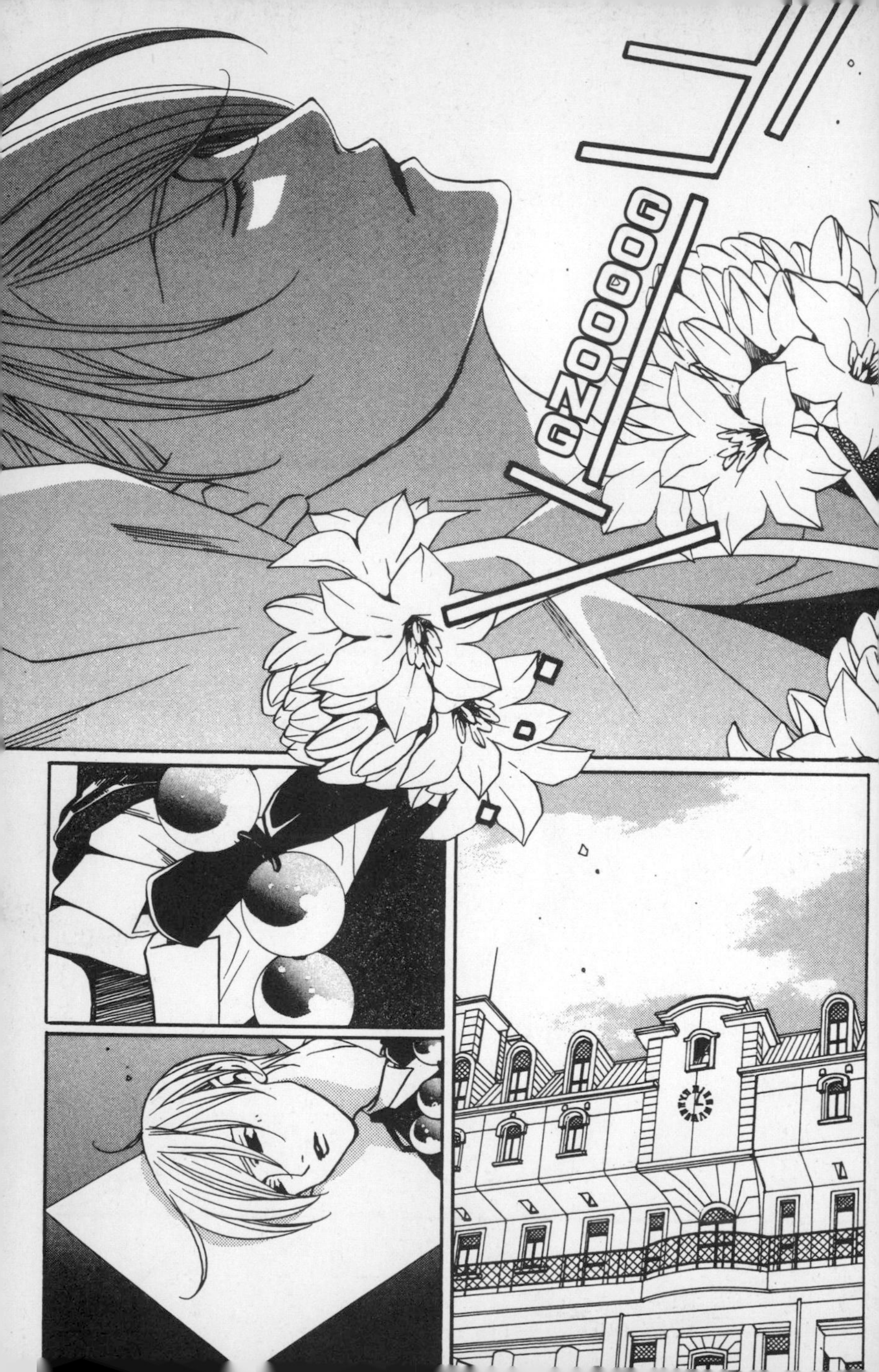
GOOOOONG

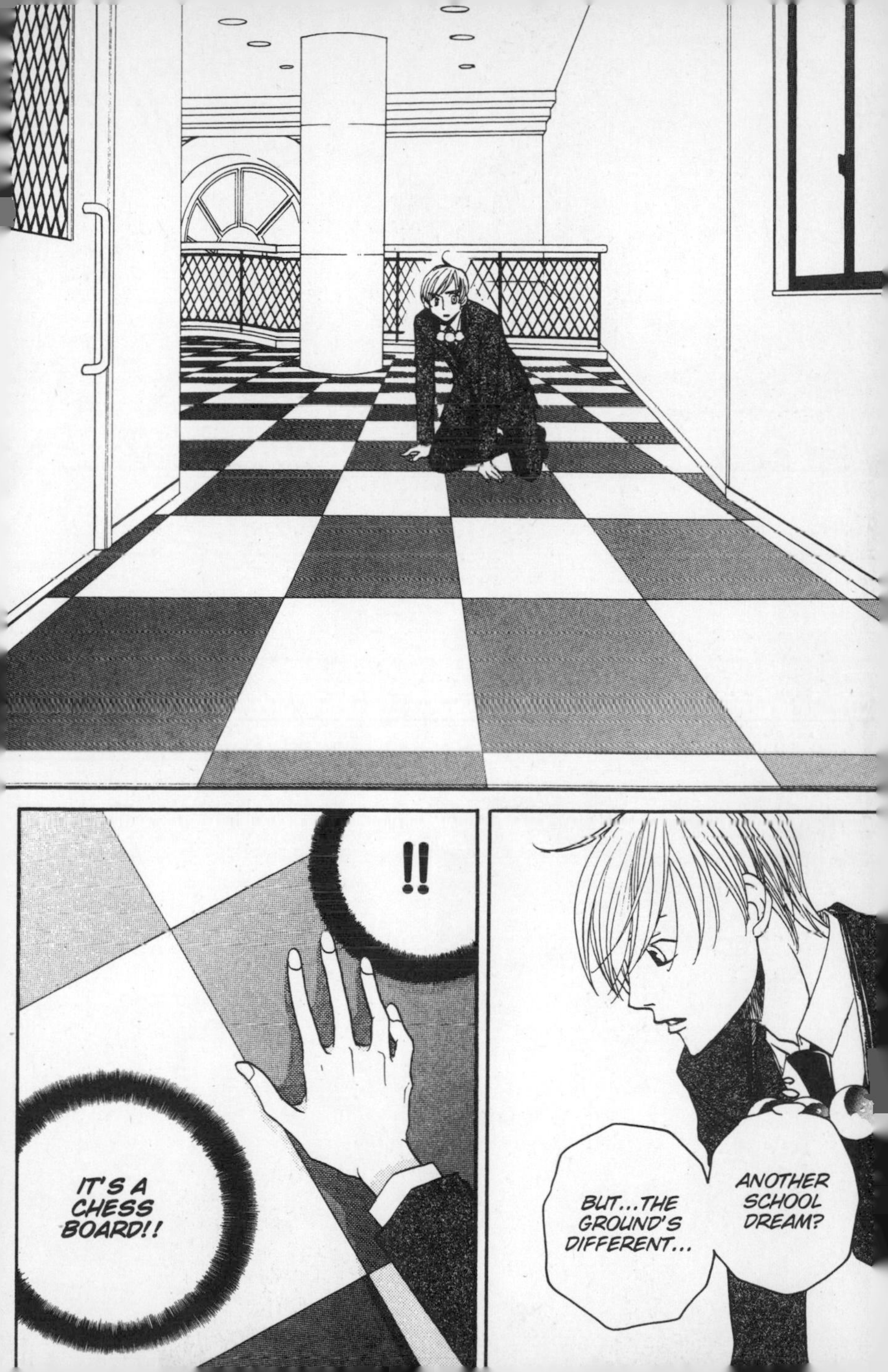
ANOTHER SCHOOL DREAM?
BUT...THE GROUND'S DIFFERENT...
!!
IT'S A CHESS BOARD!!

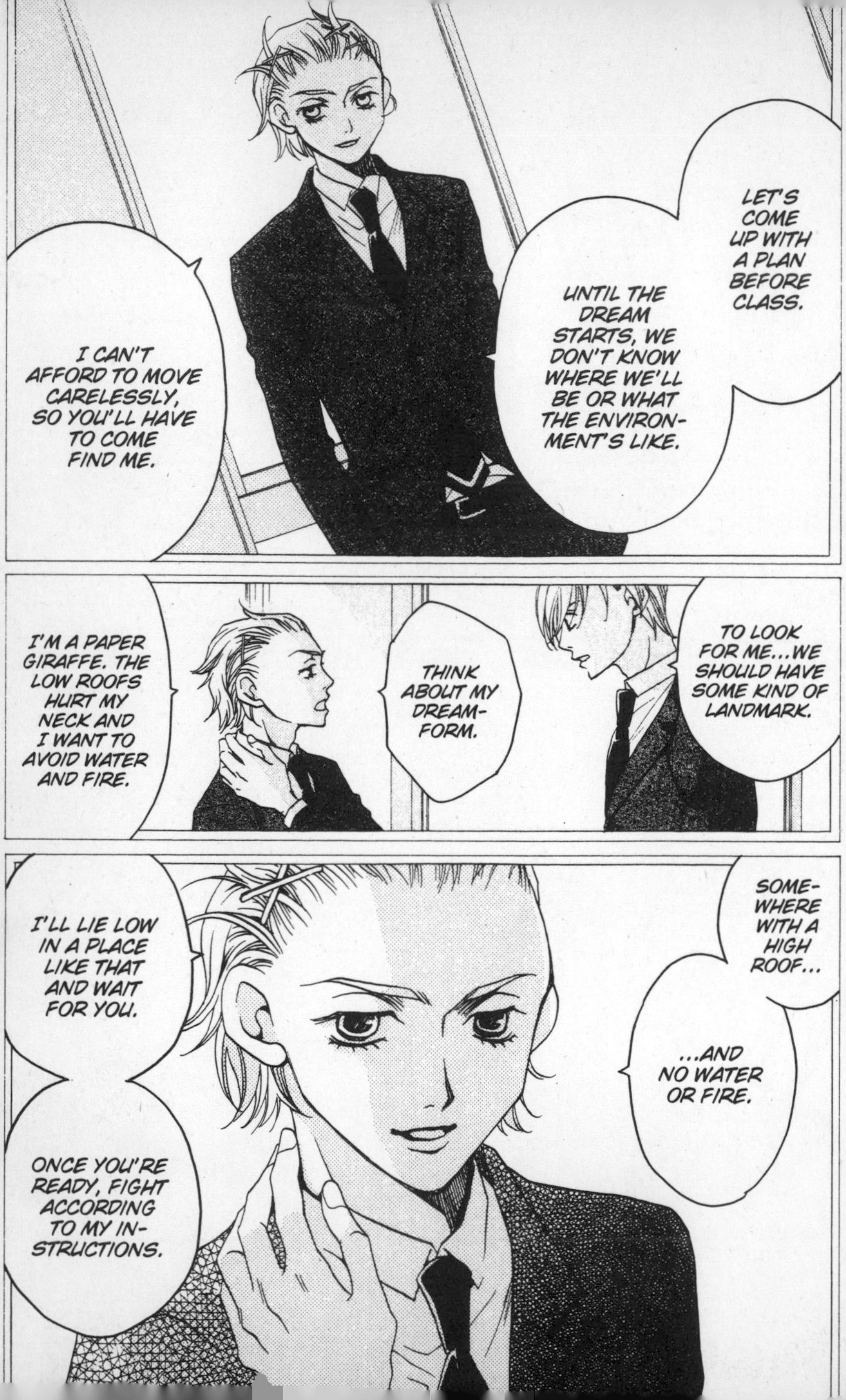
LET'S COME UP WITH A PLAN BEFORE CLASS.
UNTIL THE DREAM STARTS, WE DON'T KNOW WHERE WE'LL BE OR WHAT THE ENVIRONMENT'S LIKE.
I CAN'T AFFORD TO MOVE CARELESSLY, SO YOU'LL HAVE TO COME FIND ME.
TO LOOK FOR ME...WE SHOULD HAVE SOME KIND OF LANDMARK.
THINK ABOUT MY DREAM-FORM.
I'M A PAPER GIRAFFE. THE LOW ROOFS HURT MY NECK AND I WANT TO AVOID WATER AND FIRE.
SOMEWHERE WITH A HIGH ROOF...
...AND NO WATER OR FIRE.
I'LL LIE LOW IN A PLACE LIKE THAT AND WAIT FOR YOU.
ONCE YOU'RE READY, FIGHT ACCORDING TO MY INSTRUCTIONS.

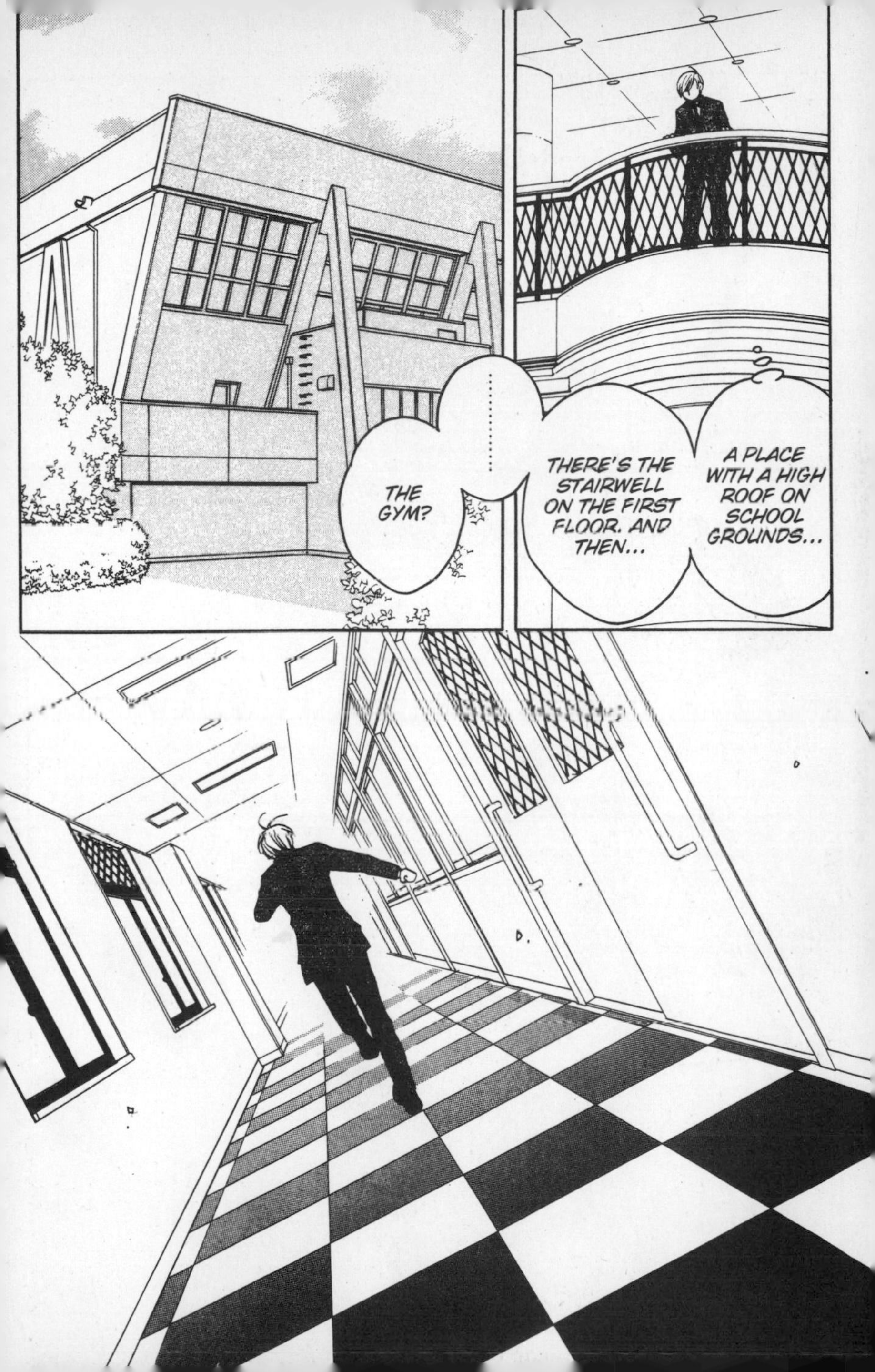
A PLACE WITH A HIGH ROOF ON SCHOOL GROUNDS...
THERE'S THE STAIRWELL ON THE FIRST FLOOR. AND THEN...
......
THE GYM?

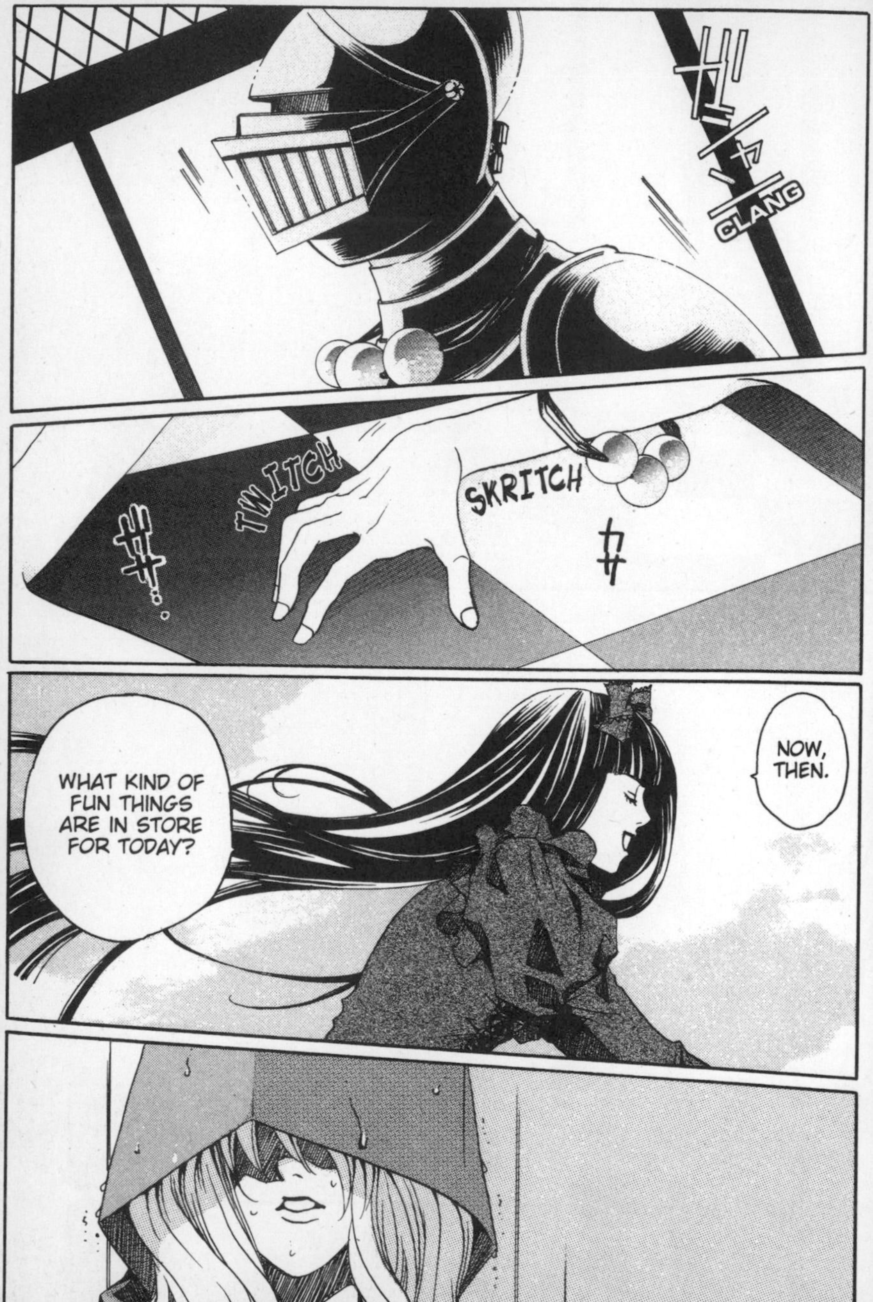
CLANG
SKRITCH
TWITCH
NOW, THEN.
WHAT KIND OF FUN THINGS ARE IN STORE FOR TODAY?

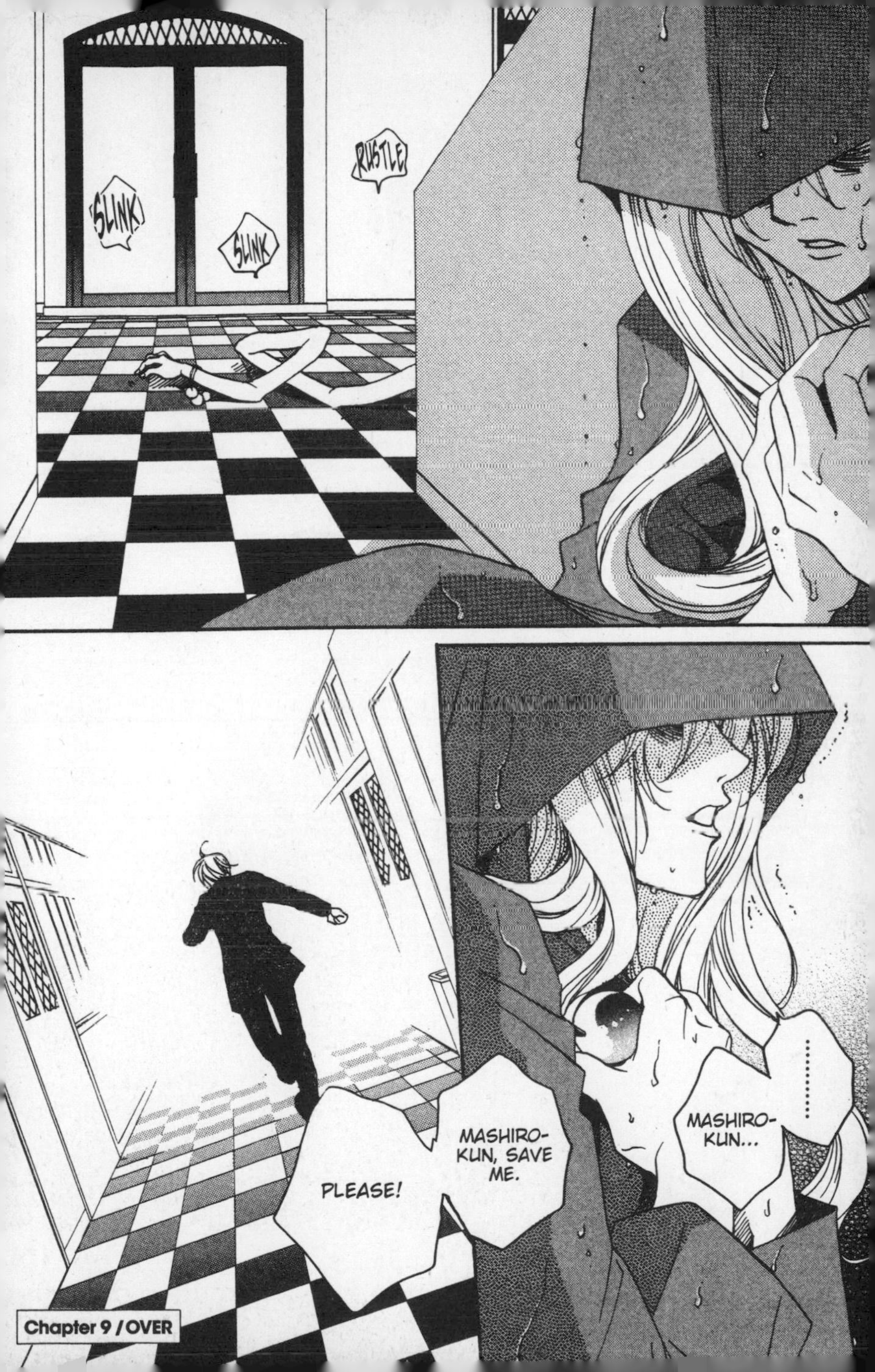
RUSTLE
SLINK
SLINK
......
MASHIRO-KUN...
MASHIRO-KUN, SAVE ME.
PLEASE!

Chapter 9 / OVER

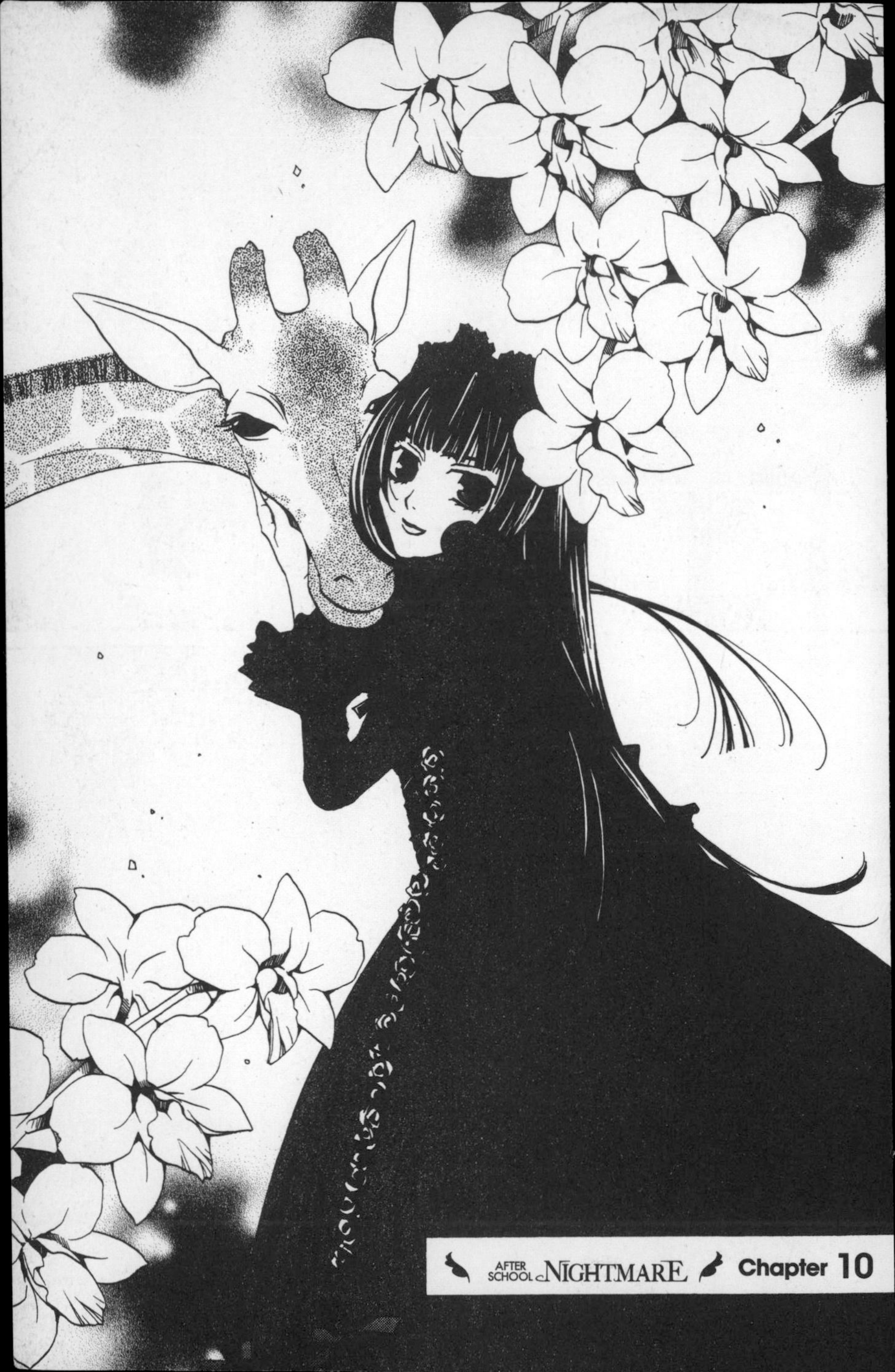
AFTER SCHOOL NIGHTMARE
Chapter 10

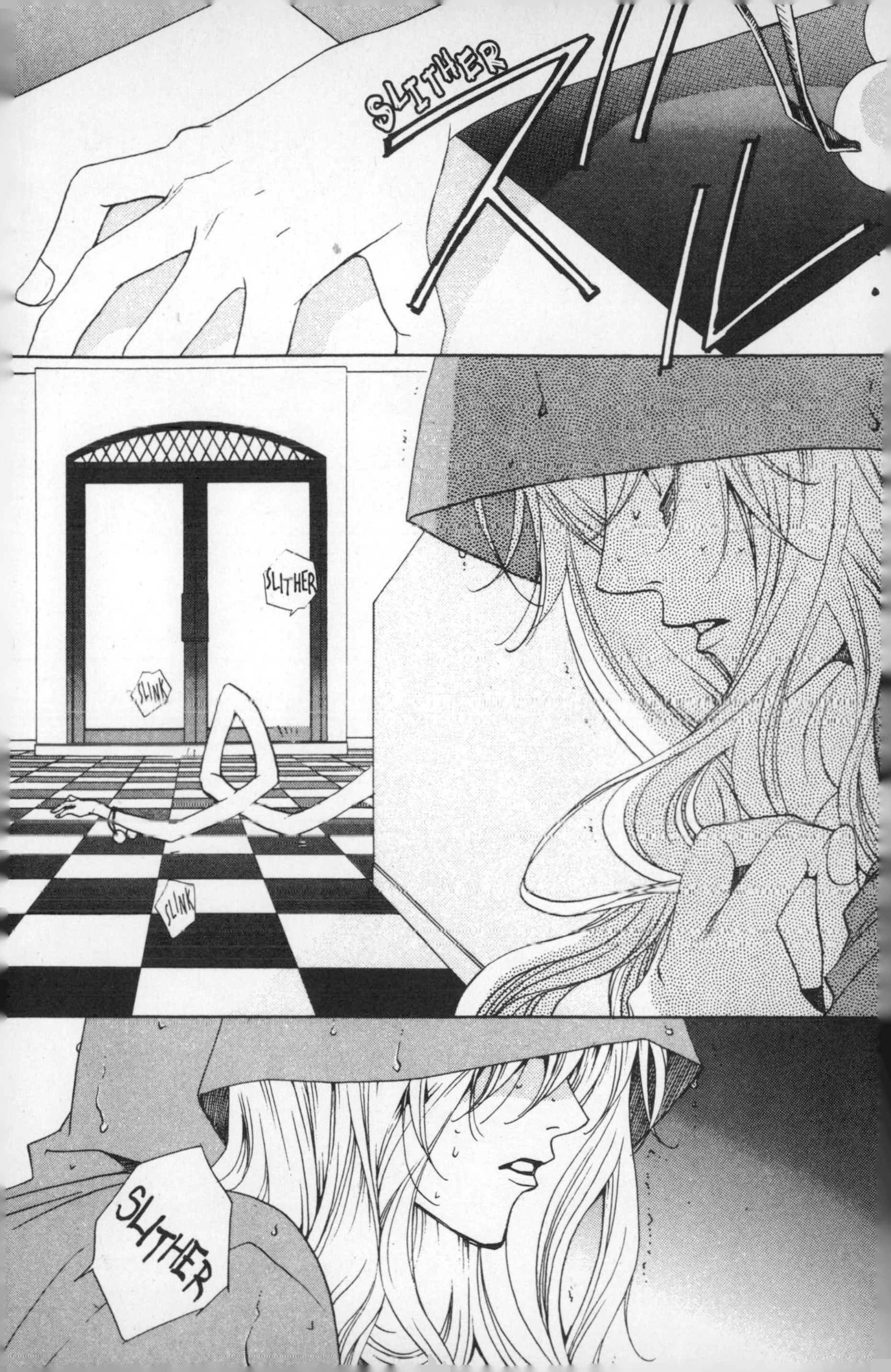
SLITHER
SLITHER
SLINK
SLINK
SLITHER

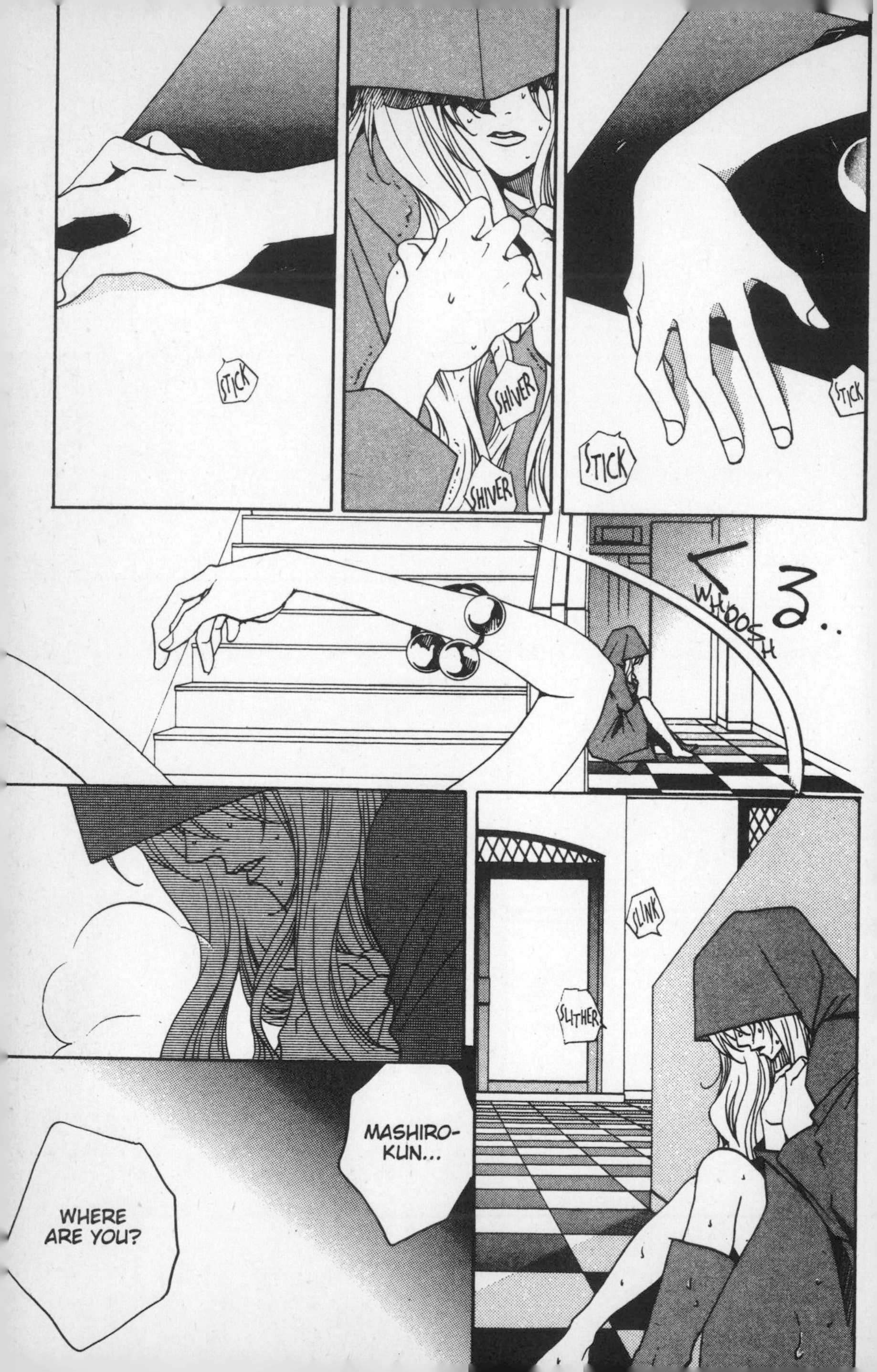
STICK
STICK
SHIVER
SHIVER
STICK
くる..
WHOOSH
SLINK
SLITHER
MASHIRO-KUN...
WHERE ARE YOU?

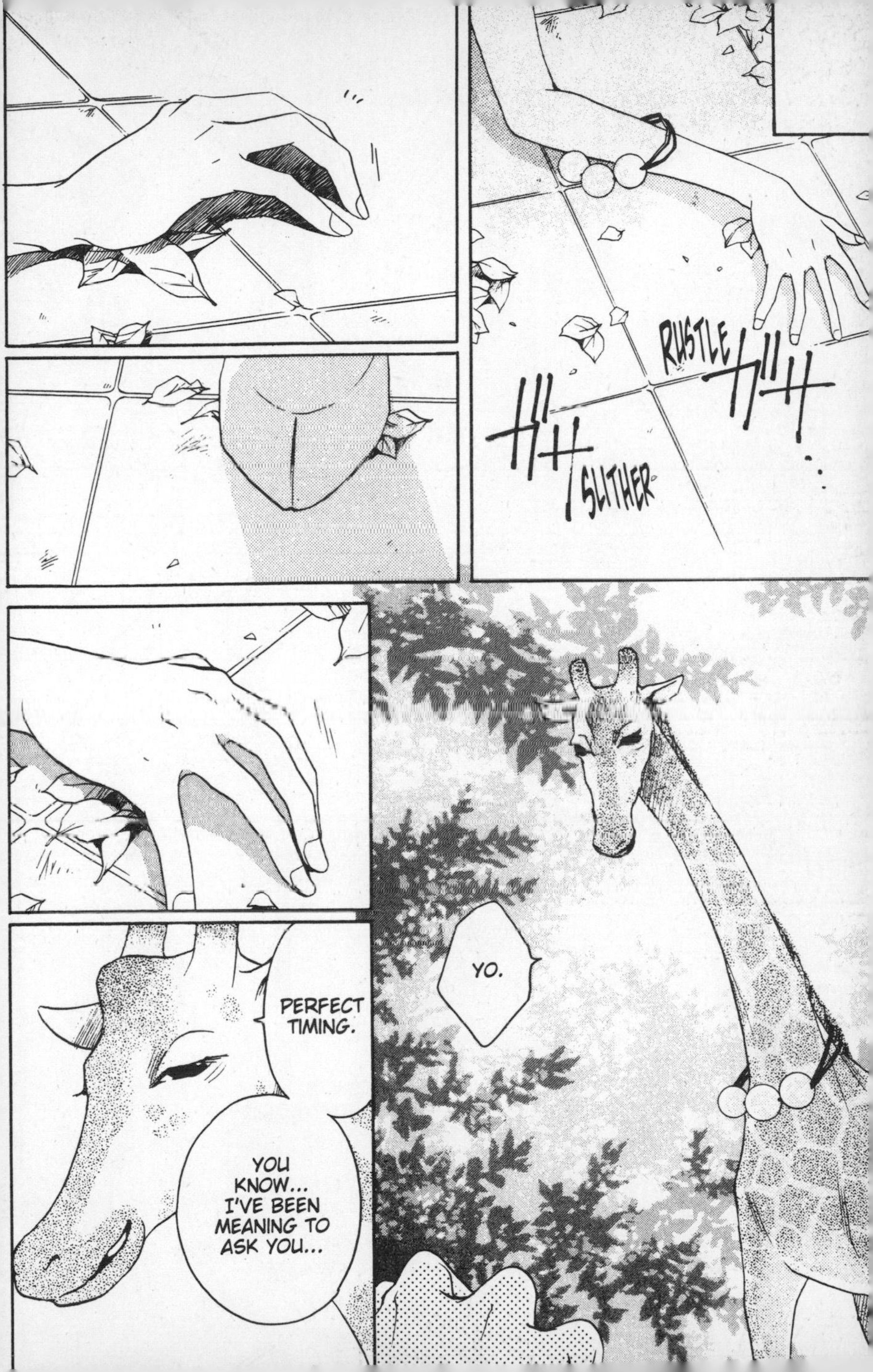
RUSTLE
SLITHER
YO.
PERFECT TIMING.
YOU KNOW... I'VE BEEN MEANING TO ASK YOU...

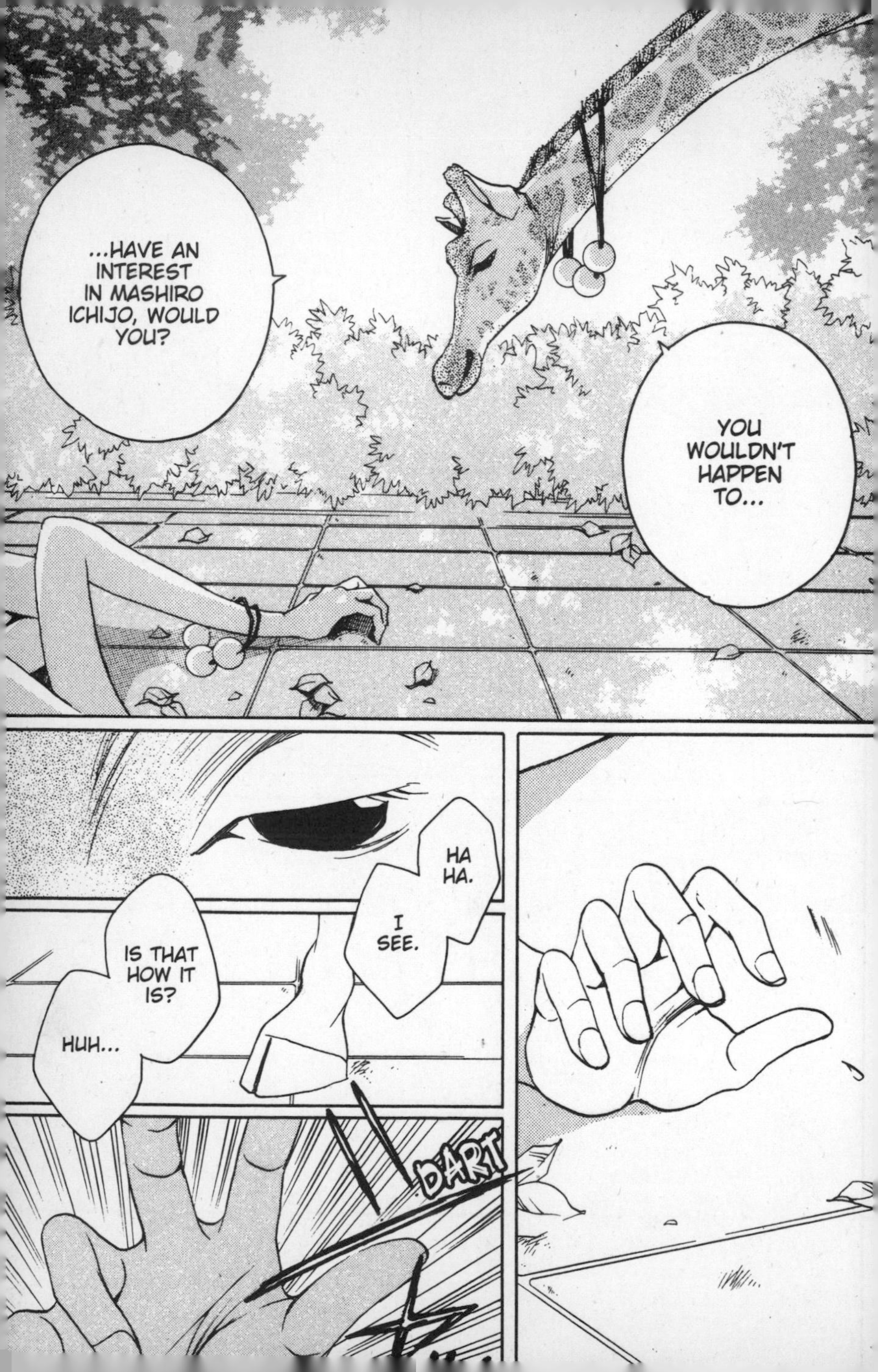
YOU WOULDN'T HAPPEN TO...
...HAVE AN INTEREST IN MASHIRO ICHIJO, WOULD YOU?
HA HA.
I SEE.
IS THAT HOW IT IS?
HUH...
DART

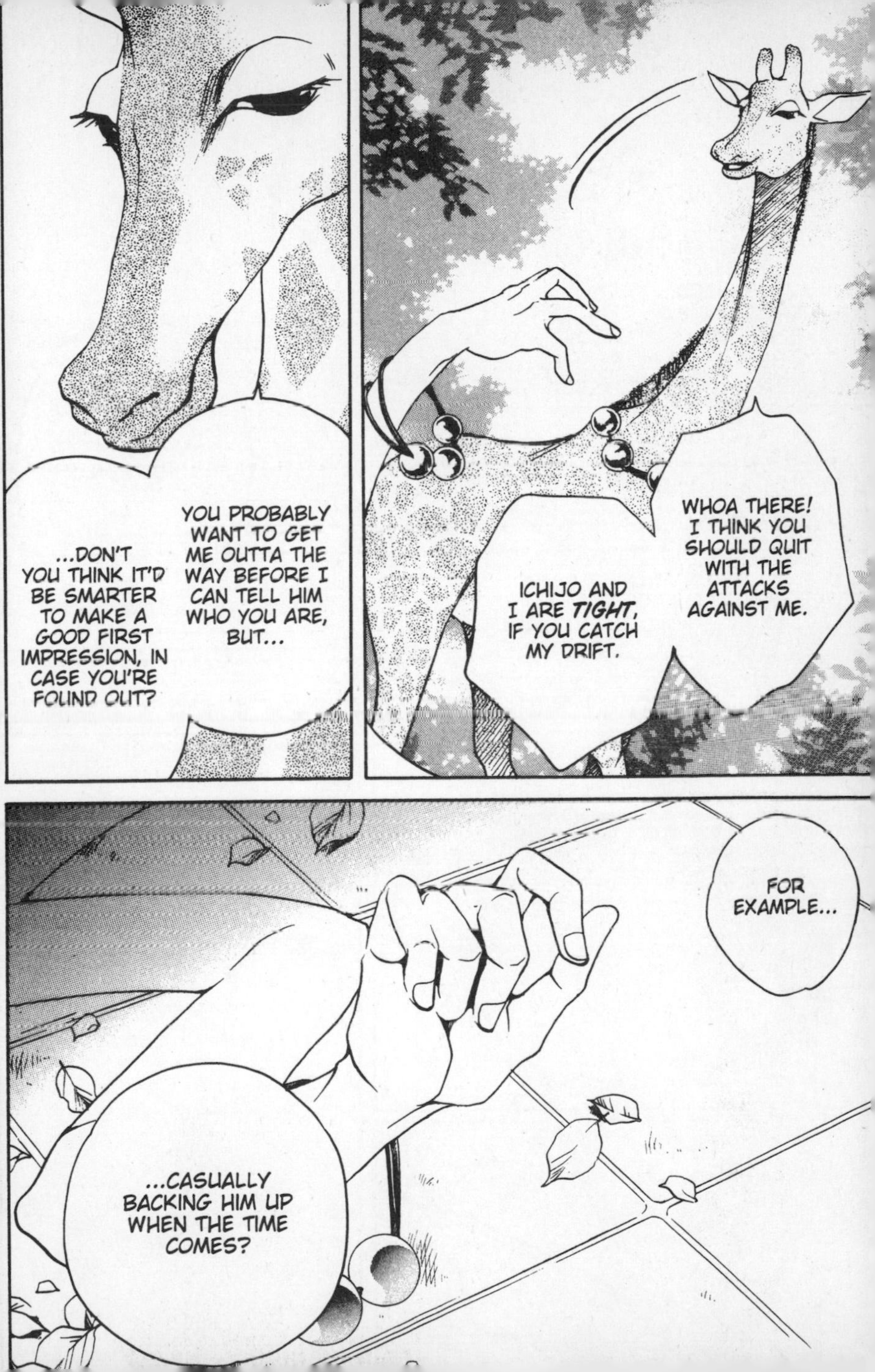
WHOA THERE! I THINK YOU SHOULD QUIT WITH THE ATTACKS AGAINST ME.
ICHIJO AND I ARE *TIGHT*, IF YOU CATCH MY DRIFT.
YOU PROBABLY WANT TO GET ME OUTTA THE WAY BEFORE I CAN TELL HIM WHO YOU ARE, BUT...
...DON'T YOU THINK IT'D BE SMARTER TO MAKE A GOOD FIRST IMPRESSION, IN CASE YOU'RE FOUND OUT?
FOR EXAMPLE...
...CASUALLY BACKING HIM UP WHEN THE TIME COMES?

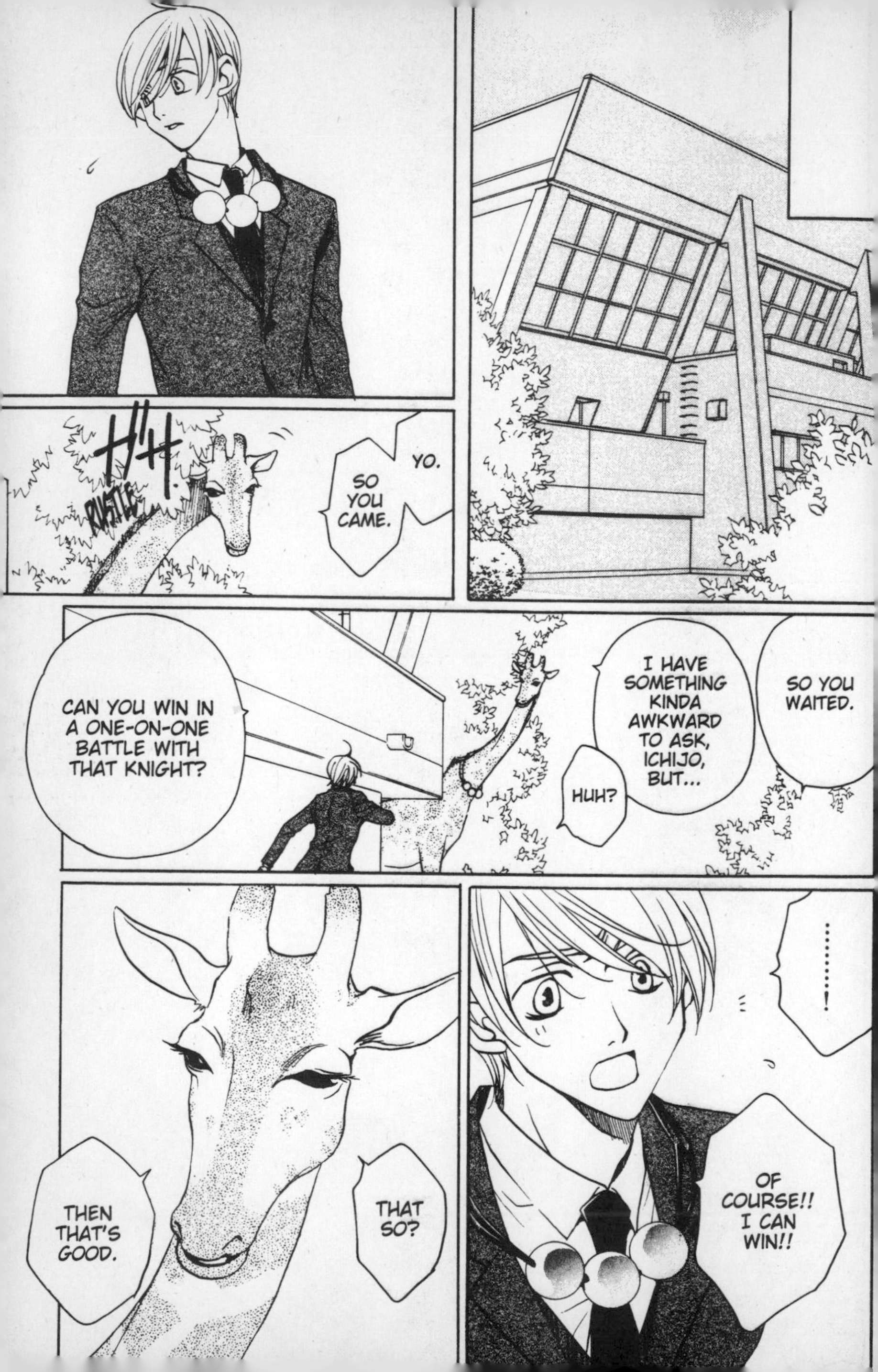
YO.
SO YOU CAME.
RUSTLE
SO YOU WAITED.
I HAVE SOMETHING KINDA AWKWARD TO ASK, ICHIJO, BUT...
HUH?
CAN YOU WIN IN A ONE-ON-ONE BATTLE WITH THAT KNIGHT?
……!
OF COURSE!! I CAN WIN!!
THAT SO?
THEN THAT'S GOOD.

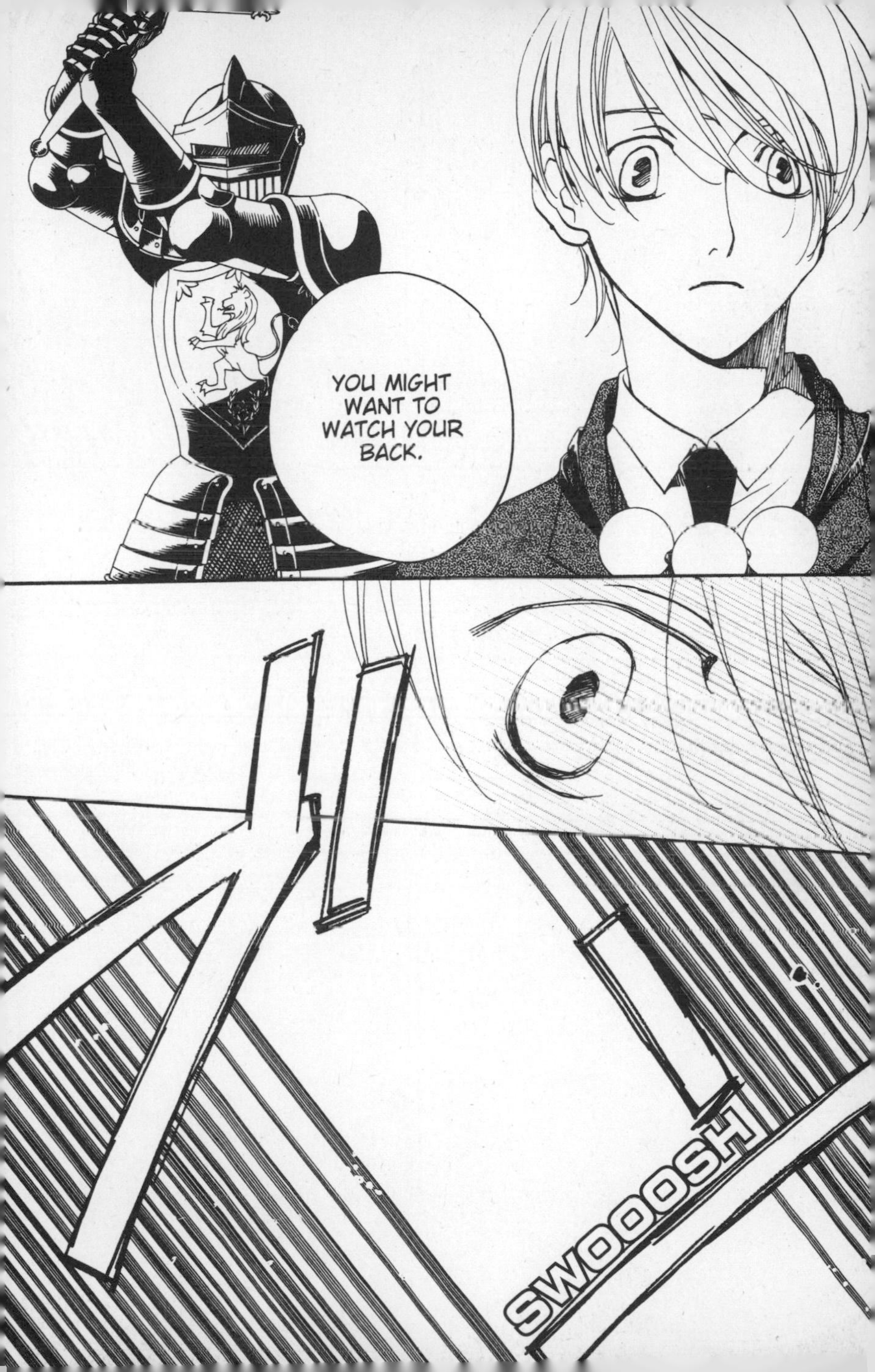
YOU MIGHT WANT TO WATCH YOUR BACK.
SWOOOSH

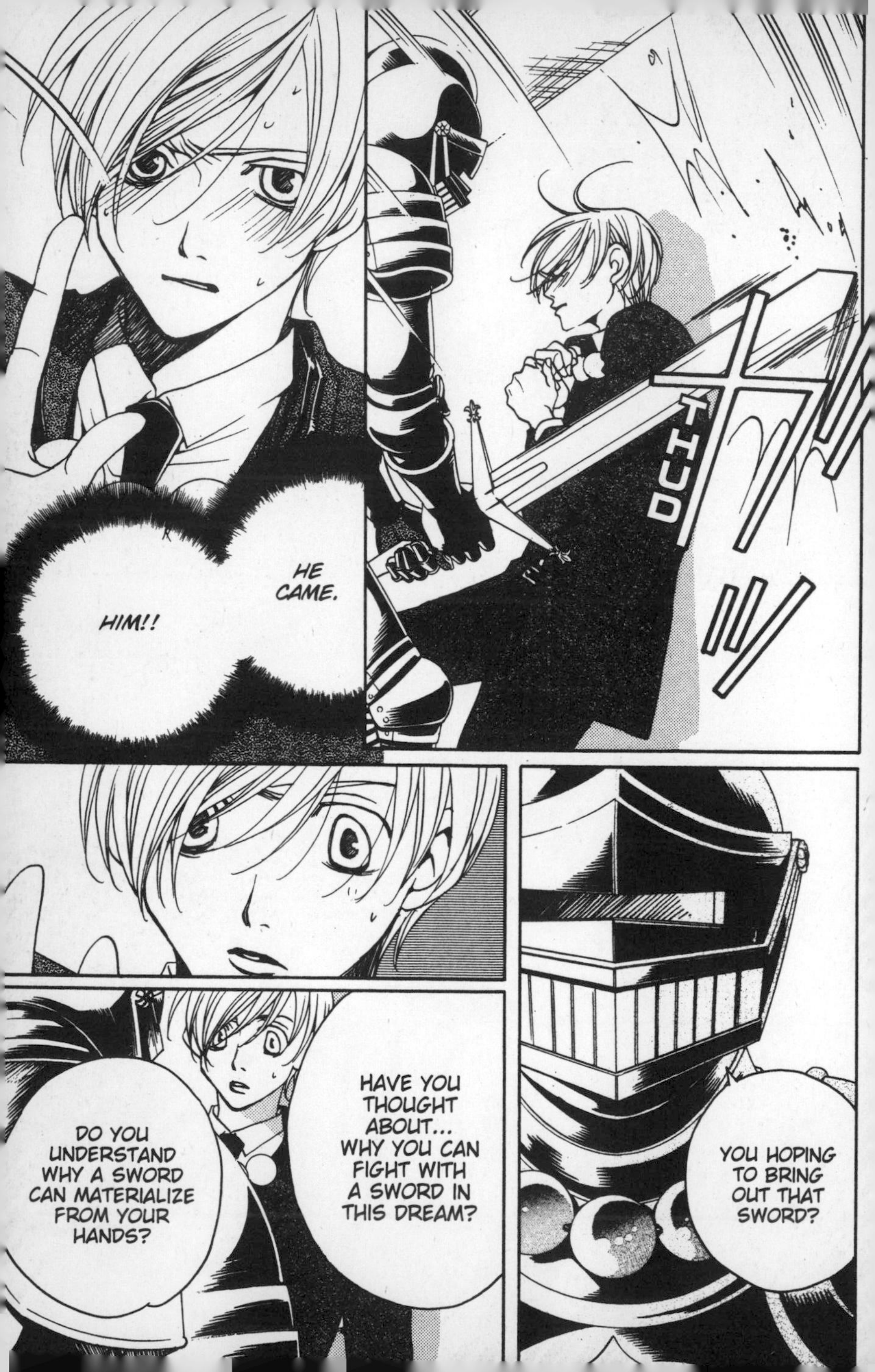
THUD
HE CAME.
HIM!!
YOU HOPING TO BRING OUT THAT SWORD?
HAVE YOU THOUGHT ABOUT... WHY YOU CAN FIGHT WITH A SWORD IN THIS DREAM?
DO YOU UNDERSTAND WHY A SWORD CAN MATERIALIZE FROM YOUR HANDS?

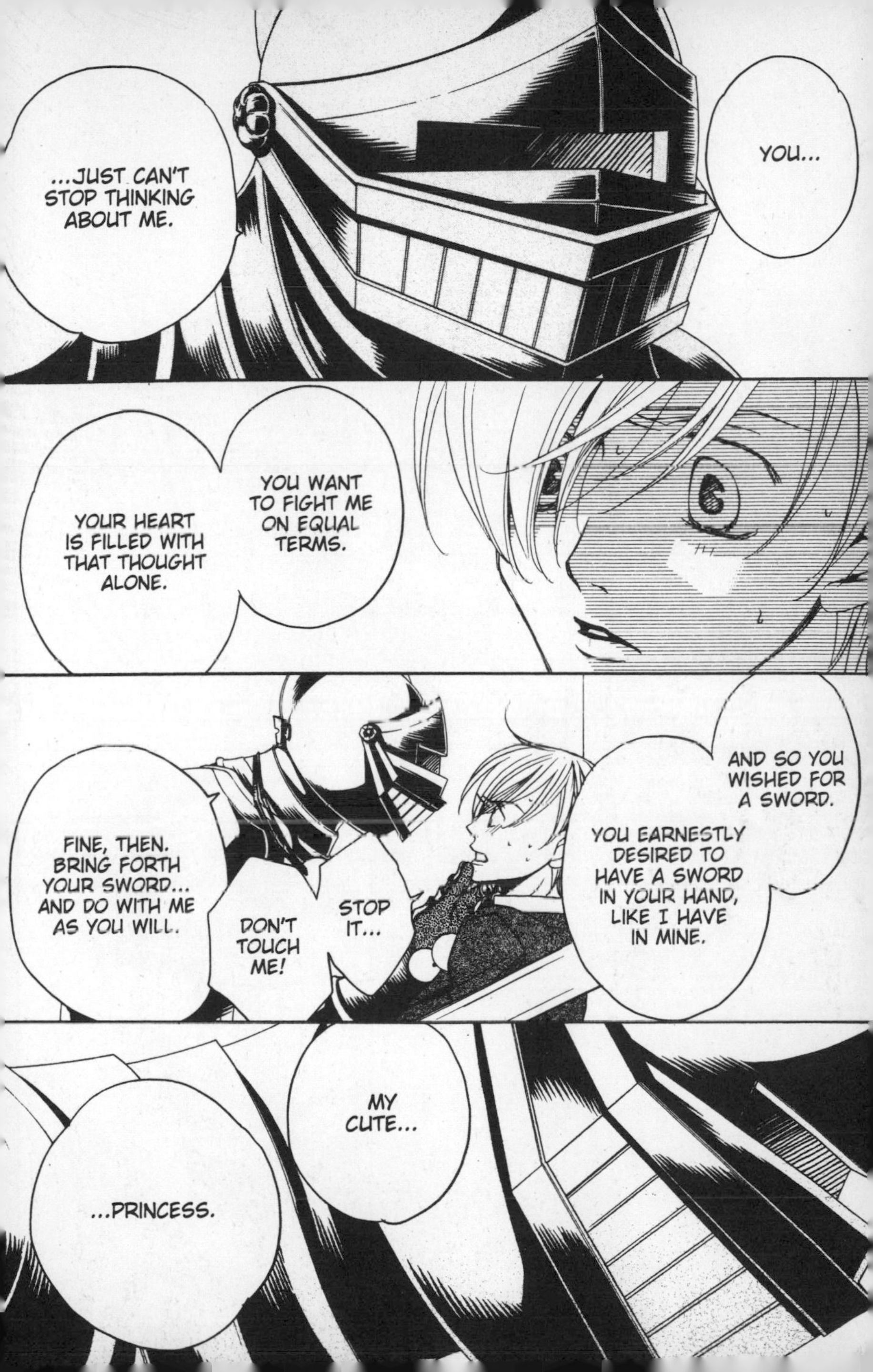
YOU...
...JUST CAN'T STOP THINKING ABOUT ME.
YOU WANT TO FIGHT ME ON EQUAL TERMS.
YOUR HEART IS FILLED WITH THAT THOUGHT ALONE.
AND SO YOU WISHED FOR A SWORD.
YOU EARNESTLY DESIRED TO HAVE A SWORD IN YOUR HAND, LIKE I HAVE IN MINE.
STOP IT...
DON'T TOUCH ME!
FINE, THEN. BRING FORTH YOUR SWORD... AND DO WITH ME AS YOU WILL.
MY CUTE...
...PRINCESS.

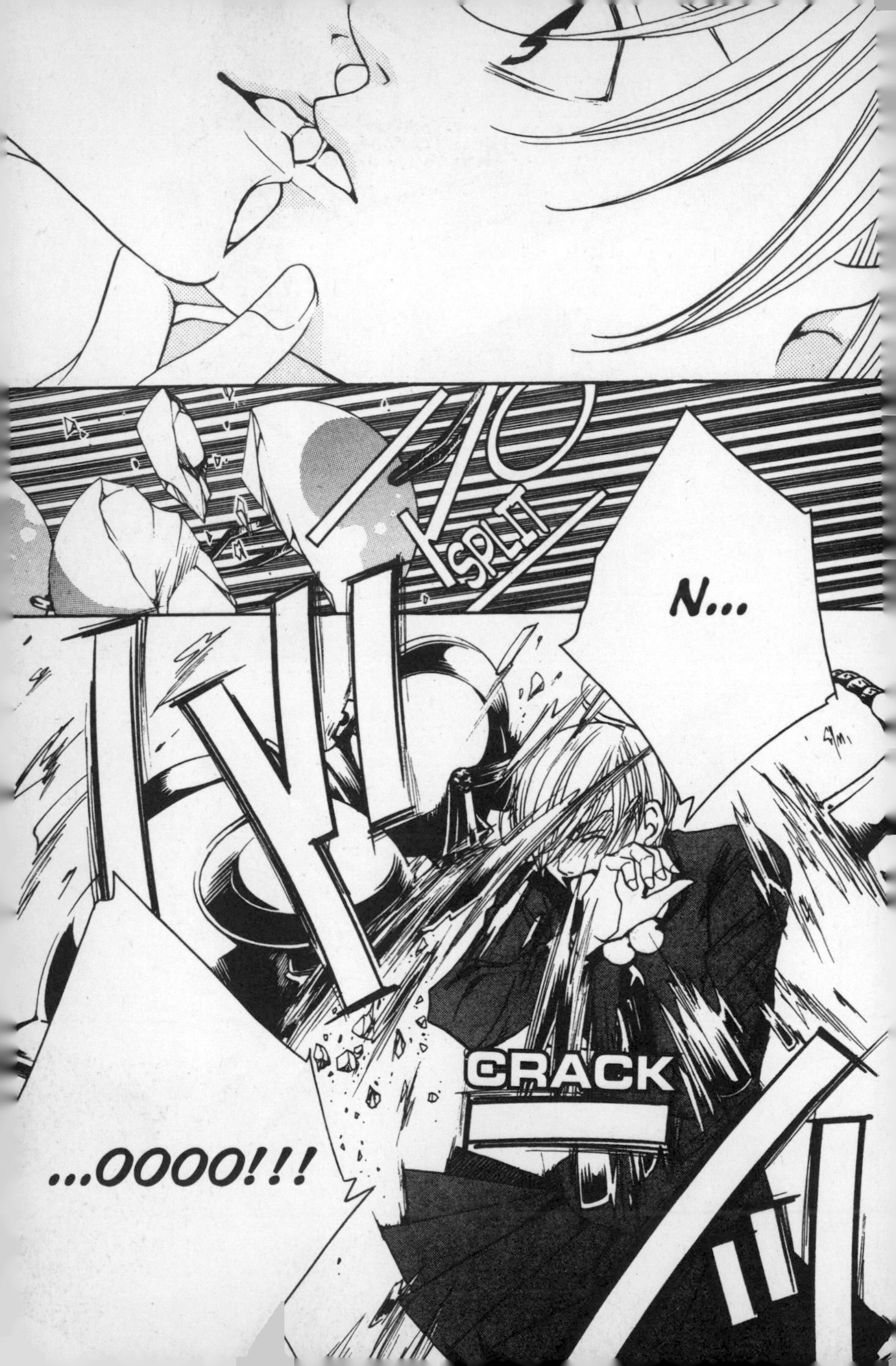
SPLIT
N...
CRACK
...OOOO!!!

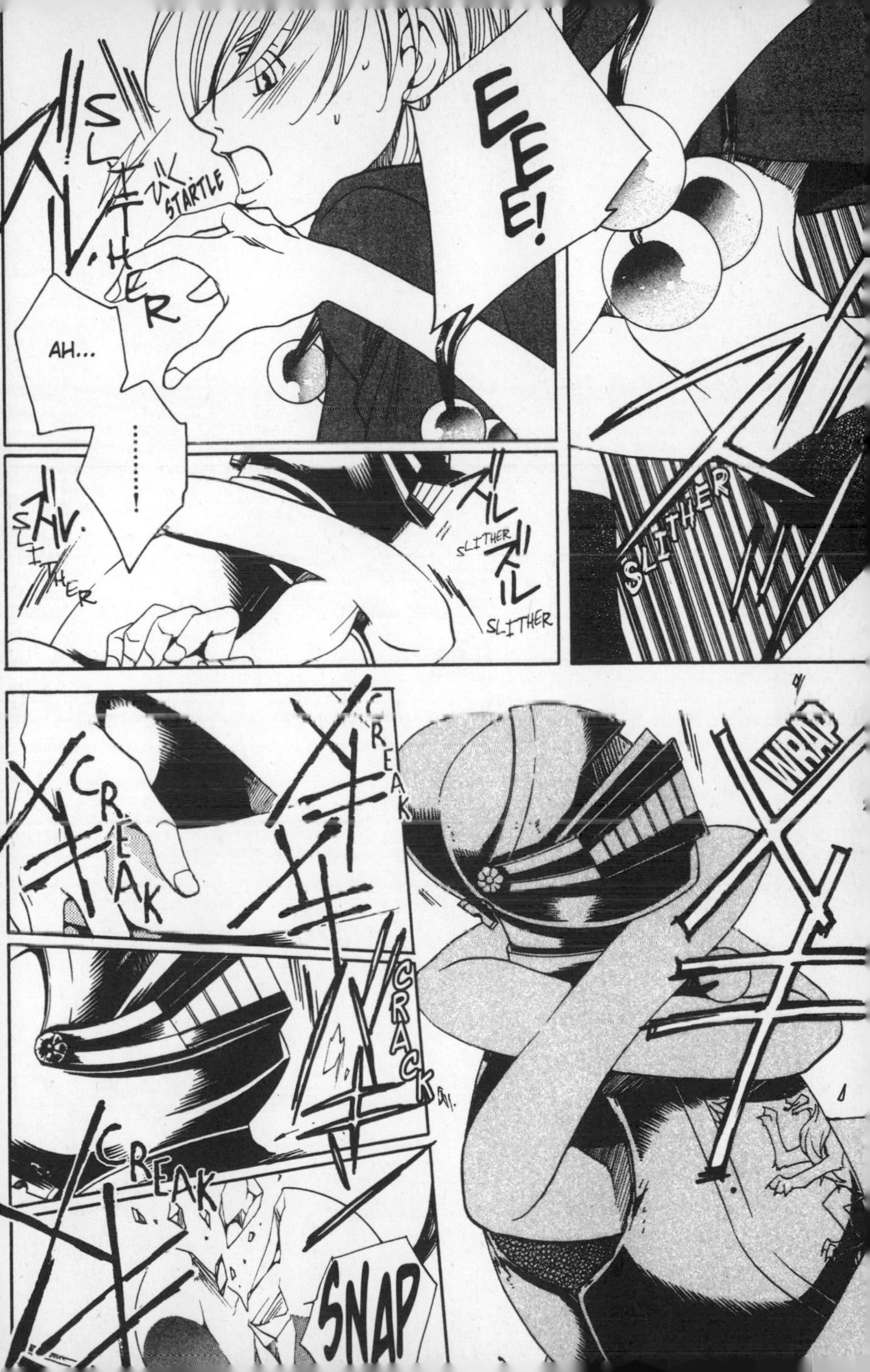
EEEE!
STARTLE
SLITHER
AH...
......!
SLITHER
SLITHER
SLITHER
SLITHER
WRAP
CREAK
CREAK
CRACK
CREAK
SNAP

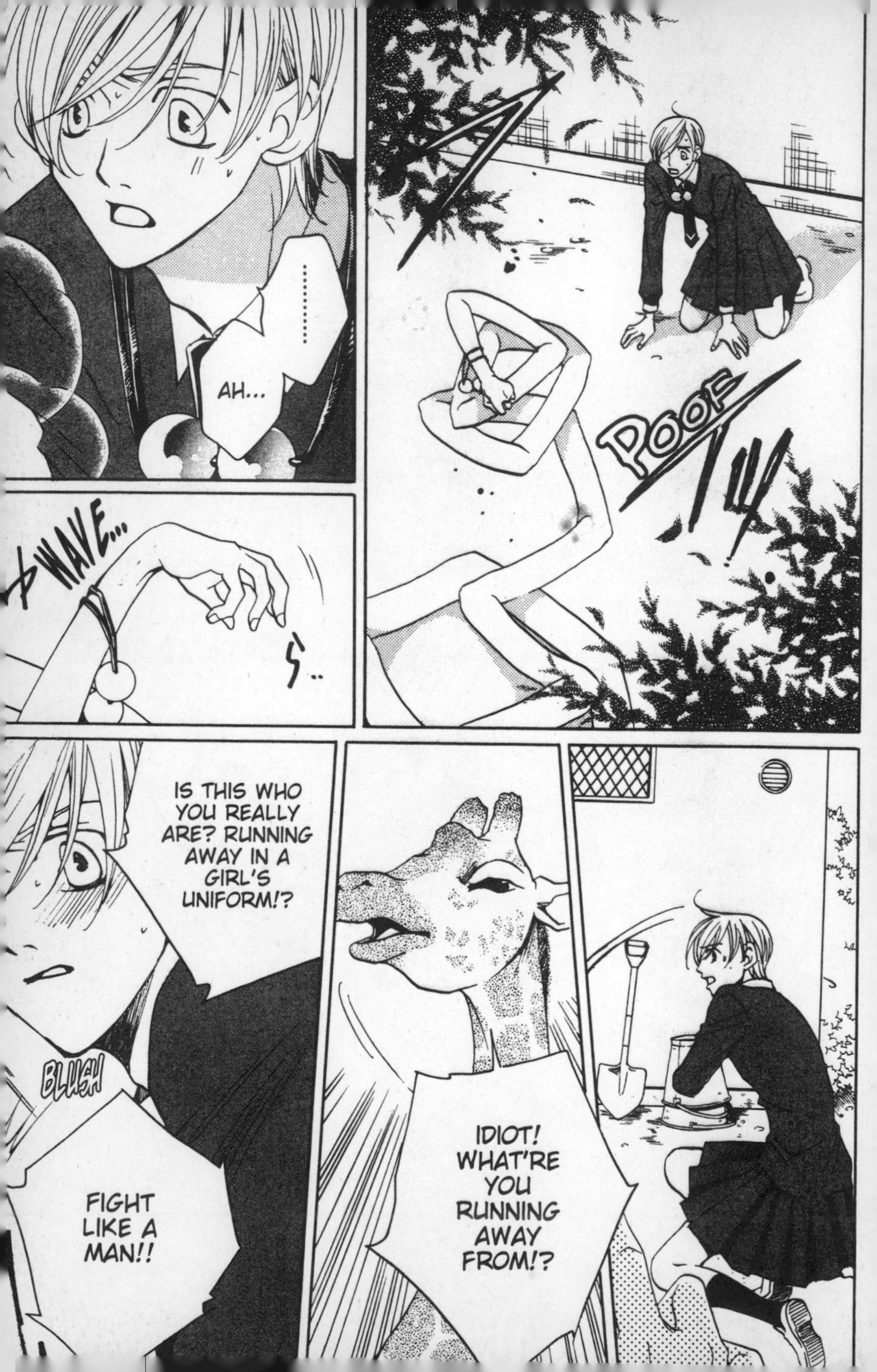
POOF
......
AH...
WAVE...
IDIOT! WHAT'RE YOU RUNNING AWAY FROM!?
IS THIS WHO YOU REALLY ARE? RUNNING AWAY IN A GIRL'S UNIFORM!?
BLUSH
FIGHT LIKE A MAN!!

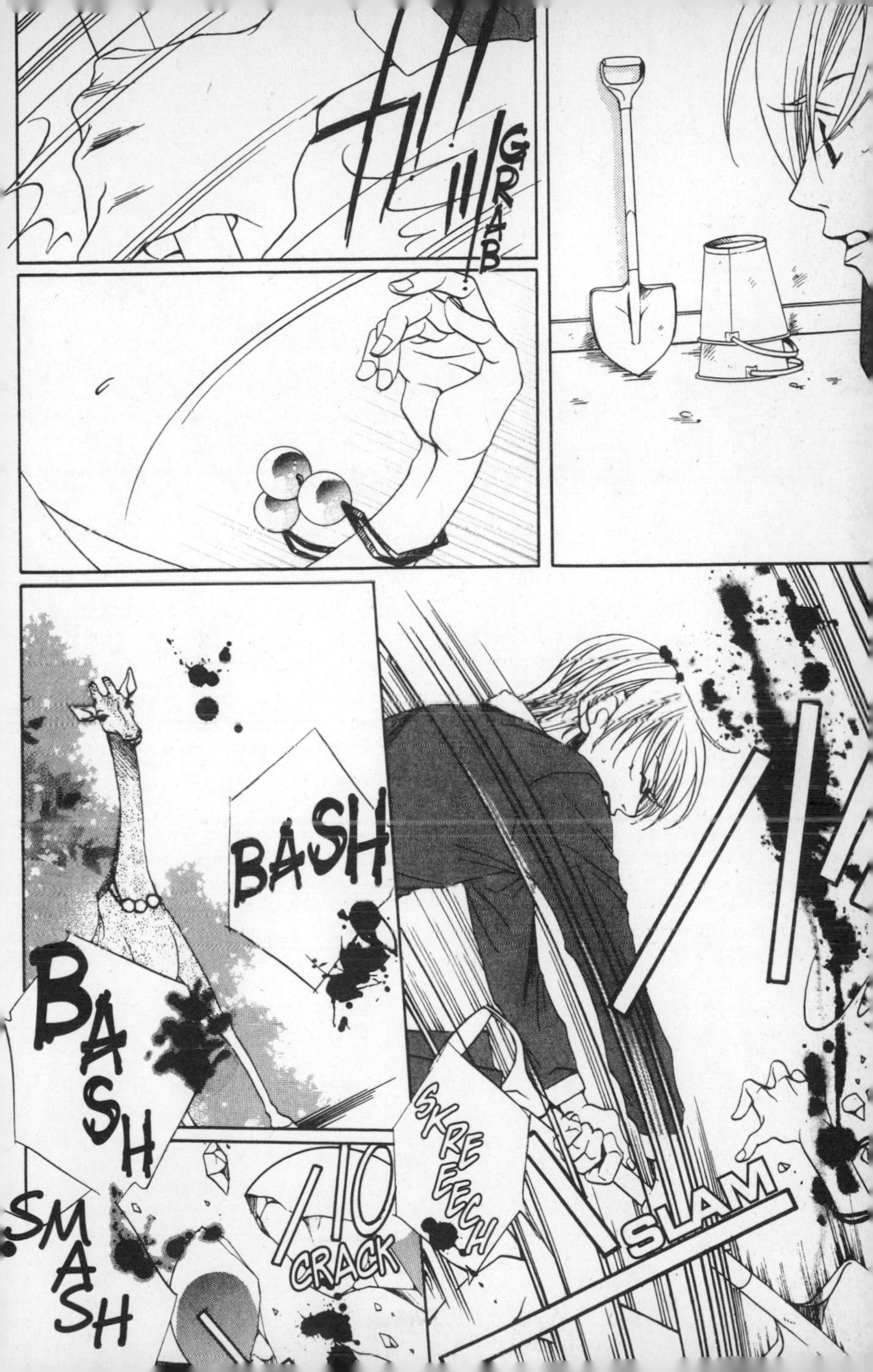
GRAB
BASH
SLAM
SKREEECH
CRACK
BASH
SMASH

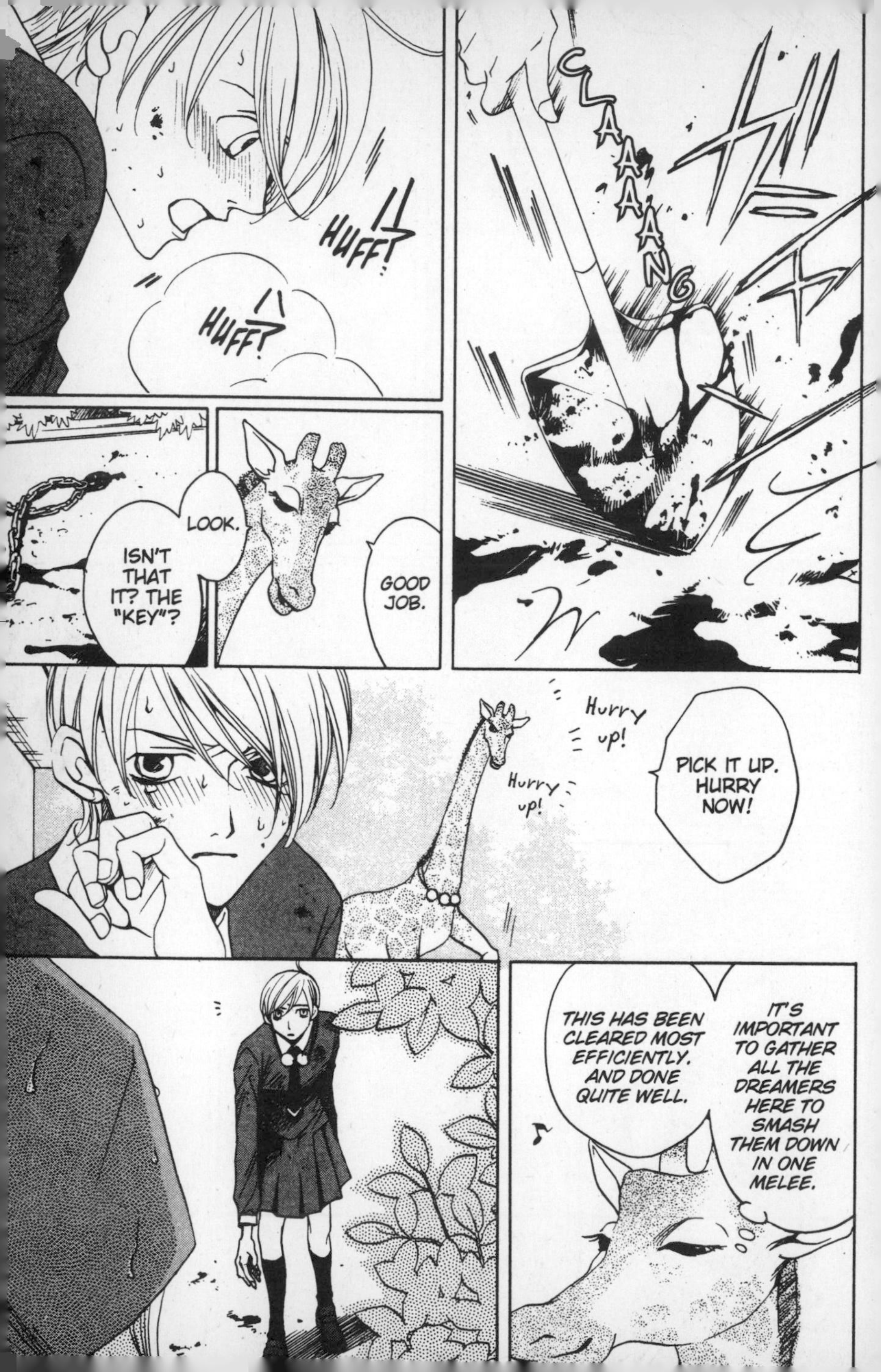
CLAAAAANG
HUFF!
HUFF!
GOOD JOB.
LOOK.
ISN'T THAT IT? THE "KEY"?
PICK IT UP. HURRY NOW!
Hurry up!
Hurry up!
THIS HAS BEEN CLEARED MOST EFFICIENTLY. AND DONE QUITE WELL.
IT'S IMPORTANT TO GATHER ALL THE DREAMERS HERE TO SMASH THEM DOWN IN ONE MELEE.

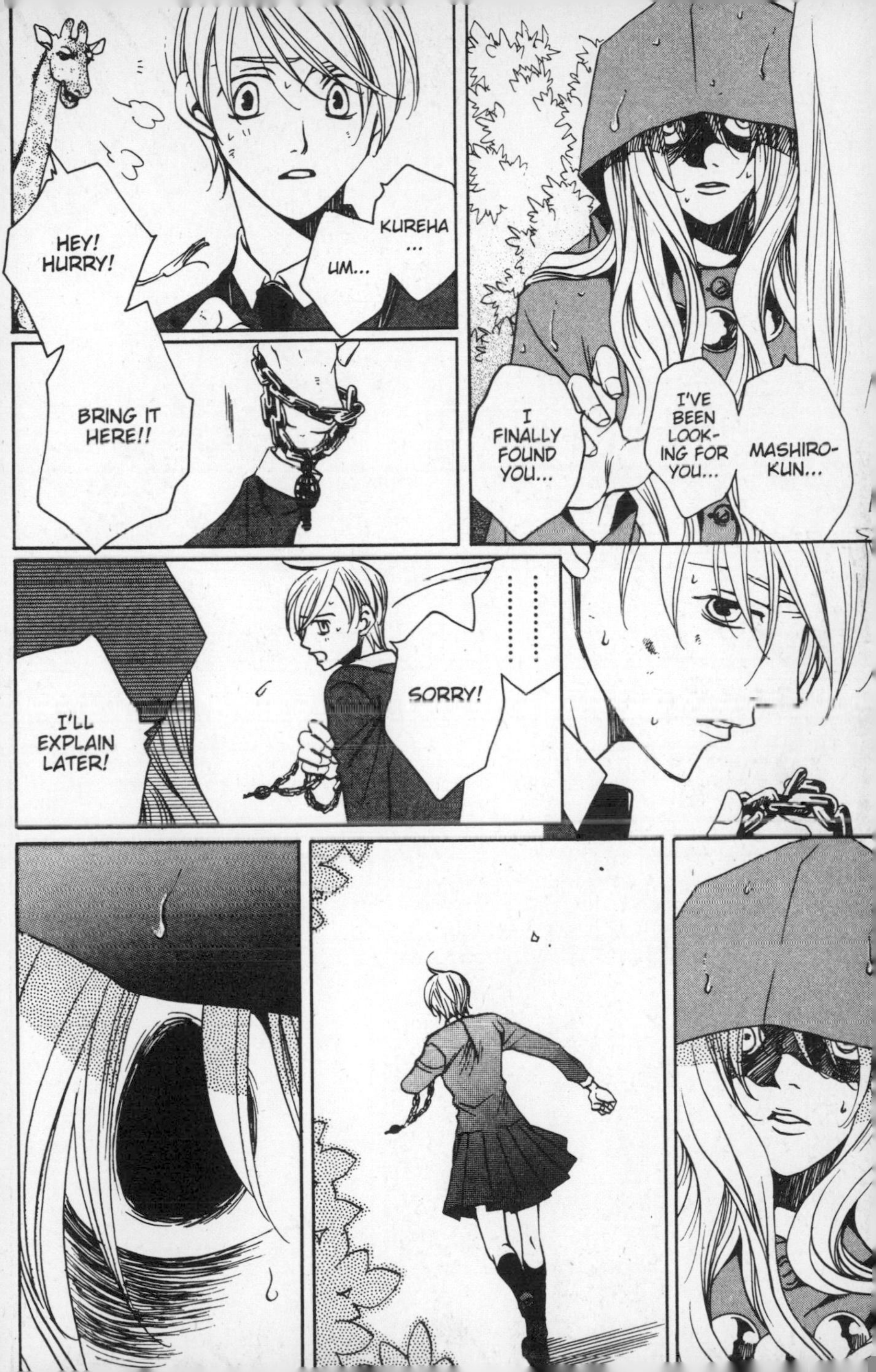

MASHIRO-KUN...
I'VE BEEN LOOKING FOR YOU...
I FINALLY FOUND YOU...
KUREHA ...
UM...
HEY! HURRY!
BRING IT HERE!!
......
SORRY!
I'LL EXPLAIN LATER!

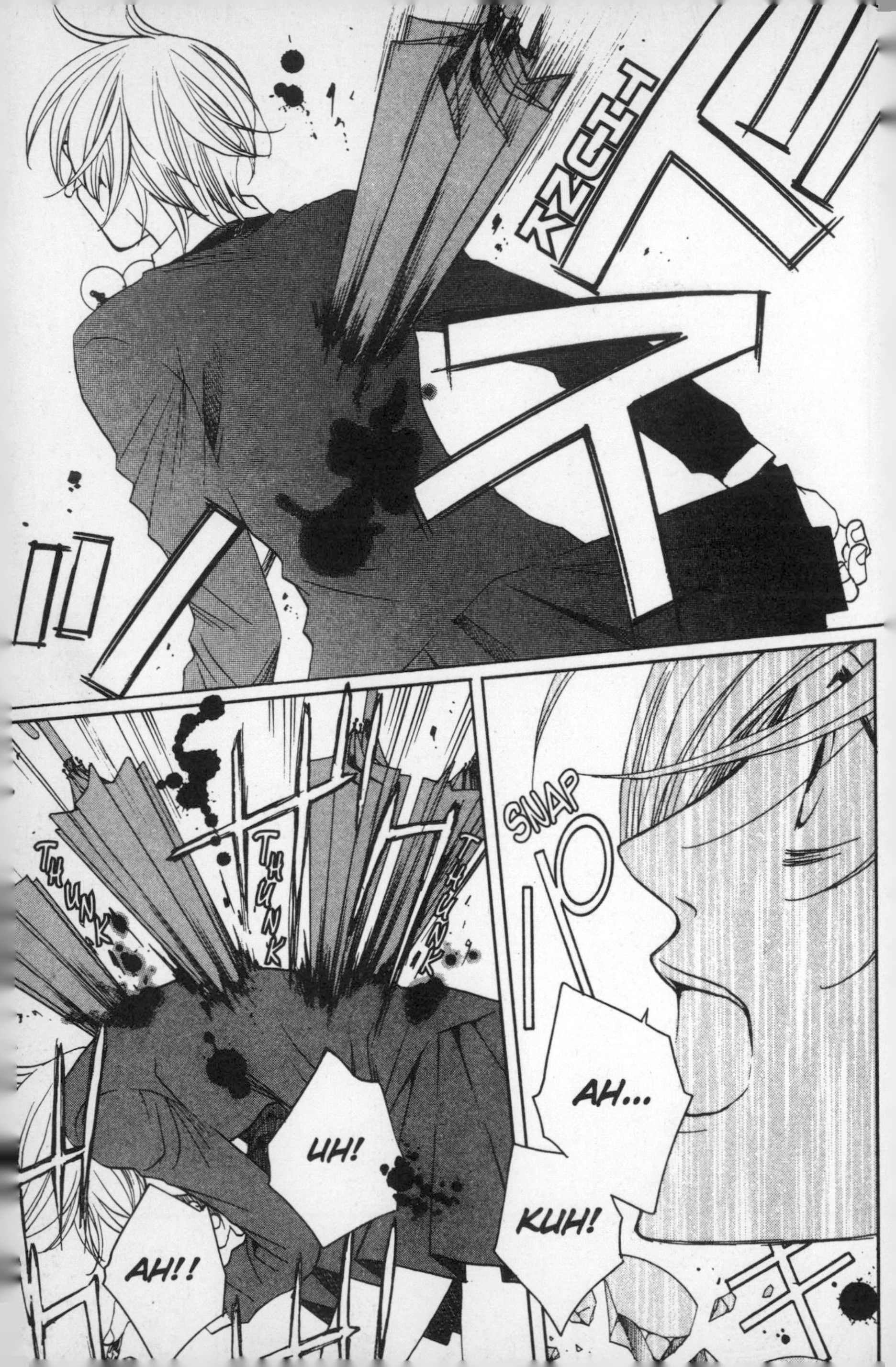
KZCHT
SNAP
AH...
KUH!
THUNK
THUNK
THUNK
UH!
AH!!

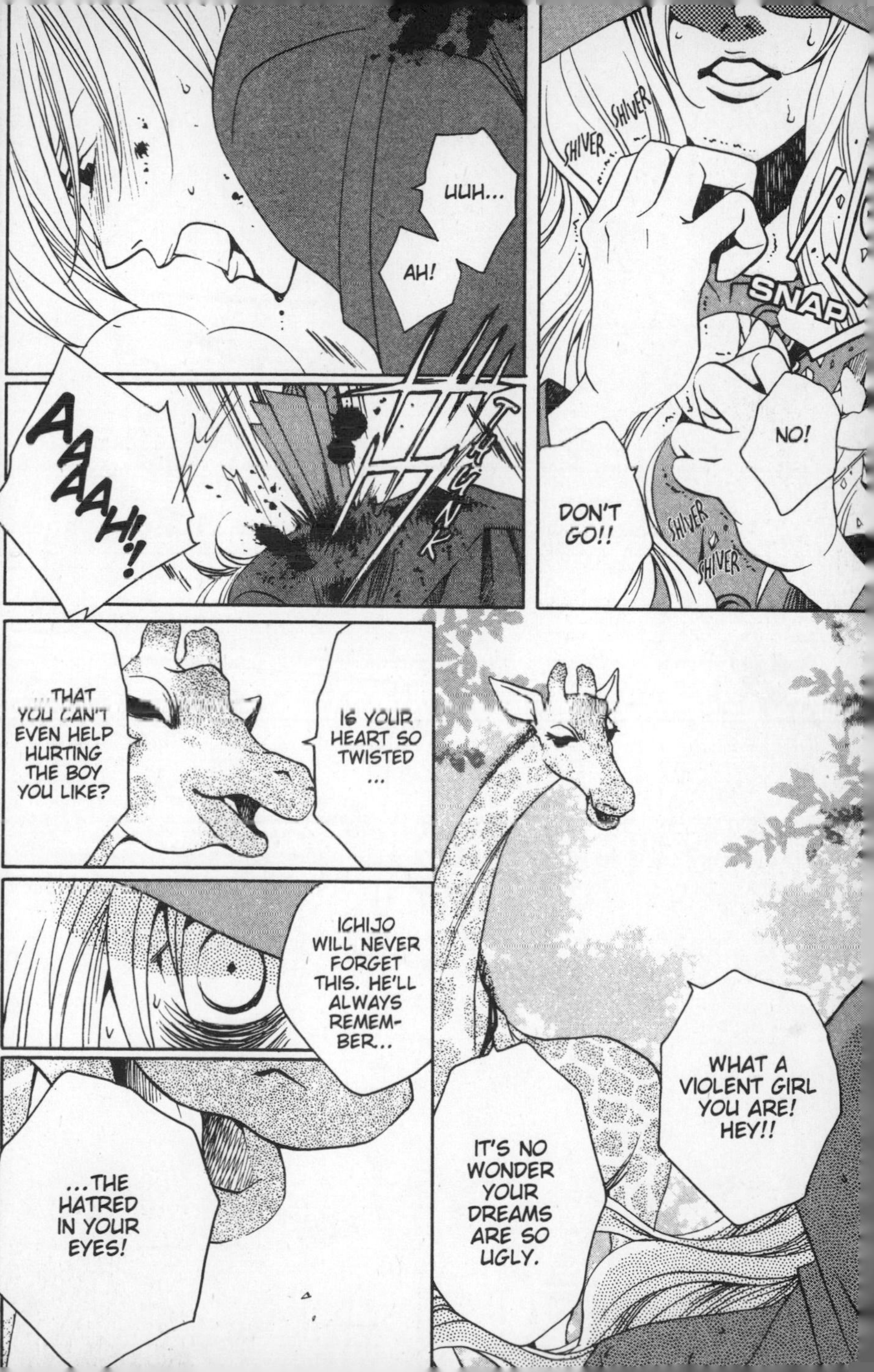
SHIVER SHIVER
SNAP
NO!
DON'T GO!!
SHIVER SHIVER
UUH...
AH!
AAAAH!!
THUNK
WHAT A VIOLENT GIRL YOU ARE! HEY!!
IT'S NO WONDER YOUR DREAMS ARE SO UGLY.
IS YOUR HEART SO TWISTED...
...THAT YOU CAN'T EVEN HELP HURTING THE BOY YOU LIKE?
ICHIJO WILL NEVER FORGET THIS. HE'LL ALWAYS REMEMBER...
...THE HATRED IN YOUR EYES!

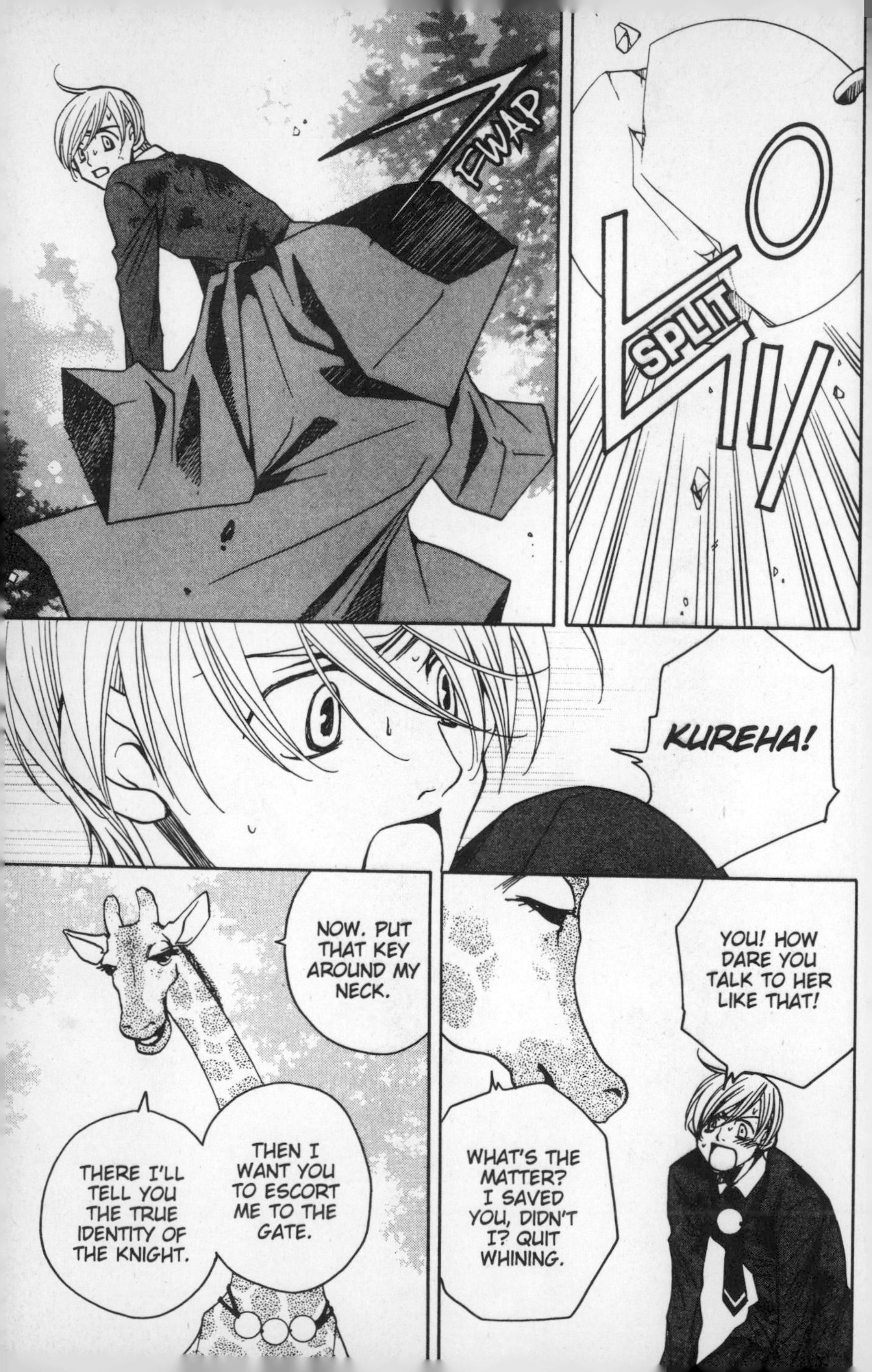
SPLIT
FWAP
KUREHA!
YOU! HOW DARE YOU TALK TO HER LIKE THAT!
WHAT'S THE MATTER? I SAVED YOU, DIDN'T I? QUIT WHINING.
NOW. PUT THAT KEY AROUND MY NECK.
THEN I WANT YOU TO ESCORT ME TO THE GATE.
THERE I'LL TELL YOU THE TRUE IDENTITY OF THE KNIGHT.

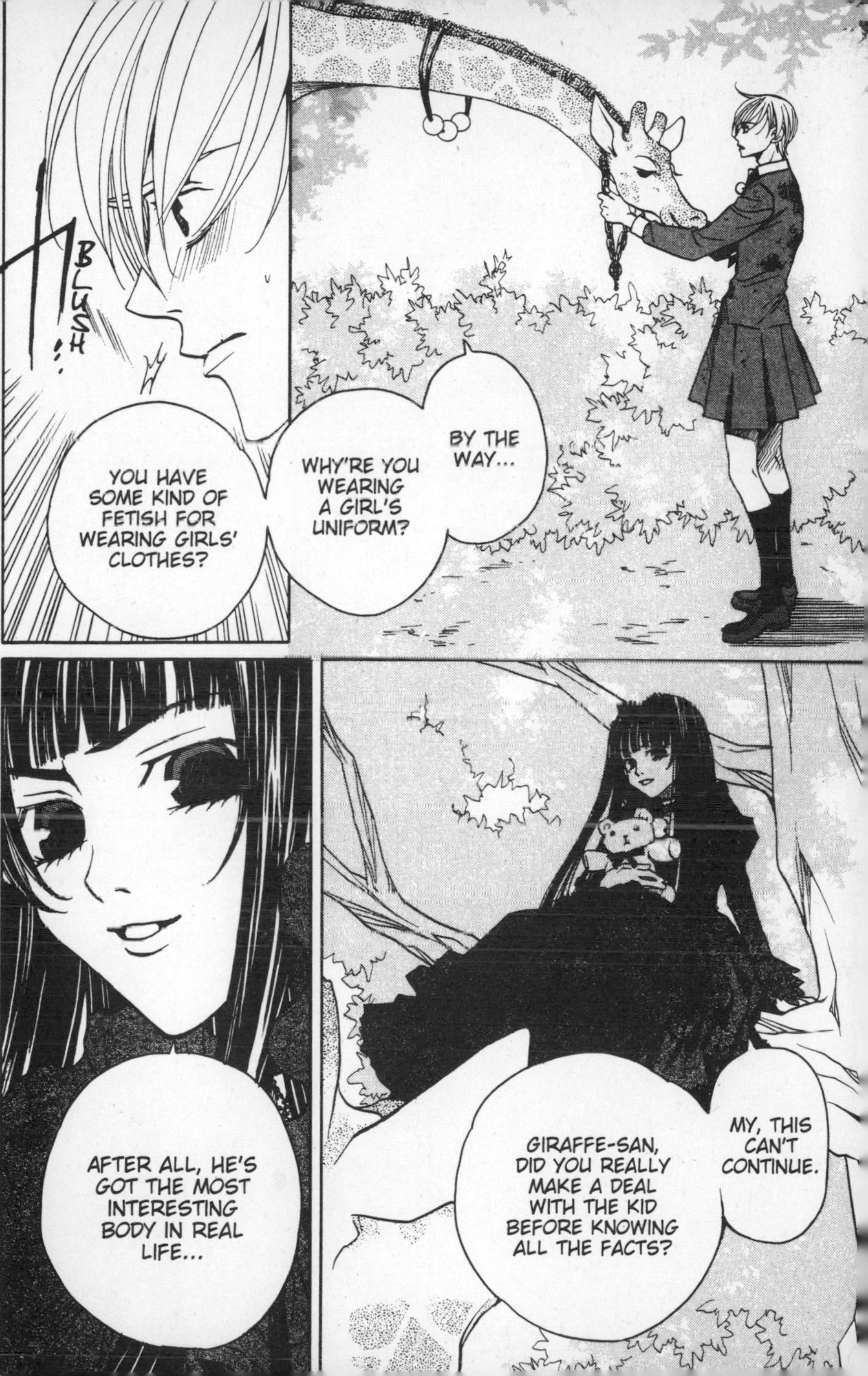
BY THE WAY...
WHY'RE YOU WEARING A GIRL'S UNIFORM?
YOU HAVE SOME KIND OF FETISH FOR WEARING GIRLS' CLOTHES?
BLUSH!!
MY, THIS CAN'T CONTINUE.
GIRAFFE-SAN, DID YOU REALLY MAKE A DEAL WITH THE KID BEFORE KNOWING ALL THE FACTS?
AFTER ALL, HE'S GOT THE MOST INTERESTING BODY IN REAL LIFE...

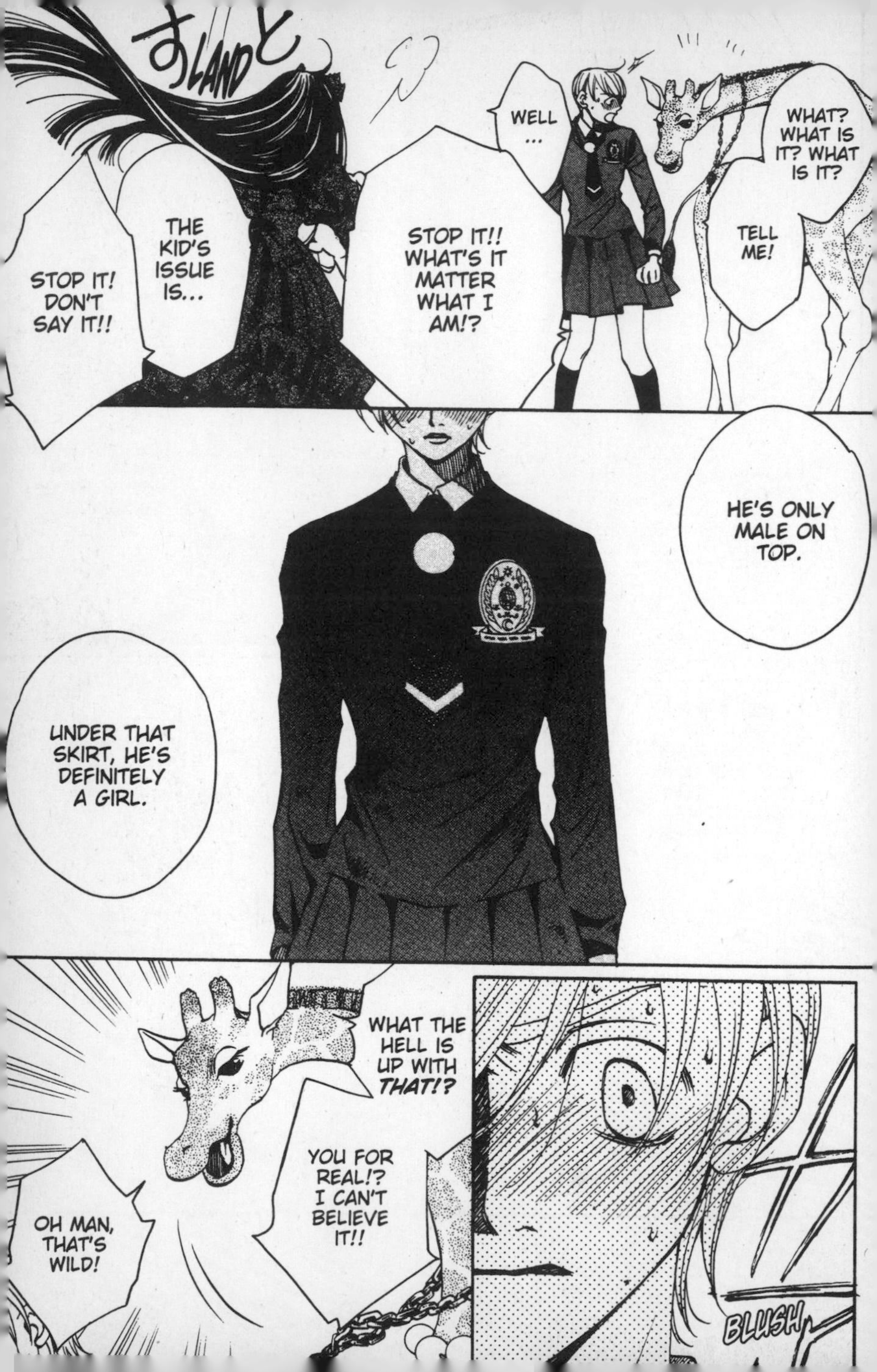
WHAT? WHAT IS IT? WHAT IS IT?
TELL ME!
WELL ...
すLANDと
STOP IT!! WHAT'S IT MATTER WHAT I AM!?
THE KID'S ISSUE IS...
STOP IT! DON'T SAY IT!!
HE'S ONLY MALE ON TOP.
UNDER THAT SKIRT, HE'S DEFINITELY A GIRL.
BLUSH
WHAT THE HELL IS UP WITH *THAT!?*
YOU FOR REAL!? I CAN'T BELIEVE IT!!
OH MAN, THAT'S WILD!

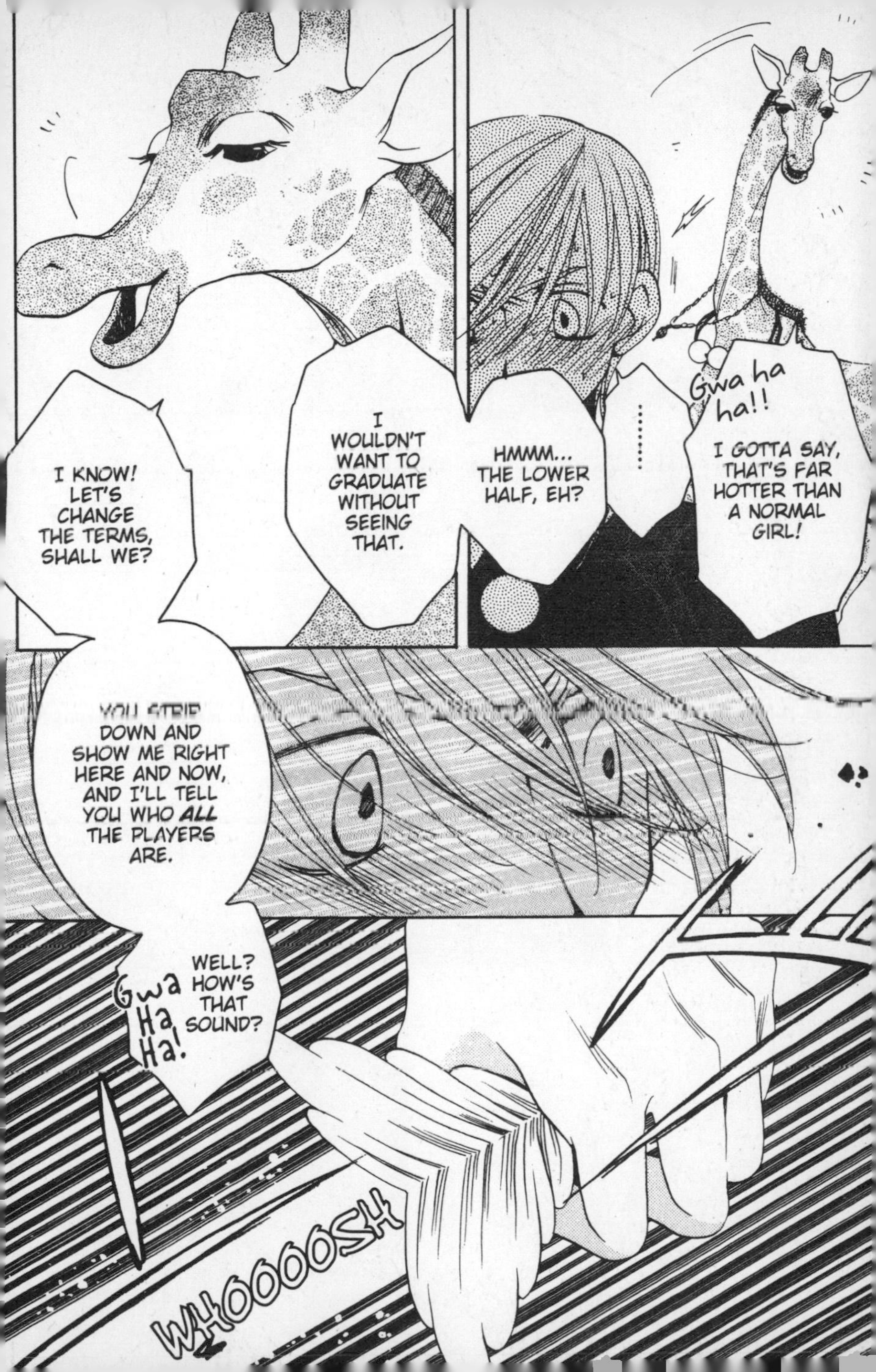
Gwa ha ha!!
I GOTTA SAY, THAT'S FAR HOTTER THAN A NORMAL GIRL!
......
HMMM... THE LOWER HALF, EH?
I WOULDN'T WANT TO GRADUATE WITHOUT SEEING THAT.
I KNOW! LET'S CHANGE THE TERMS, SHALL WE?
YOU STRIP DOWN AND SHOW ME RIGHT HERE AND NOW, AND I'LL TELL YOU WHO ALL THE PLAYERS ARE.
WELL? HOW'S THAT SOUND?
Gwa Ha Ha!
WHOOOOOSH

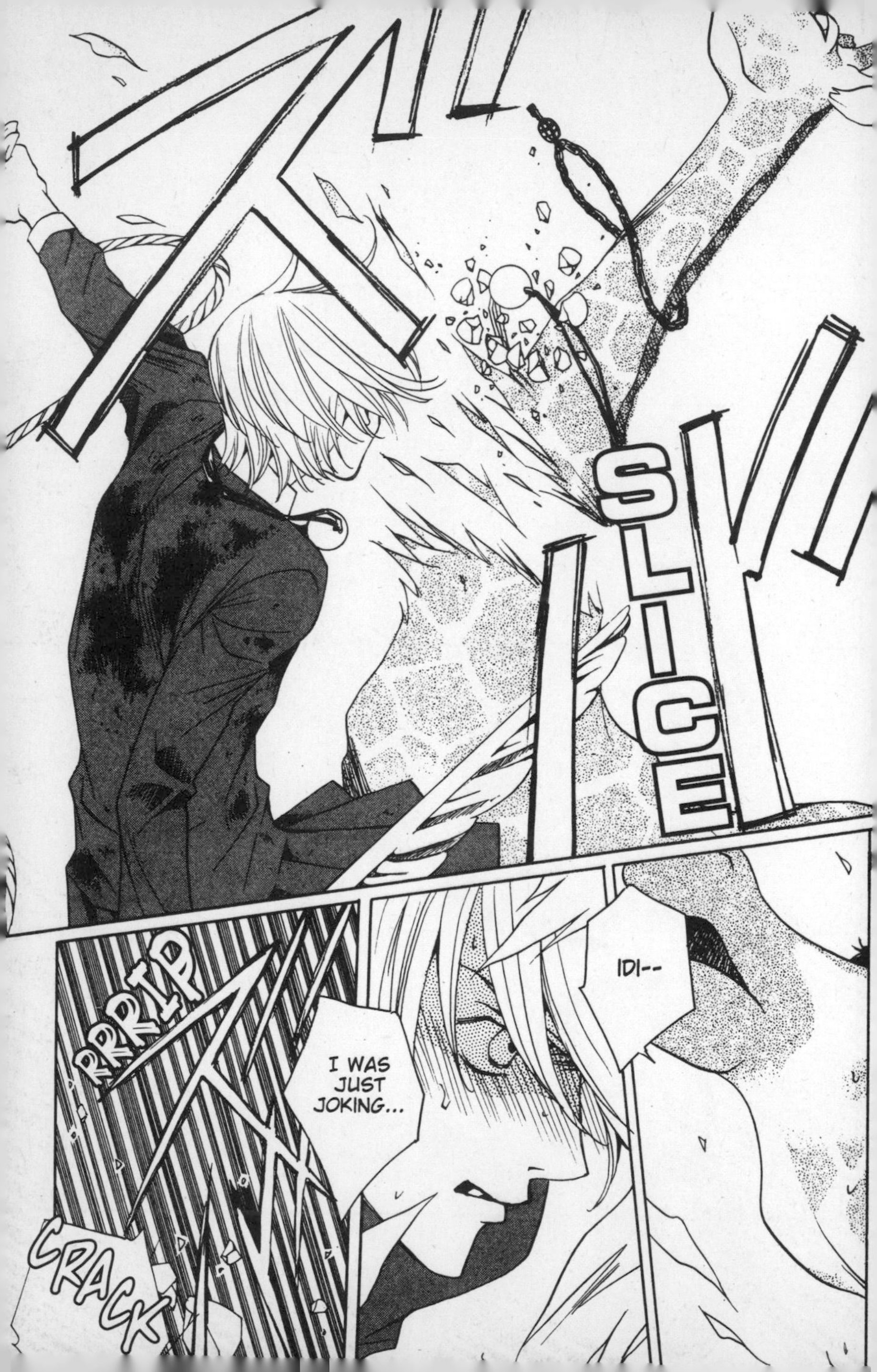
SLICE
IDI--
I WAS JUST JOKING...
RRRIP
CRACK

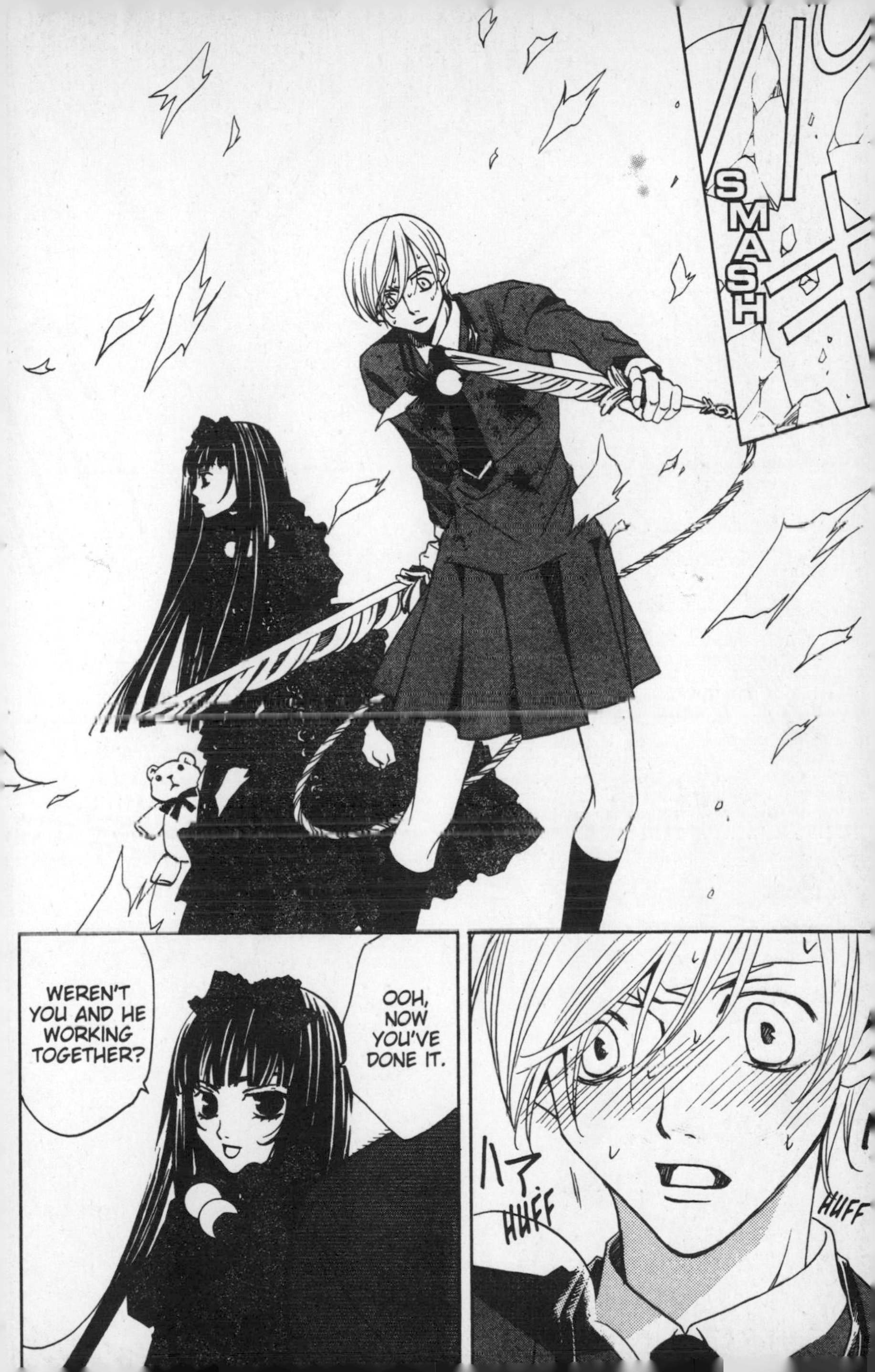
SMASH
ハア
HUFF
HUFF
OOH, NOW YOU'VE DONE IT.
WEREN'T YOU AND HE WORKING TOGETHER?

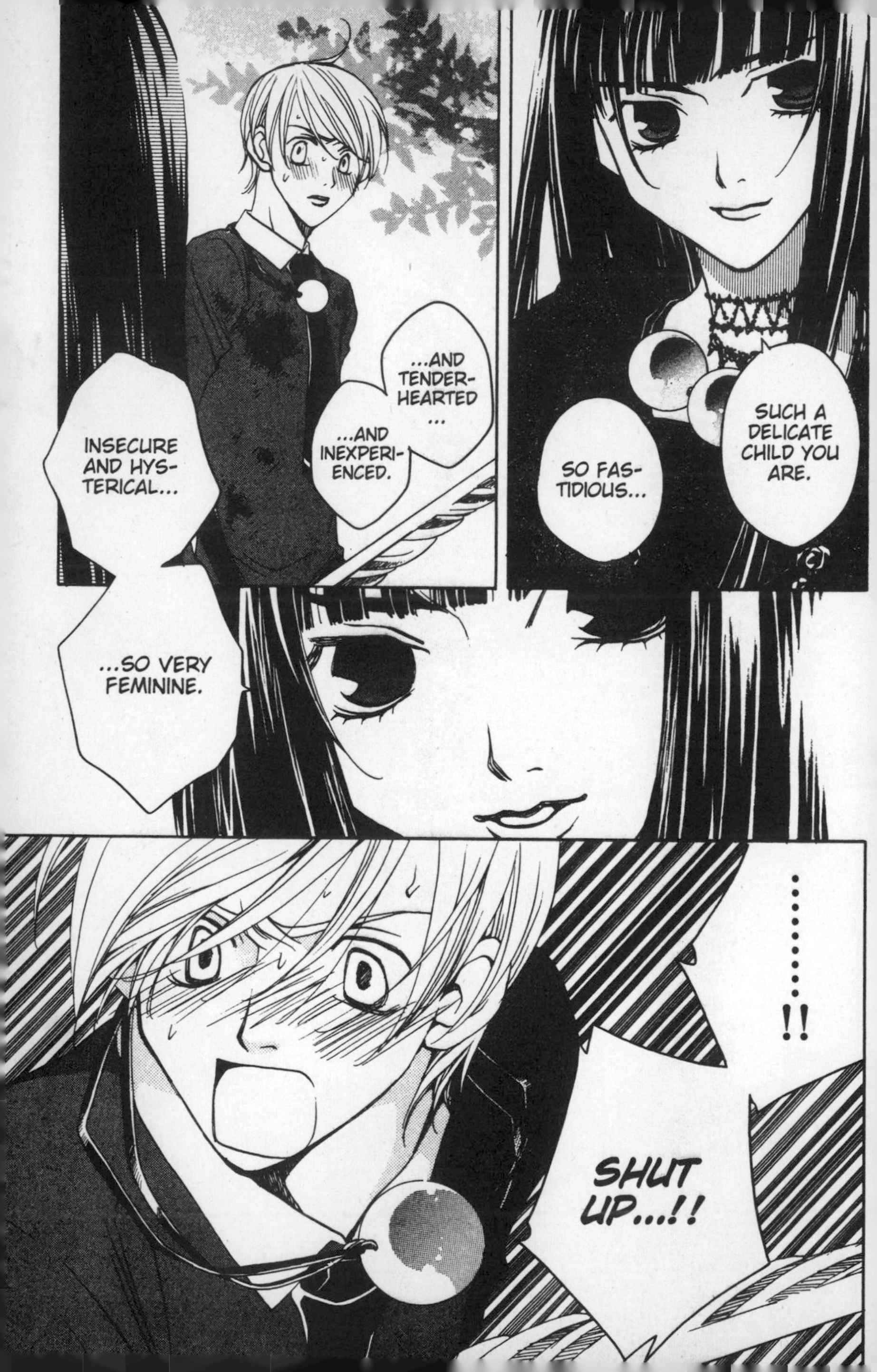
SUCH A DELICATE CHILD YOU ARE.
SO FASTIDIOUS...
...AND TENDER-HEARTED...
...AND INEXPERIENCED.
INSECURE AND HYSTERICAL...
...SO VERY FEMININE.
......!!
SHUT UP...!!

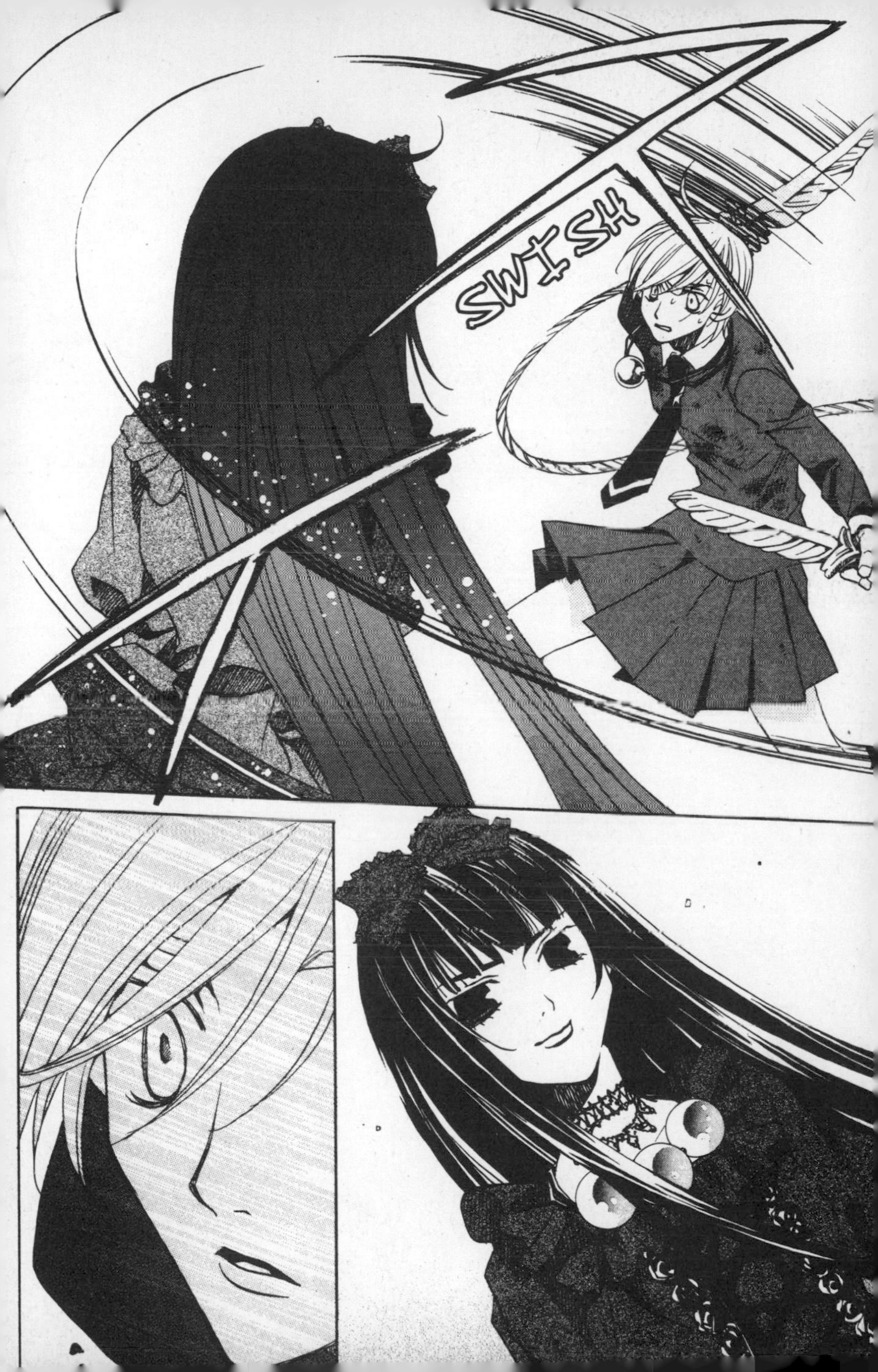
SWISH

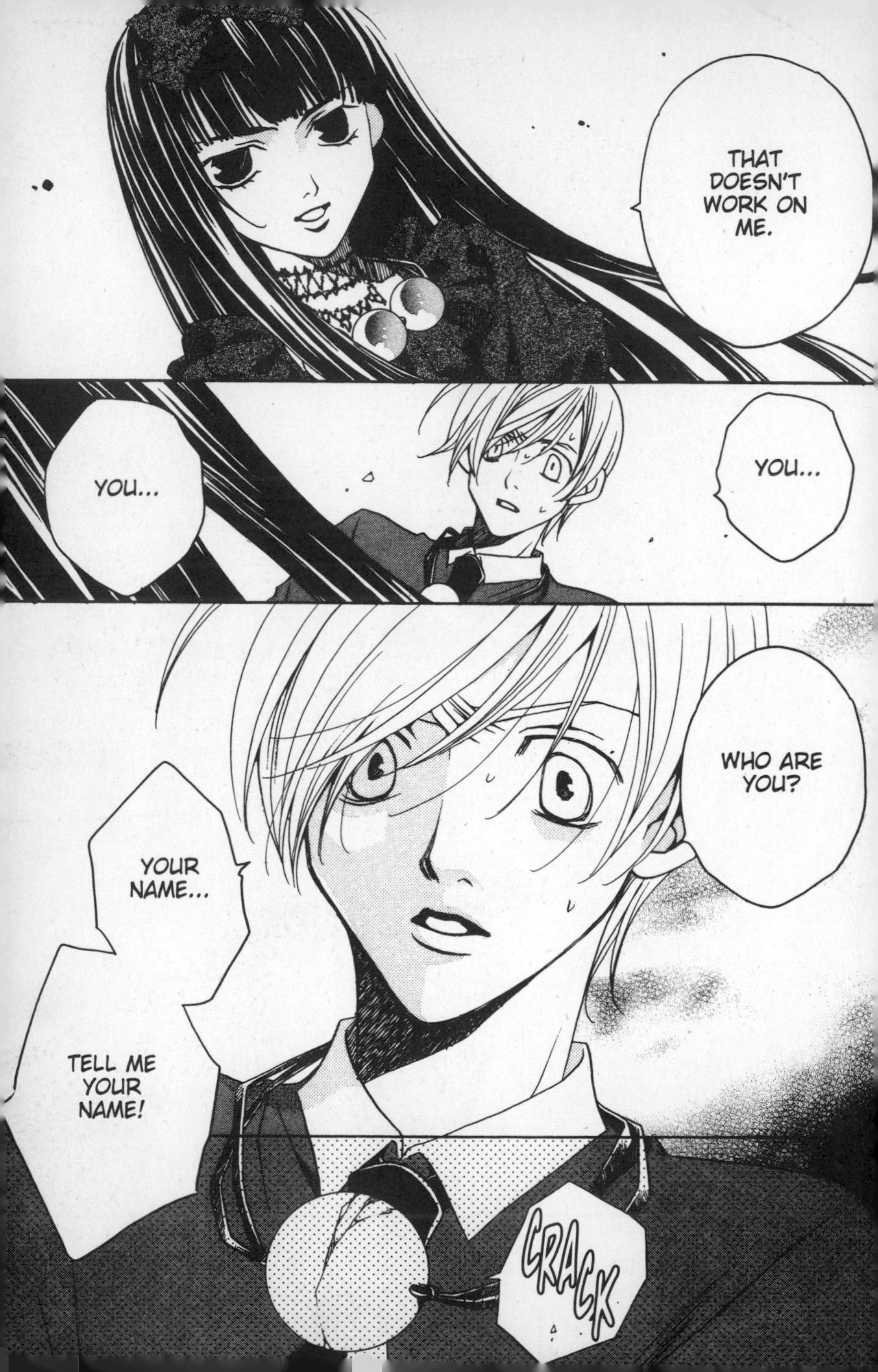
THAT DOESN'T WORK ON ME.
YOU...
YOU...
WHO ARE YOU?
YOUR NAME...
TELL ME YOUR NAME!
CRACK

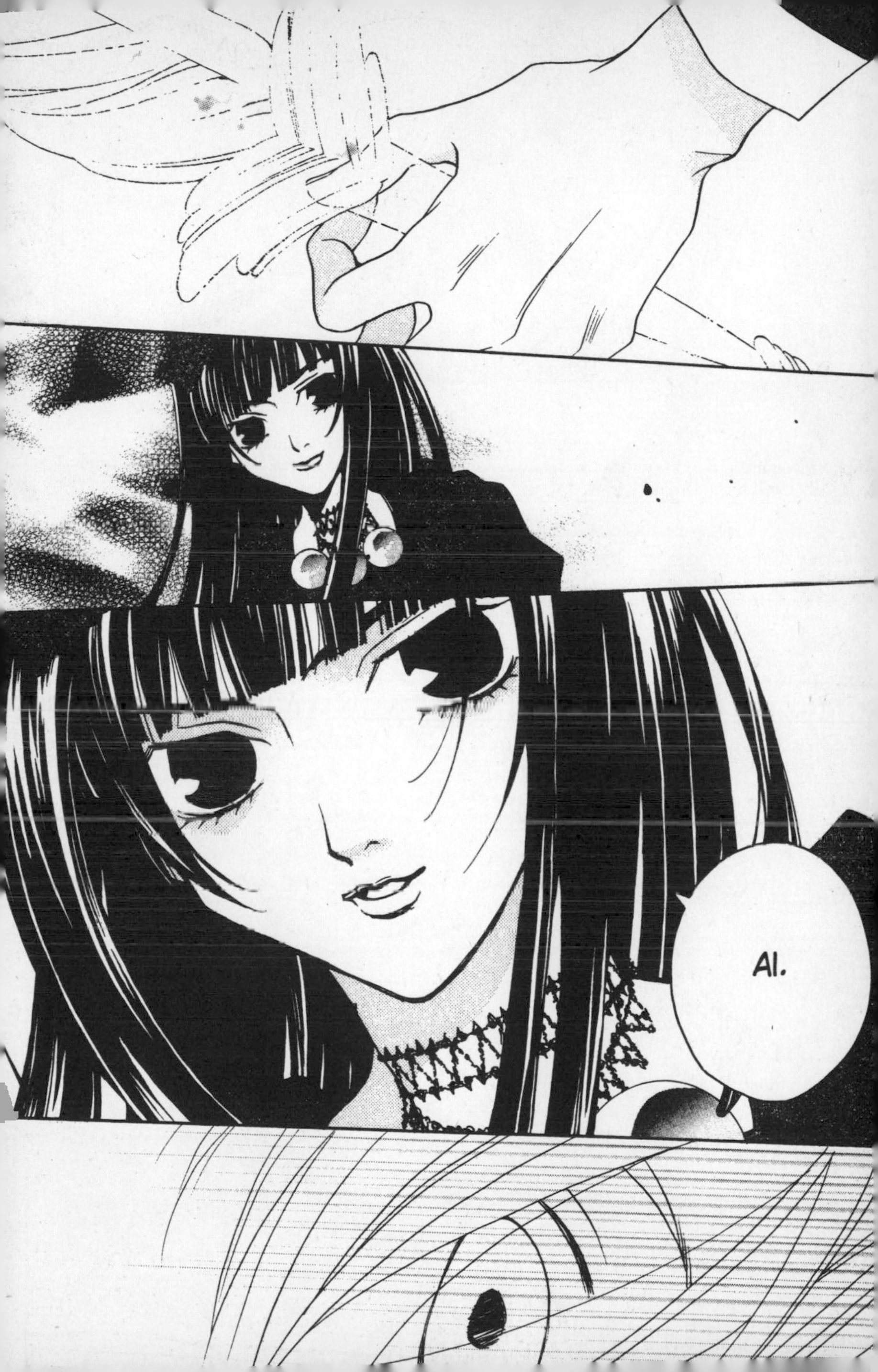
AI.

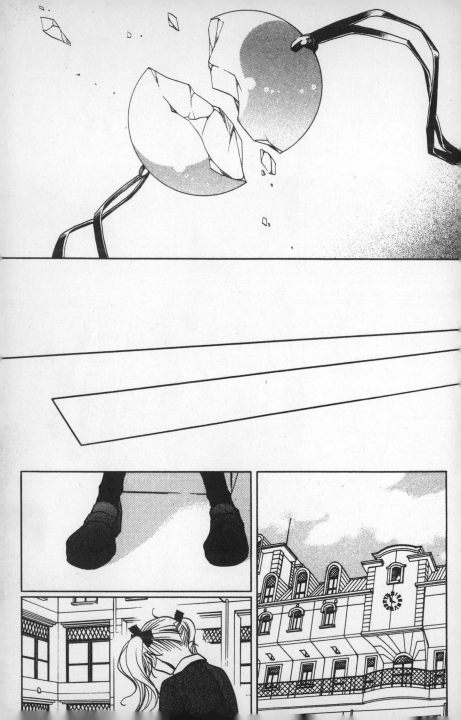

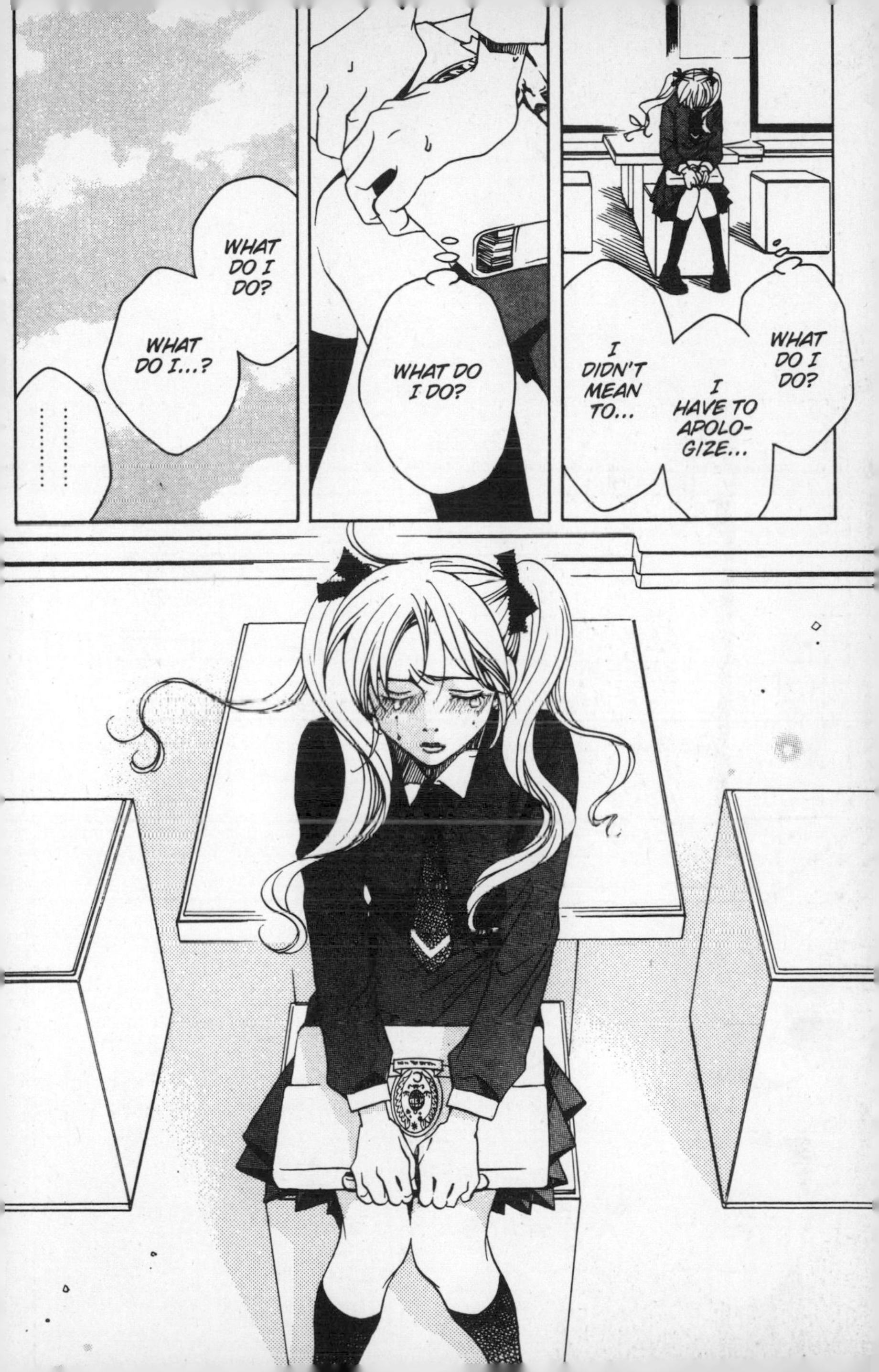
WHAT DO I DO?
I HAVE TO APOLOGIZE...
I DIDN'T MEAN TO...
WHAT DO I DO?
WHAT DO I DO?
WHAT DO I...?

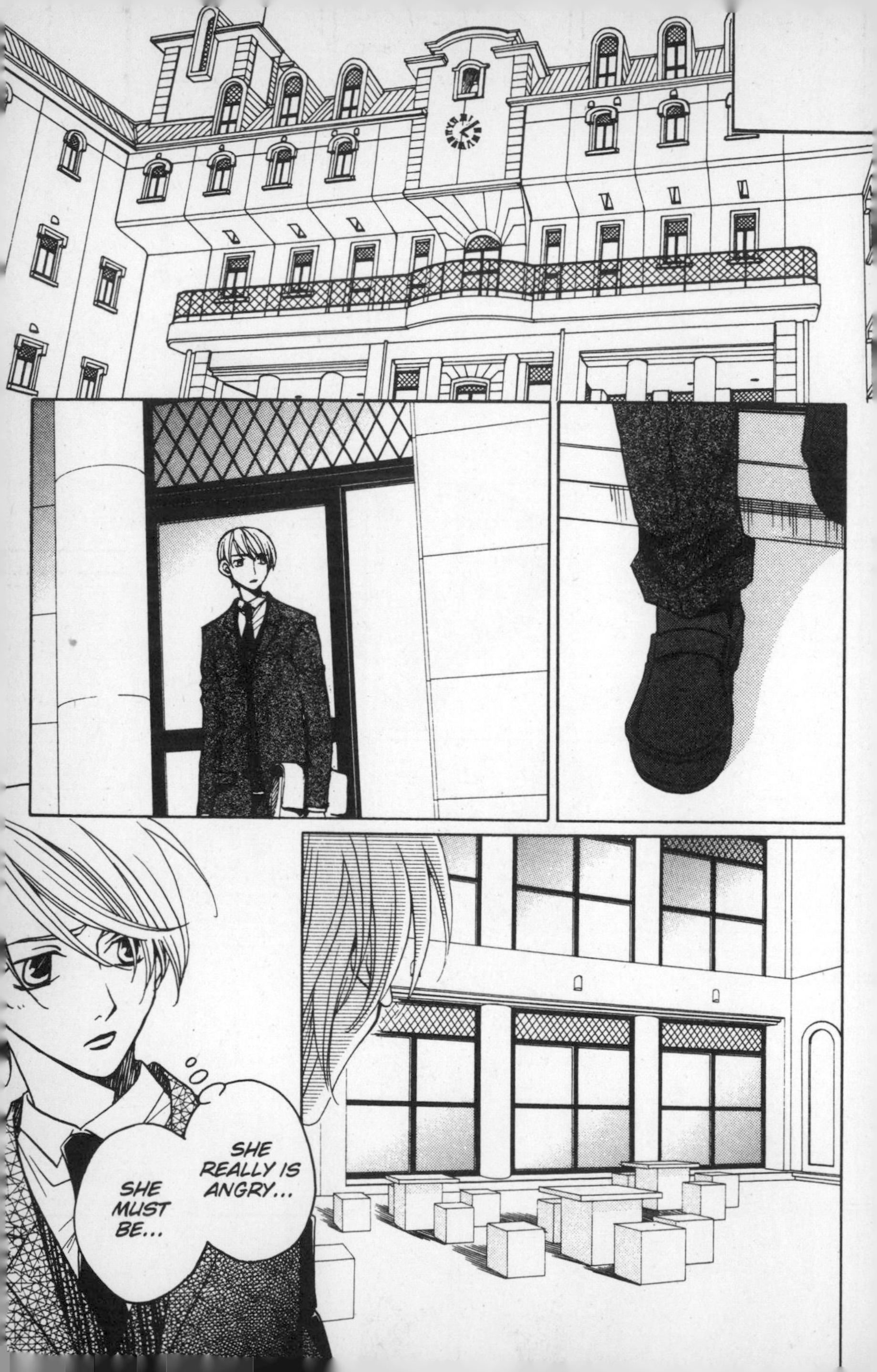
SHE REALLY IS ANGRY...
SHE MUST BE...

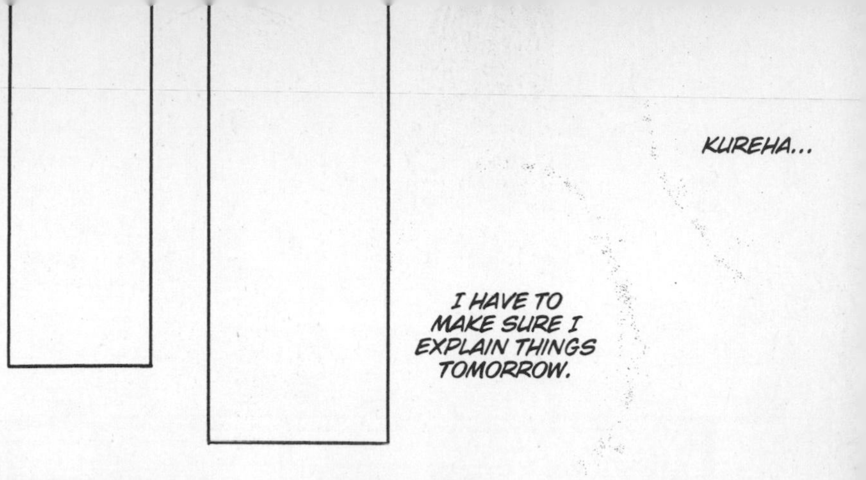
KUREHA...
I HAVE TO MAKE SURE I EXPLAIN THINGS TOMORROW.

*SEE TRANSLATOR'S NOTES

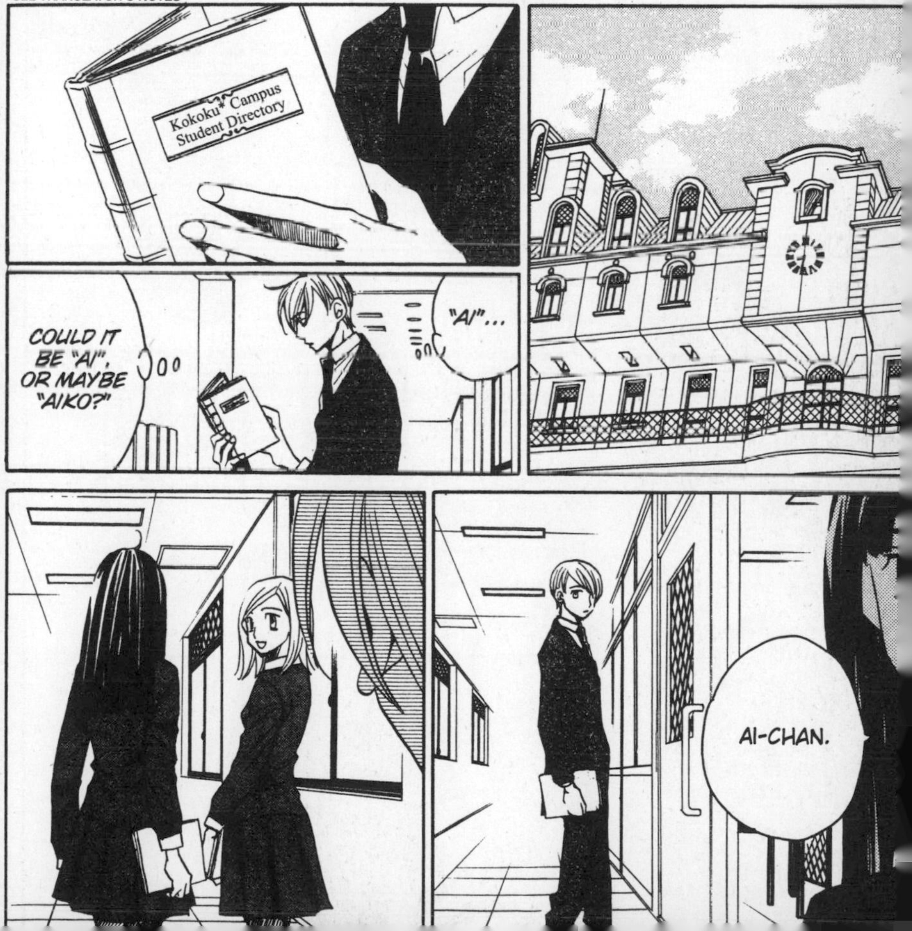
Kokoku* Campus Student Directory
"AI"...
COULD IT BE "AI", OR MAYBE "AIKO?"
AI-CHAN.

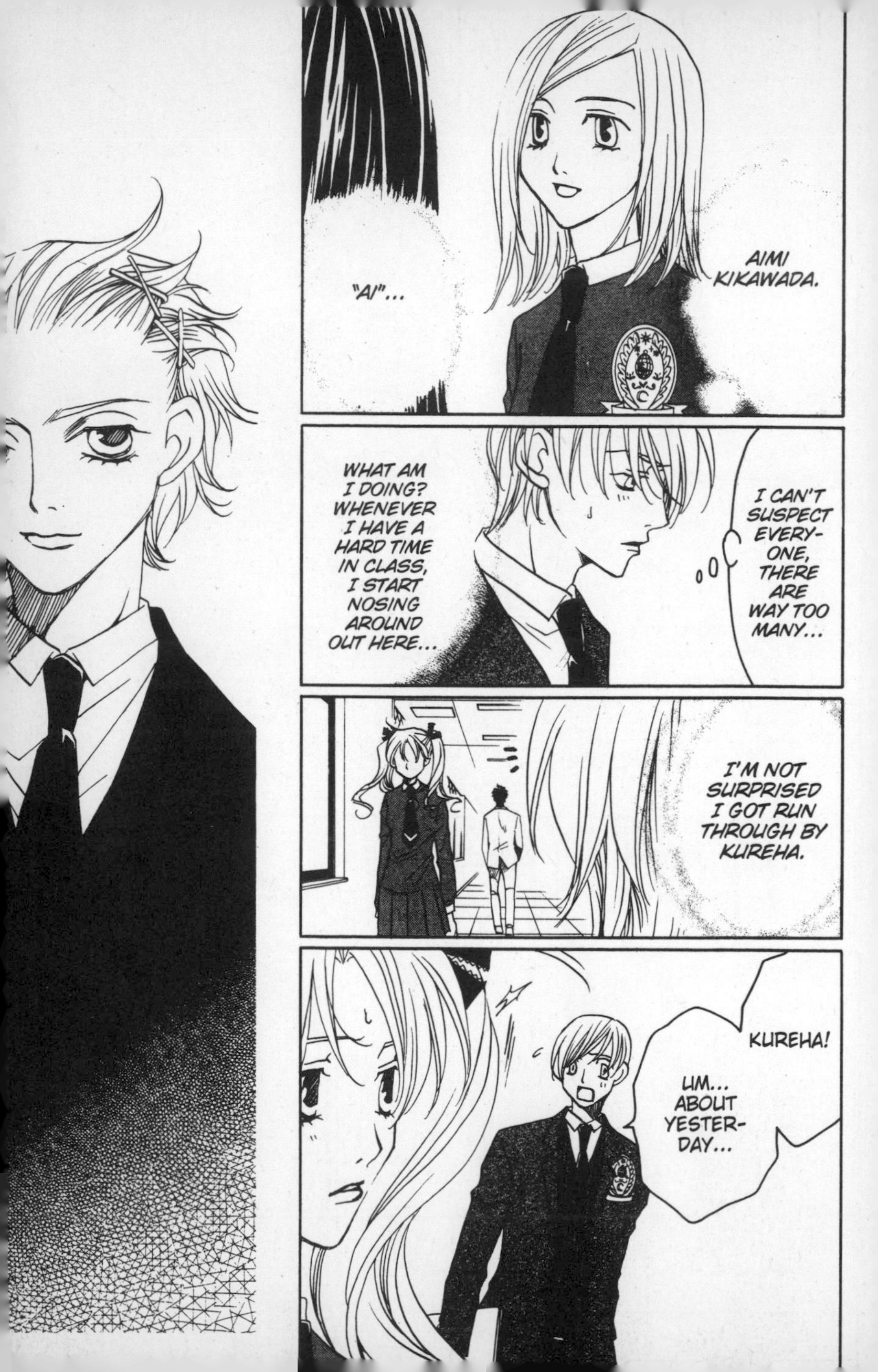
AIMI KIKAWADA.
"AI"...
I CAN'T SUSPECT EVERY-ONE, THERE ARE WAY TOO MANY...
WHAT AM I DOING? WHENEVER I HAVE A HARD TIME IN CLASS, I START NOSING AROUND OUT HERE...
I'M NOT SURPRISED I GOT RUN THROUGH BY KUREHA.
KUREHA!
UM... ABOUT YESTER-DAY...

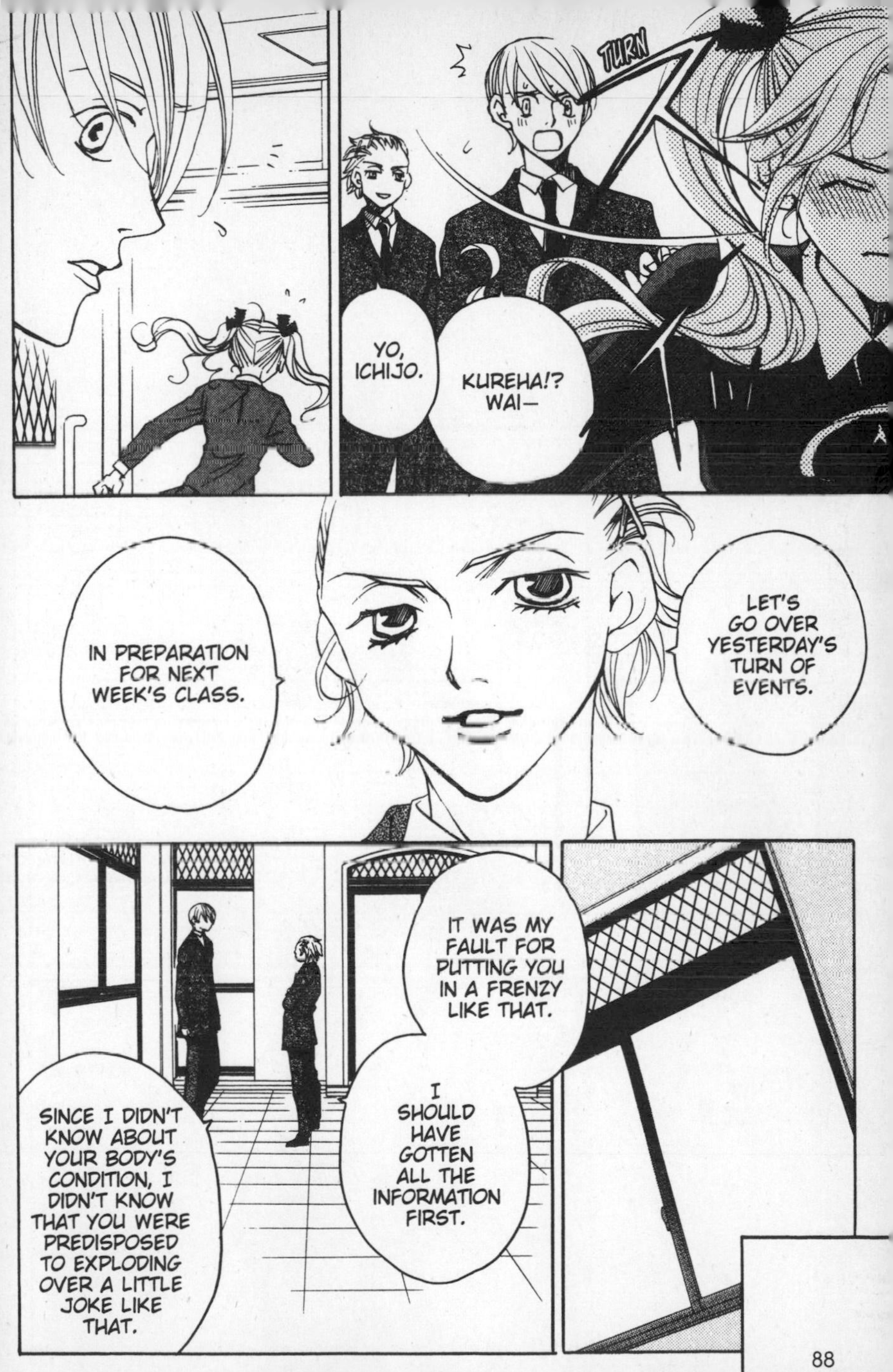
TURN
KUREHA!? WAI—
YO, ICHIJO.
LET'S GO OVER YESTERDAY'S TURN OF EVENTS.
IN PREPARATION FOR NEXT WEEK'S CLASS.
IT WAS MY FAULT FOR PUTTING YOU IN A FRENZY LIKE THAT.
I SHOULD HAVE GOTTEN ALL THE INFORMATION FIRST.
SINCE I DIDN'T KNOW ABOUT YOUR BODY'S CONDITION, I DIDN'T KNOW THAT YOU WERE PREDISPOSED TO EXPLODING OVER A LITTLE JOKE LIKE THAT.

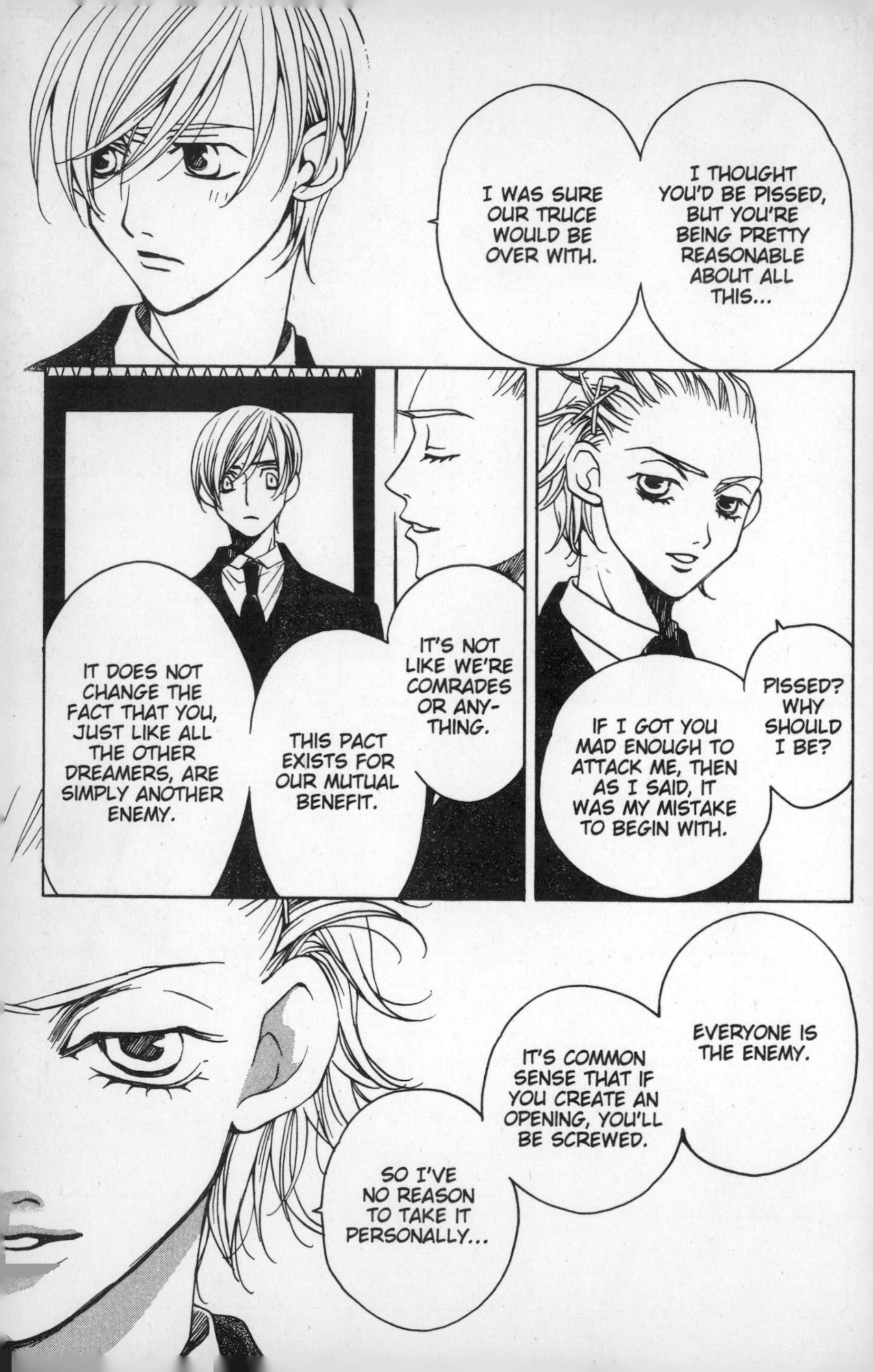
I THOUGHT YOU'D BE PISSED, BUT YOU'RE BEING PRETTY REASONABLE ABOUT ALL THIS...
I WAS SURE OUR TRUCE WOULD BE OVER WITH.
PISSED? WHY SHOULD I BE?
IF I GOT YOU MAD ENOUGH TO ATTACK ME, THEN AS I SAID, IT WAS MY MISTAKE TO BEGIN WITH.
IT'S NOT LIKE WE'RE COMRADES OR ANY-THING.
THIS PACT EXISTS FOR OUR MUTUAL BENEFIT.
IT DOES NOT CHANGE THE FACT THAT YOU, JUST LIKE ALL THE OTHER DREAMERS, ARE SIMPLY ANOTHER ENEMY.
EVERYONE IS THE ENEMY.
IT'S COMMON SENSE THAT IF YOU CREATE AN OPENING, YOU'LL BE SCREWED.
SO I'VE NO REASON TO TAKE IT PERSONALLY...

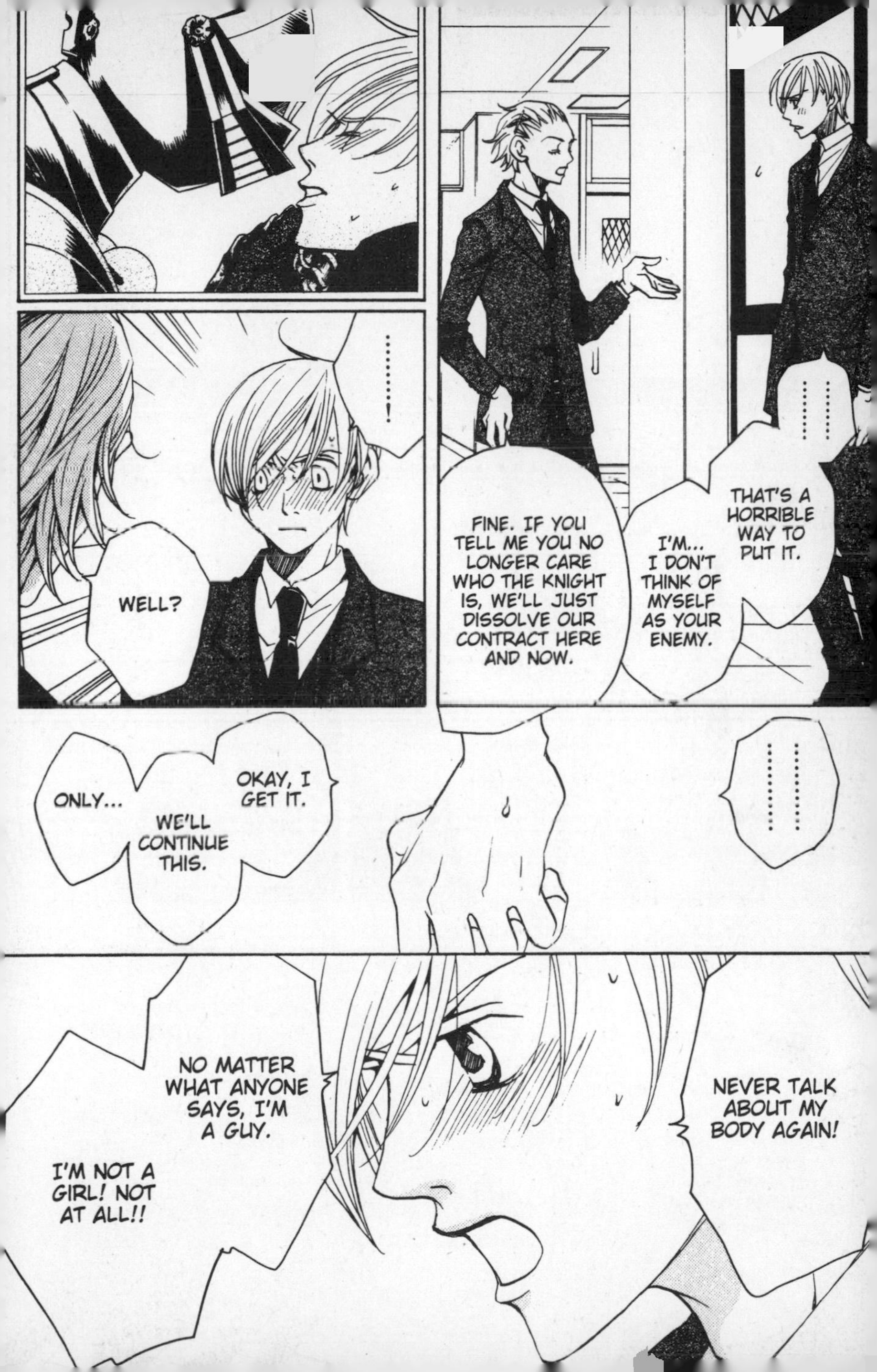
......
THAT'S A HORRIBLE WAY TO PUT IT.
I'M... I DON'T THINK OF MYSELF AS YOUR ENEMY.
FINE. IF YOU TELL ME YOU NO LONGER CARE WHO THE KNIGHT IS, WE'LL JUST DISSOLVE OUR CONTRACT HERE AND NOW.
......!
WELL?
......
OKAY, I GET IT.
WE'LL CONTINUE THIS.
ONLY...
NEVER TALK ABOUT MY BODY AGAIN!
NO MATTER WHAT ANYONE SAYS, I'M A GUY.
I'M NOT A GIRL! NOT AT ALL!!

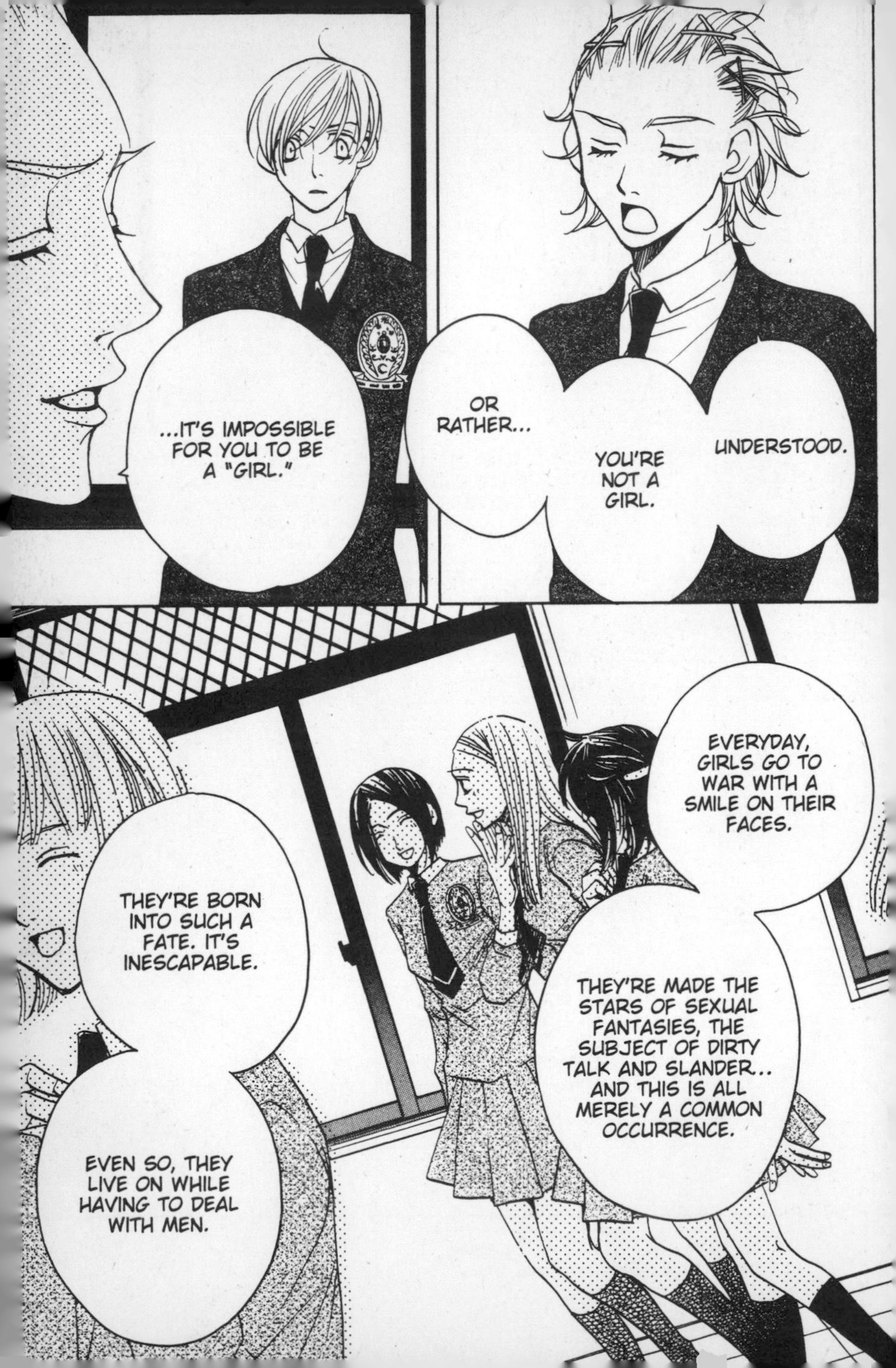
UNDERSTOOD.
YOU'RE NOT A GIRL.
OR RATHER...
...IT'S IMPOSSIBLE FOR YOU TO BE A "GIRL."
EVERYDAY, GIRLS GO TO WAR WITH A SMILE ON THEIR FACES.
THEY'RE MADE THE STARS OF SEXUAL FANTASIES, THE SUBJECT OF DIRTY TALK AND SLANDER... AND THIS IS ALL MERELY A COMMON OCCURRENCE.
THEY'RE BORN INTO SUCH A FATE. IT'S INESCAPABLE.
EVEN SO, THEY LIVE ON WHILE HAVING TO DEAL WITH MEN.

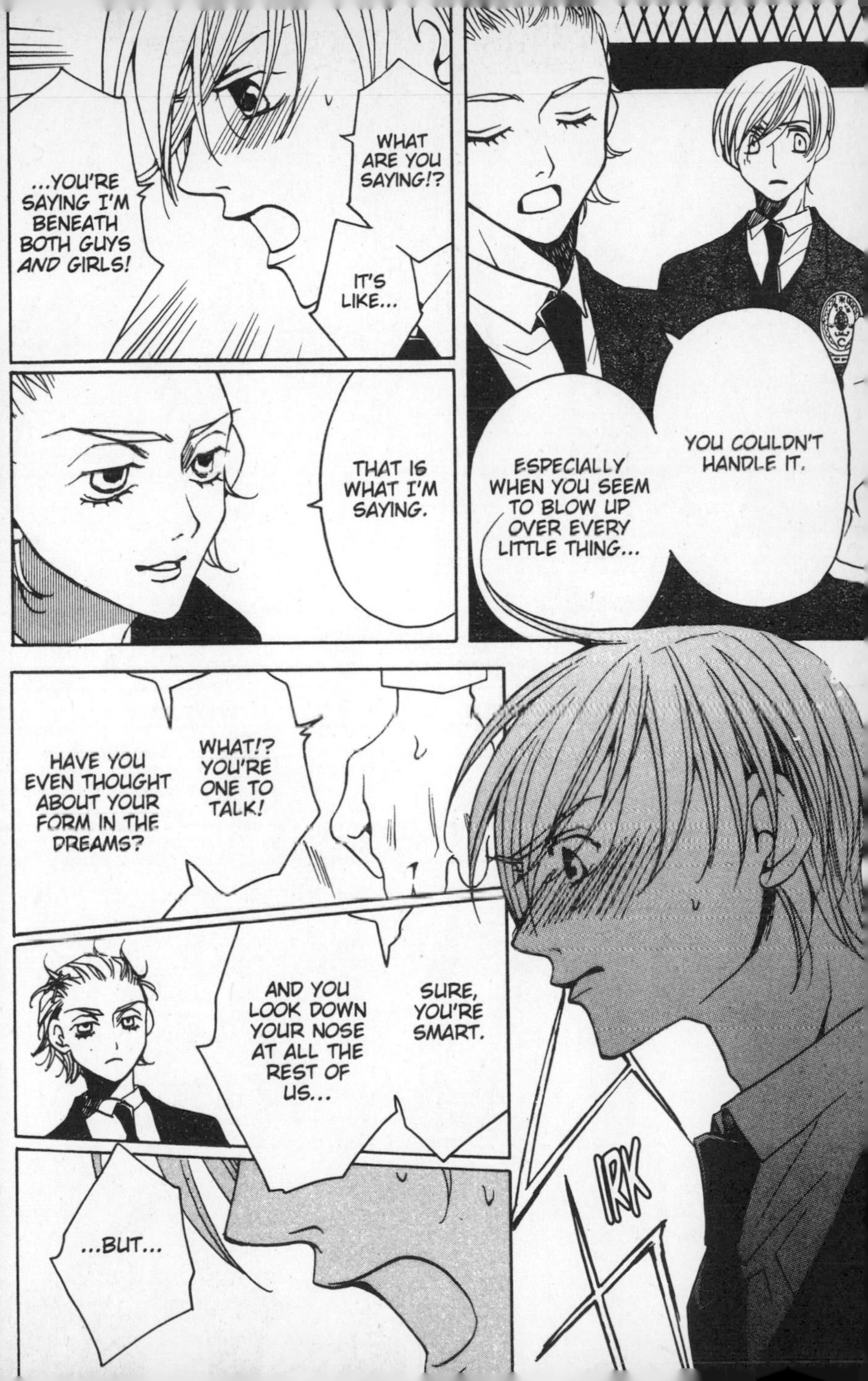
YOU COULDN'T HANDLE IT.
ESPECIALLY WHEN YOU SEEM TO BLOW UP OVER EVERY LITTLE THING...
WHAT ARE YOU SAYING!?
IT'S LIKE...
...YOU'RE SAYING I'M BENEATH BOTH GUYS AND GIRLS!
THAT IS WHAT I'M SAYING.
IRK
WHAT!? YOU'RE ONE TO TALK!
HAVE YOU EVEN THOUGHT ABOUT YOUR FORM IN THE DREAMS?
SURE, YOU'RE SMART.
AND YOU LOOK DOWN YOUR NOSE AT ALL THE REST OF US...
...BUT...

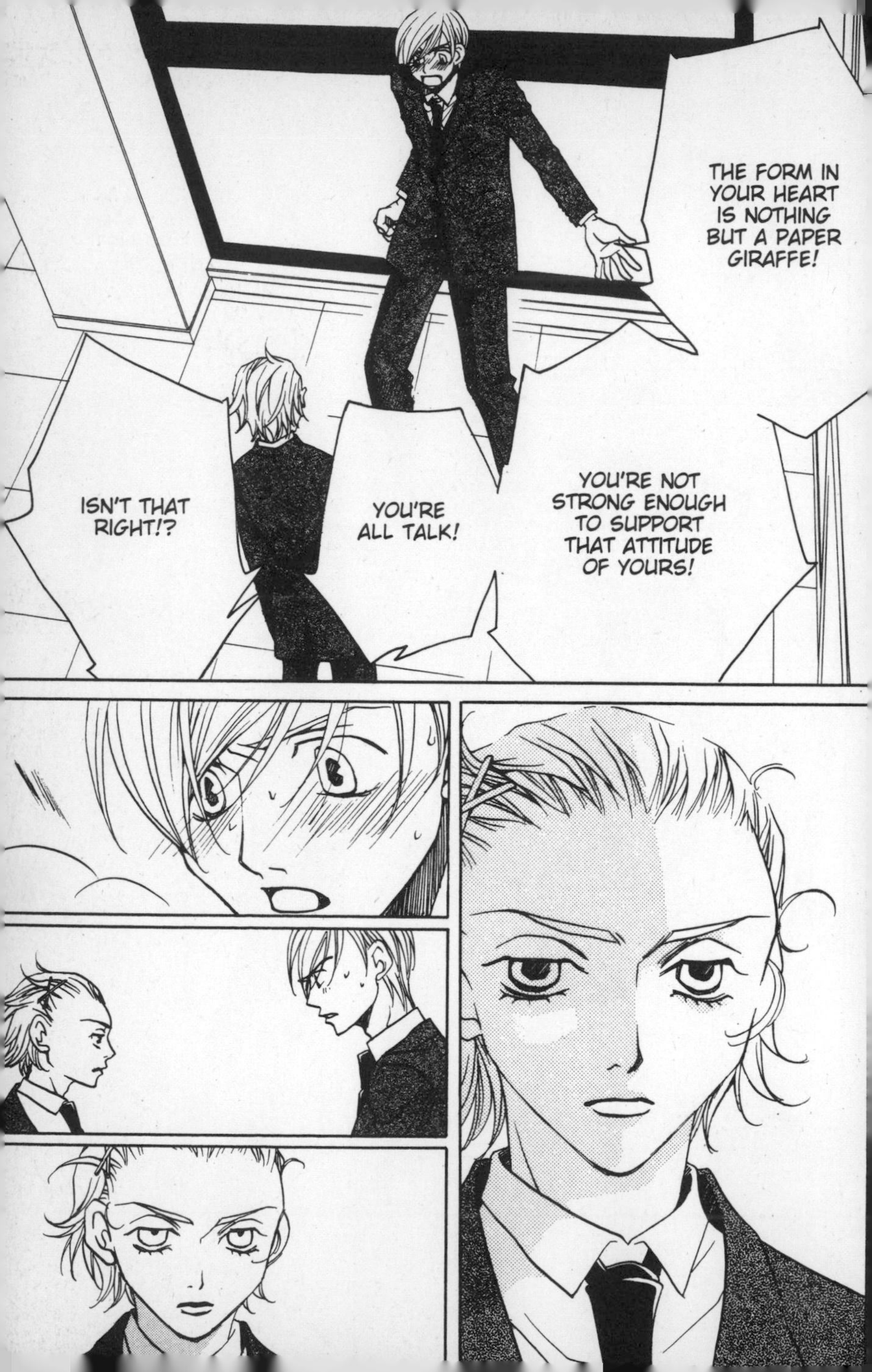
THE FORM IN YOUR HEART IS NOTHING BUT A PAPER GIRAFFE!
YOU'RE NOT STRONG ENOUGH TO SUPPORT THAT ATTITUDE OF YOURS!
YOU'RE ALL TALK!
ISN'T THAT RIGHT!?

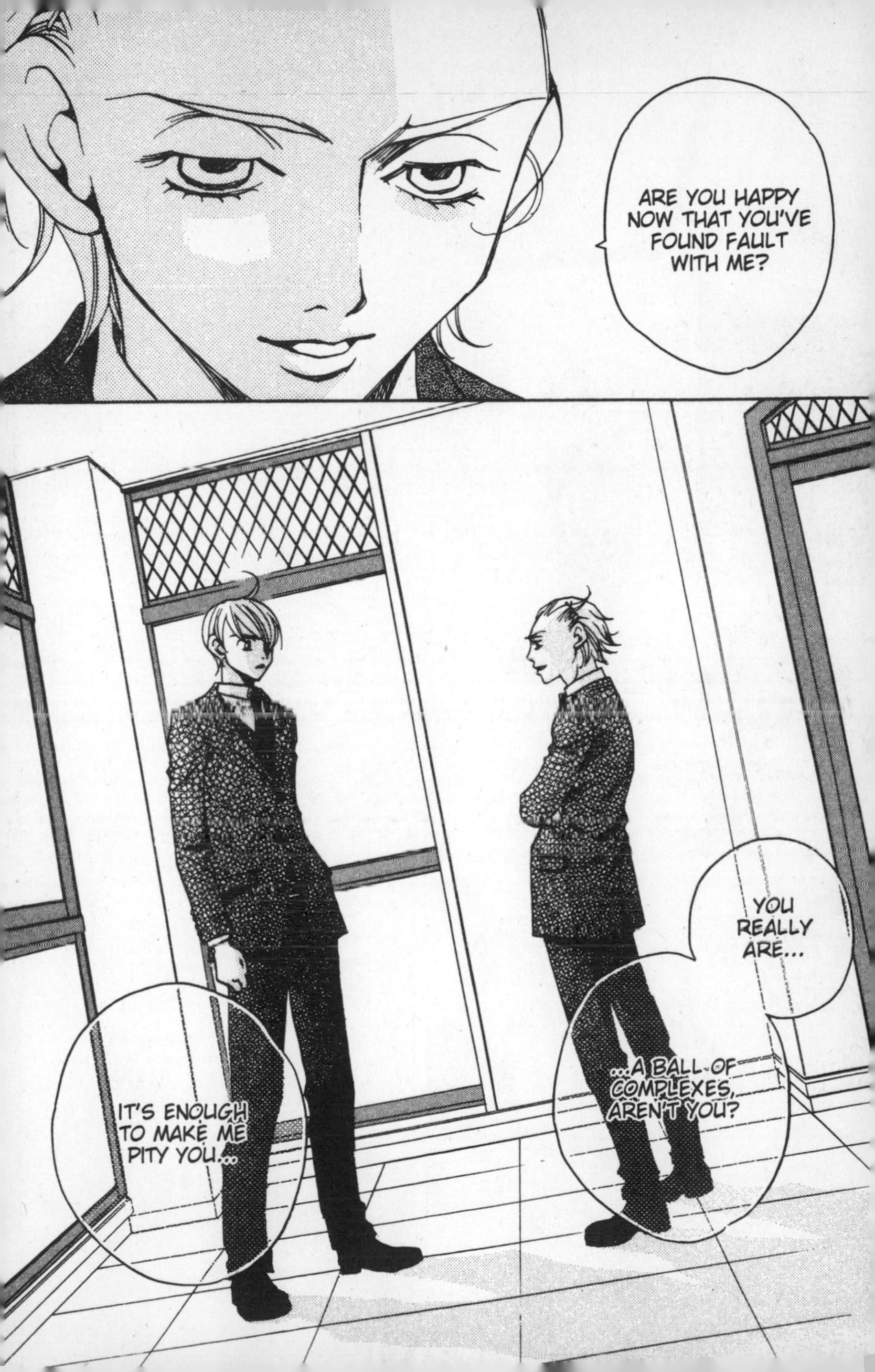
ARE YOU HAPPY NOW THAT YOU'VE FOUND FAULT WITH ME?
YOU REALLY ARE...
...A BALL OF COMPLEXES, AREN'T YOU?
IT'S ENOUGH TO MAKE ME PITY YOU...

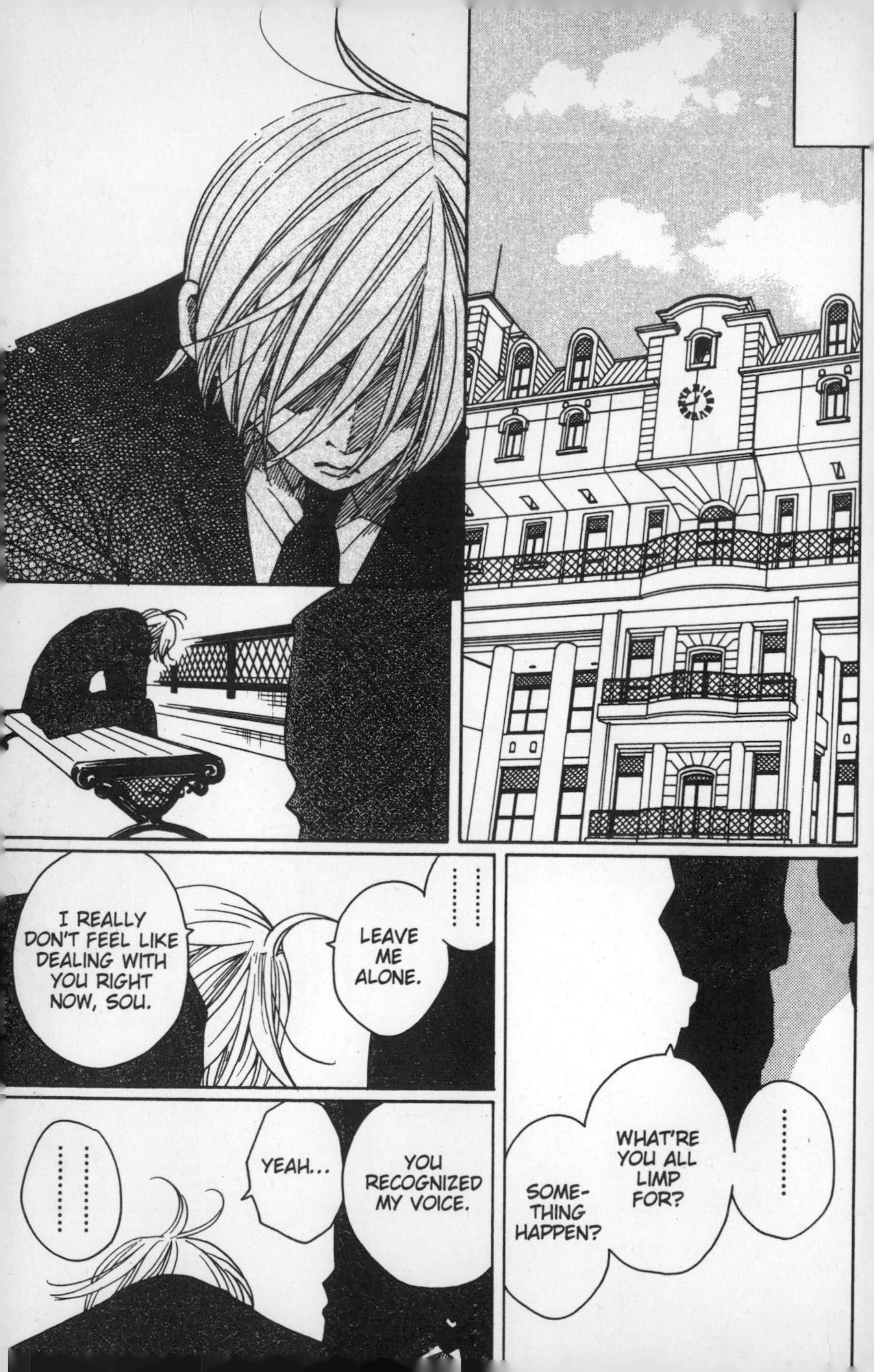
......
WHAT'RE YOU ALL LIMP FOR?
SOME-THING HAPPEN?
......
LEAVE ME ALONE.
I REALLY DON'T FEEL LIKE DEALING WITH YOU RIGHT NOW, SOU.
YOU RECOGNIZED MY VOICE.
YEAH...
......

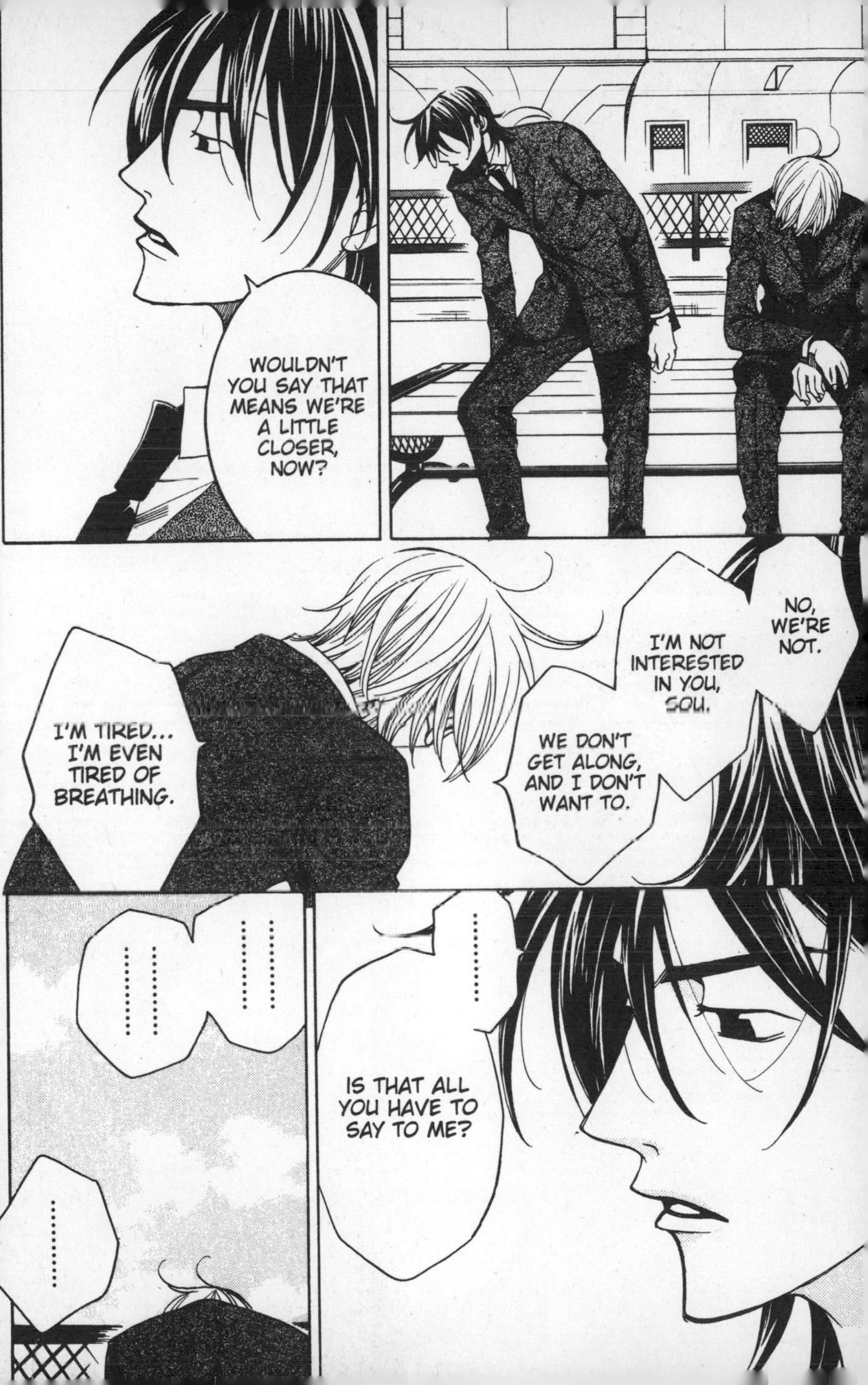
WOULDN'T YOU SAY THAT MEANS WE'RE A LITTLE CLOSER, NOW?
NO, WE'RE NOT.
I'M NOT INTERESTED IN YOU, SOU.
WE DON'T GET ALONG, AND I DON'T WANT TO.
I'M TIRED... I'M EVEN TIRED OF BREATHING.
......
IS THAT ALL YOU HAVE TO SAY TO ME?
......
......
......

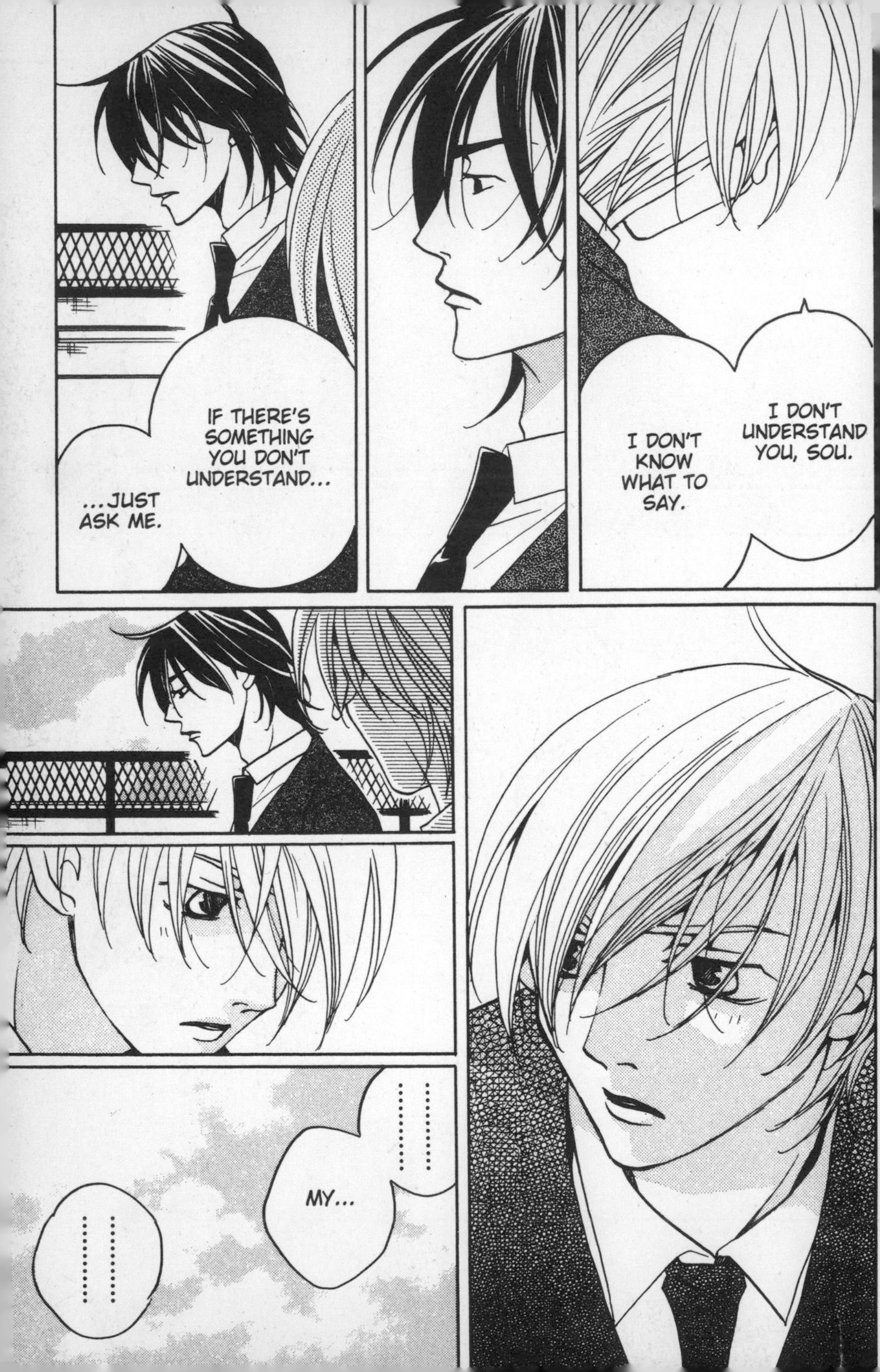
I DON'T UNDERSTAND YOU, SOU.
I DON'T KNOW WHAT TO SAY.
IF THERE'S SOMETHING YOU DON'T UNDERSTAND...
...JUST ASK ME.
......
MY...
......

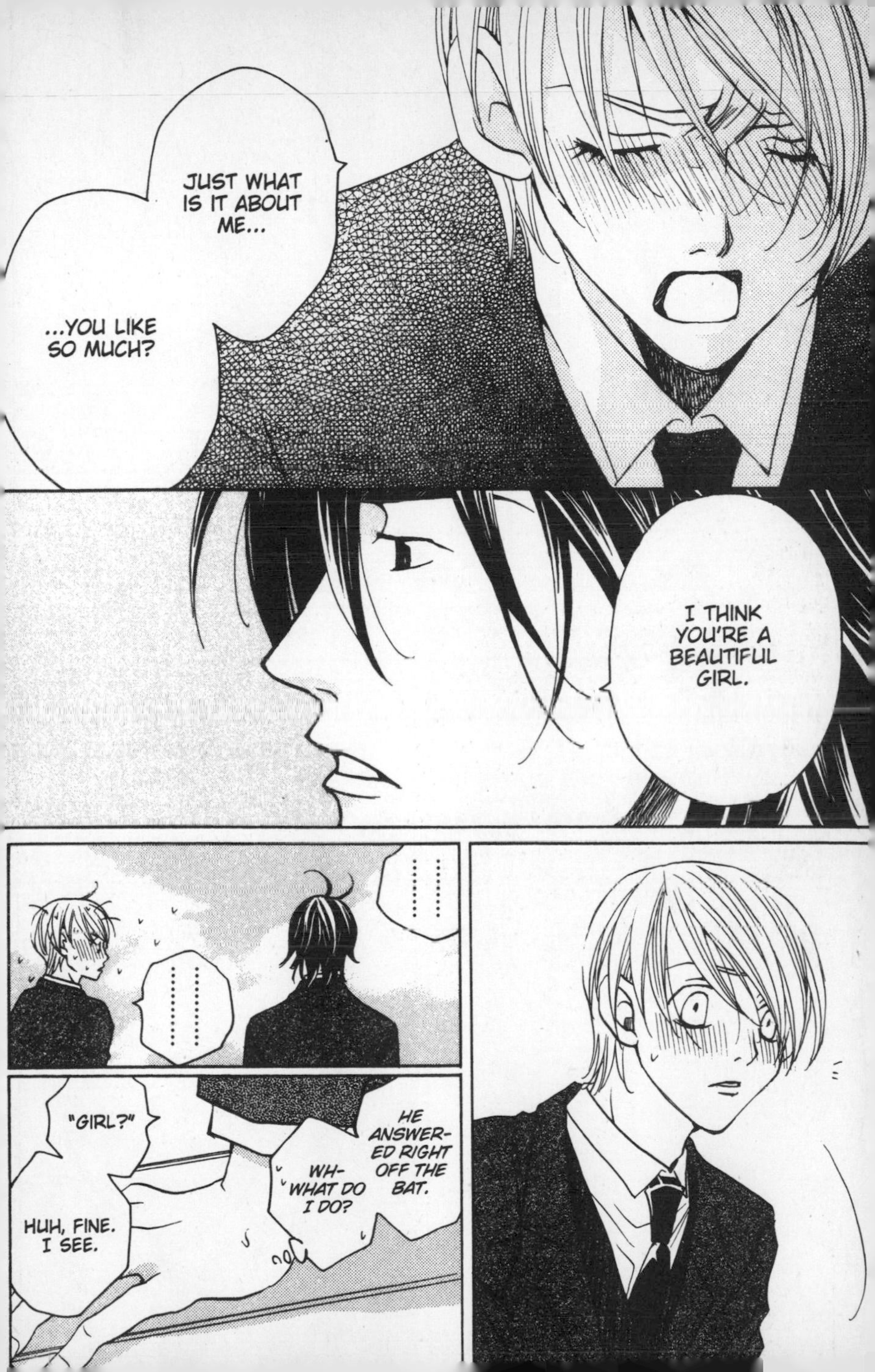
JUST WHAT IS IT ABOUT ME...
...YOU LIKE SO MUCH?
I THINK YOU'RE A BEAUTIFUL GIRL.
......
......
HE ANSWER-ED RIGHT OFF THE BAT.
WH-WHAT DO I DO?
"GIRL?"
HUH, FINE. I SEE.

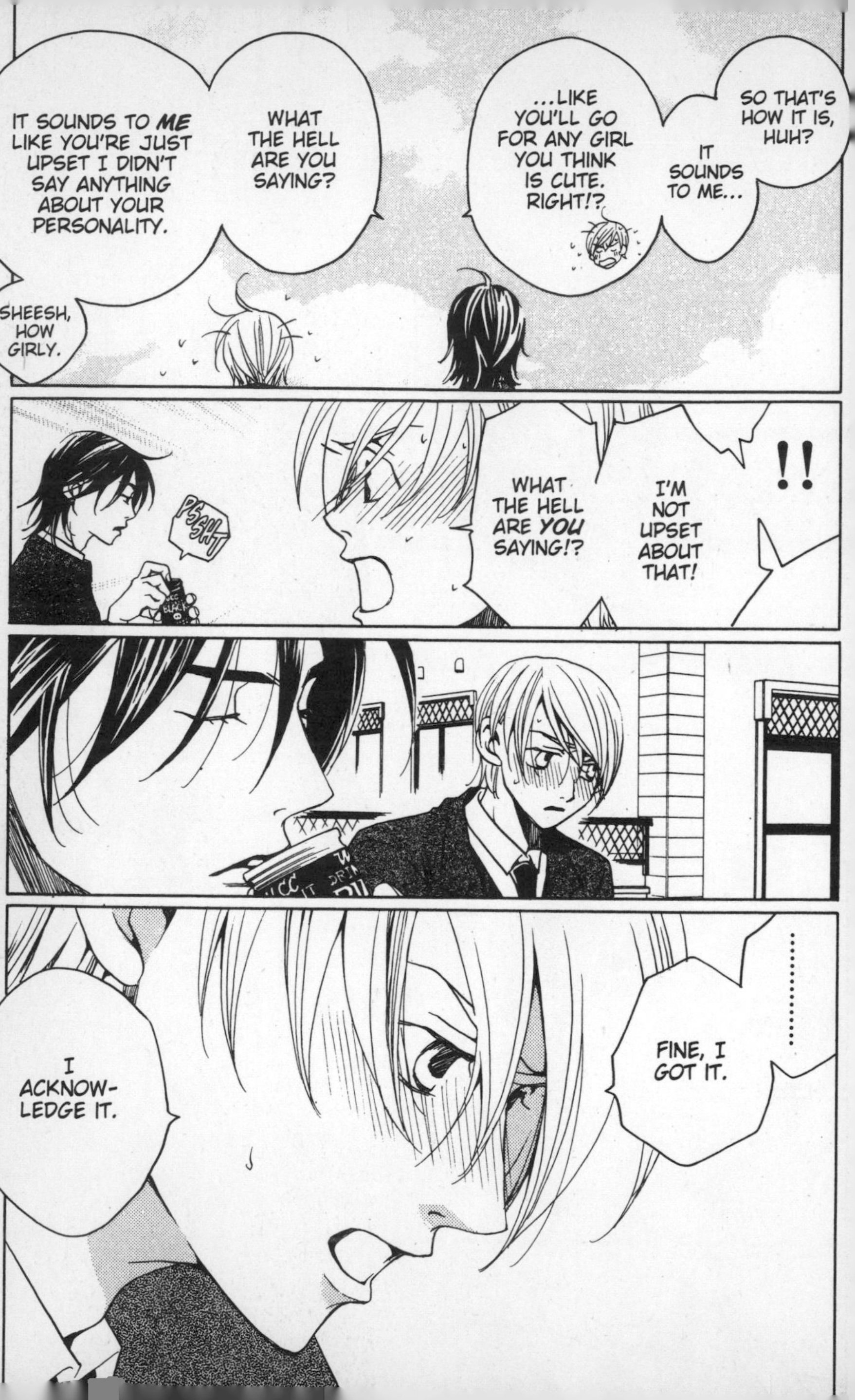
SO THAT'S HOW IT IS, HUH?
IT SOUNDS TO ME...
...LIKE YOU'LL GO FOR ANY GIRL YOU THINK IS CUTE. RIGHT!?
WHAT THE HELL ARE YOU SAYING?
IT SOUNDS TO *ME* LIKE YOU'RE JUST UPSET I DIDN'T SAY ANYTHING ABOUT YOUR PERSONALITY.
SHEESH, HOW GIRLY.
!!
I'M NOT UPSET ABOUT THAT!
WHAT THE HELL ARE *YOU* SAYING!?
PSSHT
......
FINE, I GOT IT.
I ACKNOWLEDGE IT.

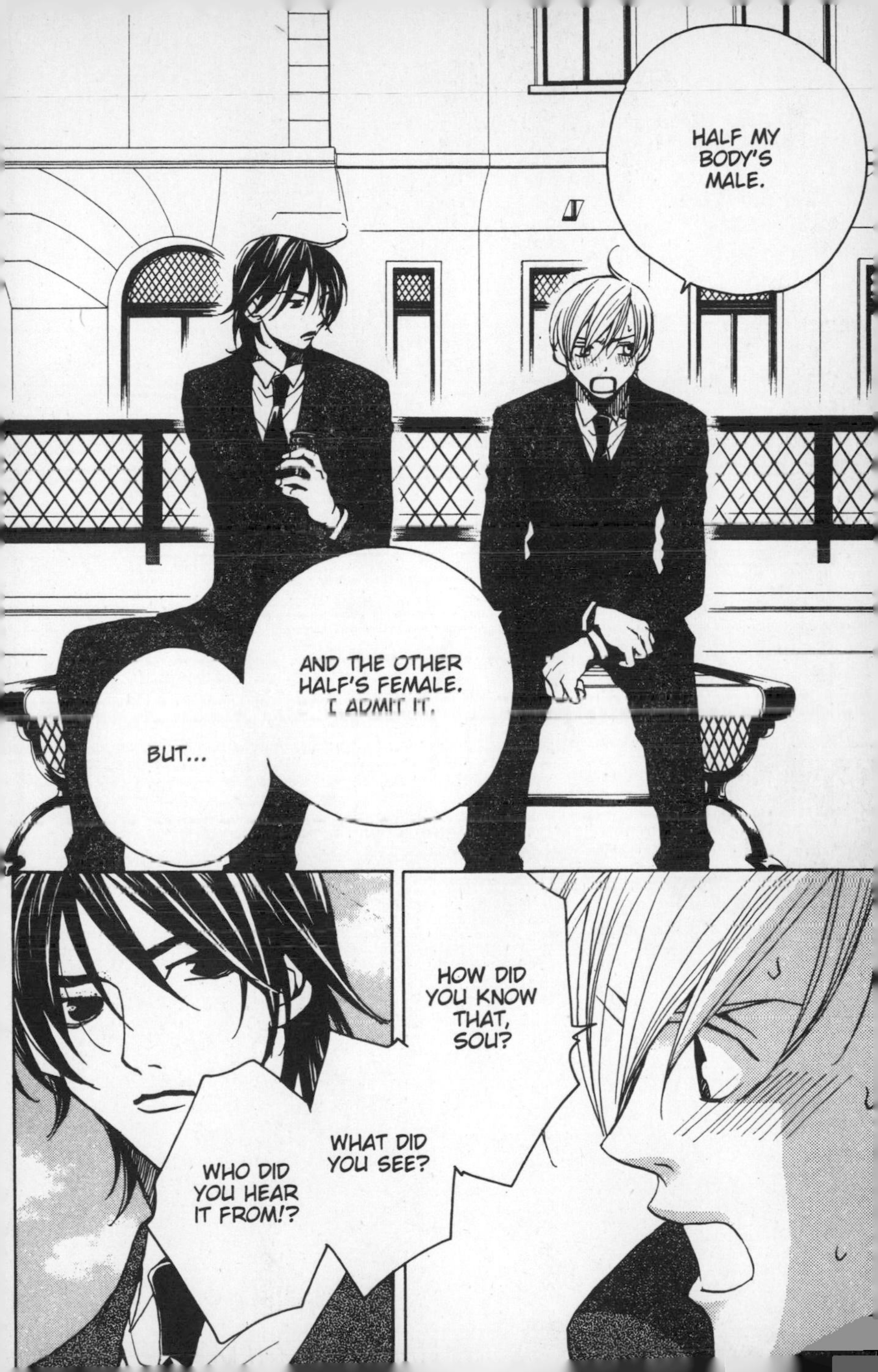
HALF MY BODY'S MALE.
AND THE OTHER HALF'S FEMALE. I ADMIT IT.
BUT...
HOW DID YOU KNOW THAT, SOU?
WHAT DID YOU SEE?
WHO DID YOU HEAR IT FROM!?

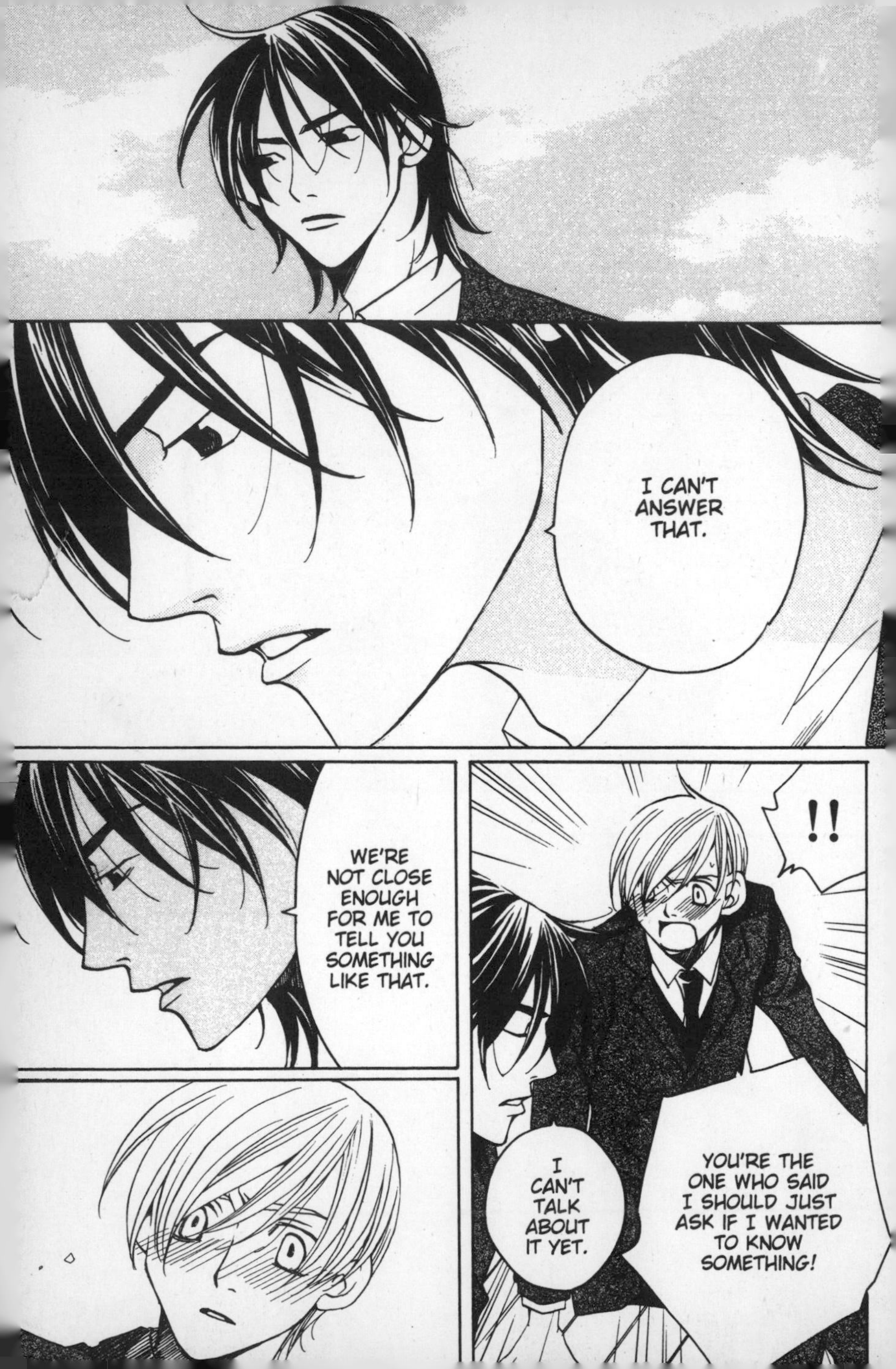
I CAN'T ANSWER THAT.
!!
YOU'RE THE ONE WHO SAID I SHOULD JUST ASK IF I WANTED TO KNOW SOMETHING!
I CAN'T TALK ABOUT IT YET.
WE'RE NOT CLOSE ENOUGH FOR ME TO TELL YOU SOMETHING LIKE THAT.

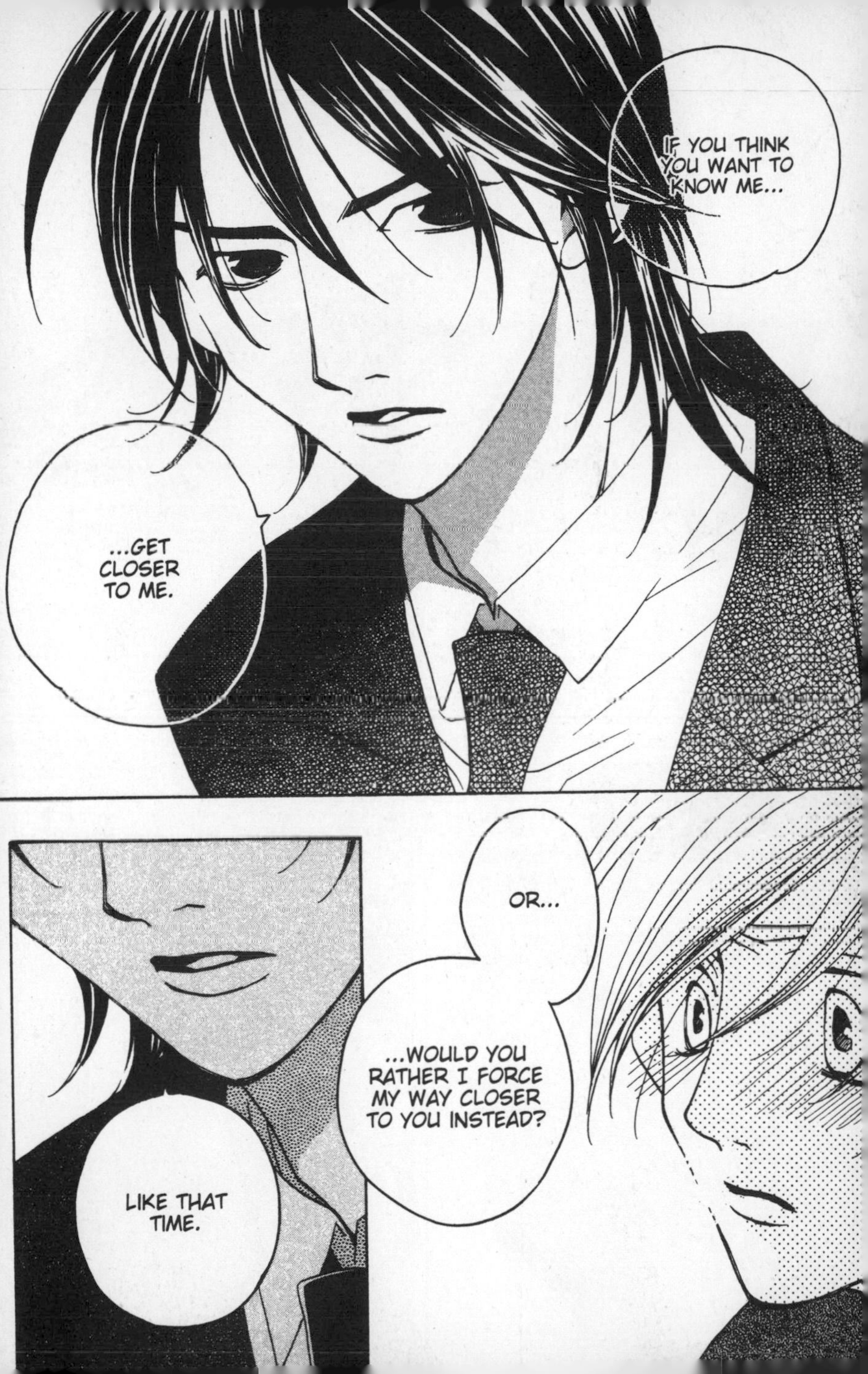
IF YOU THINK YOU WANT TO KNOW ME...
...GET CLOSER TO ME.
OR...
...WOULD YOU RATHER I FORCE MY WAY CLOSER TO YOU INSTEAD?
LIKE THAT TIME.

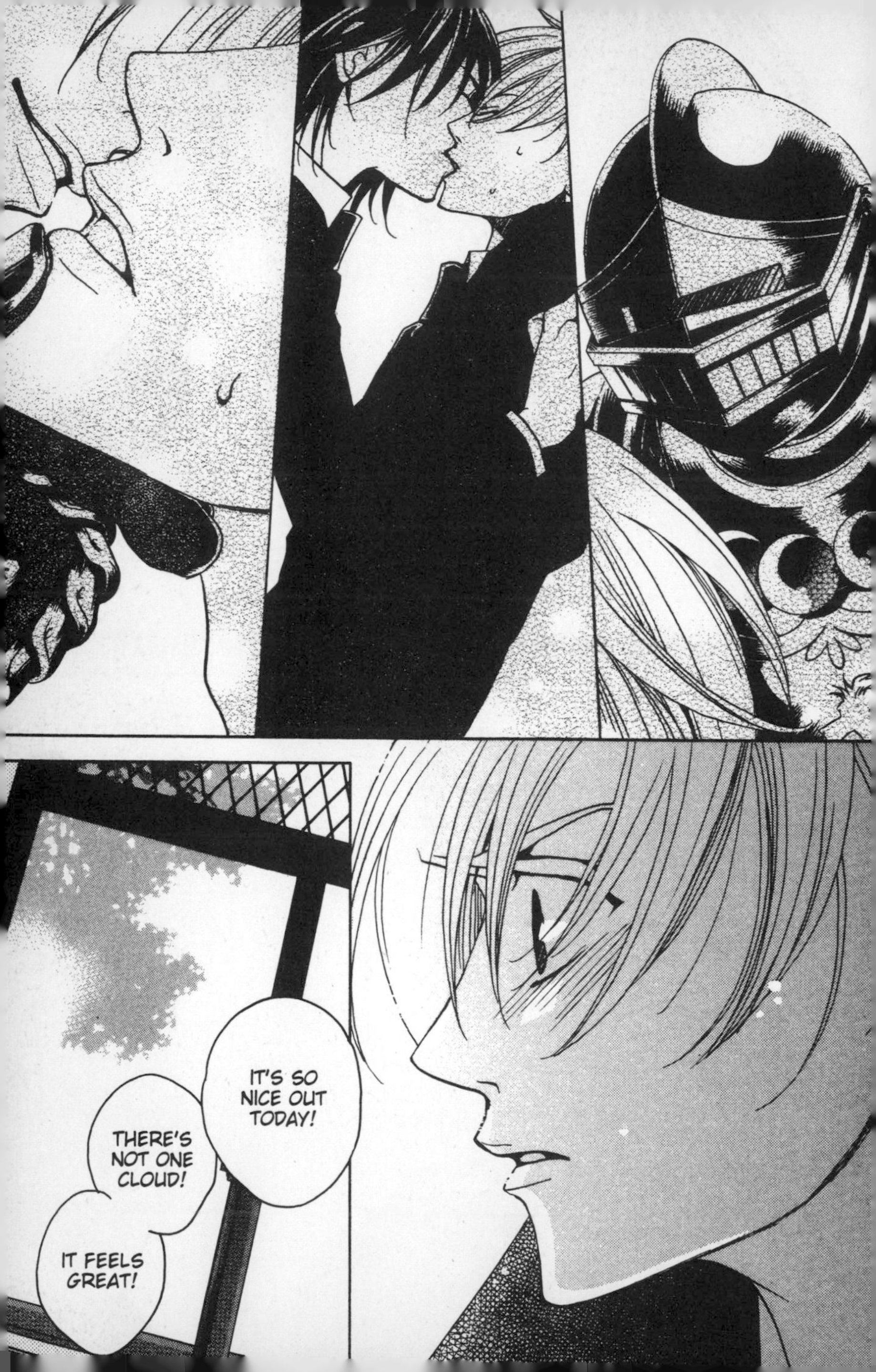
IT'S SO NICE OUT TODAY!
THERE'S NOT ONE CLOUD!
IT FEELS GREAT!

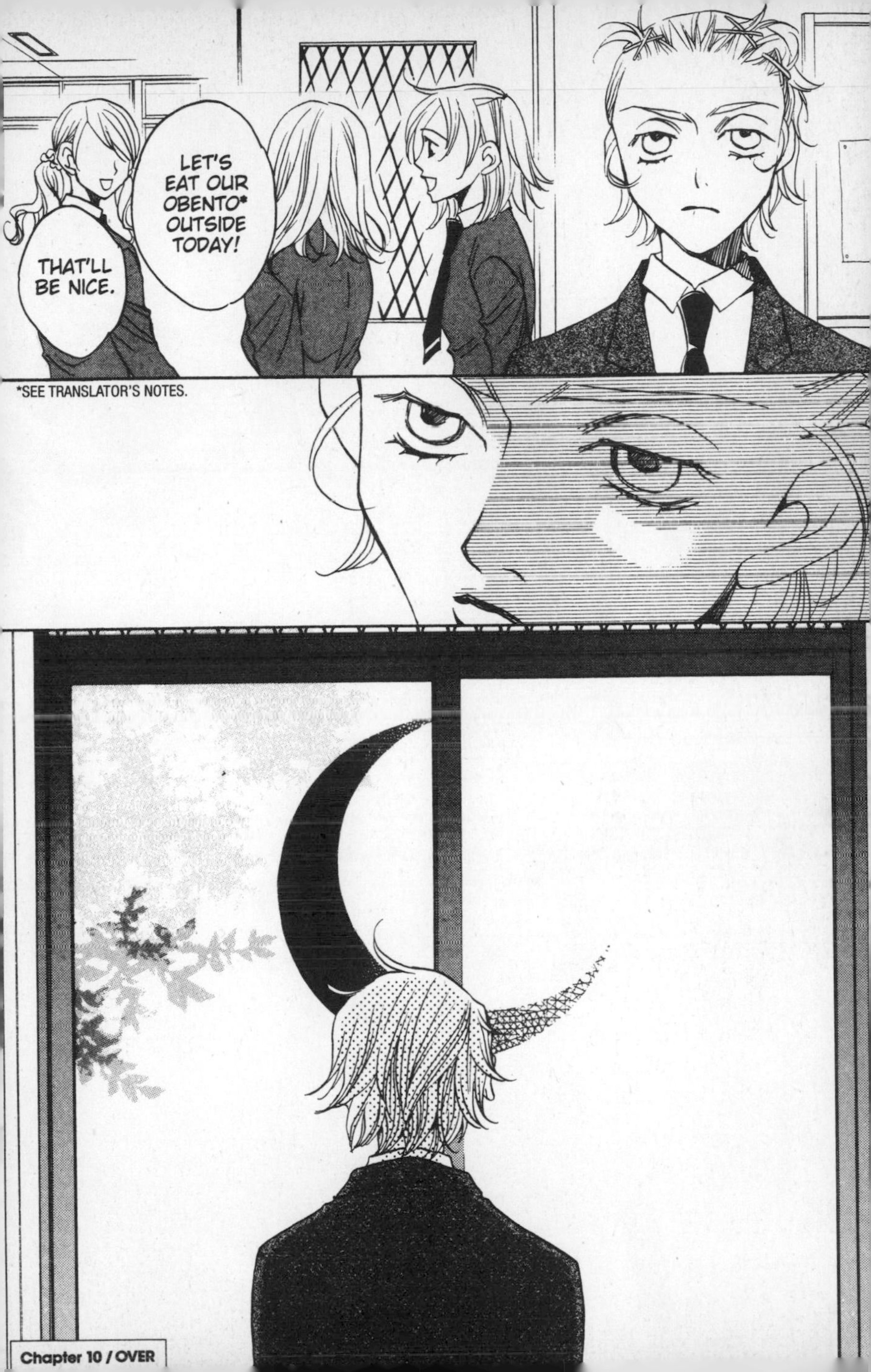
LET'S EAT OUR OBENTO* OUTSIDE TODAY!
THAT'LL BE NICE.
*SEE TRANSLATOR'S NOTES.
Chapter 10 / OVER

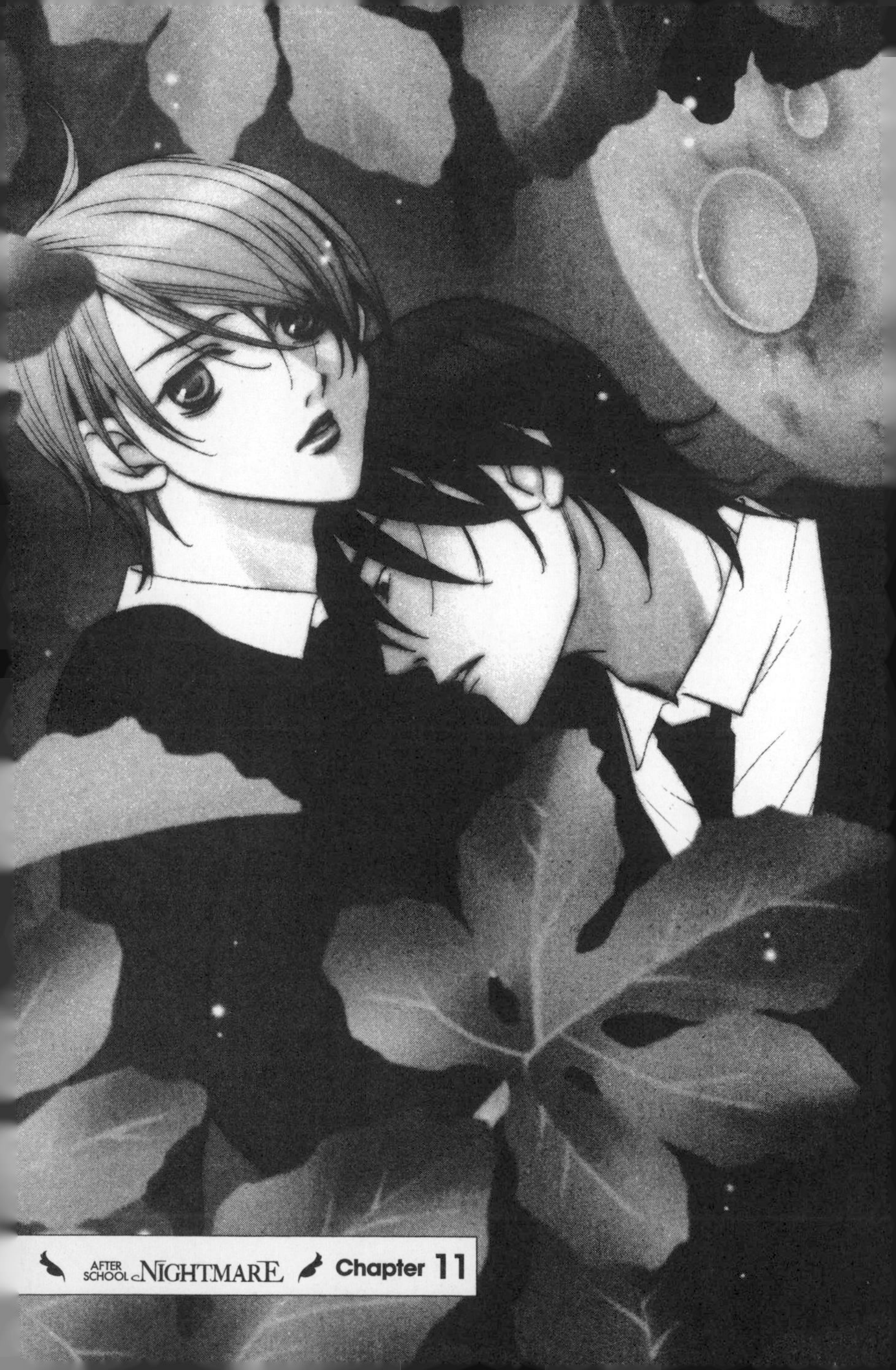
AFTER SCHOOL NIGHTMARE
Chapter 11

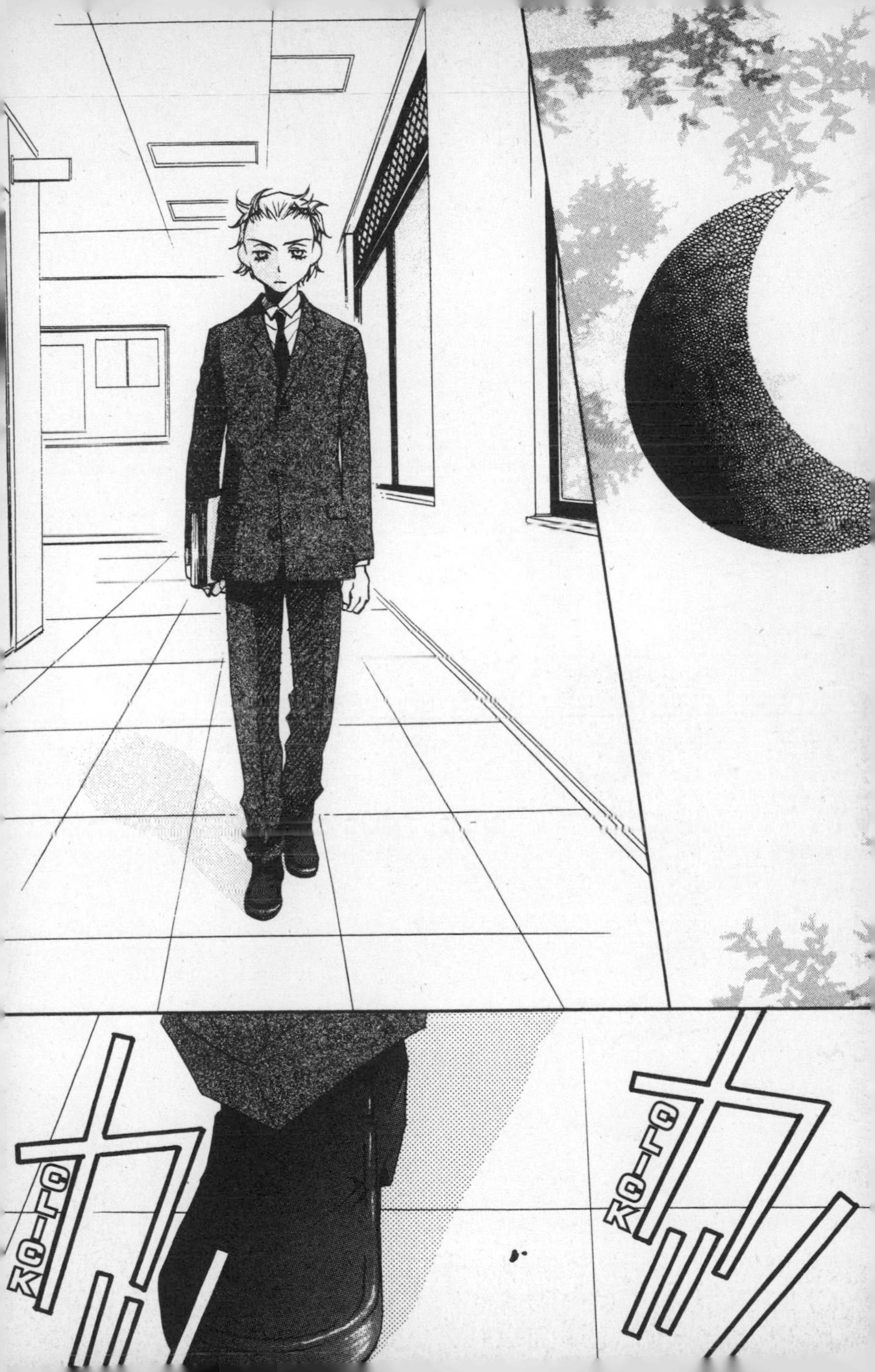
カッ
CLICK
カッ
CLICK

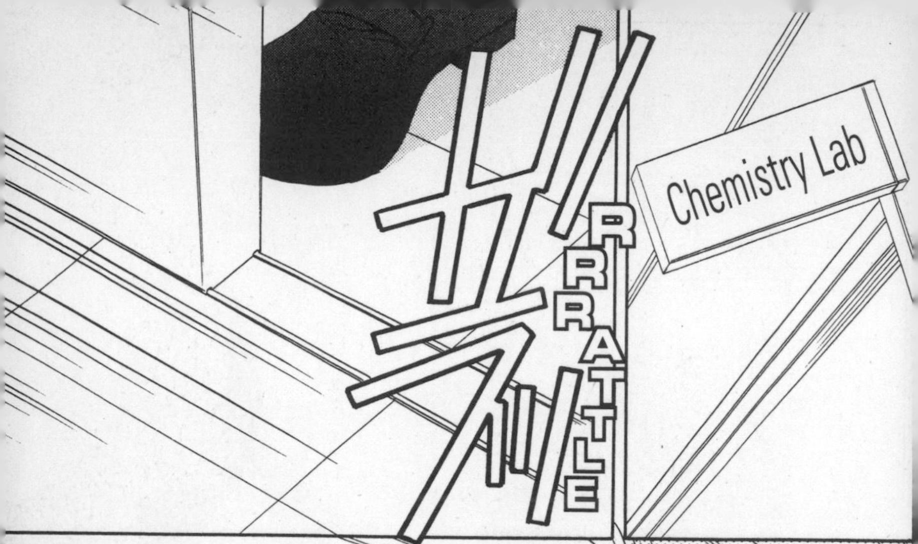
Chemistry Lab
RRRATTLE
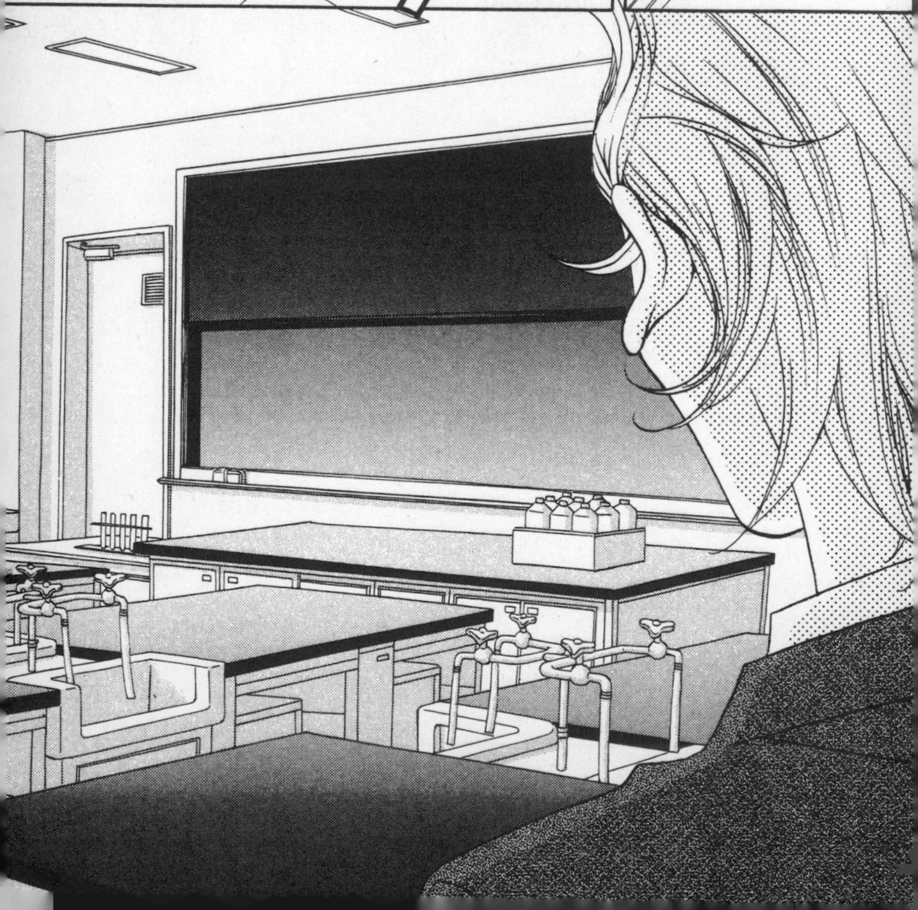

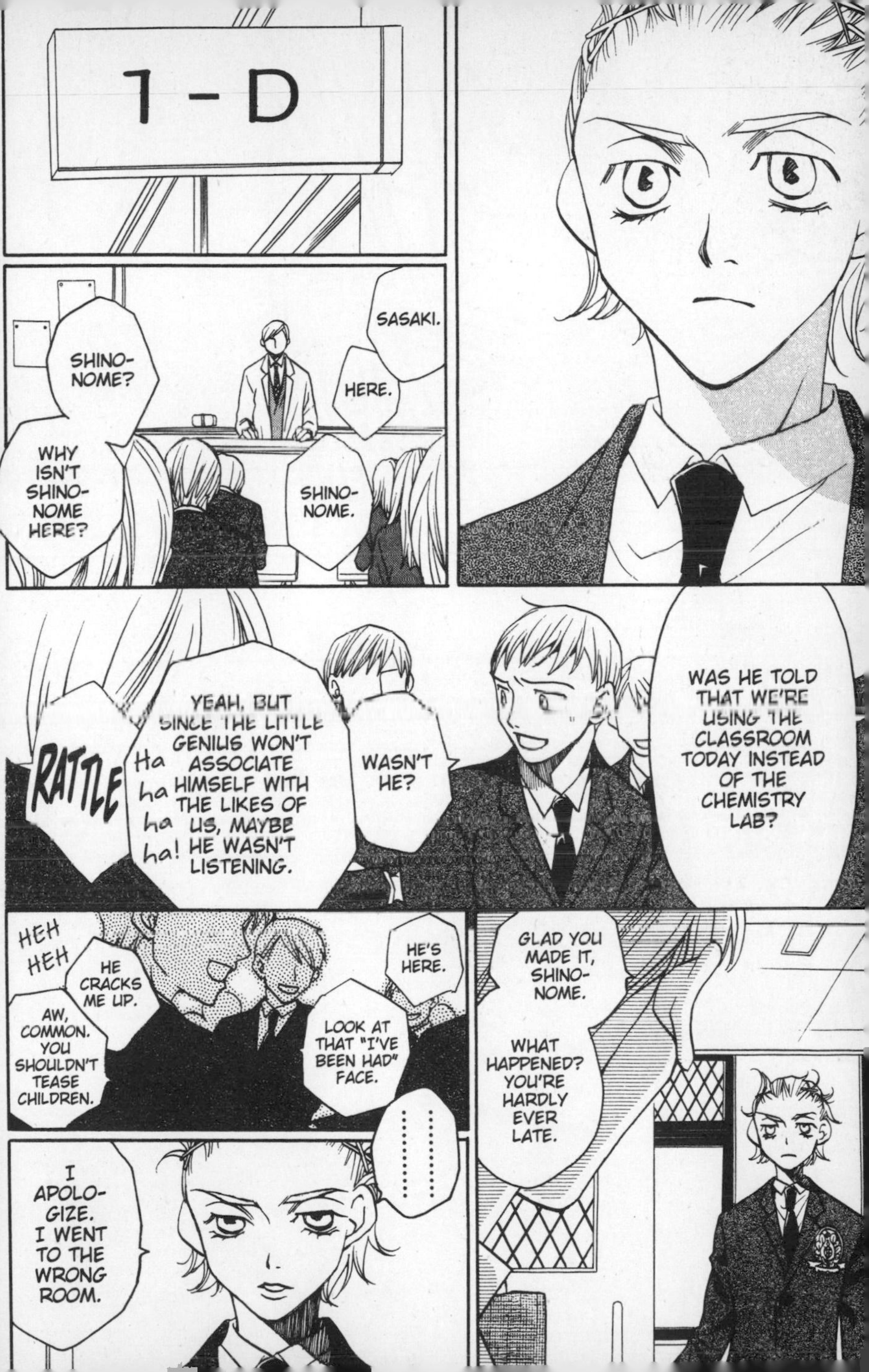
1-D
SASAKI.
HERE.
SHINO-NOME.
SHINO-NOME?
WHY ISN'T SHINO-NOME HERE?
WAS HE TOLD THAT WE'RE USING THE CLASSROOM TODAY INSTEAD OF THE CHEMISTRY LAB?
WASN'T HE?
YEAH, BUT SINCE THE LITTLE GENIUS WON'T ASSOCIATE HIMSELF WITH THE LIKES OF US, MAYBE HE WASN'T LISTENING.
Ha ha ha ha!
RATTLE
GLAD YOU MADE IT, SHINO-NOME.
WHAT HAPPENED? YOU'RE HARDLY EVER LATE.
HE'S HERE.
LOOK AT THAT "I'VE BEEN HAD" FACE.
HEH HEH
HE CRACKS ME UP.
AW, COMMON. YOU SHOULDN'T TEASE CHILDREN.
......
I APOLO-GIZE. I WENT TO THE WRONG ROOM.

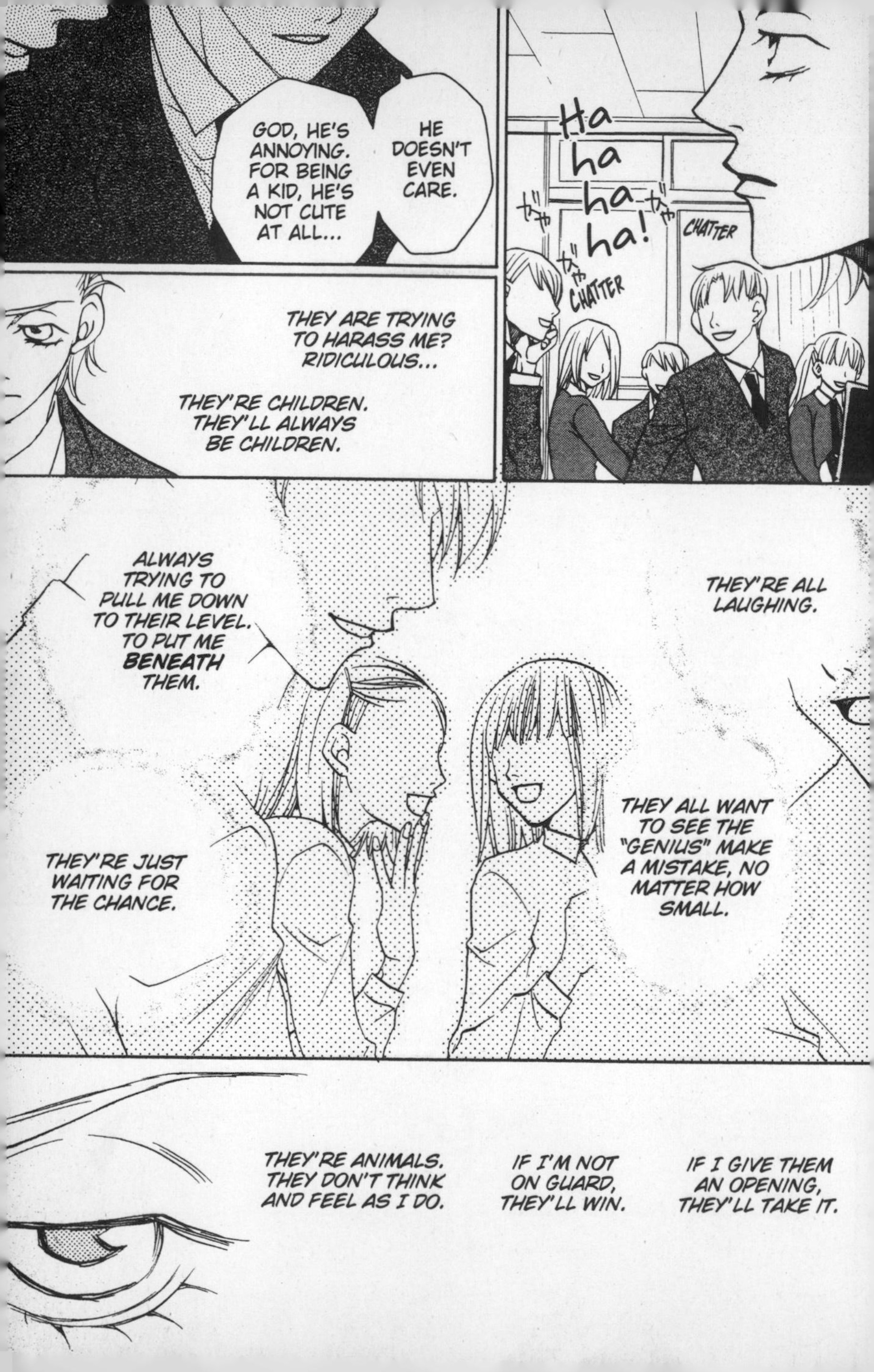
Ha ha ha ha!
ガヤ
ガヤ
ガヤ
CHATTER
CHATTER
HE DOESN'T EVEN CARE.
GOD, HE'S ANNOYING. FOR BEING A KID, HE'S NOT CUTE AT ALL...
THEY ARE TRYING TO HARASS ME? RIDICULOUS...
THEY'RE CHILDREN. THEY'LL ALWAYS BE CHILDREN.
THEY'RE ALL LAUGHING.
THEY ALL WANT TO SEE THE "GENIUS" MAKE A MISTAKE, NO MATTER HOW SMALL.
ALWAYS TRYING TO PULL ME DOWN TO THEIR LEVEL. TO PUT ME BENEATH THEM.
THEY'RE JUST WAITING FOR THE CHANCE.
IF I GIVE THEM AN OPENING, THEY'LL TAKE IT.
IF I'M NOT ON GUARD, THEY'LL WIN.
THEY'RE ANIMALS. THEY DON'T THINK AND FEEL AS I DO.

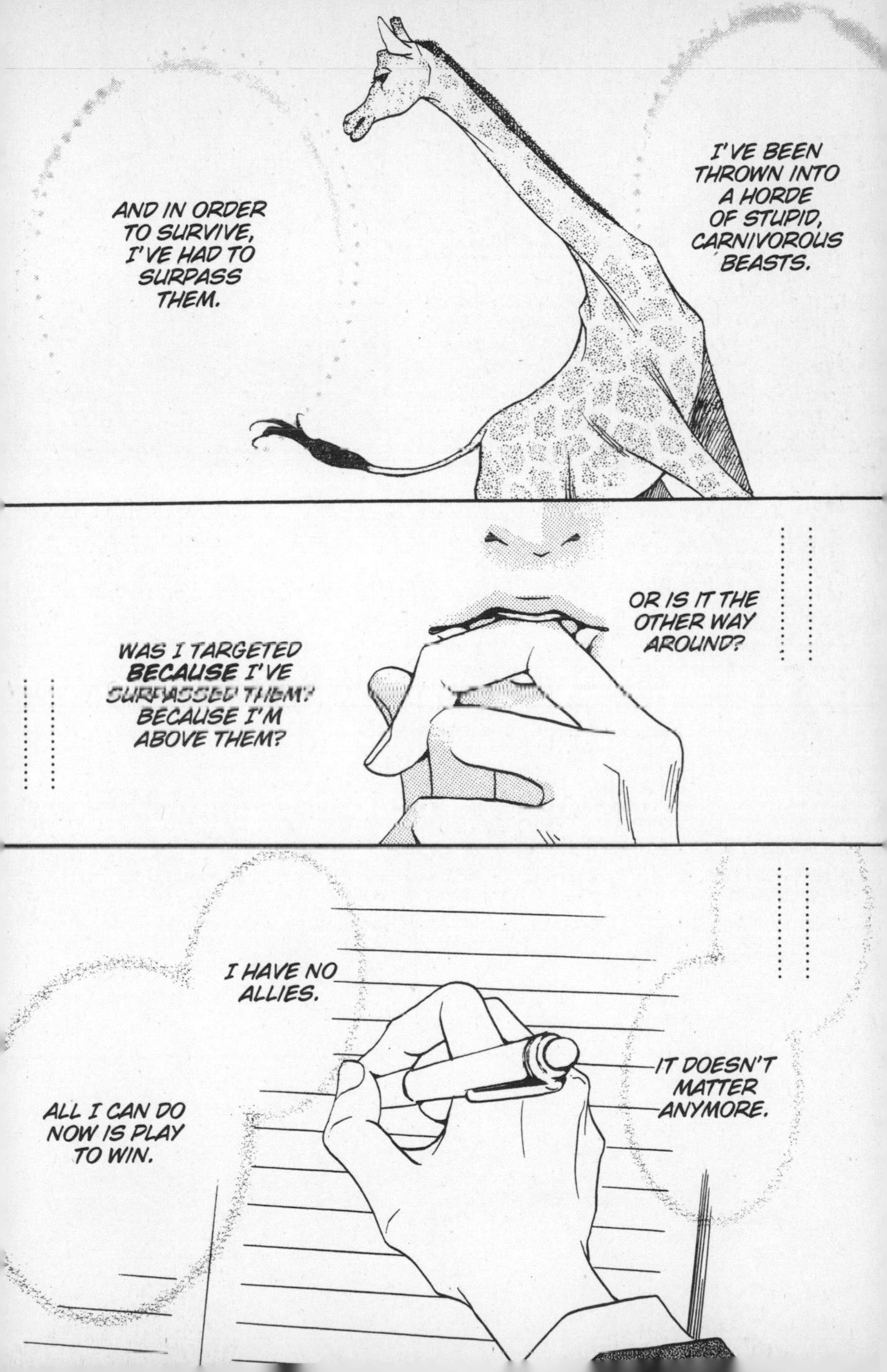
I'VE BEEN THROWN INTO A HORDE OF STUPID, CARNIVOROUS BEASTS.
AND IN ORDER TO SURVIVE, I'VE HAD TO SURPASS THEM.
WAS I TARGETED BECAUSE I'VE SURPASSED THEM? BECAUSE I'M ABOVE THEM?
OR IS IT THE OTHER WAY AROUND?
I HAVE NO ALLIES.
IT DOESN'T MATTER ANYMORE.
ALL I CAN DO NOW IS PLAY TO WIN.

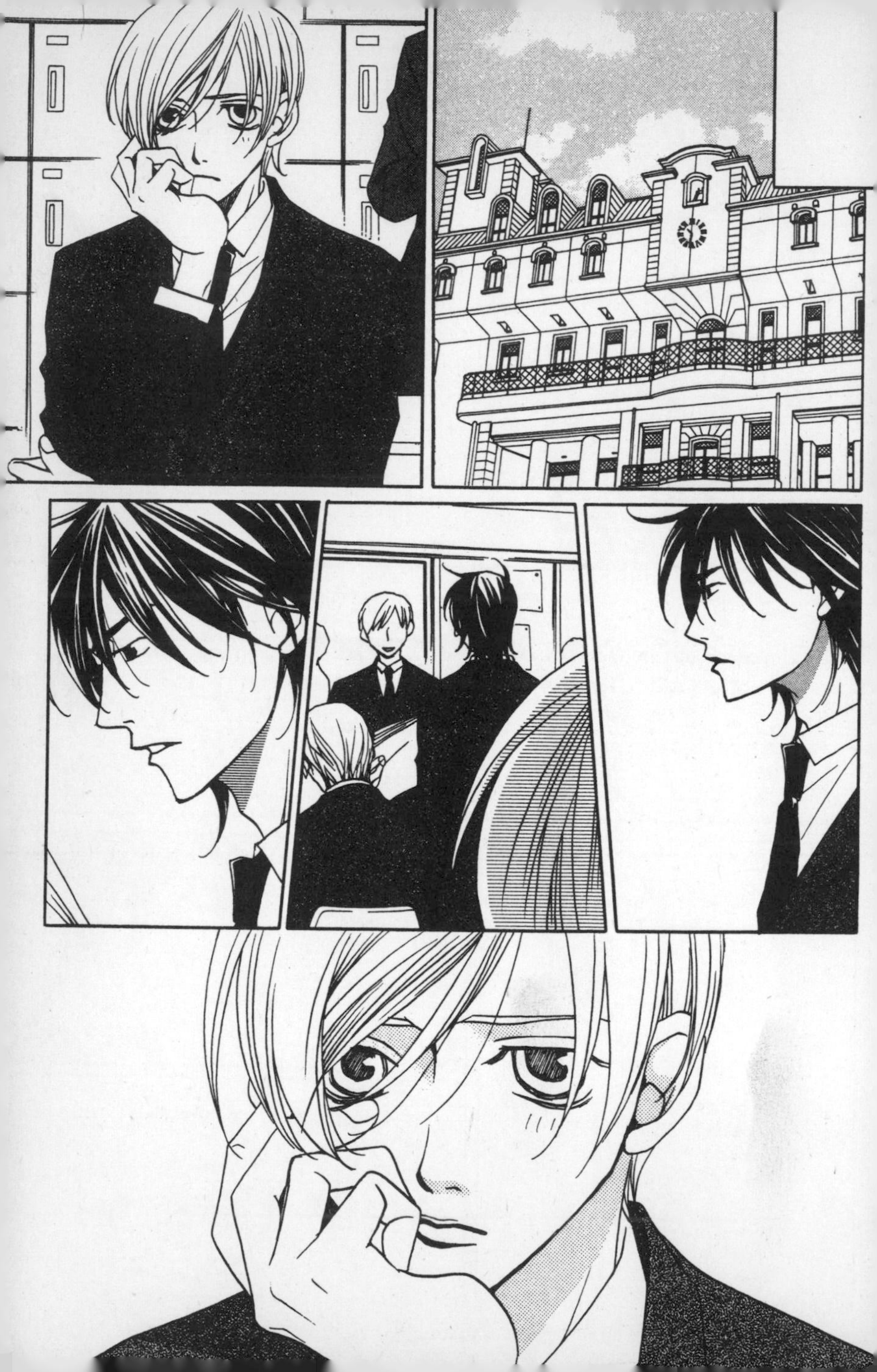

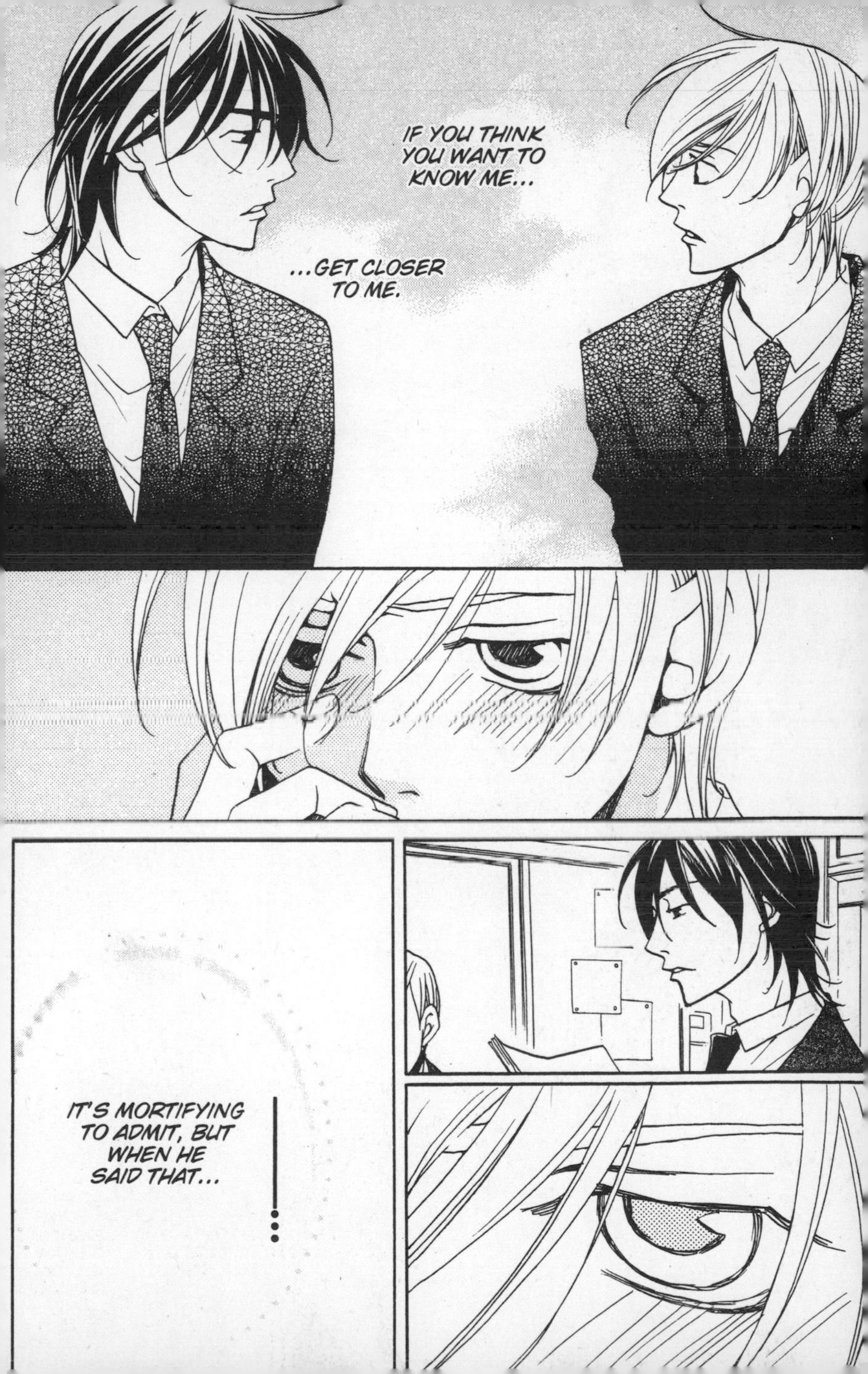
IF YOU THINK YOU WANT TO KNOW ME...
...GET CLOSER TO ME.
IT'S MORTIFYING TO ADMIT, BUT WHEN HE SAID THAT...

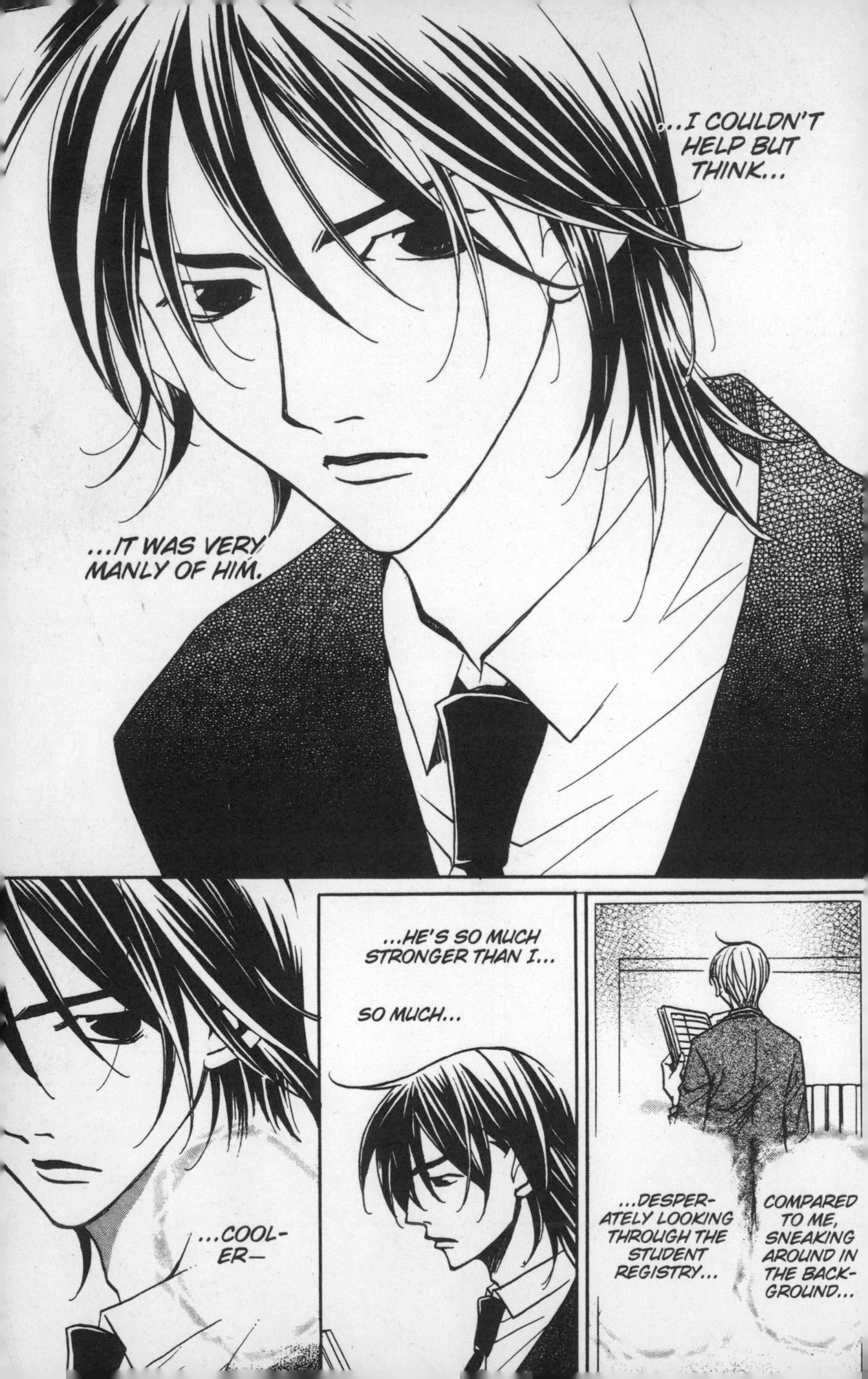
...I COULDN'T HELP BUT THINK...
...IT WAS VERY MANLY OF HIM.
COMPARED TO ME, SNEAKING AROUND IN THE BACK-GROUND...
...DESPER-ATELY LOOKING THROUGH THE STUDENT REGISTRY...
...HE'S SO MUCH STRONGER THAN I...
SO MUCH...
...COOL-ER—

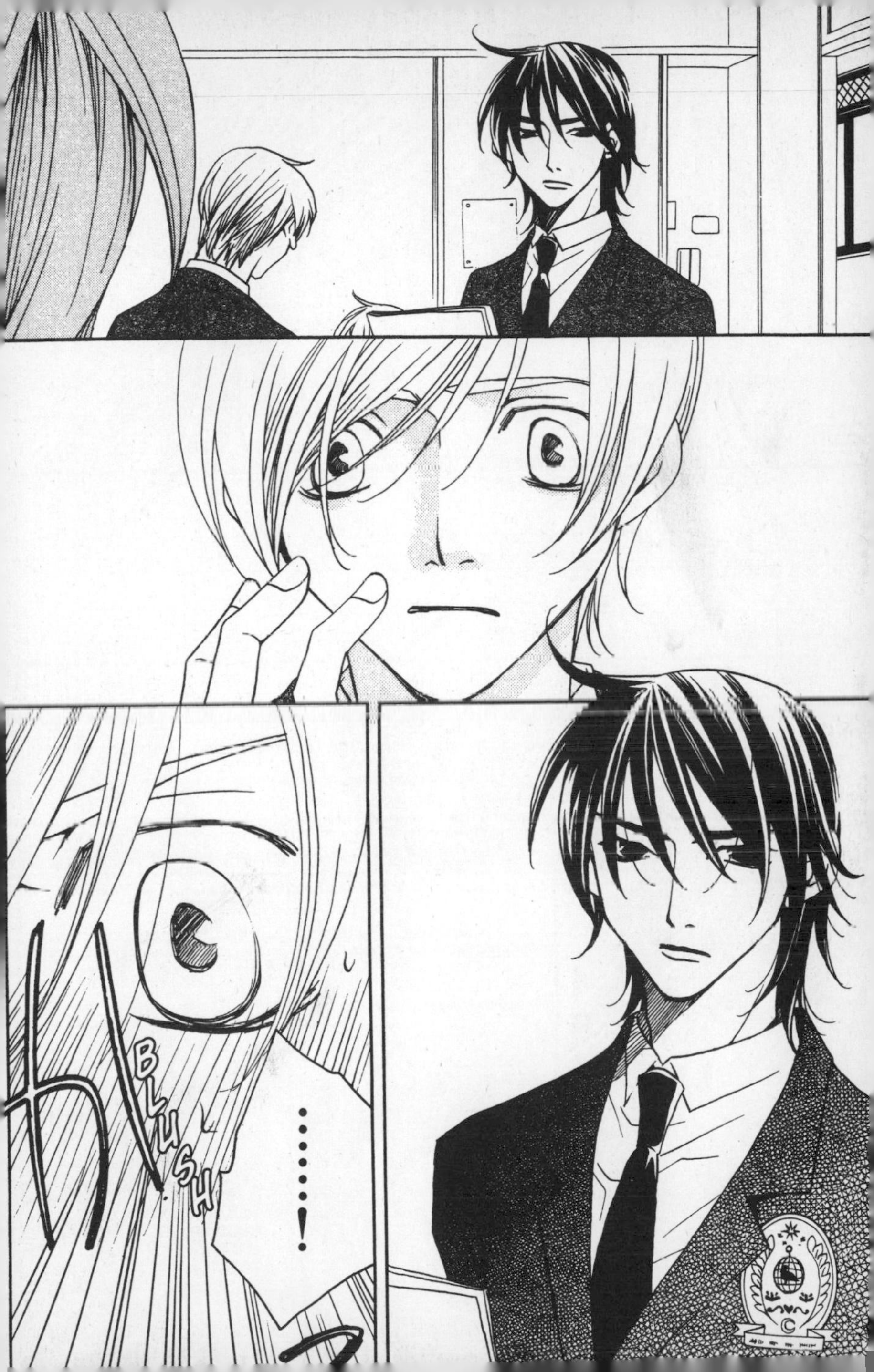
......!
BLUSH

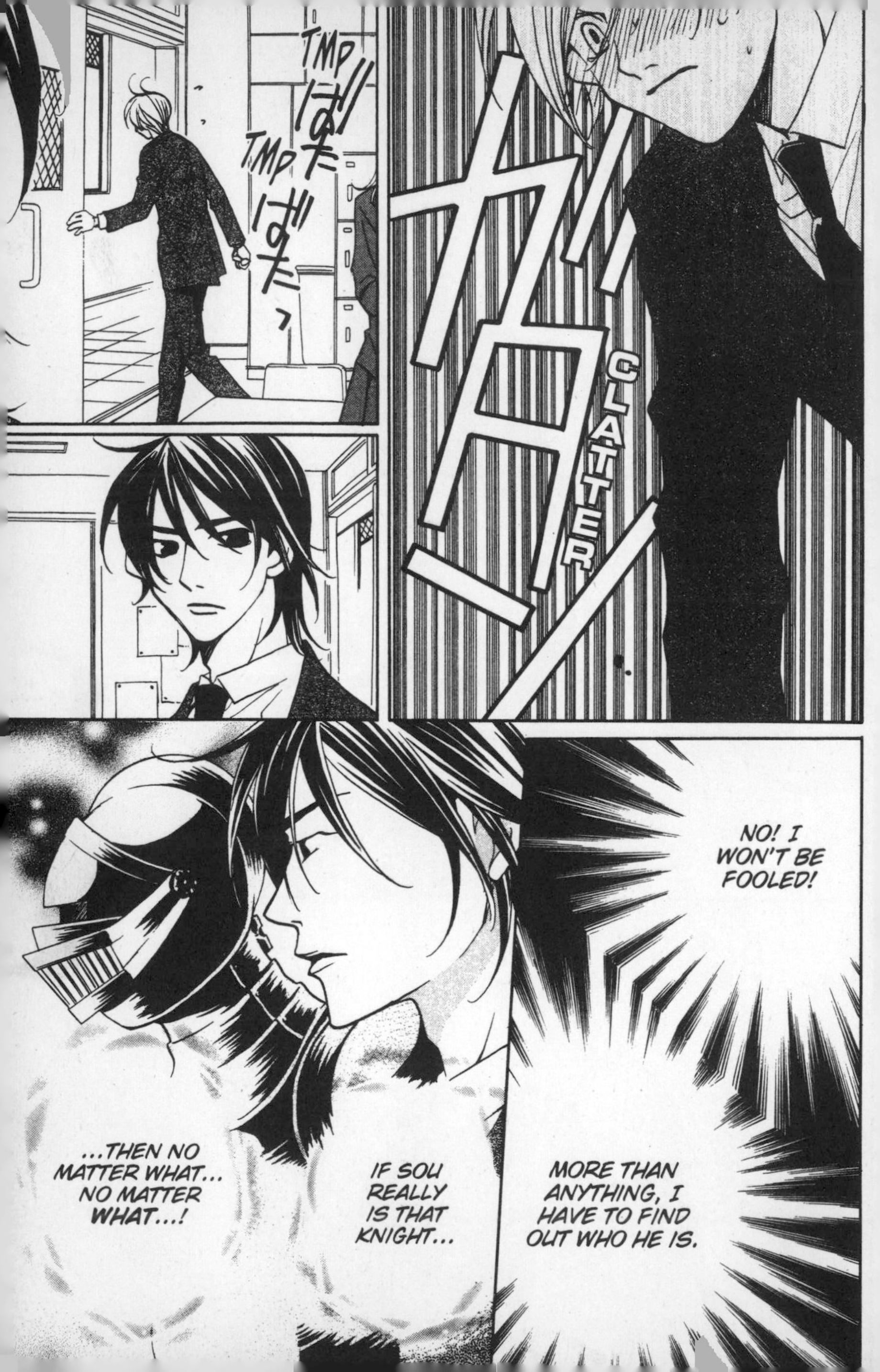
CLATTER
TMP
TMP
NO! I WON'T BE FOOLED!
MORE THAN ANYTHING, I HAVE TO FIND OUT WHO HE IS.
IF SOU REALLY IS THAT KNIGHT...
...THEN NO MATTER WHAT... NO MATTER WHAT...!

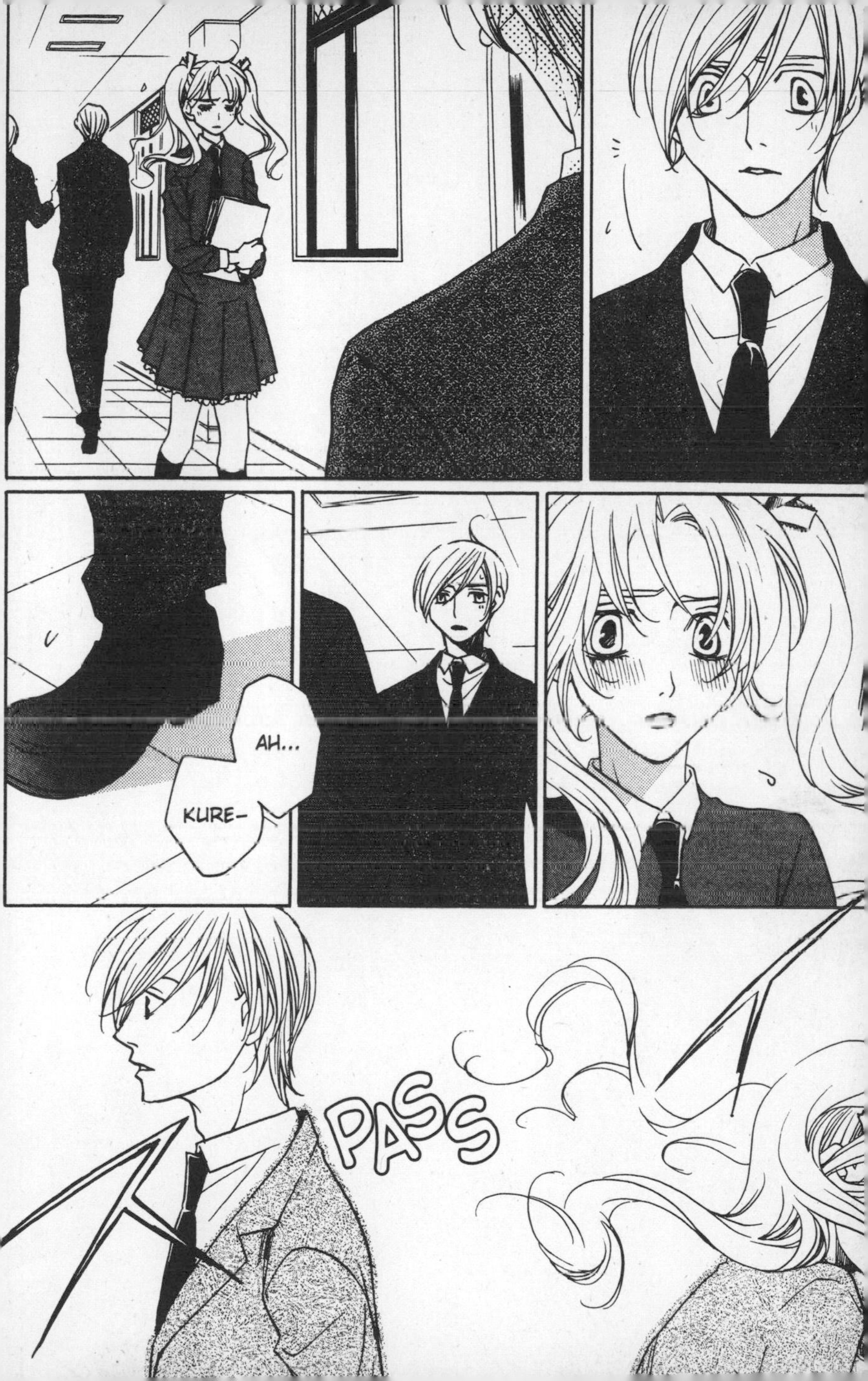
AH...
KURE-
PASS

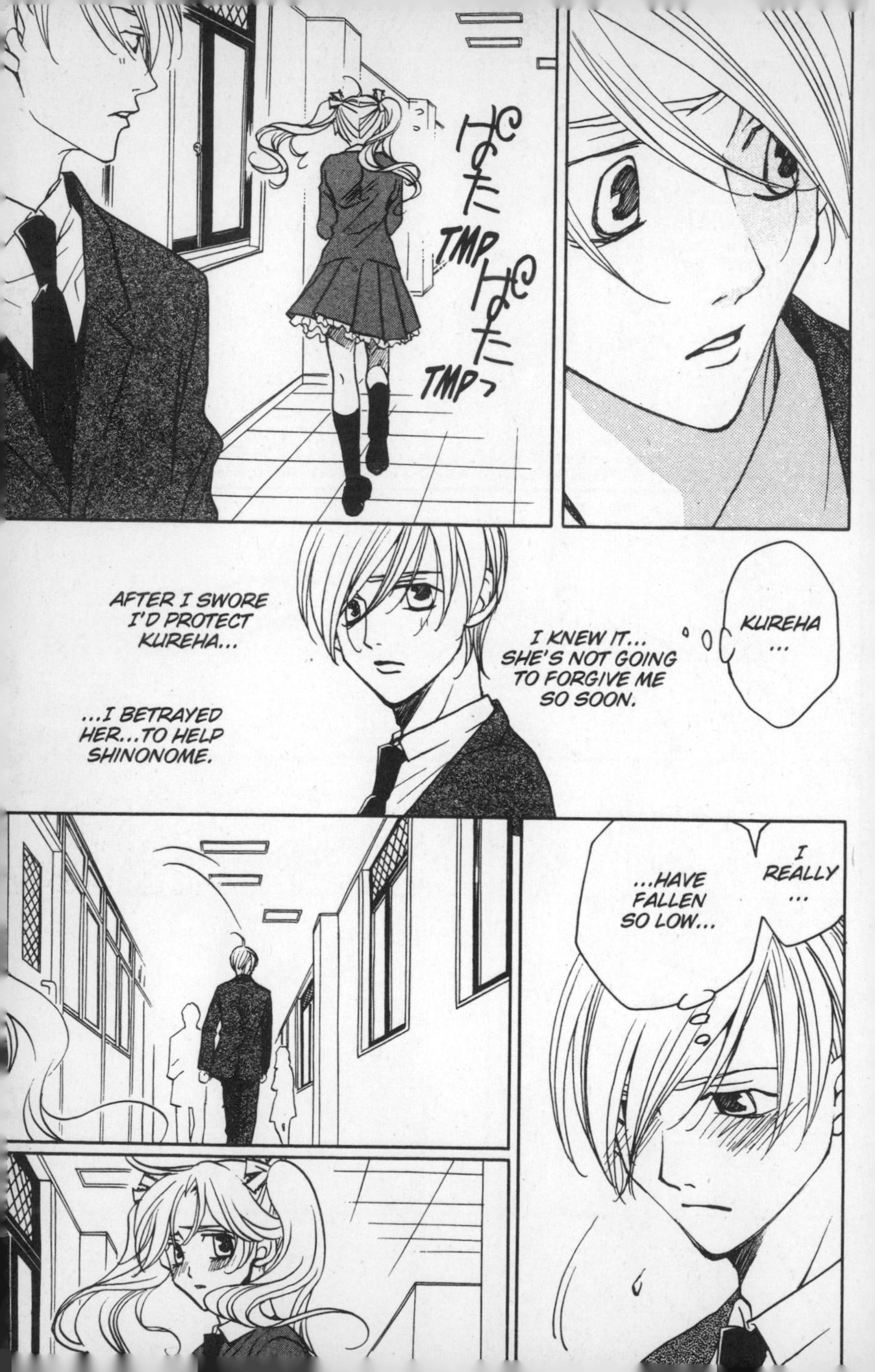
TMP
TMP
KUREHA ...
I KNEW IT... SHE'S NOT GOING TO FORGIVE ME SO SOON.
AFTER I SWORE I'D PROTECT KUREHA...
...I BETRAYED HER...TO HELP SHINONOME.
I REALLY ...
...HAVE FALLEN SO LOW...

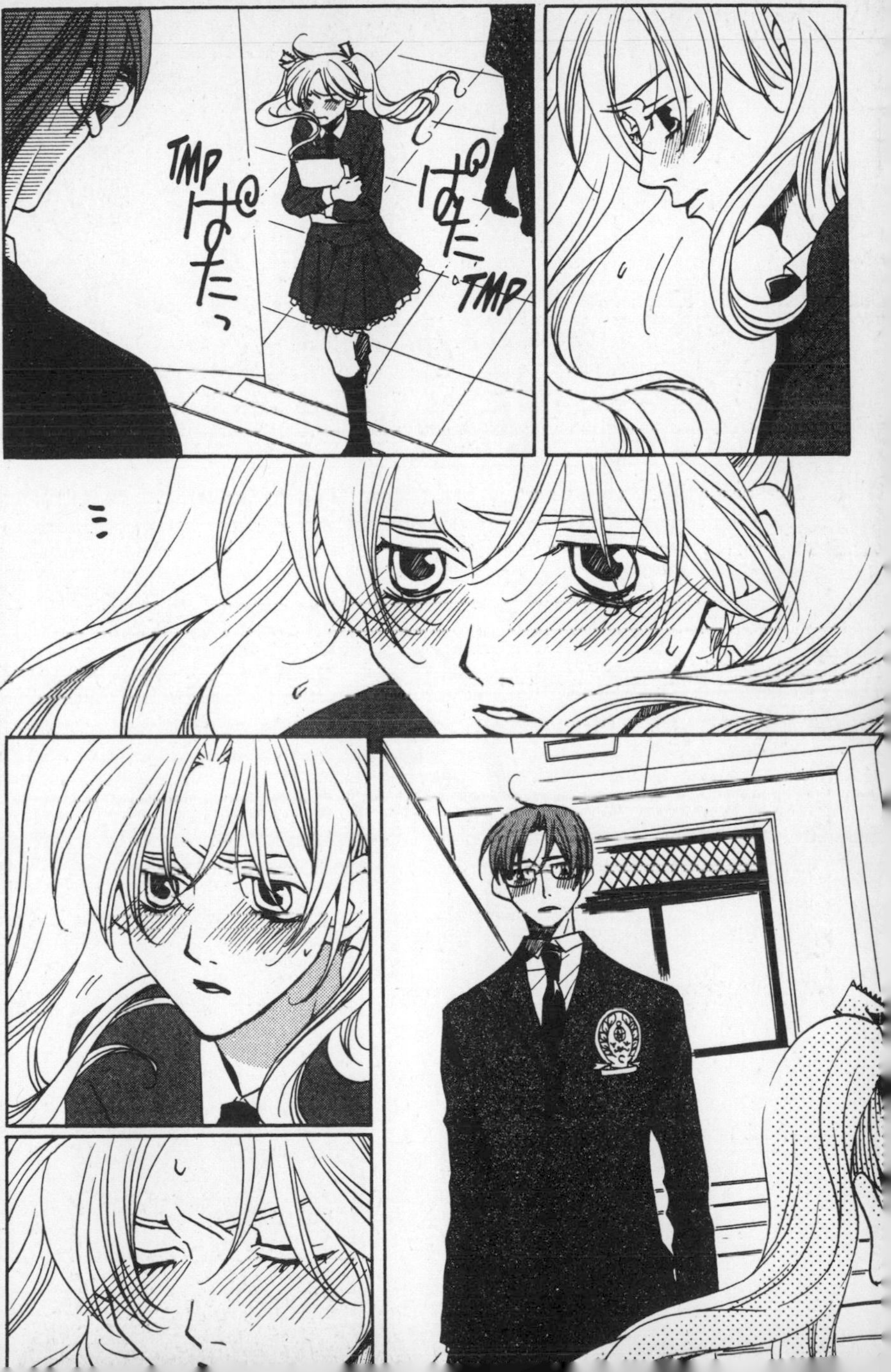
ぱた
TMP
TMP
ぱたっ

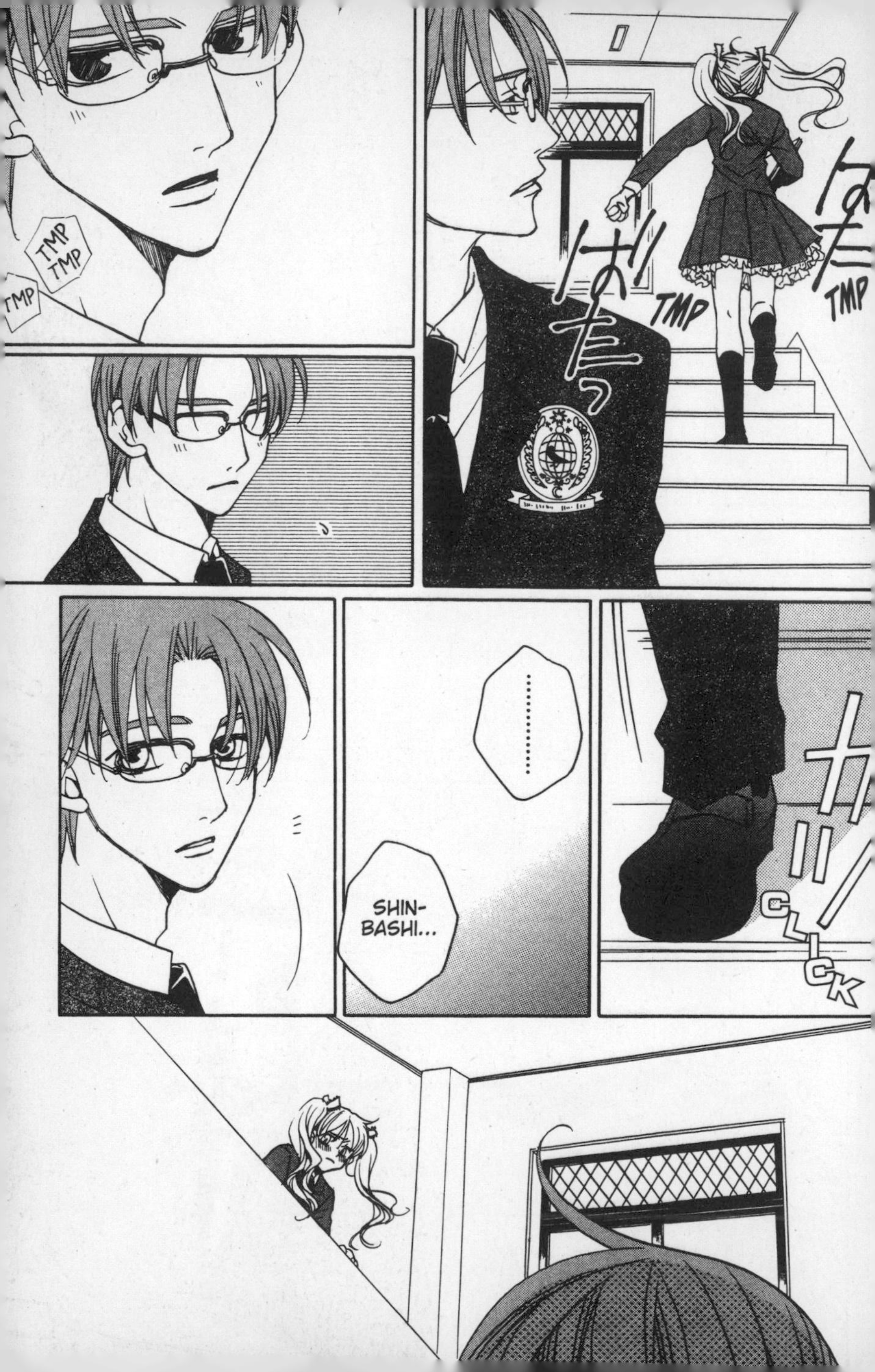
TMP
TMP
TMP TMP
TMP
CLICK
......
SHIN-BASHI...

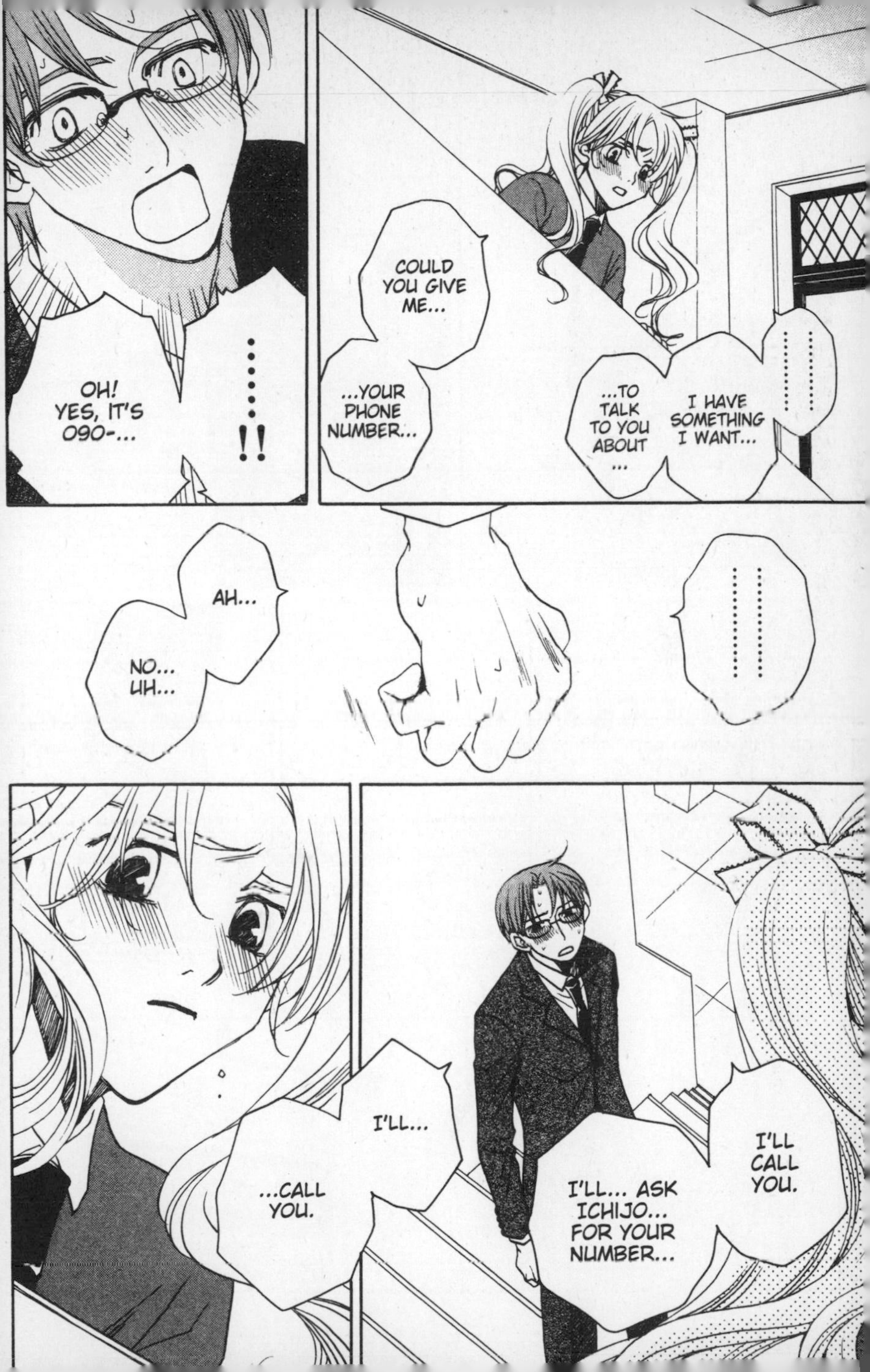
......
I HAVE SOMETHING I WANT...
...TO TALK TO YOU ABOUT...
COULD YOU GIVE ME...
...YOUR PHONE NUMBER...
......!!
OH! YES, IT'S 090-...
......
AH...
NO... UH...
I'LL CALL YOU.
I'LL... ASK ICHIJO... FOR YOUR NUMBER...
I'LL...
...CALL YOU.

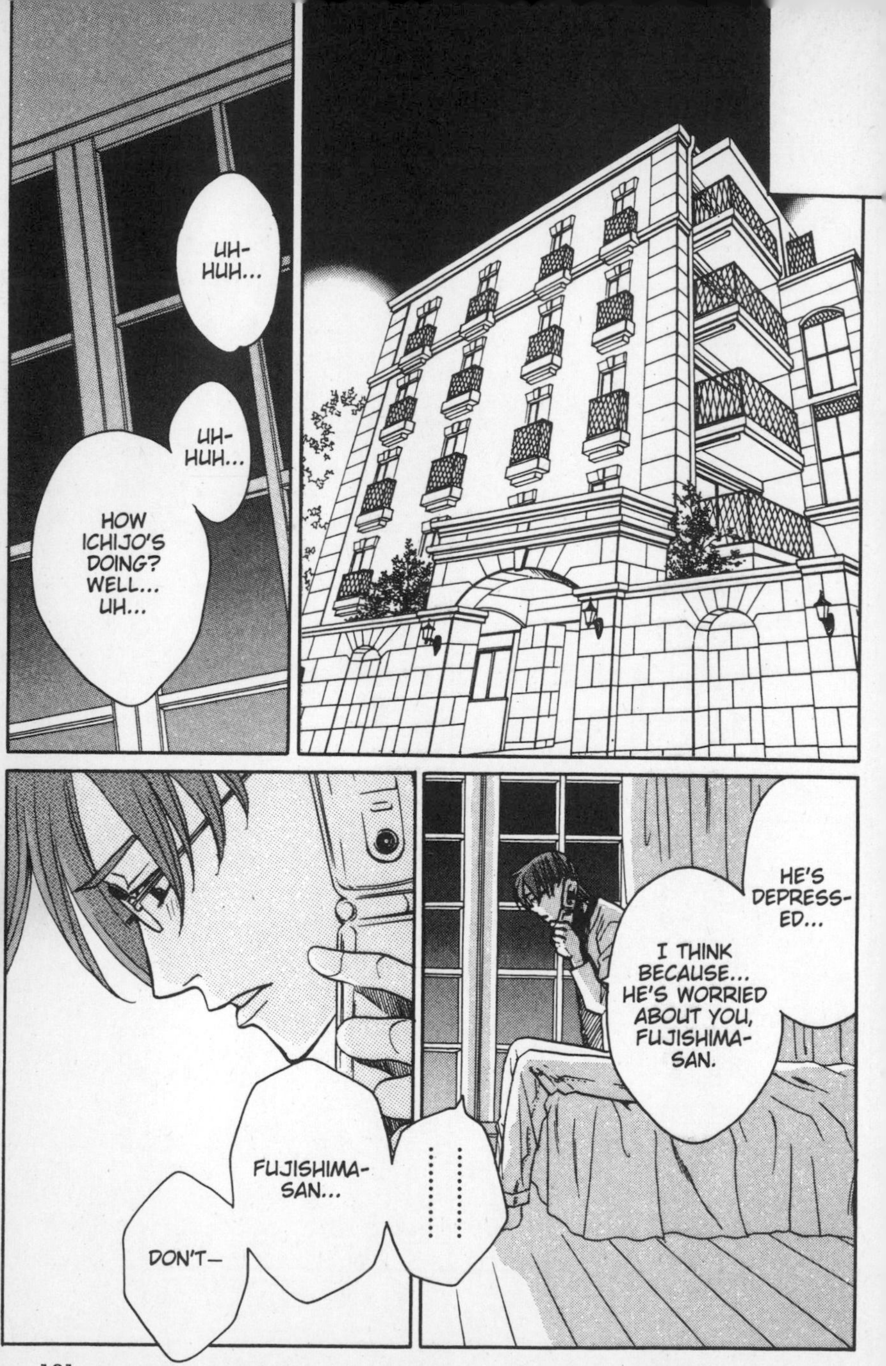
UH-HUH...
UH-HUH...
HOW ICHIJO'S DOING? WELL... UH...
HE'S DEPRESS-ED...
I THINK BECAUSE... HE'S WORRIED ABOUT YOU, FUJISHIMA-SAN.
......
FUJISHIMA-SAN...
DON'T—

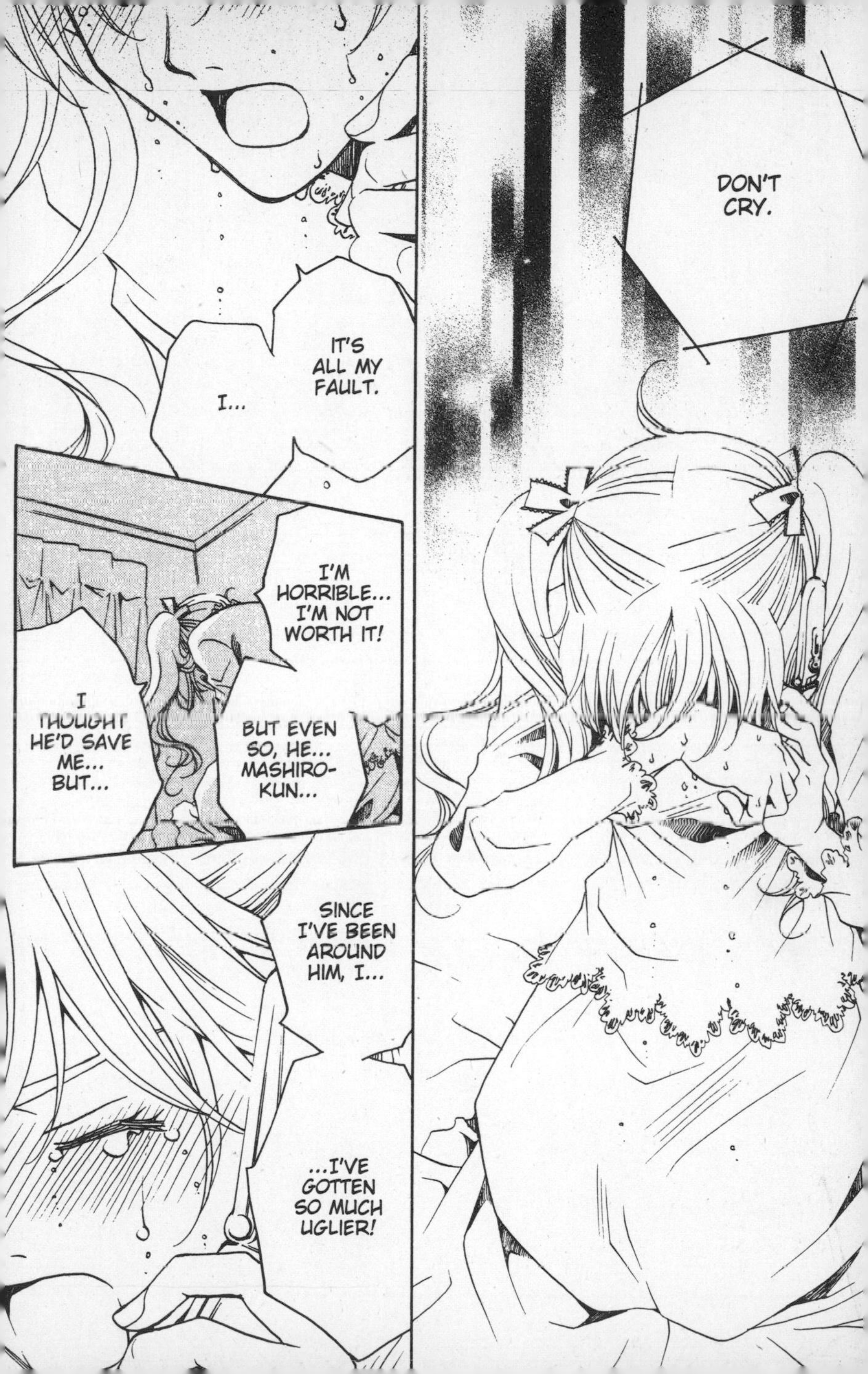
DON'T CRY.
IT'S ALL MY FAULT.
I...
I'M HORRIBLE... I'M NOT WORTH IT!
BUT EVEN SO, HE... MASHIRO-KUN...
I THOUGHT HE'D SAVE ME... BUT...
SINCE I'VE BEEN AROUND HIM, I...
...I'VE GOTTEN SO MUCH UGLIER!

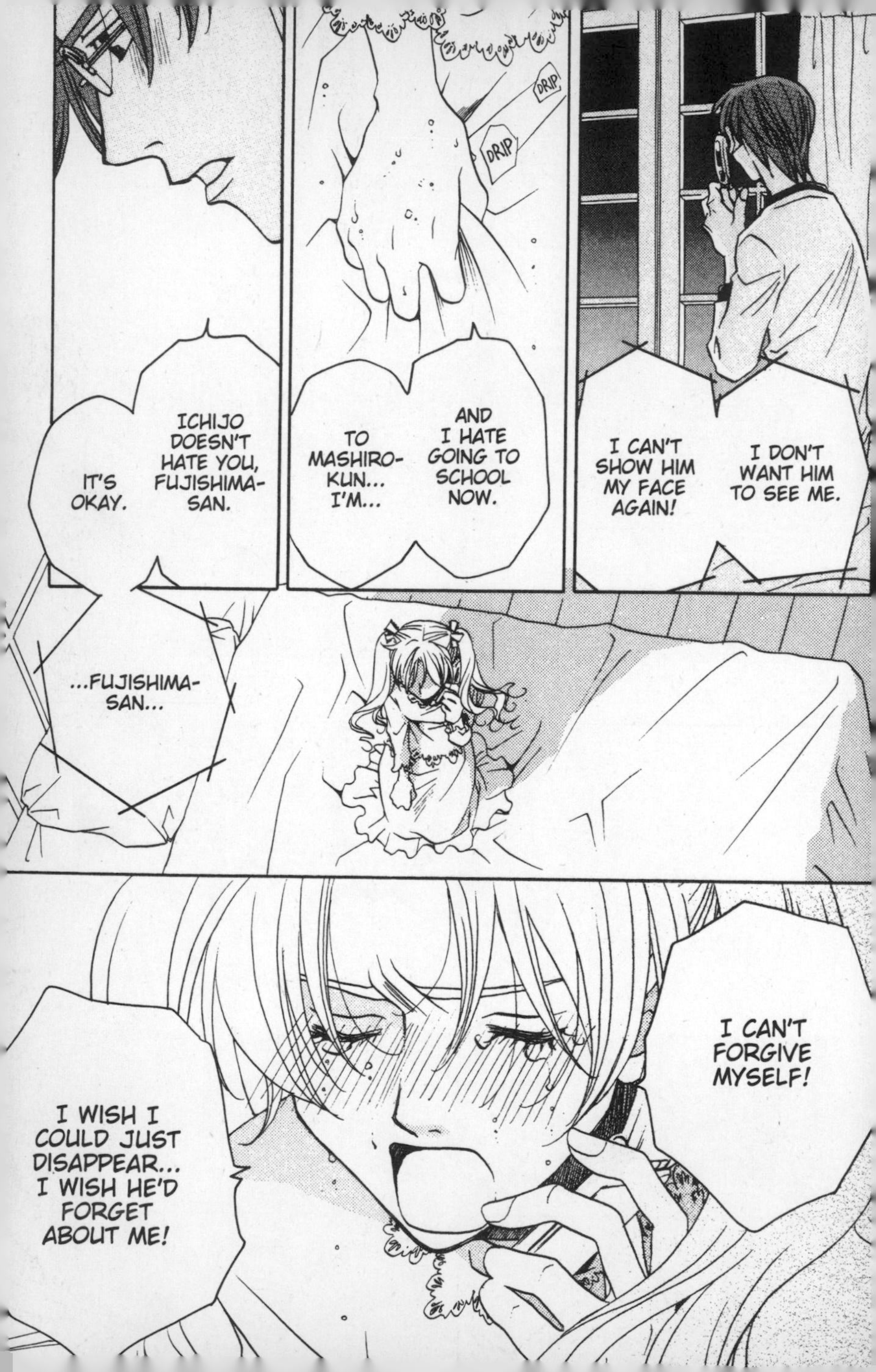
I DON'T WANT HIM TO SEE ME.
I CAN'T SHOW HIM MY FACE AGAIN!
DRIP
DRIP
AND I HATE GOING TO SCHOOL NOW.
TO MASHIRO-KUN... I'M...
ICHIJO DOESN'T HATE YOU, FUJISHIMA-SAN.
IT'S OKAY.
...FUJISHIMA-SAN...
I CAN'T FORGIVE MYSELF!
I WISH I COULD JUST DISAPPEAR... I WISH HE'D FORGET ABOUT ME!

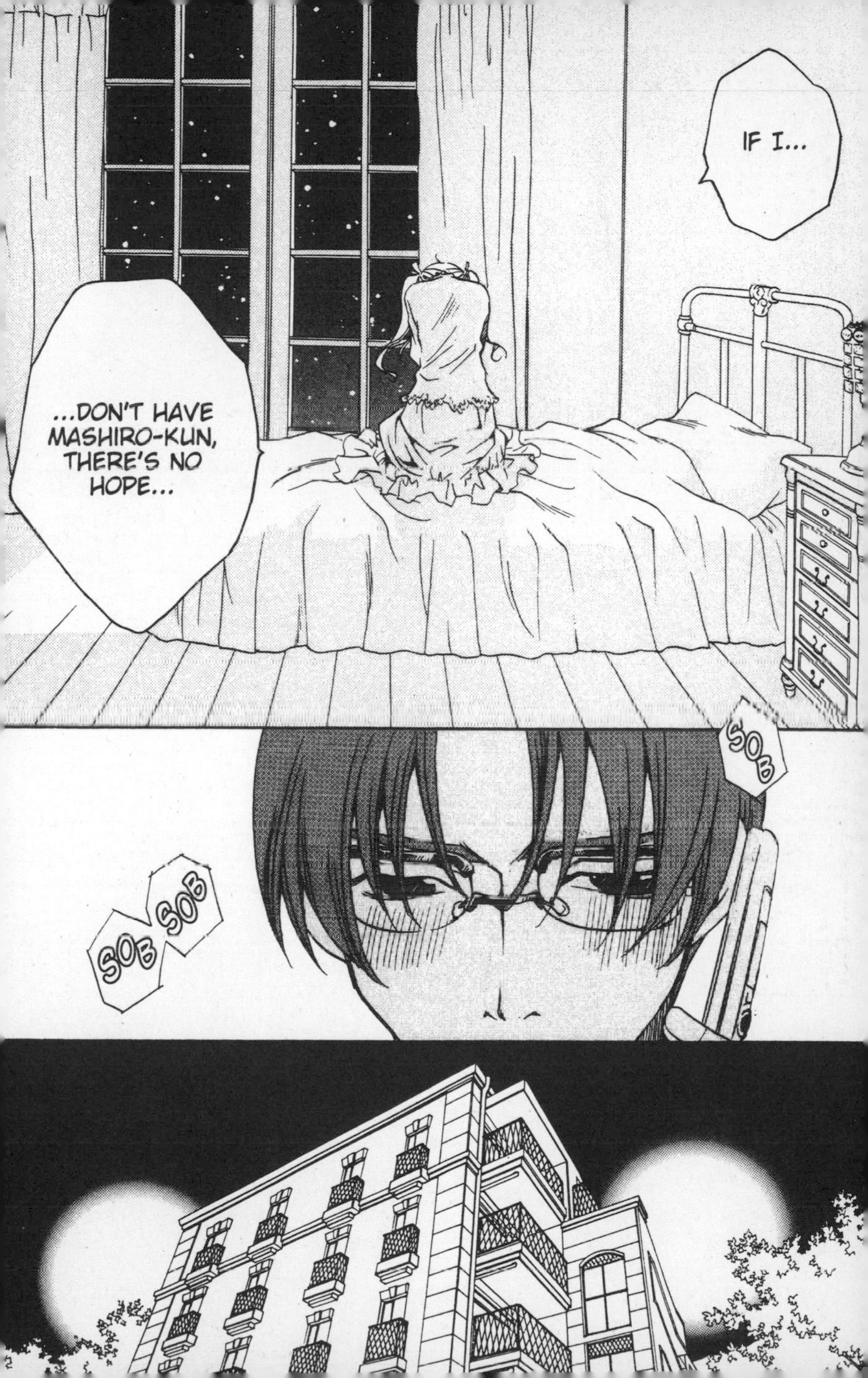
IF I...
...DON'T HAVE MASHIRO-KUN, THERE'S NO HOPE...
SOB
SOB SOB

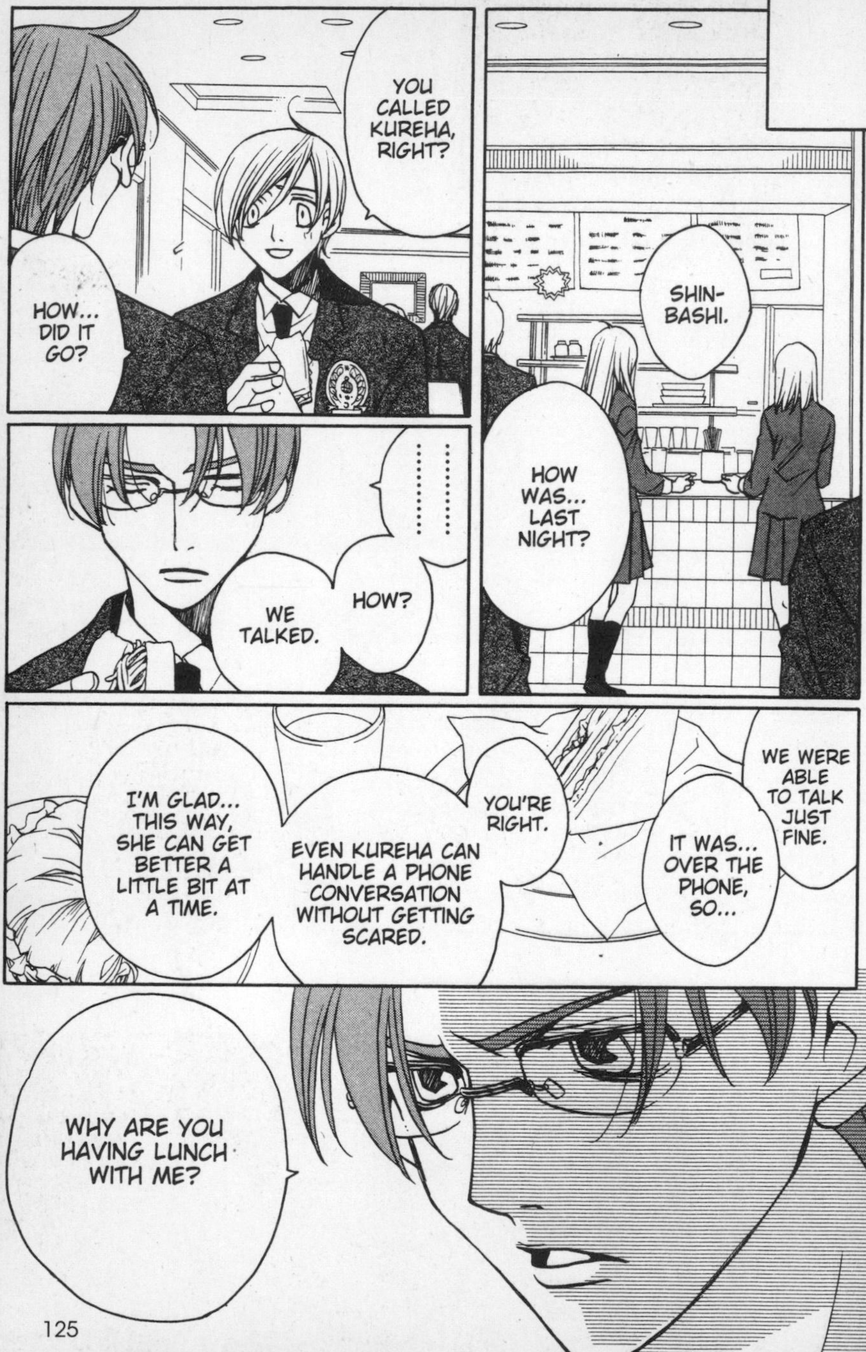
SHIN-BASHI.
HOW WAS... LAST NIGHT?
YOU CALLED KUREHA, RIGHT?
HOW... DID IT GO?
......
HOW?
WE TALKED.
WE WERE ABLE TO TALK JUST FINE.
IT WAS... OVER THE PHONE, SO...
YOU'RE RIGHT.
EVEN KUREHA CAN HANDLE A PHONE CONVERSATION WITHOUT GETTING SCARED.
I'M GLAD... THIS WAY, SHE CAN GET BETTER A LITTLE BIT AT A TIME.
WHY ARE YOU HAVING LUNCH WITH ME?

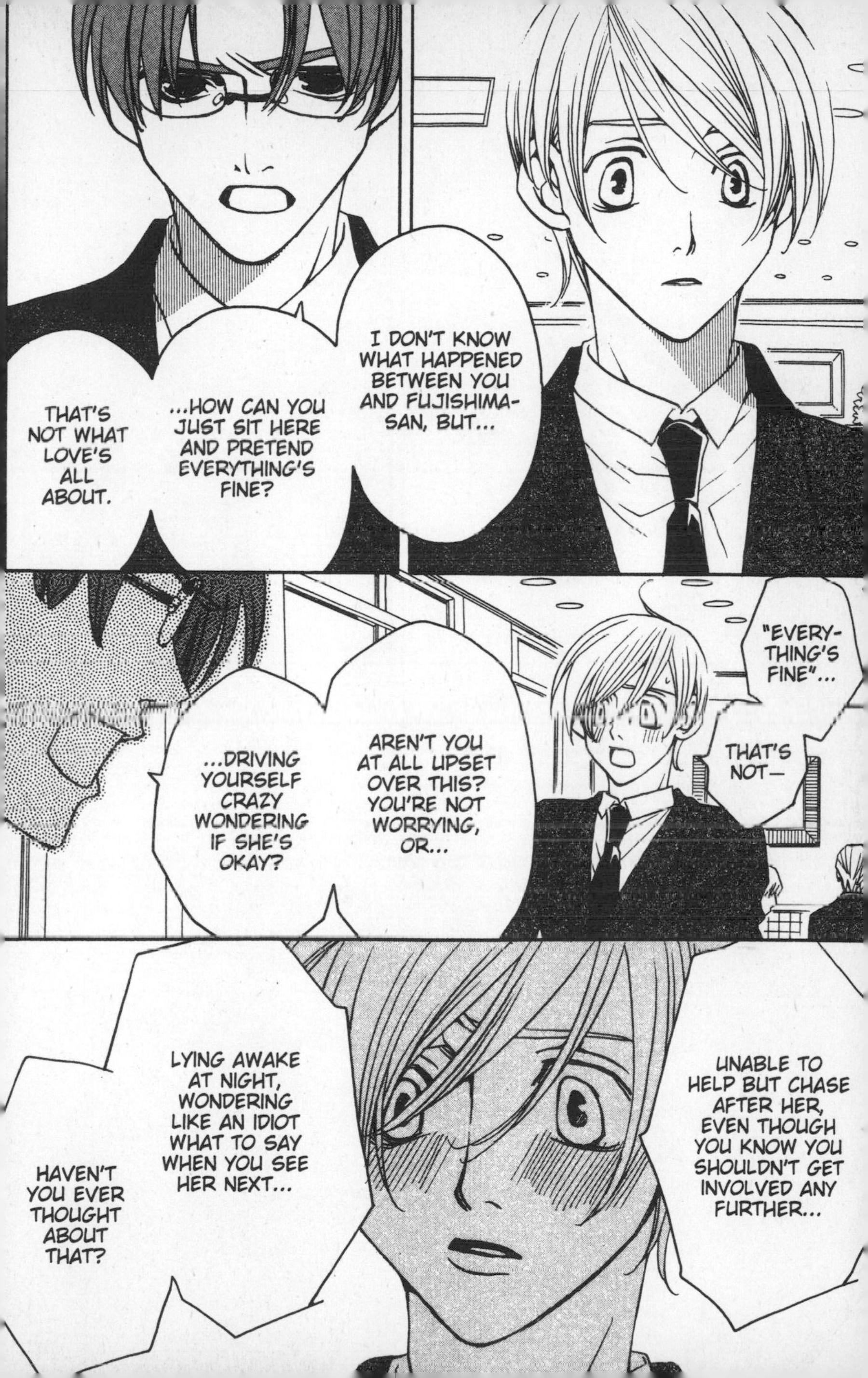
I DON'T KNOW WHAT HAPPENED BETWEEN YOU AND FUJISHIMA-SAN, BUT...
...HOW CAN YOU JUST SIT HERE AND PRETEND EVERYTHING'S FINE?
THAT'S NOT WHAT LOVE'S ALL ABOUT.
"EVERY-THING'S FINE"...
THAT'S NOT—
AREN'T YOU AT ALL UPSET OVER THIS? YOU'RE NOT WORRYING, OR...
...DRIVING YOURSELF CRAZY WONDERING IF SHE'S OKAY?
UNABLE TO HELP BUT CHASE AFTER HER, EVEN THOUGH YOU KNOW YOU SHOULDN'T GET INVOLVED ANY FURTHER...
LYING AWAKE AT NIGHT, WONDERING LIKE AN IDIOT WHAT TO SAY WHEN YOU SEE HER NEXT...
HAVEN'T YOU EVER THOUGHT ABOUT THAT?

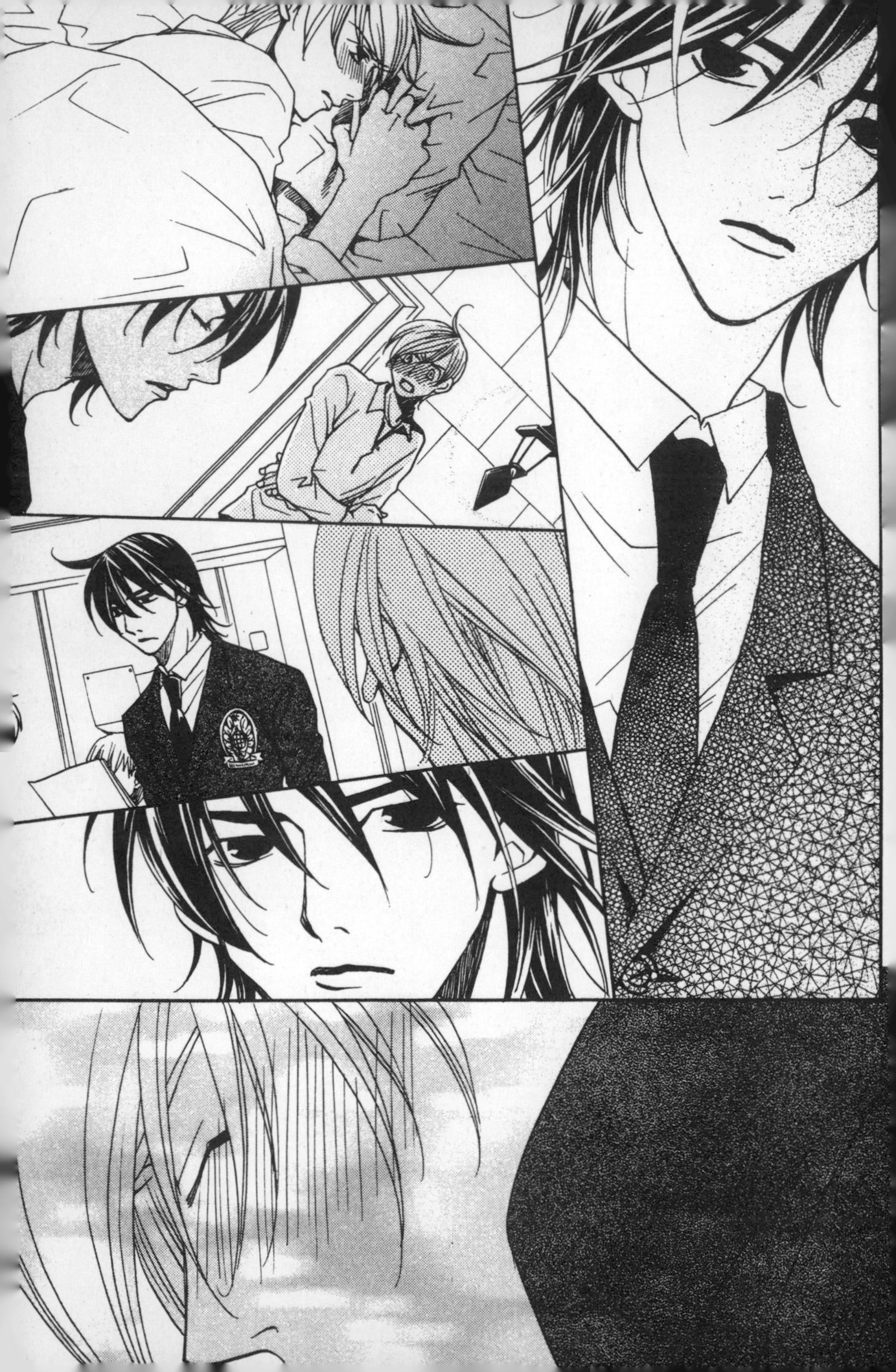

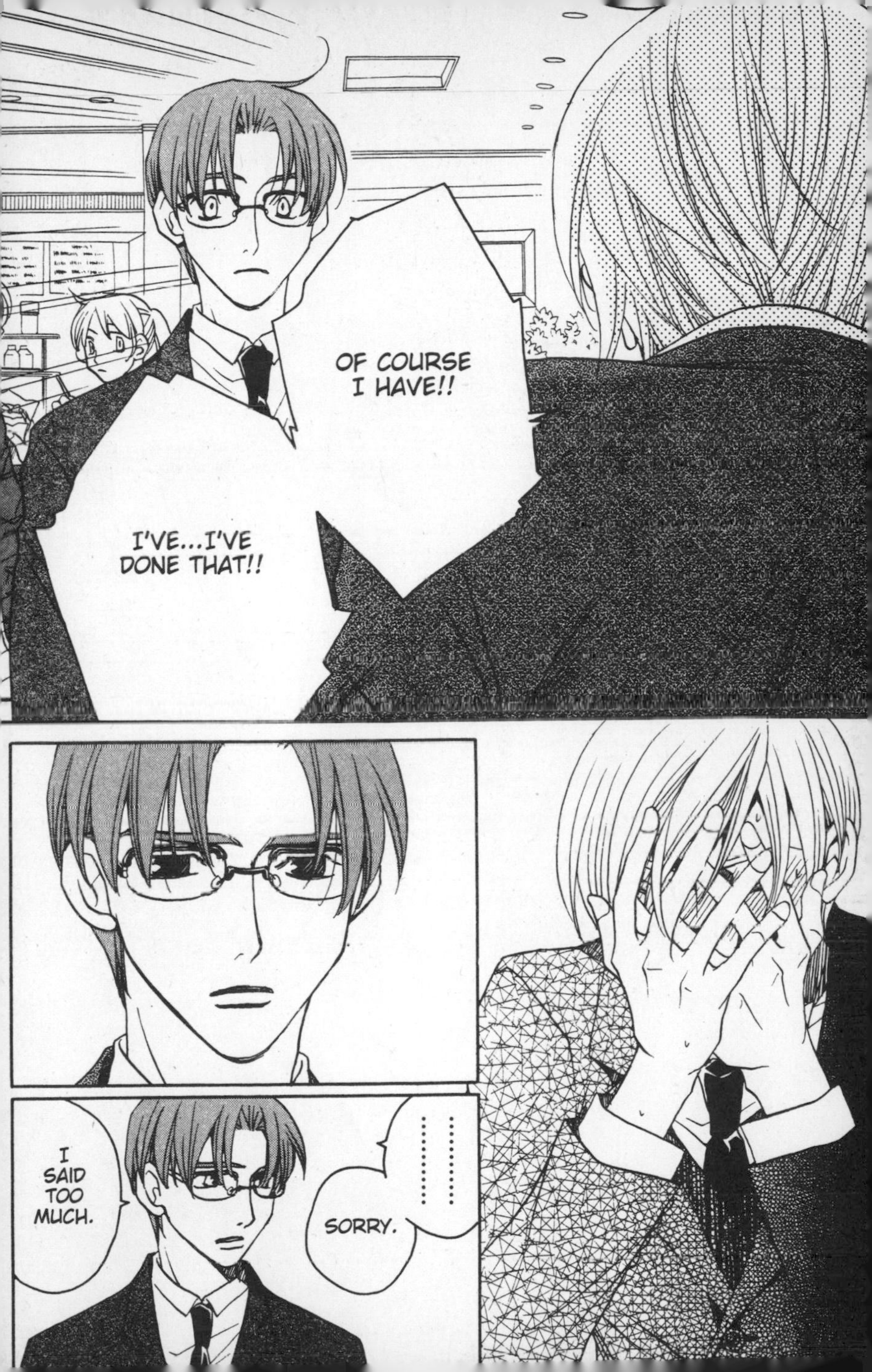
OF COURSE I HAVE!!
I'VE...I'VE DONE THAT!!
......
I SAID TOO MUCH.
SORRY.

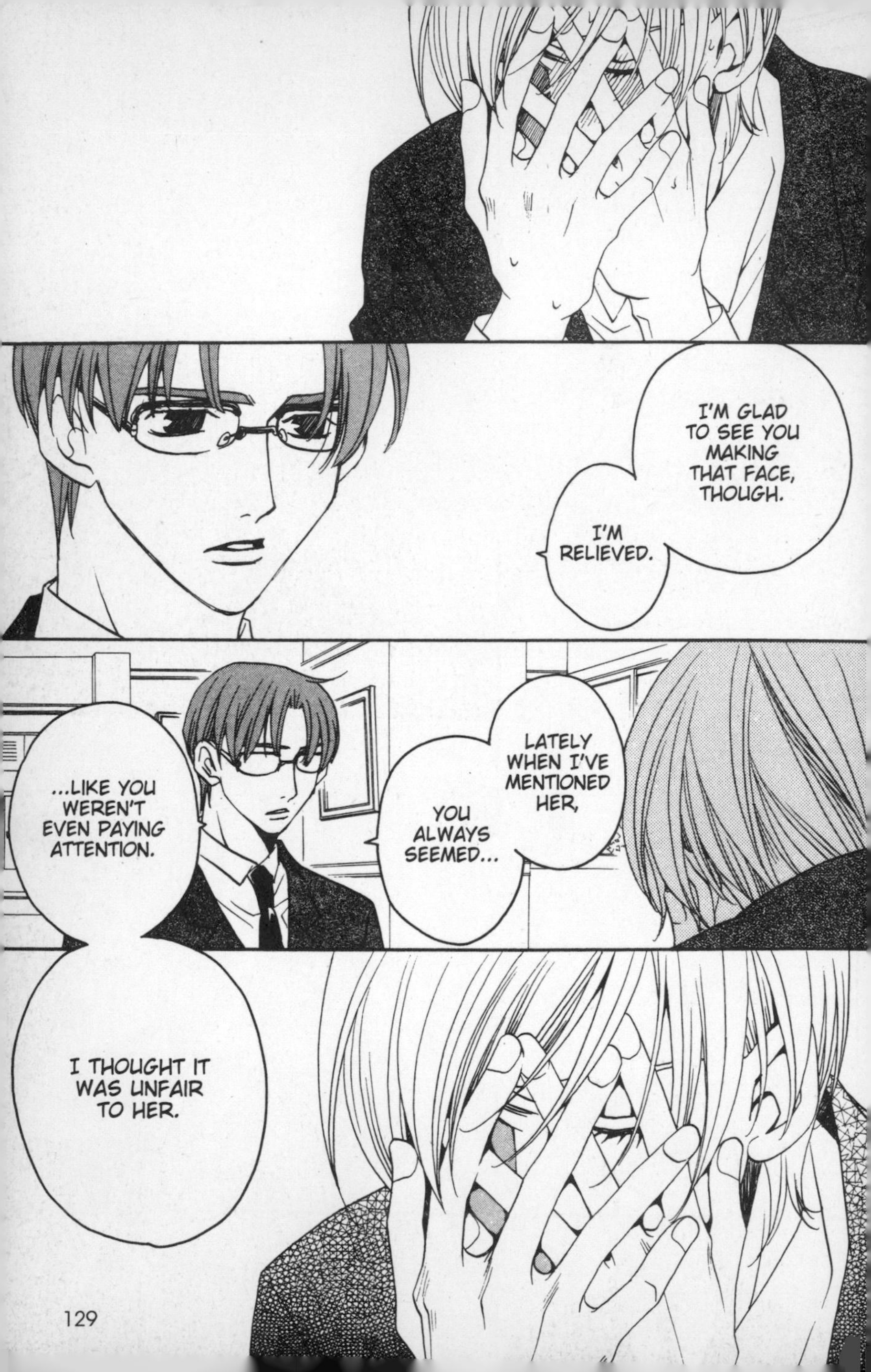
I'M GLAD TO SEE YOU MAKING THAT FACE, THOUGH.
I'M RELIEVED.
LATELY WHEN I'VE MENTIONED HER,
YOU ALWAYS SEEMED...
...LIKE YOU WEREN'T EVEN PAYING ATTENTION.
I THOUGHT IT WAS UNFAIR TO HER.

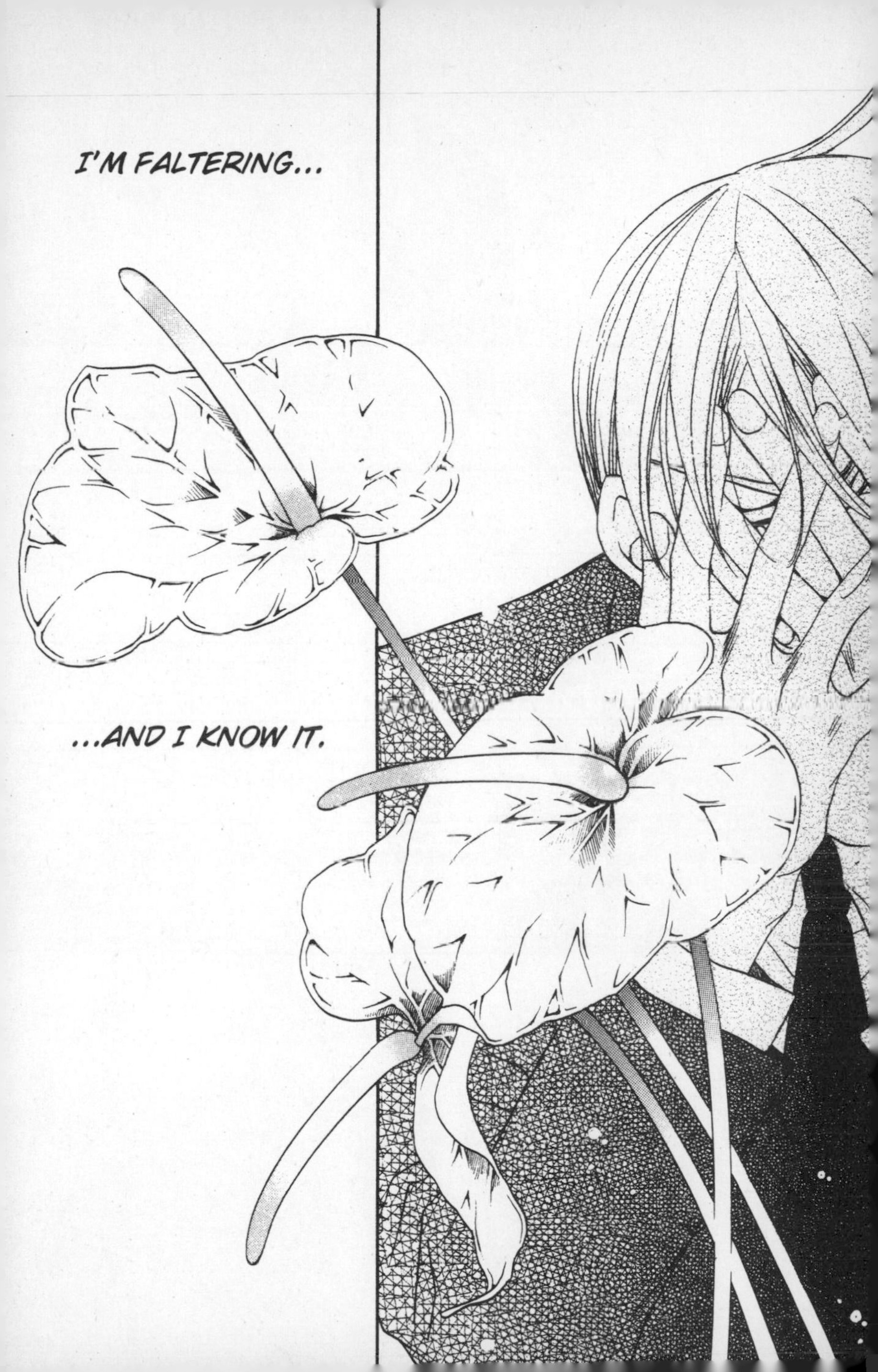
I'M FALTERING...
...AND I KNOW IT.

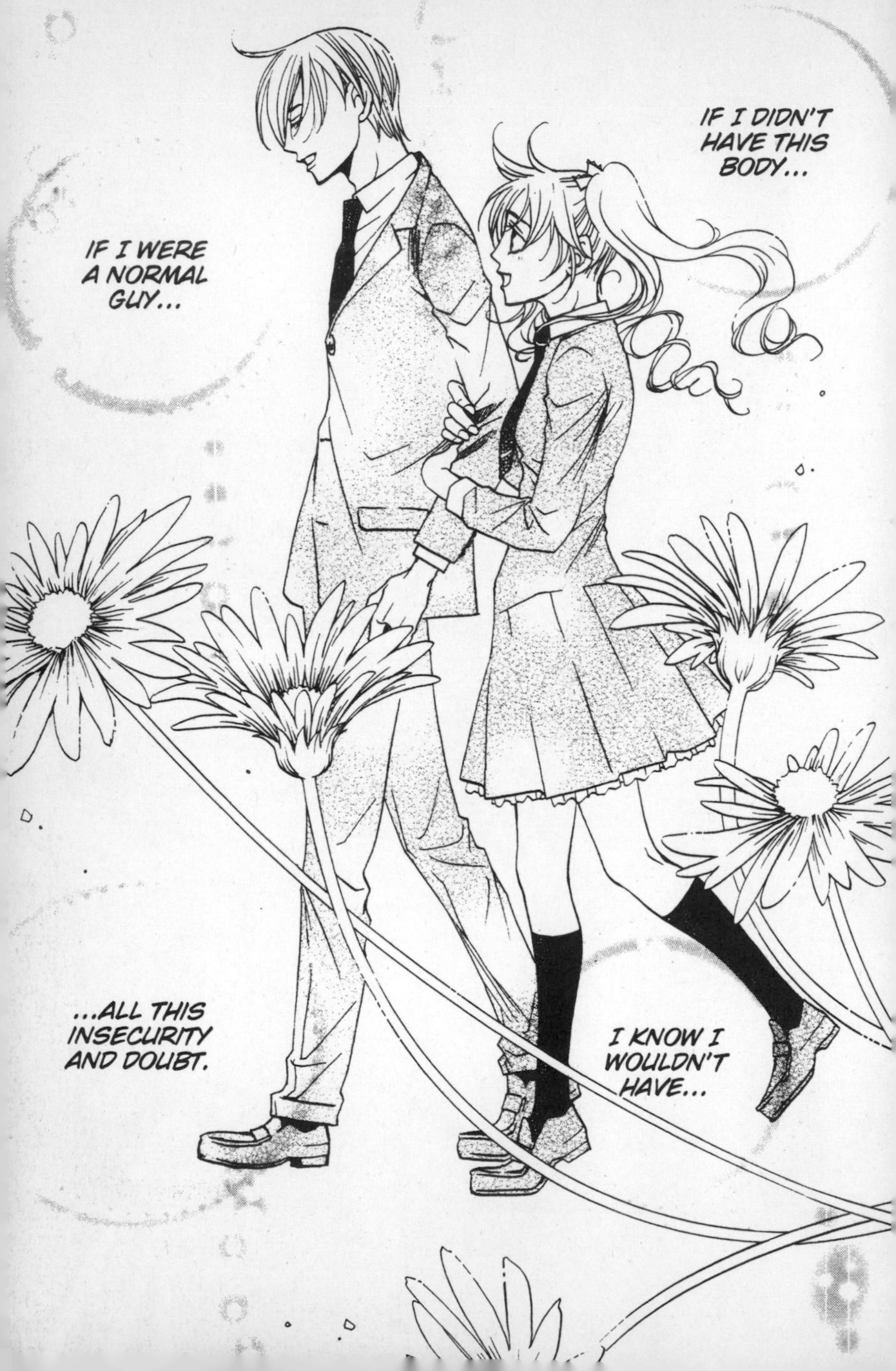
IF I DIDN'T HAVE THIS BODY...
IF I WERE A NORMAL GUY...
I KNOW I WOULDN'T HAVE...
...ALL THIS INSECURITY AND DOUBT.

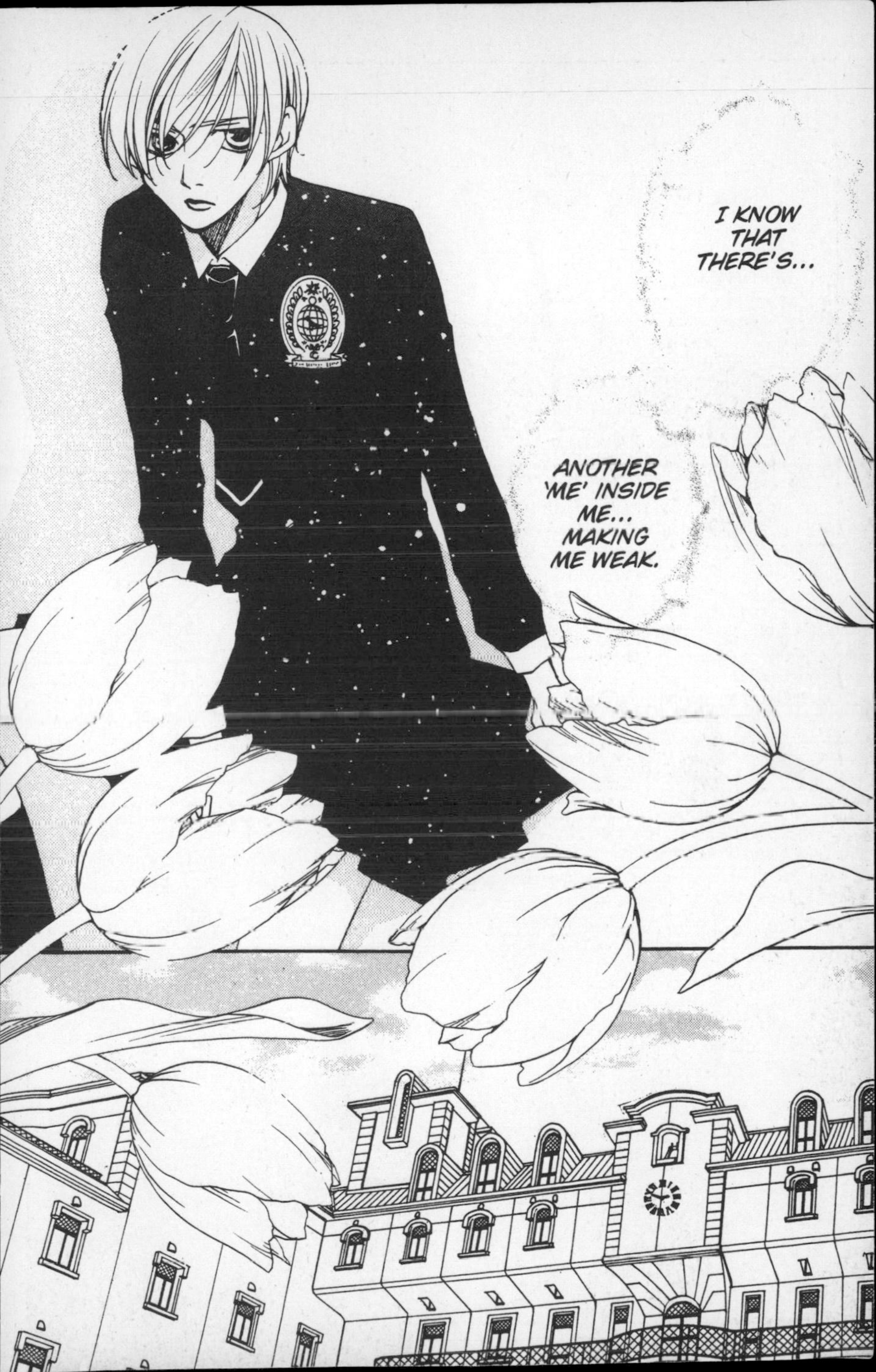
I KNOW THAT THERE'S...
ANOTHER 'ME' INSIDE ME... MAKING ME WEAK.

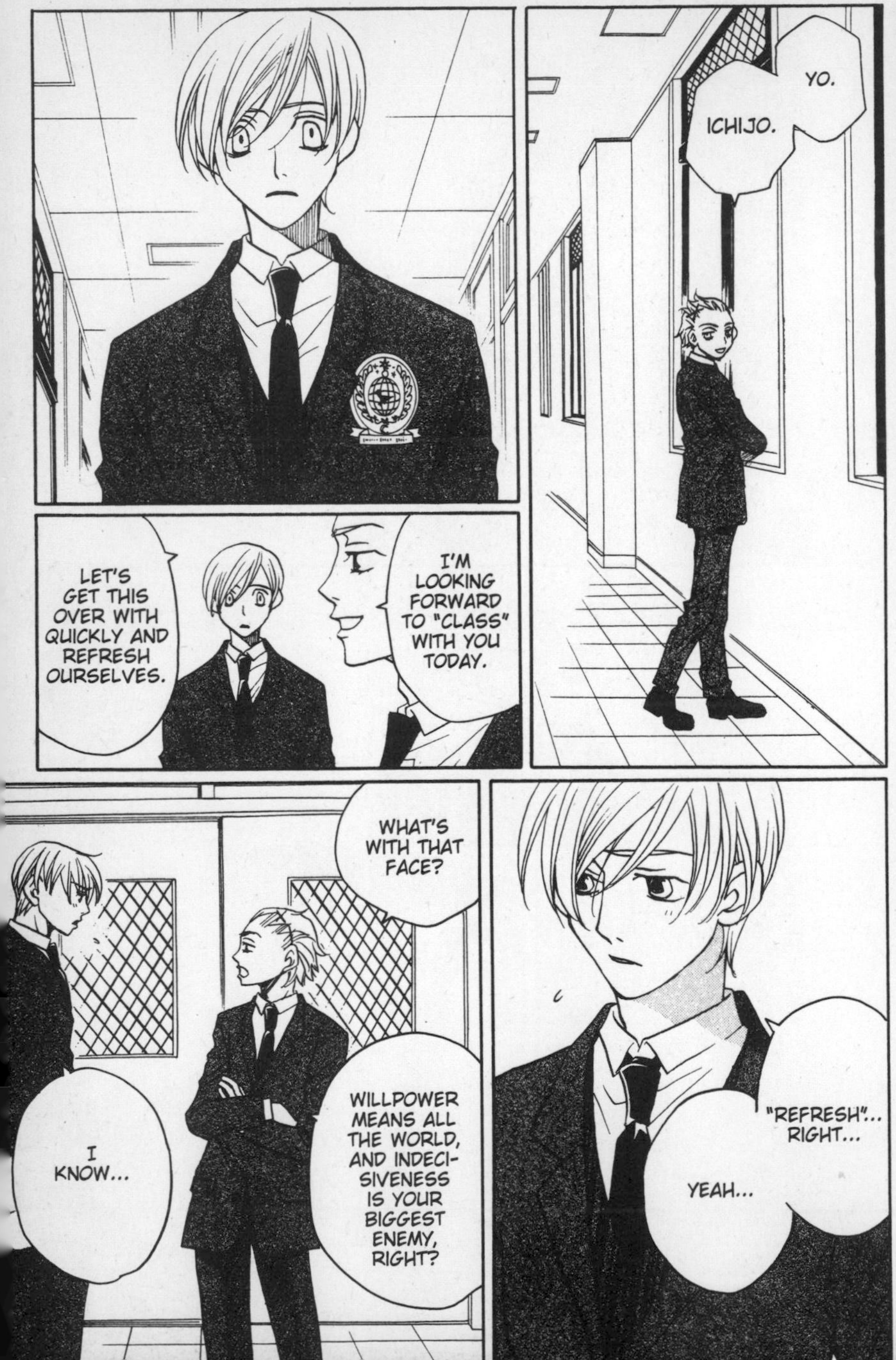
YO.
ICHIJO.
I'M LOOKING FORWARD TO "CLASS" WITH YOU TODAY.
LET'S GET THIS OVER WITH QUICKLY AND REFRESH OURSELVES.
"REFRESH"... RIGHT...
YEAH...
WHAT'S WITH THAT FACE?
WILLPOWER MEANS ALL THE WORLD, AND INDECI-SIVENESS IS YOUR BIGGEST ENEMY, RIGHT?
I KNOW...

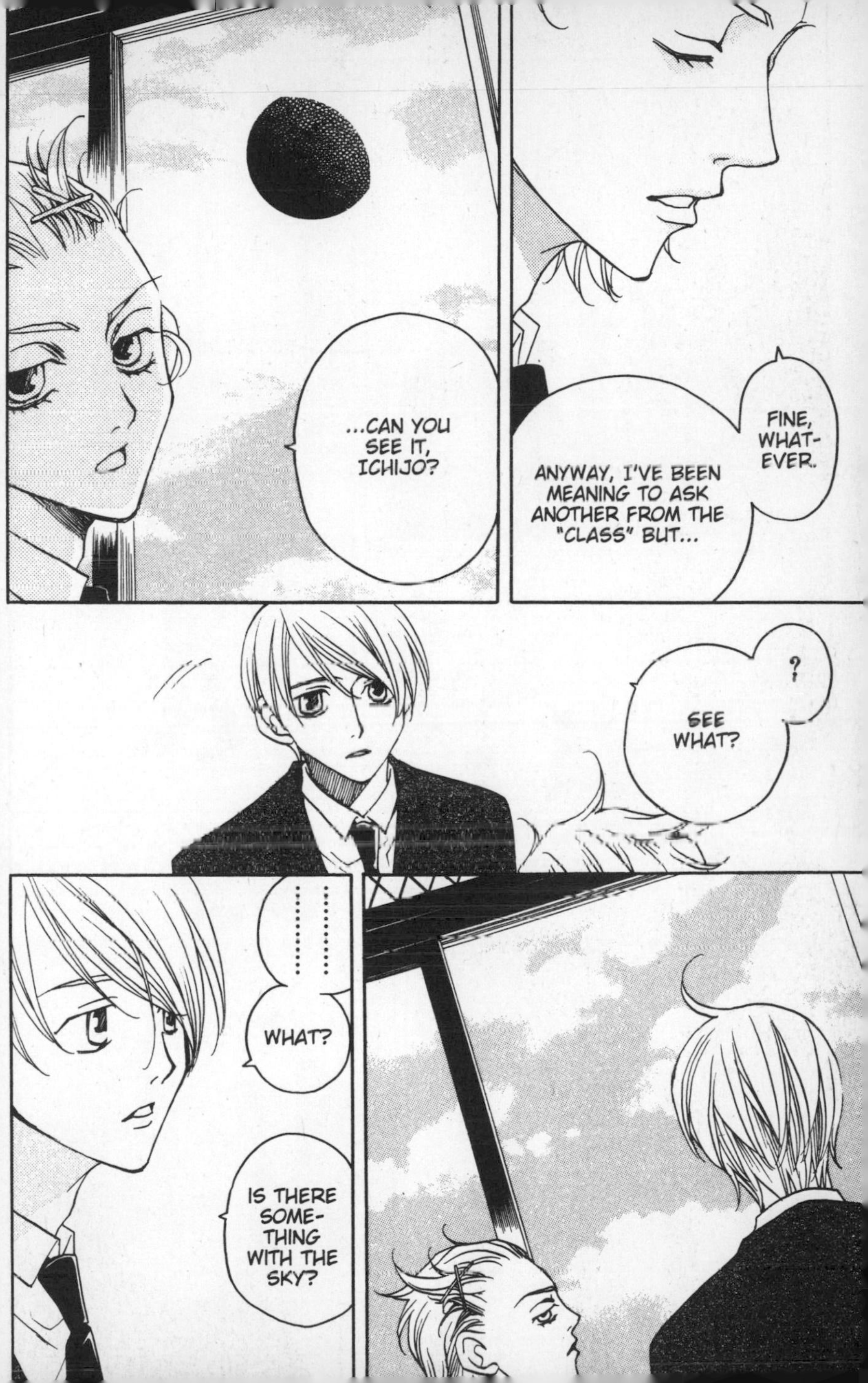
FINE, WHAT-EVER.
ANYWAY, I'VE BEEN MEANING TO ASK ANOTHER FROM THE "CLASS" BUT...
...CAN YOU SEE IT, ICHIJO?
? SEE WHAT?
......
WHAT?
IS THERE SOME-THING WITH THE SKY?

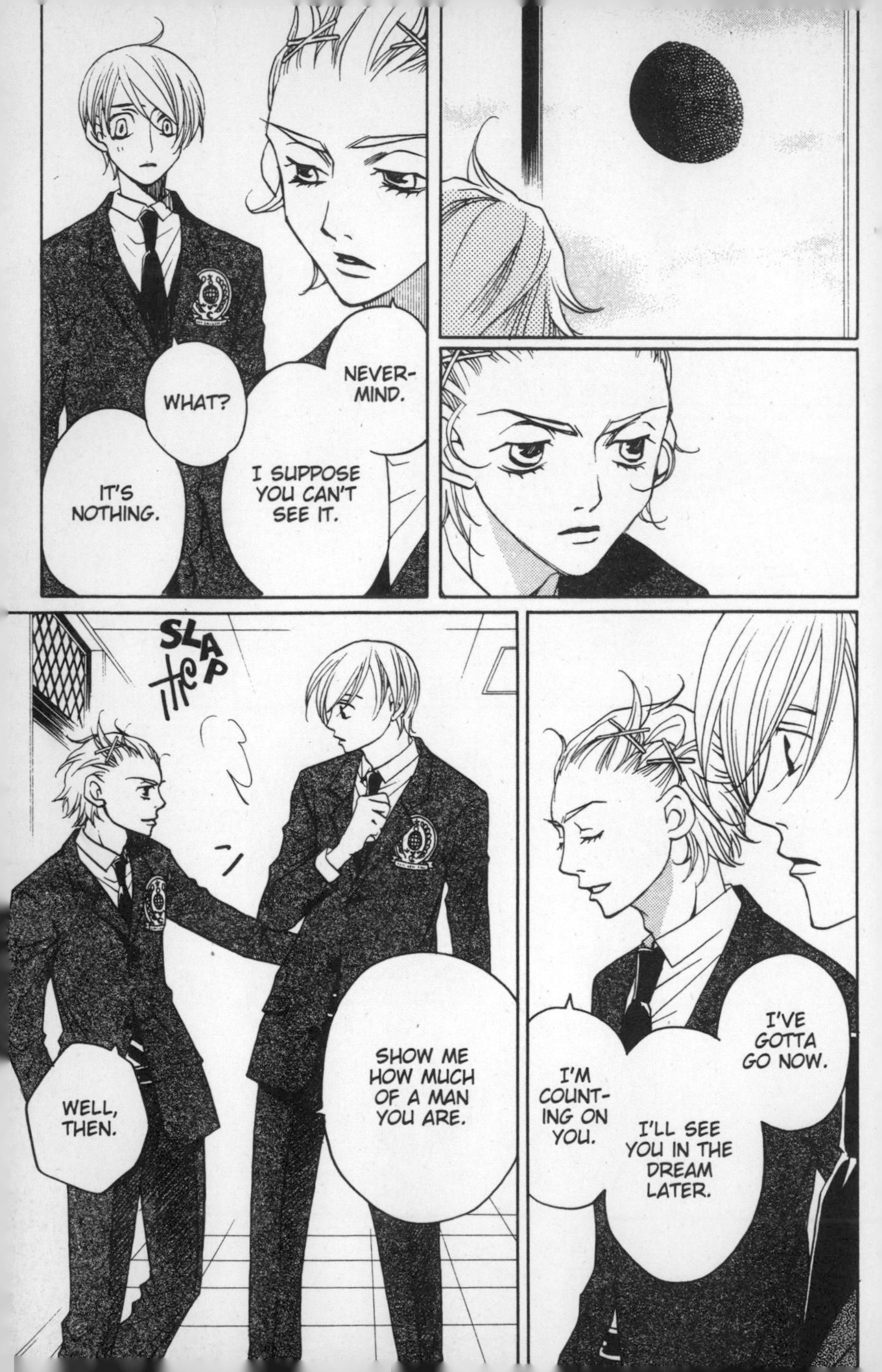
NEVER-MIND.
WHAT?
I SUPPOSE YOU CAN'T SEE IT.
IT'S NOTHING.
I'VE GOTTA GO NOW.
I'LL SEE YOU IN THE DREAM LATER.
I'M COUNTING ON YOU.
SLAP
SHOW ME HOW MUCH OF A MAN YOU ARE.
WELL, THEN.

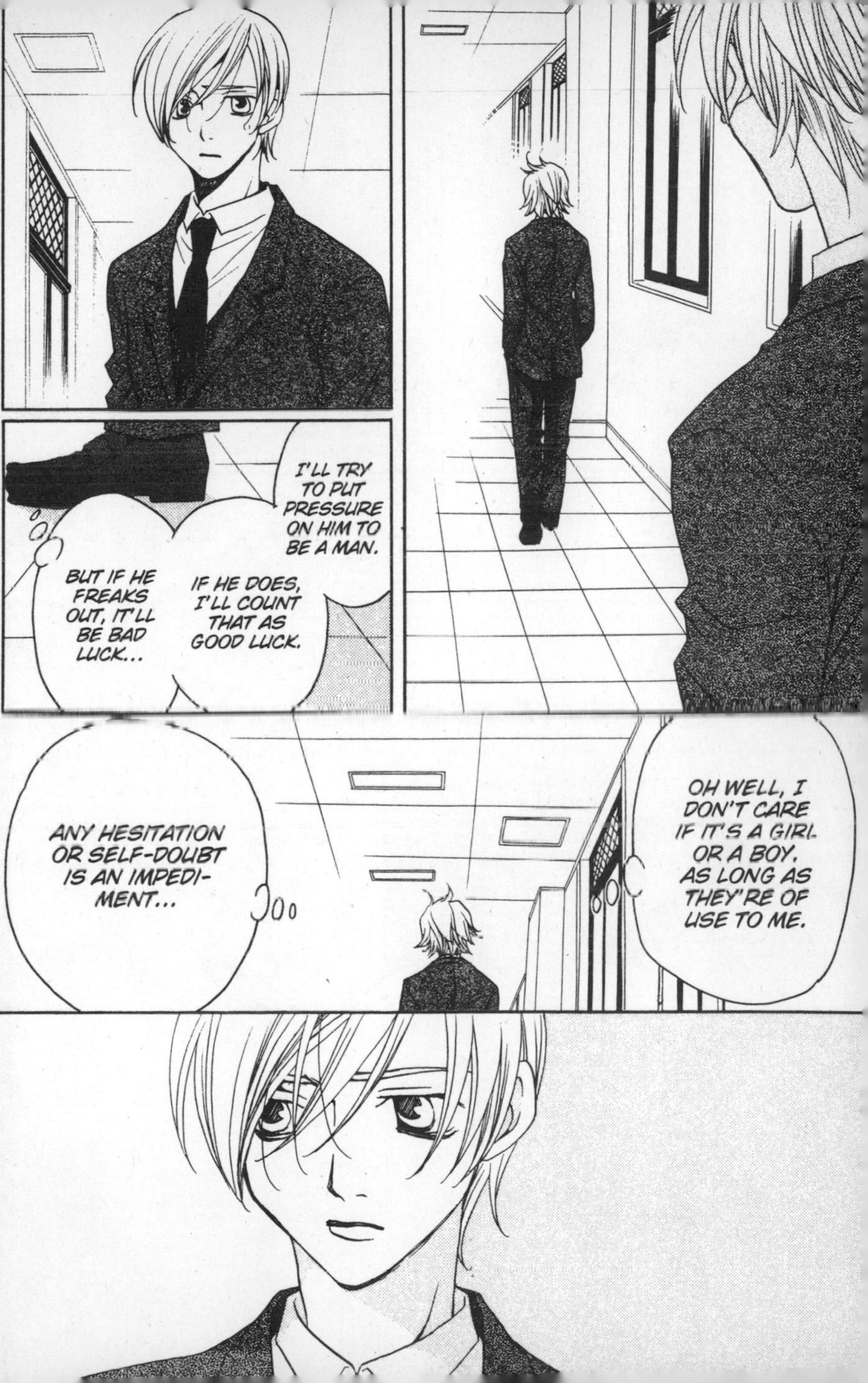
I'LL TRY TO PUT PRESSURE ON HIM TO BE A MAN.
IF HE DOES, I'LL COUNT THAT AS GOOD LUCK.
BUT IF HE FREAKS OUT, IT'LL BE BAD LUCK...
OH WELL, I DON'T CARE IF IT'S A GIRL OR A BOY. AS LONG AS THEY'RE OF USE TO ME.
ANY HESITATION OR SELF-DOUBT IS AN IMPEDIMENT...

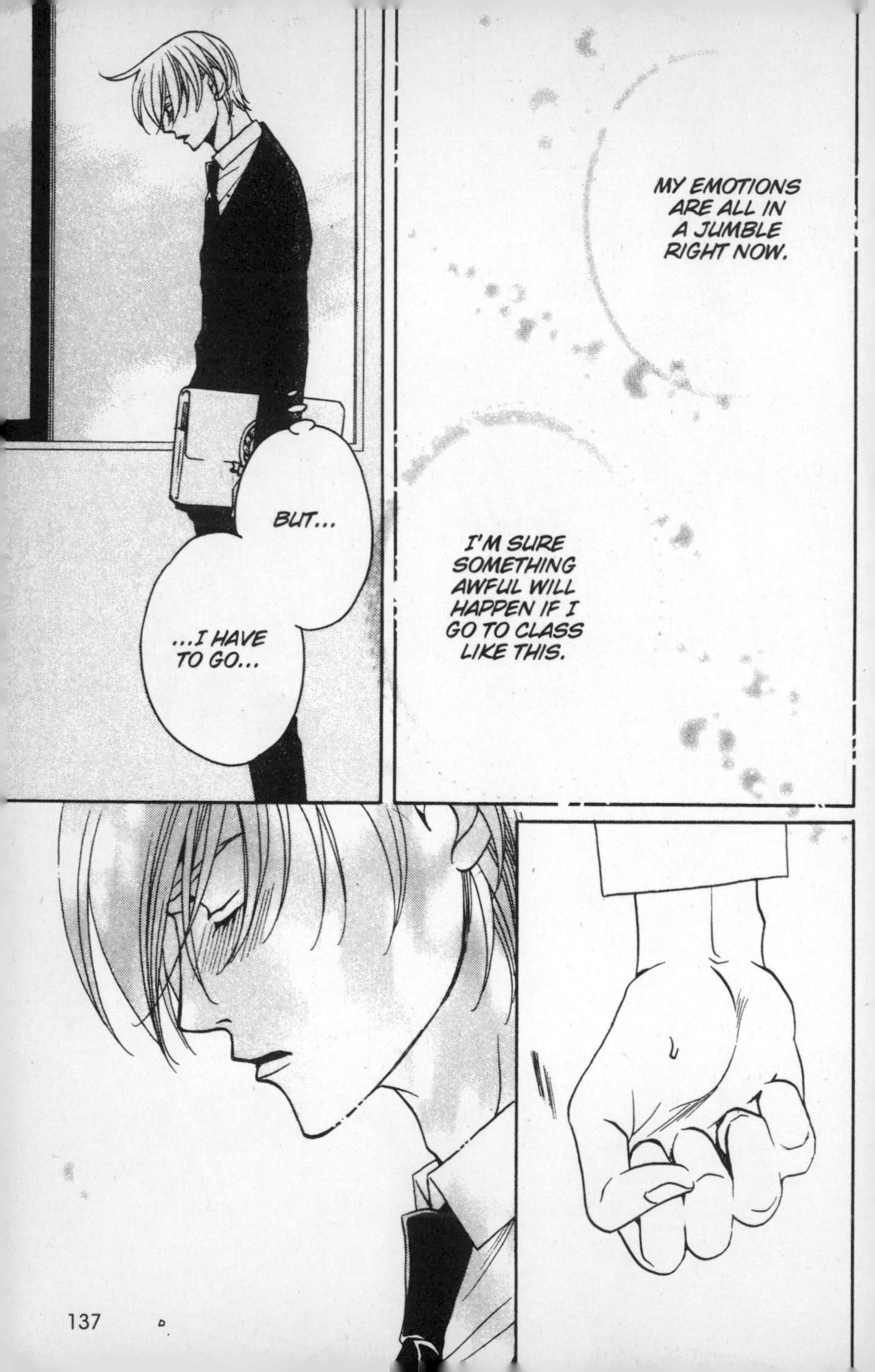
MY EMOTIONS ARE ALL IN A JUMBLE RIGHT NOW.
I'M SURE SOMETHING AWFUL WILL HAPPEN IF I GO TO CLASS LIKE THIS.
BUT...
...I HAVE TO GO...

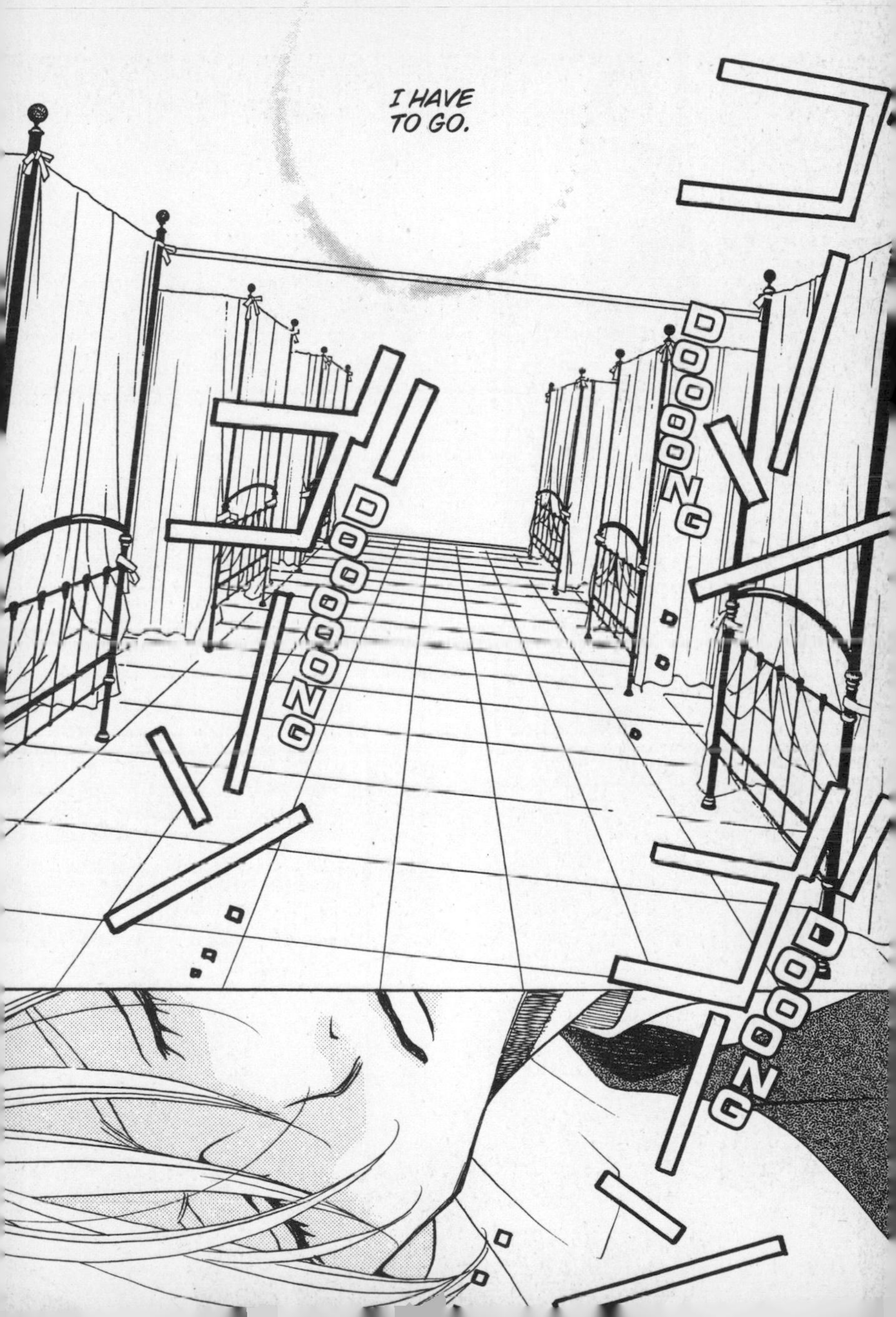
I HAVE TO GO.
DOOOONG
DOOOOONG
DOOONG

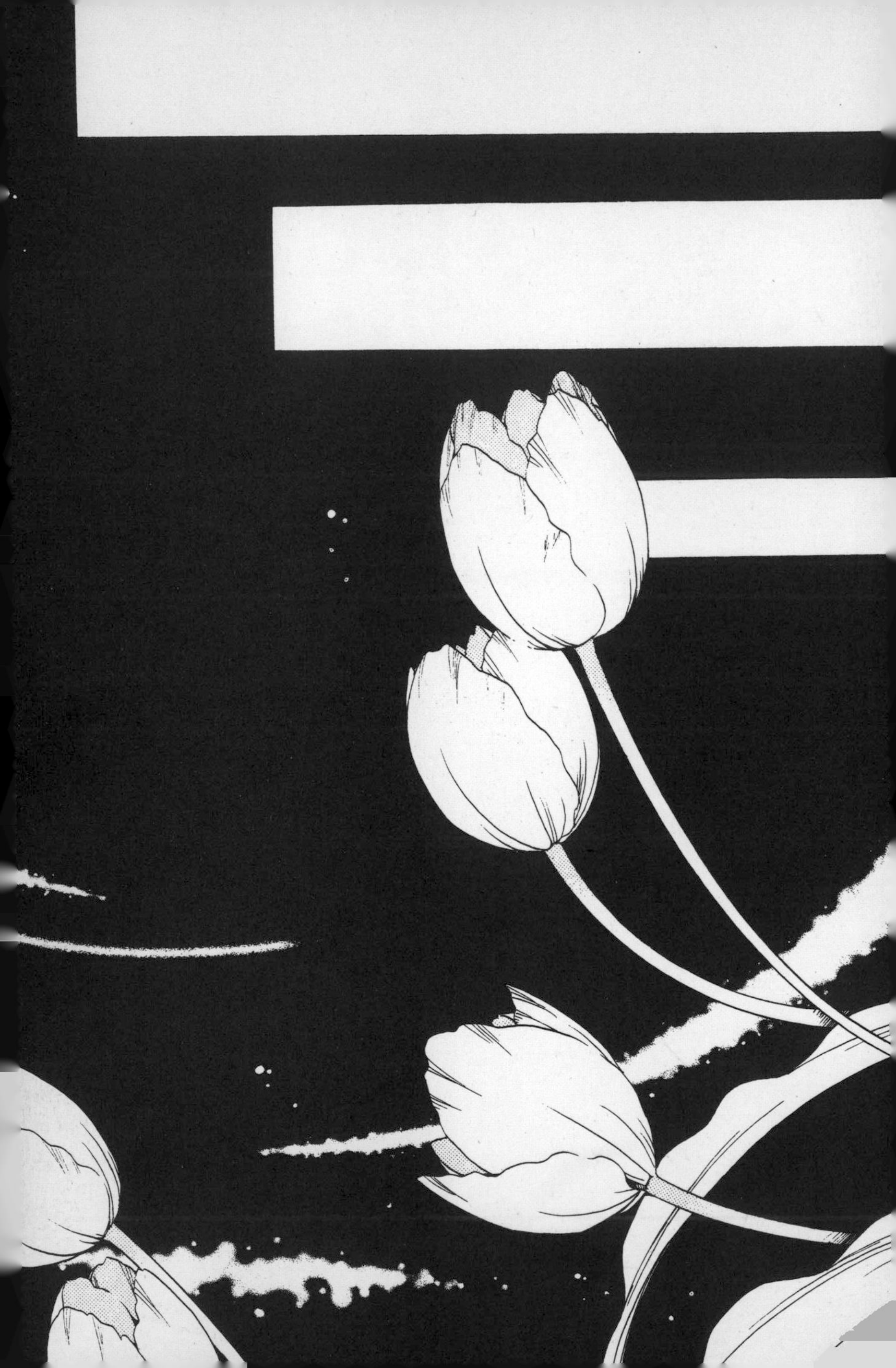

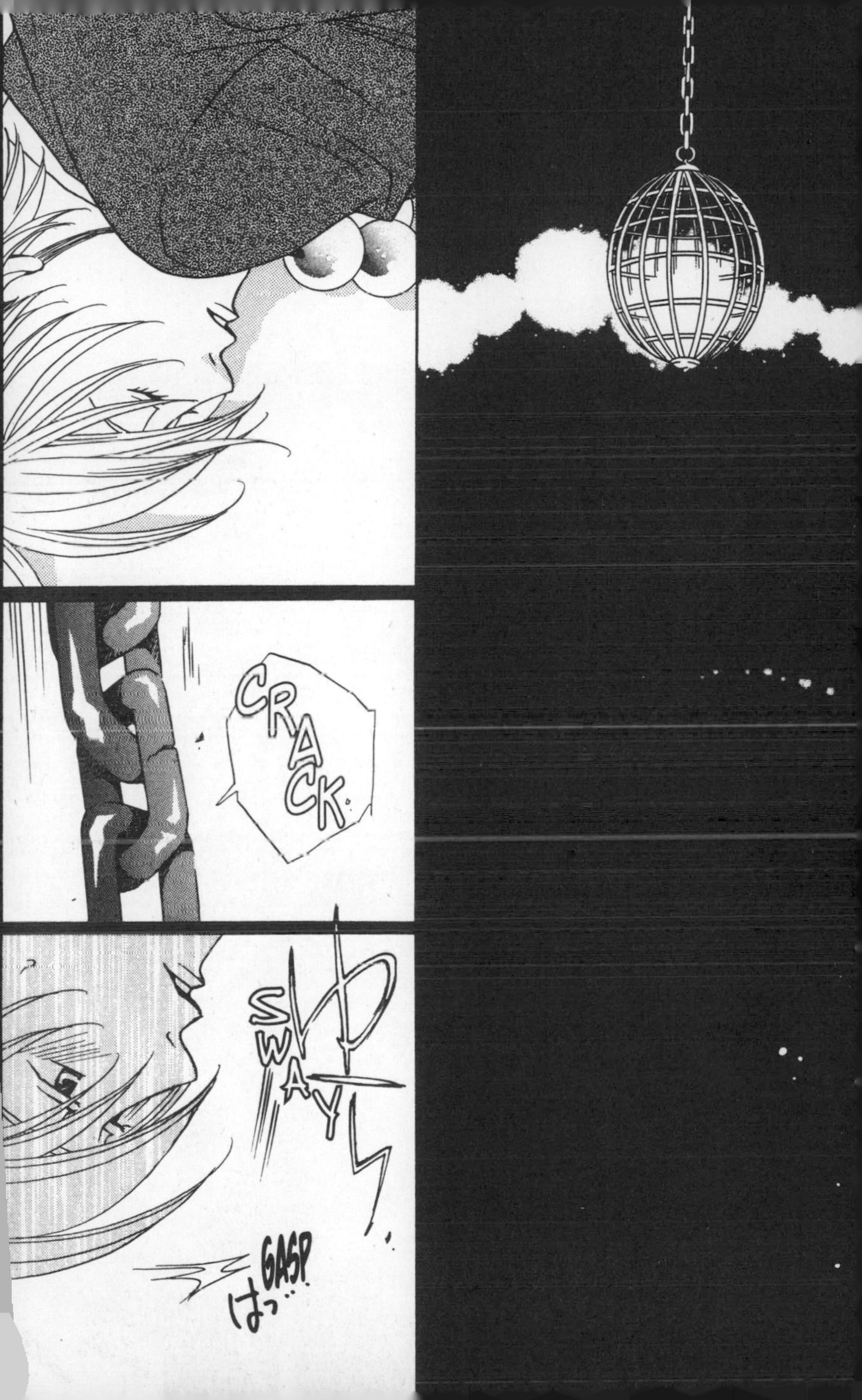
CRACK.
SWAY
GASP
はっ…

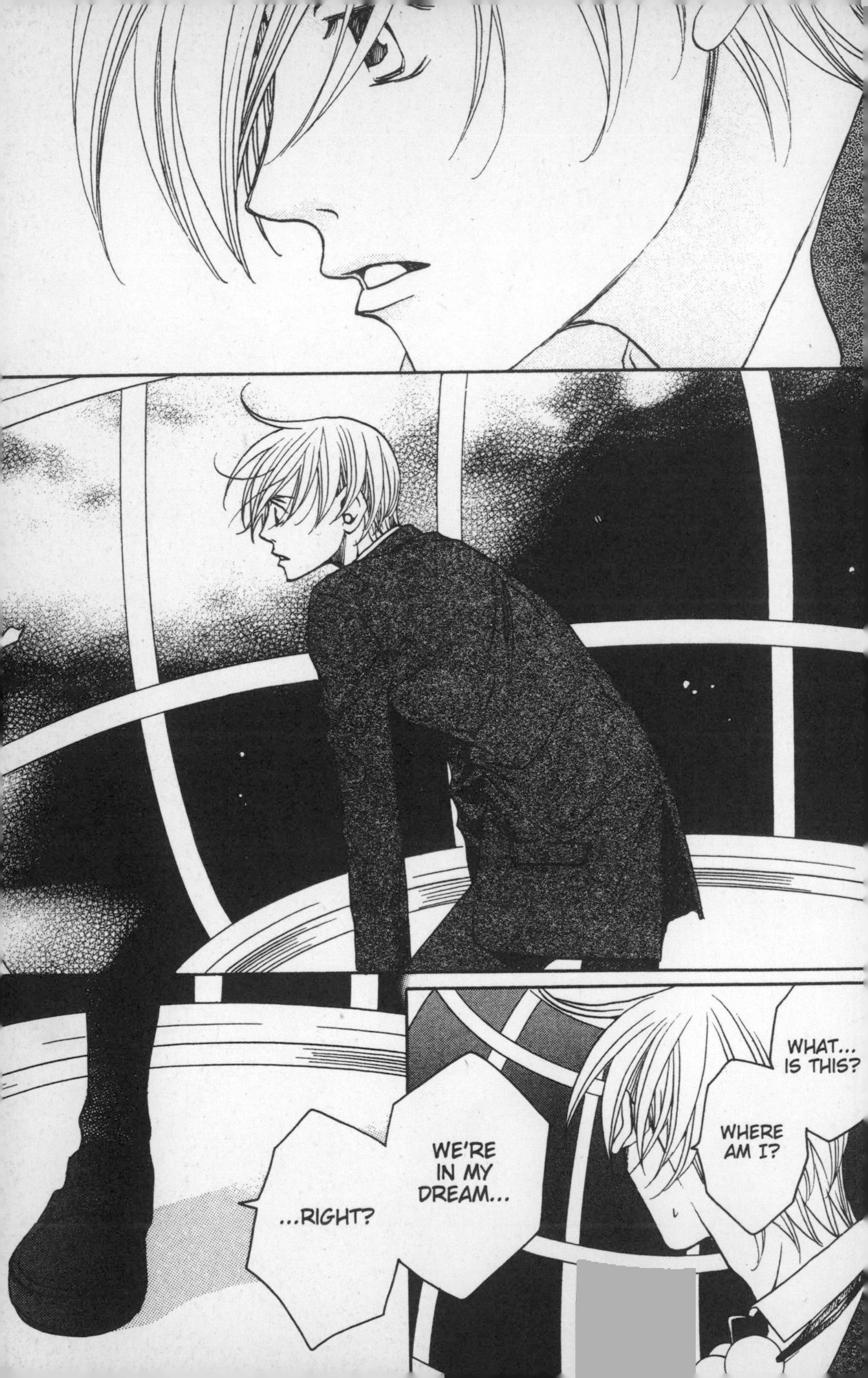
WHAT... IS THIS?
WHERE AM I?
WE'RE IN MY DREAM...
...RIGHT?

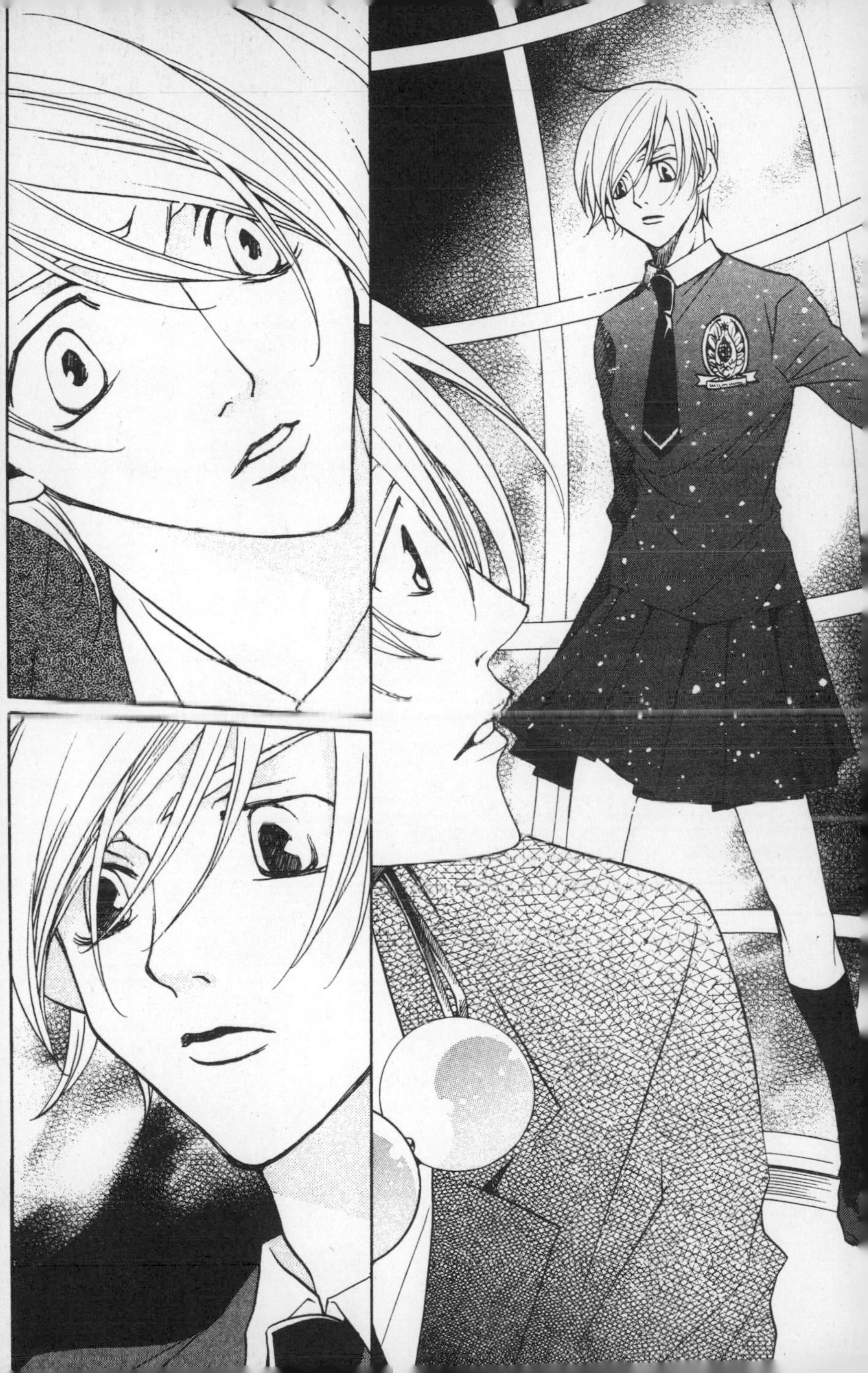

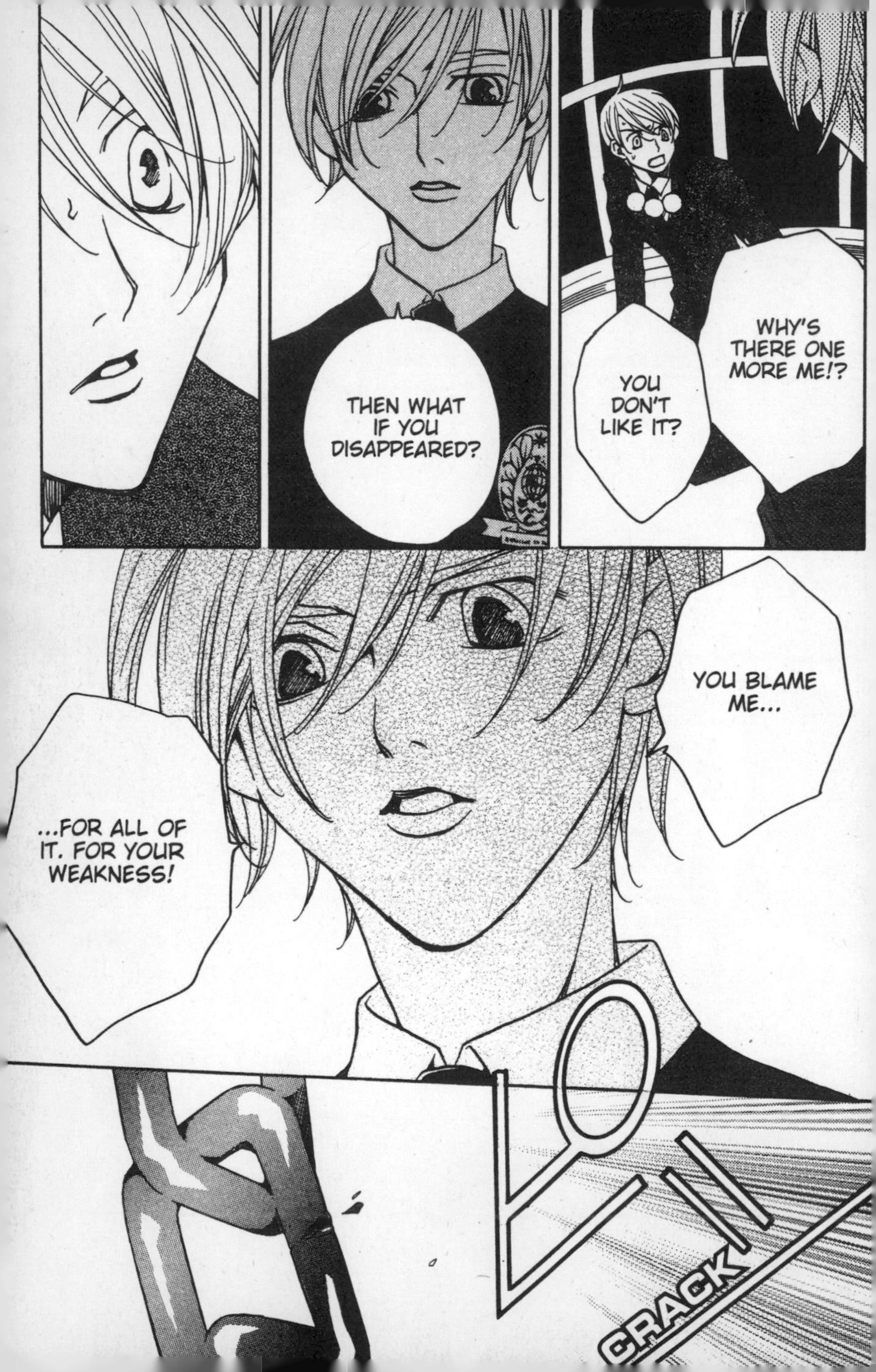
WHY'S THERE ONE MORE ME!?
YOU DON'T LIKE IT?
THEN WHAT IF YOU DISAPPEARED?
YOU BLAME ME...
...FOR ALL OF IT. FOR YOUR WEAKNESS!
CRACK

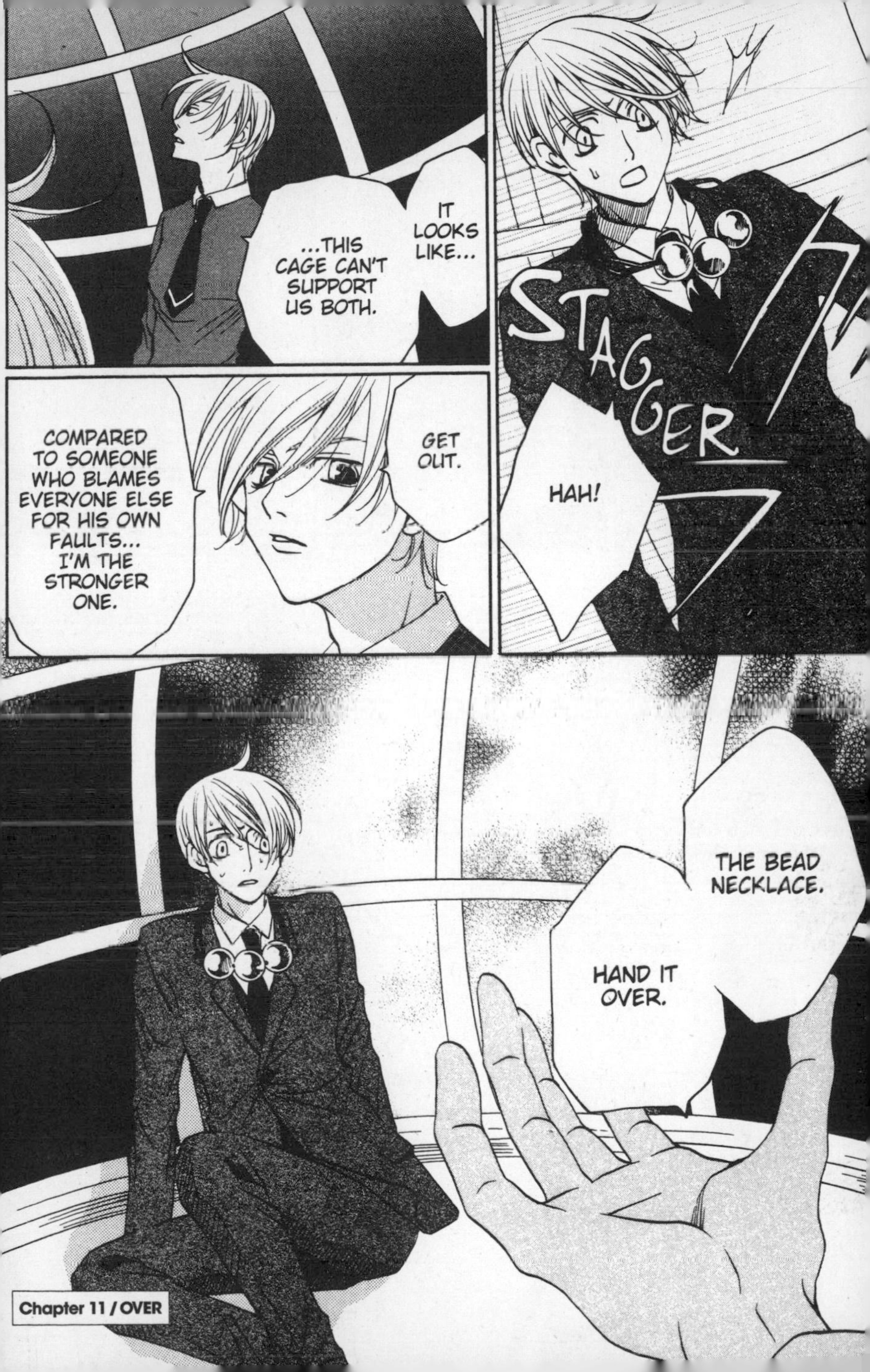
STAGGER
HAH!
IT LOOKS LIKE...
...THIS CAGE CAN'T SUPPORT US BOTH.
GET OUT.
COMPARED TO SOMEONE WHO BLAMES EVERYONE ELSE FOR HIS OWN FAULTS... I'M THE STRONGER ONE.
THE BEAD NECKLACE.
HAND IT OVER.
Chapter 11 / OVER

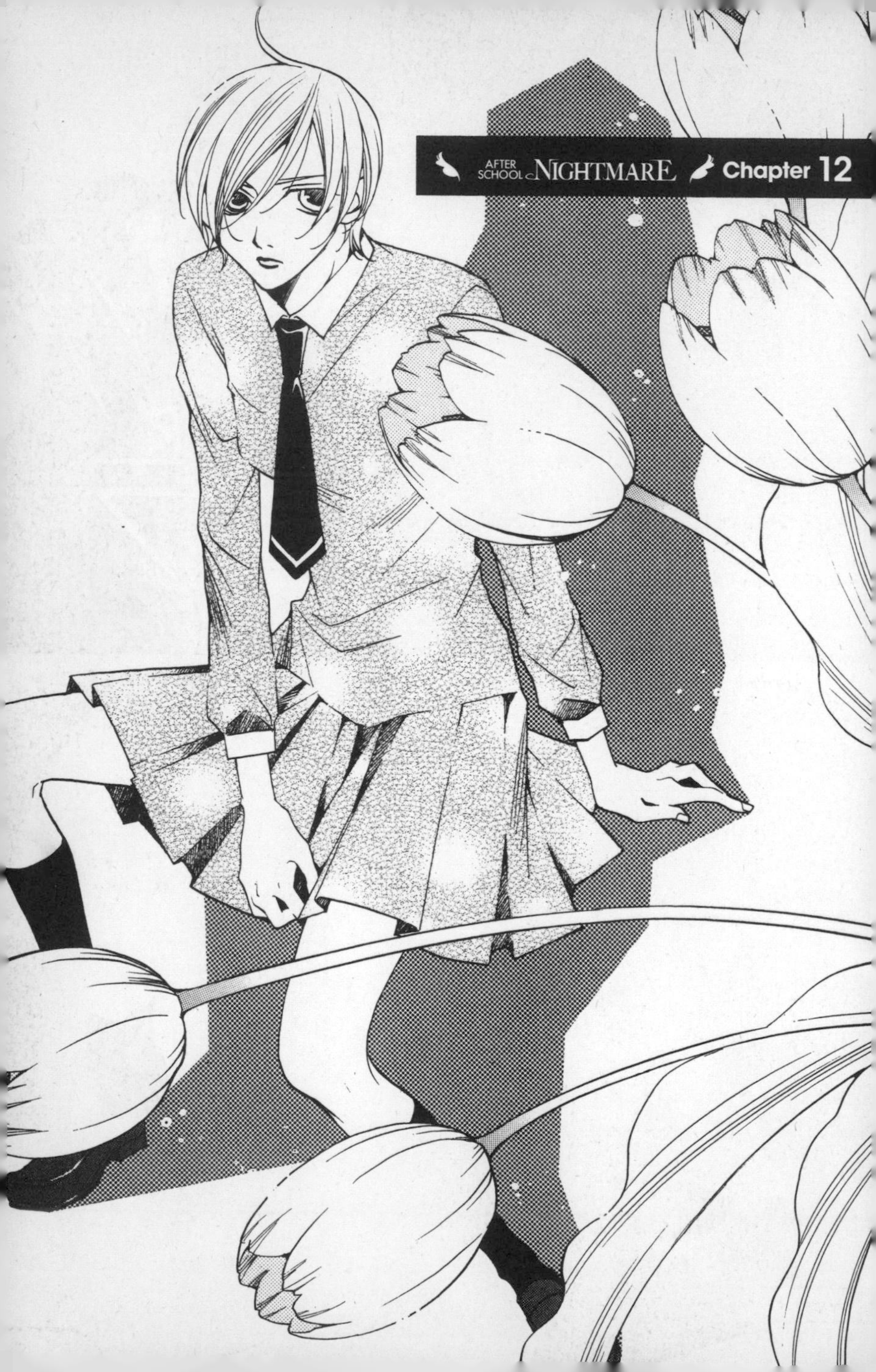
AFTER SCHOOL NIGHTMARE
Chapter 12

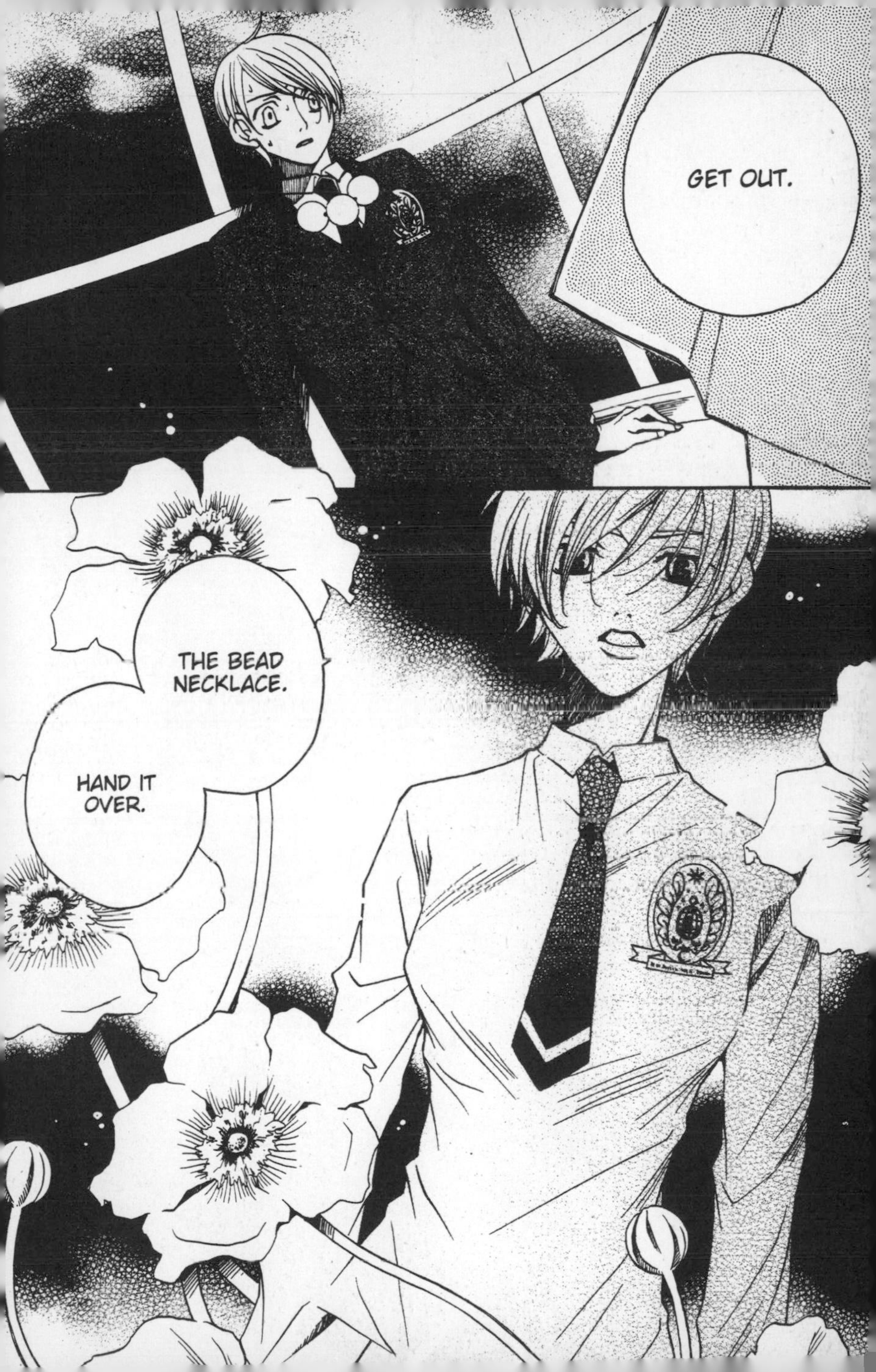
GET OUT.
THE BEAD NECKLACE.
HAND IT OVER.

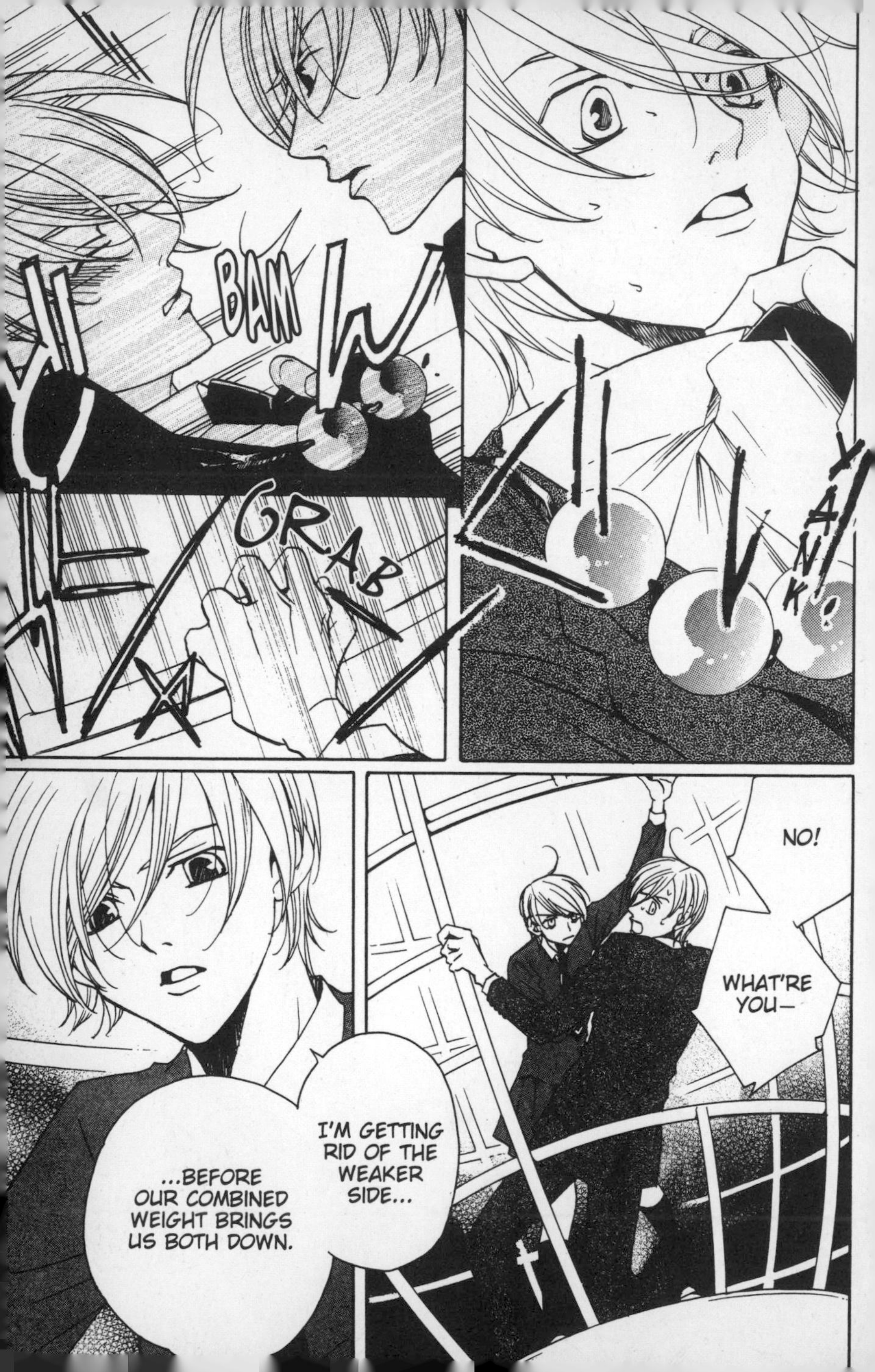
YANK!
BAM
GRAB
NO!
WHAT'RE YOU—
I'M GETTING RID OF THE WEAKER SIDE...
...BEFORE OUR COMBINED WEIGHT BRINGS US BOTH DOWN.

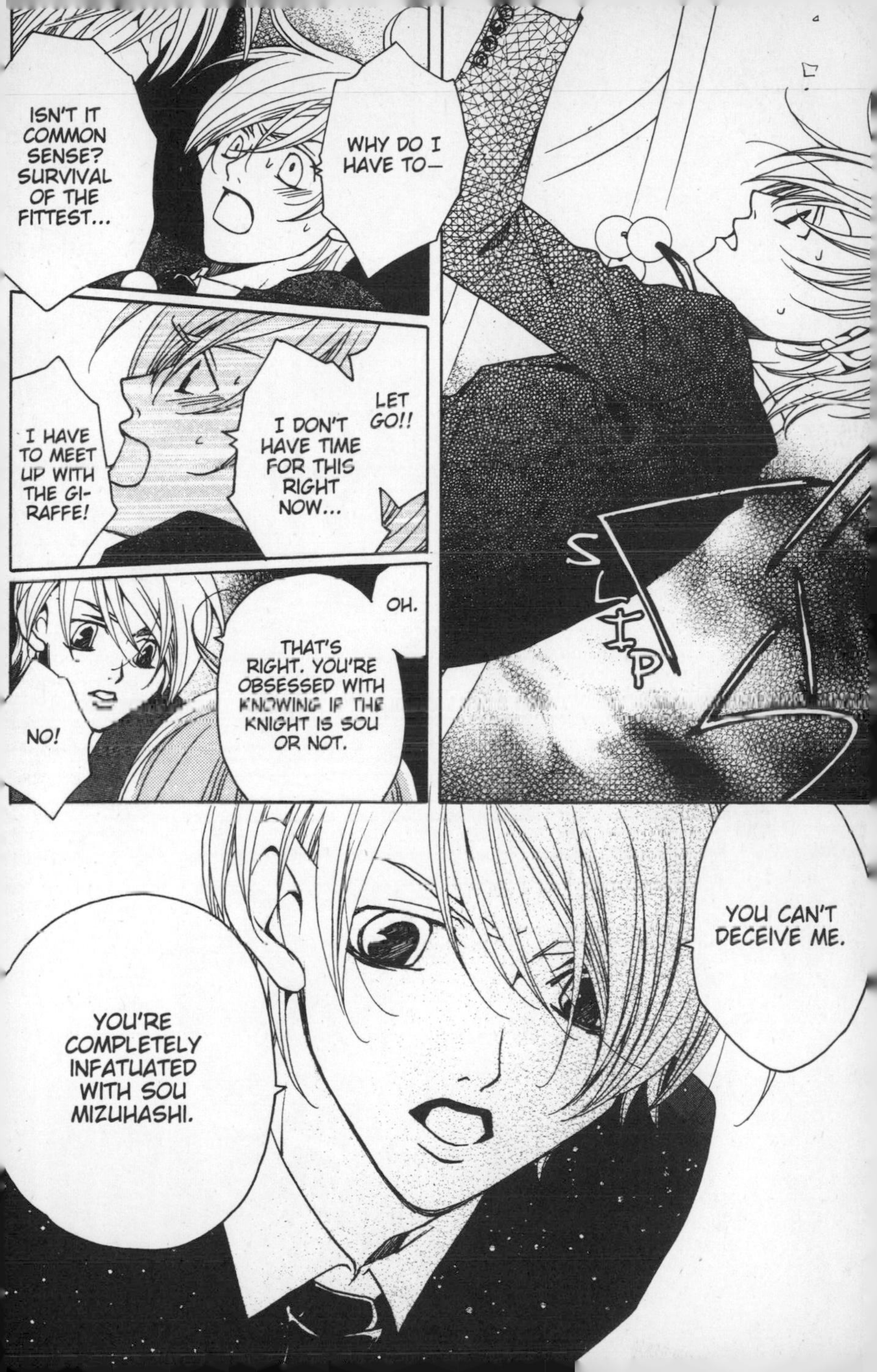
SLIP
WHY DO I HAVE TO—
ISN'T IT COMMON SENSE? SURVIVAL OF THE FITTEST...
LET GO!!
I DON'T HAVE TIME FOR THIS RIGHT NOW...
I HAVE TO MEET UP WITH THE GI-RAFFE!
OH.
THAT'S RIGHT. YOU'RE OBSESSED WITH KNOWING IF THE KNIGHT IS SOU OR NOT.
NO!
YOU CAN'T DECEIVE ME.
YOU'RE COMPLETELY INFATUATED WITH SOU MIZUHASHI.

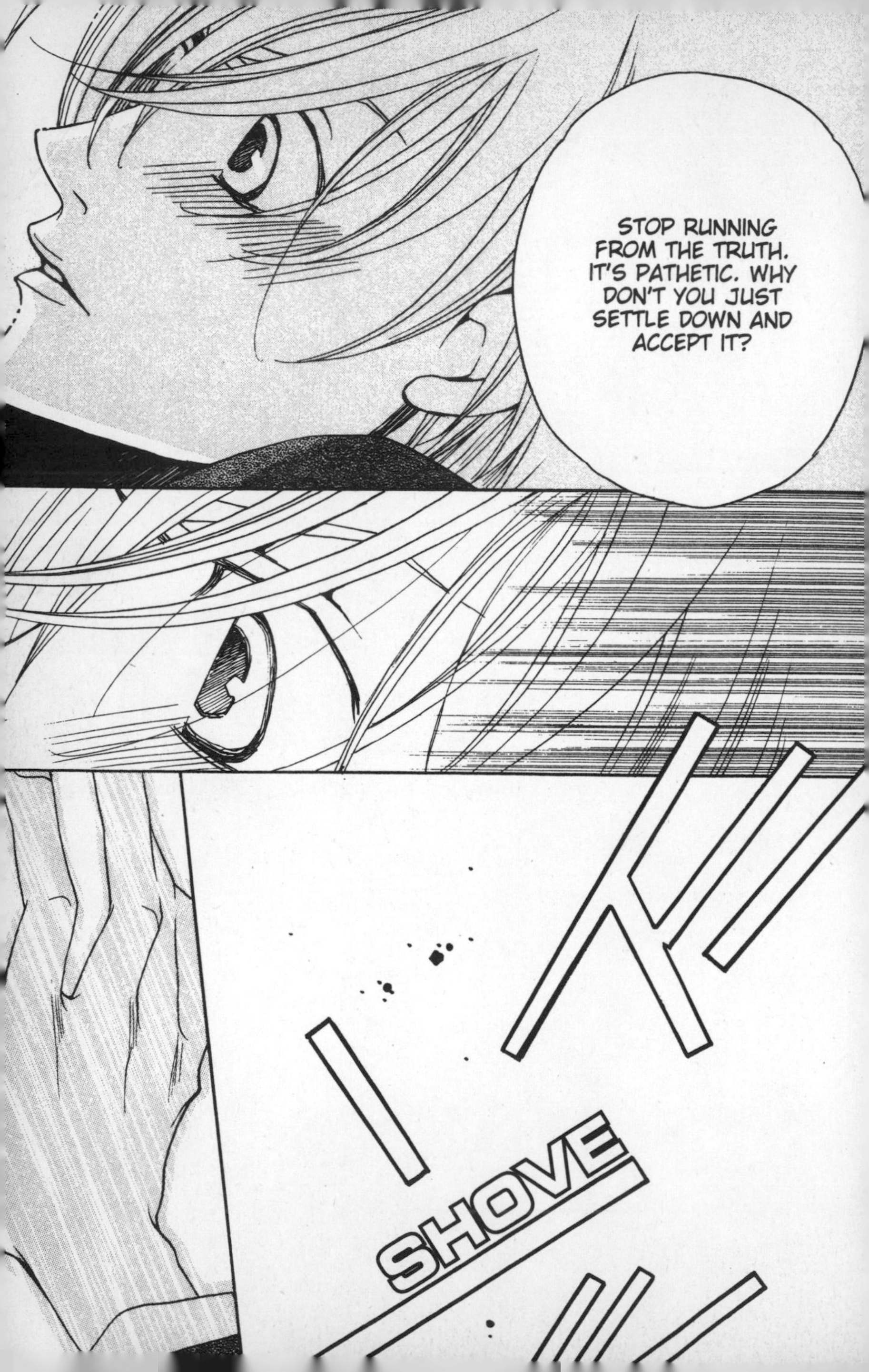
STOP RUNNING FROM THE TRUTH. IT'S PATHETIC. WHY DON'T YOU JUST SETTLE DOWN AND ACCEPT IT?
SHOVE

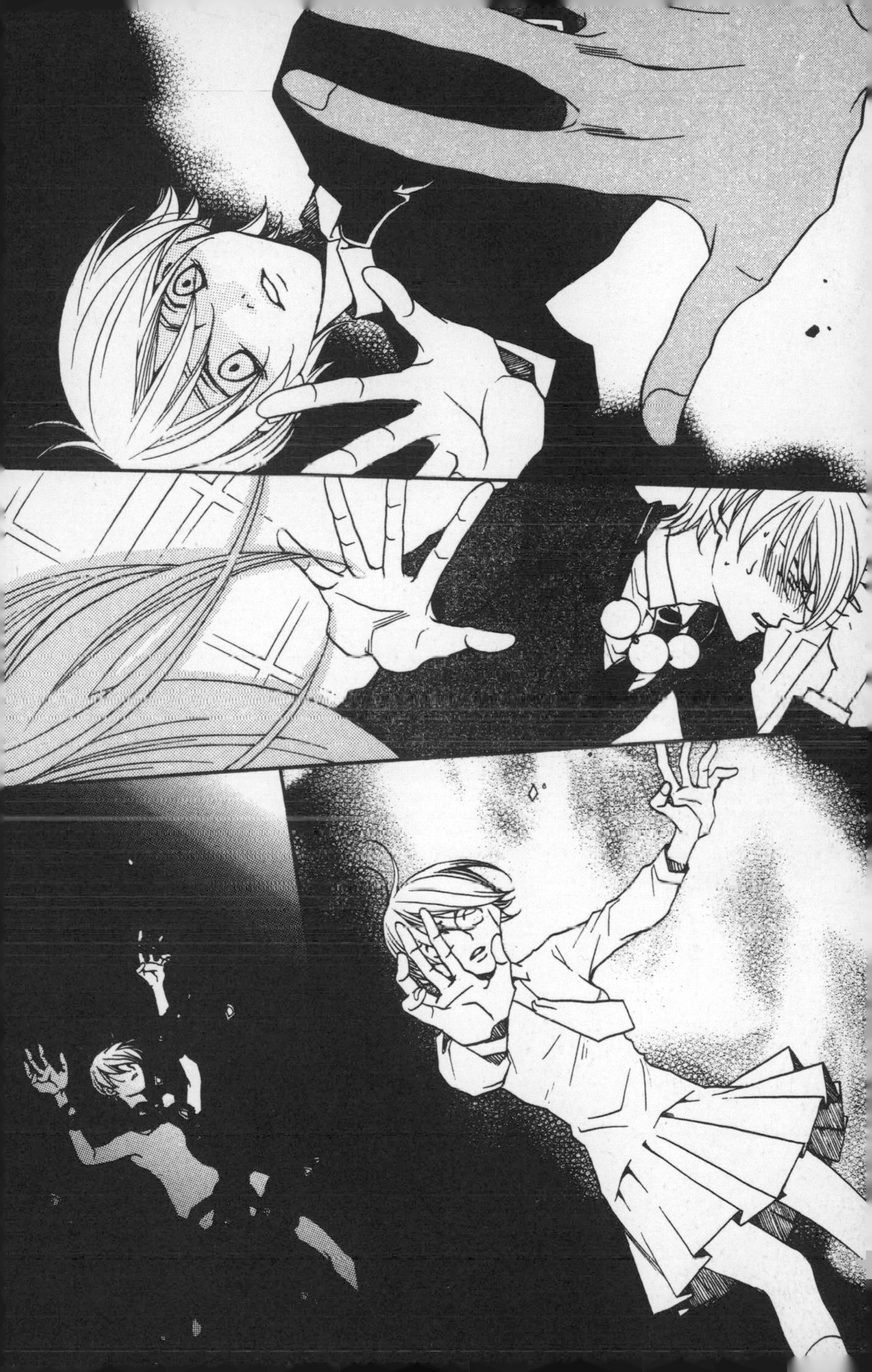

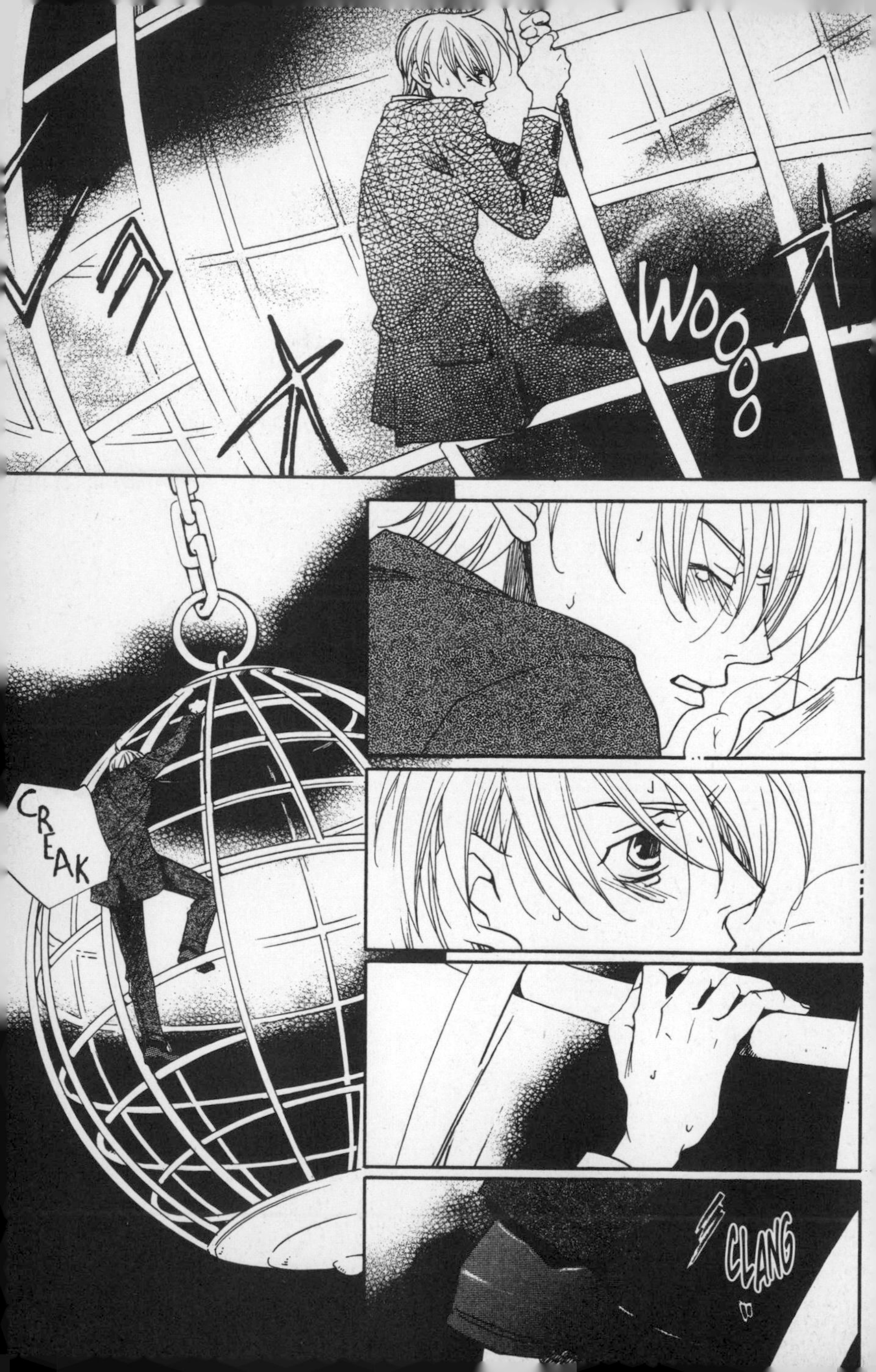
WOOOO
CLANG
CREAK

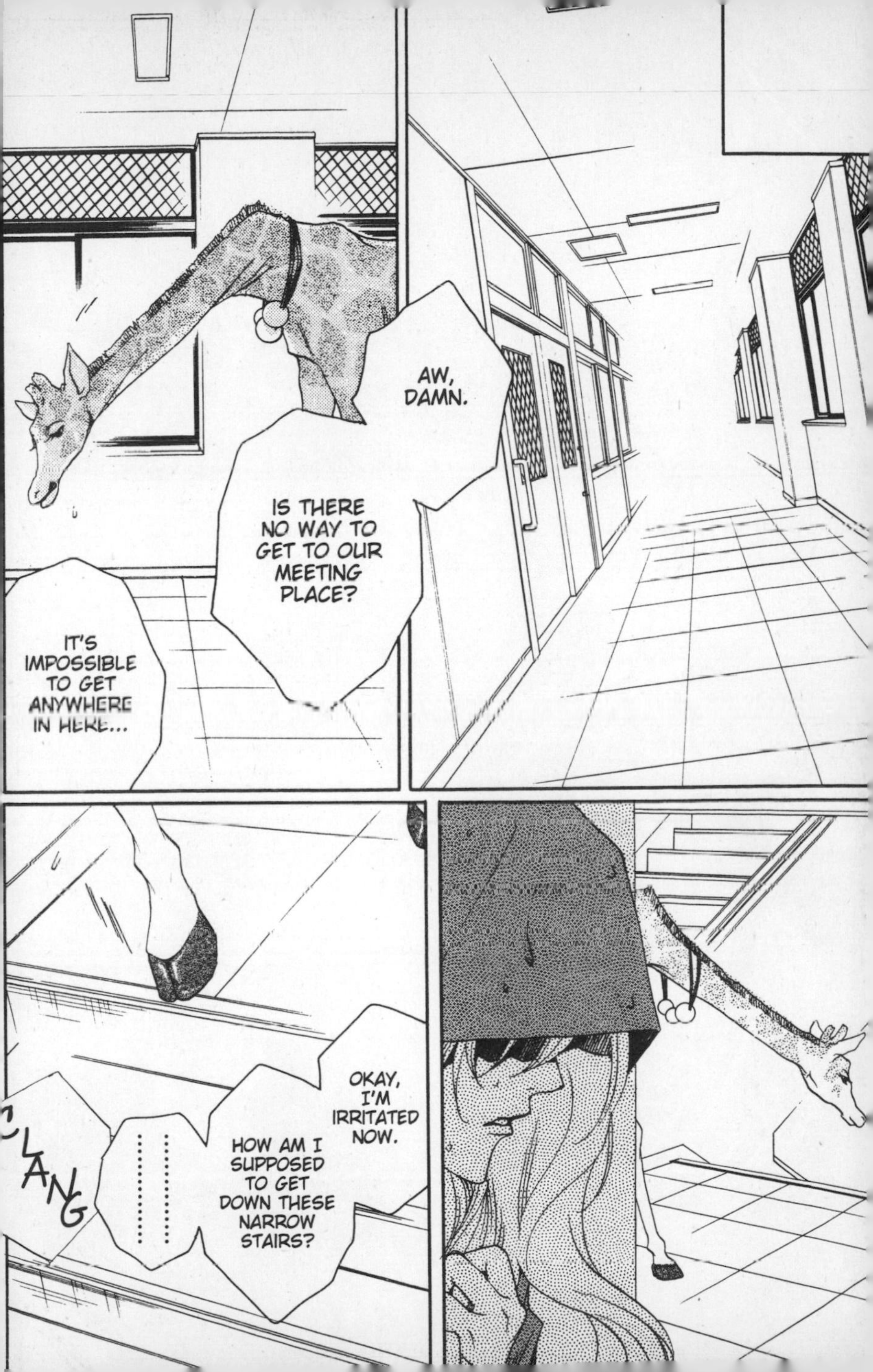
AW, DAMN.
IS THERE NO WAY TO GET TO OUR MEETING PLACE?
IT'S IMPOSSIBLE TO GET ANYWHERE IN HERE...
OKAY, I'M IRRITATED NOW.
HOW AM I SUPPOSED TO GET DOWN THESE NARROW STAIRS?
......
CLANG

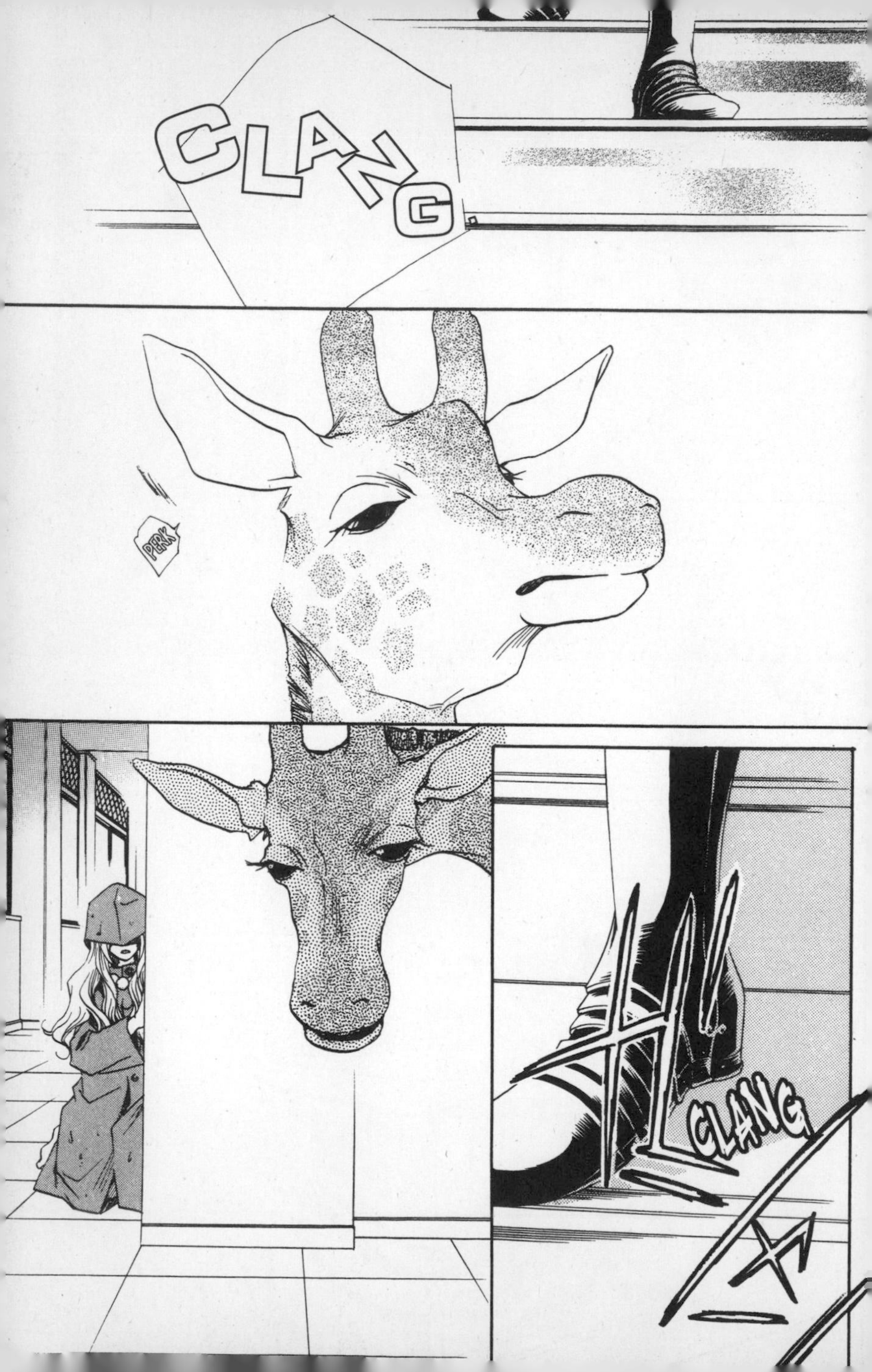
CLANG.
PERK
CLANG

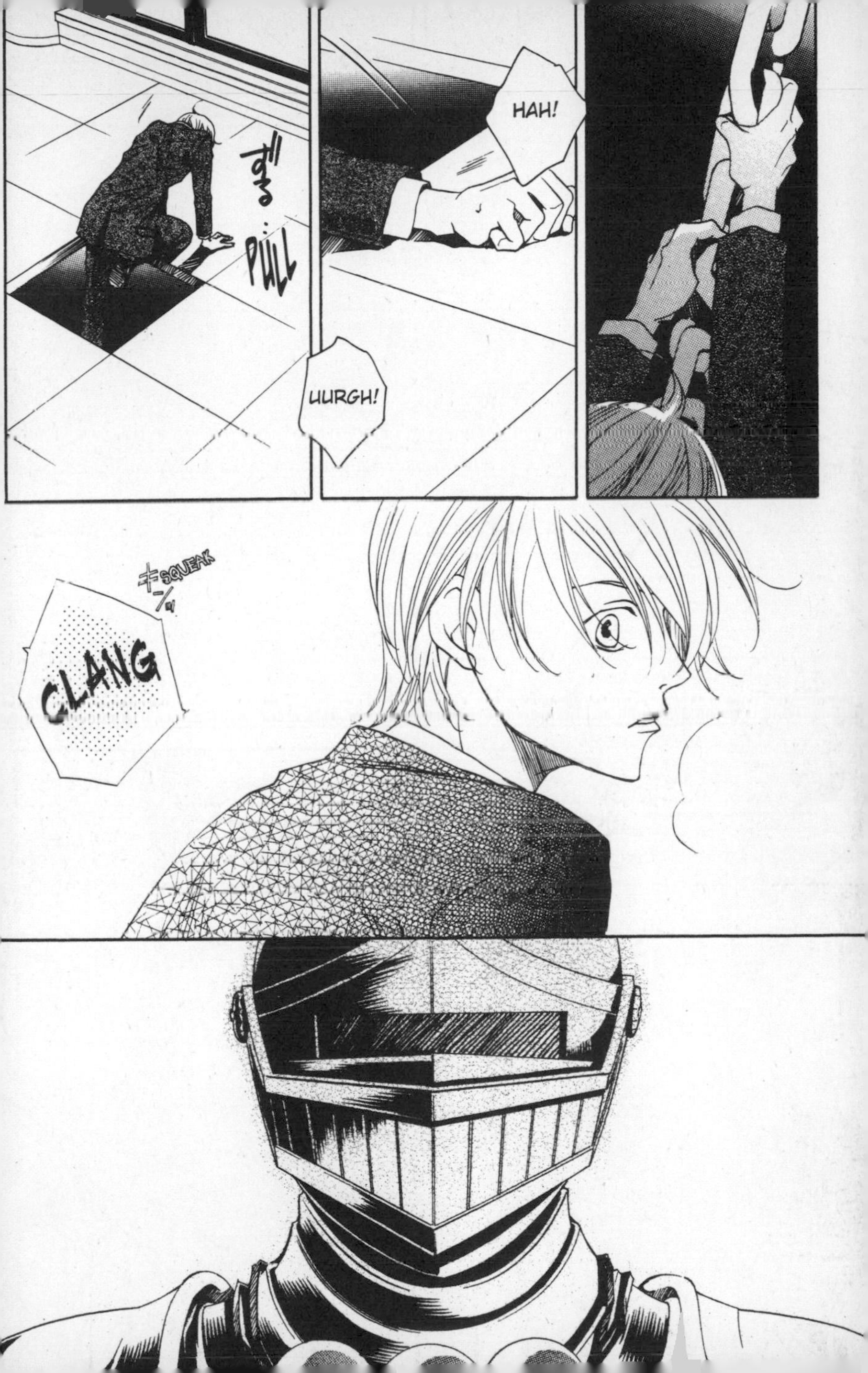
HAH!
UURGH!
ずる
PULL
SQUEAK
CLANG

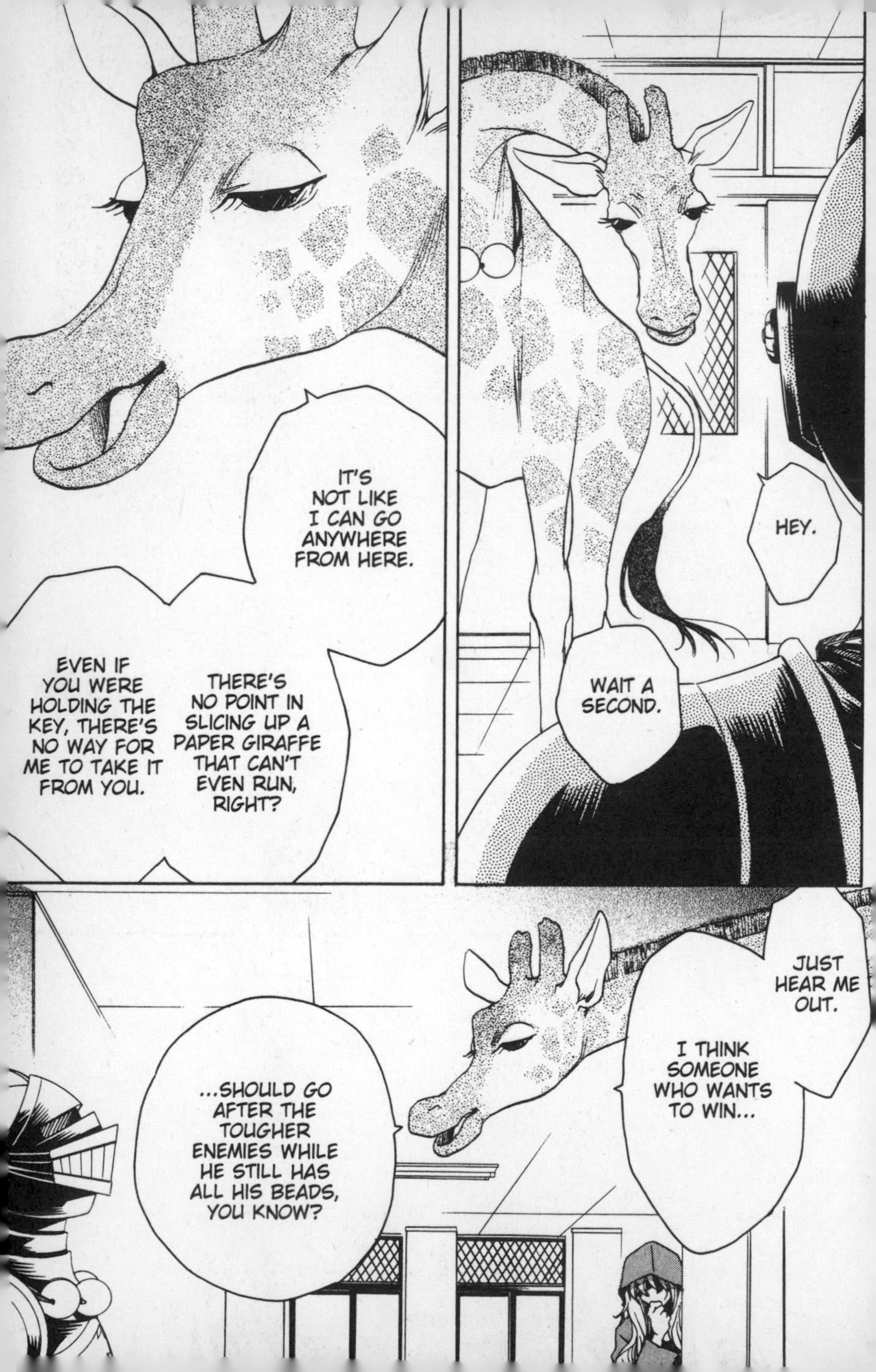
HEY.
WAIT A SECOND.
IT'S NOT LIKE I CAN GO ANYWHERE FROM HERE.
THERE'S NO POINT IN SLICING UP A PAPER GIRAFFE THAT CAN'T EVEN RUN, RIGHT?
EVEN IF YOU WERE HOLDING THE KEY, THERE'S NO WAY FOR ME TO TAKE IT FROM YOU.
JUST HEAR ME OUT.
I THINK SOMEONE WHO WANTS TO WIN...
...SHOULD GO AFTER THE TOUGHER ENEMIES WHILE HE STILL HAS ALL HIS BEADS, YOU KNOW?

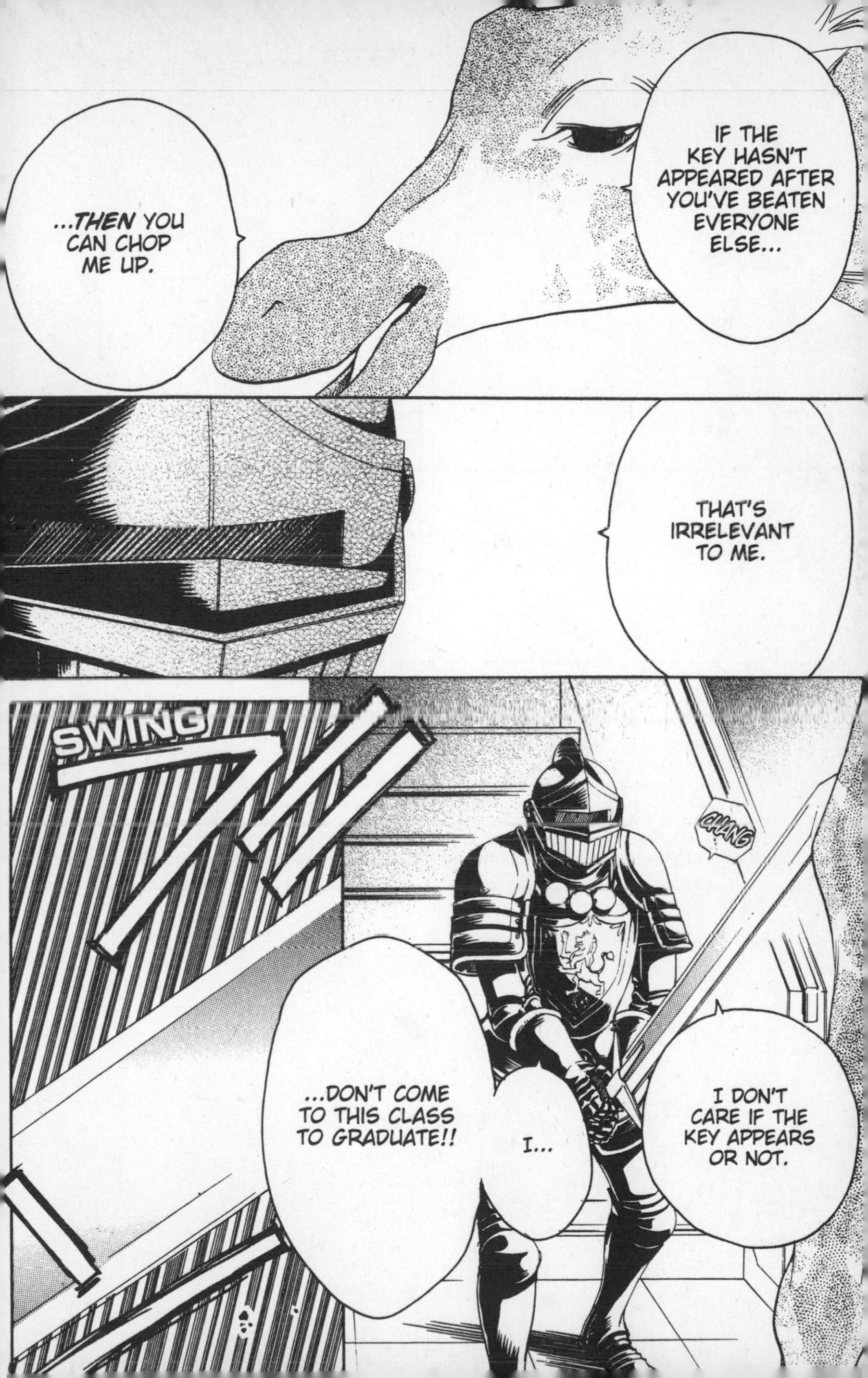
IF THE KEY HASN'T APPEARED AFTER YOU'VE BEATEN EVERYONE ELSE...
...*THEN* YOU CAN CHOP ME UP.
THAT'S IRRELEVANT TO ME.
CHANG
SWING
I DON'T CARE IF THE KEY APPEARS OR NOT.
I...
...DON'T COME TO THIS CLASS TO GRADUATE!!

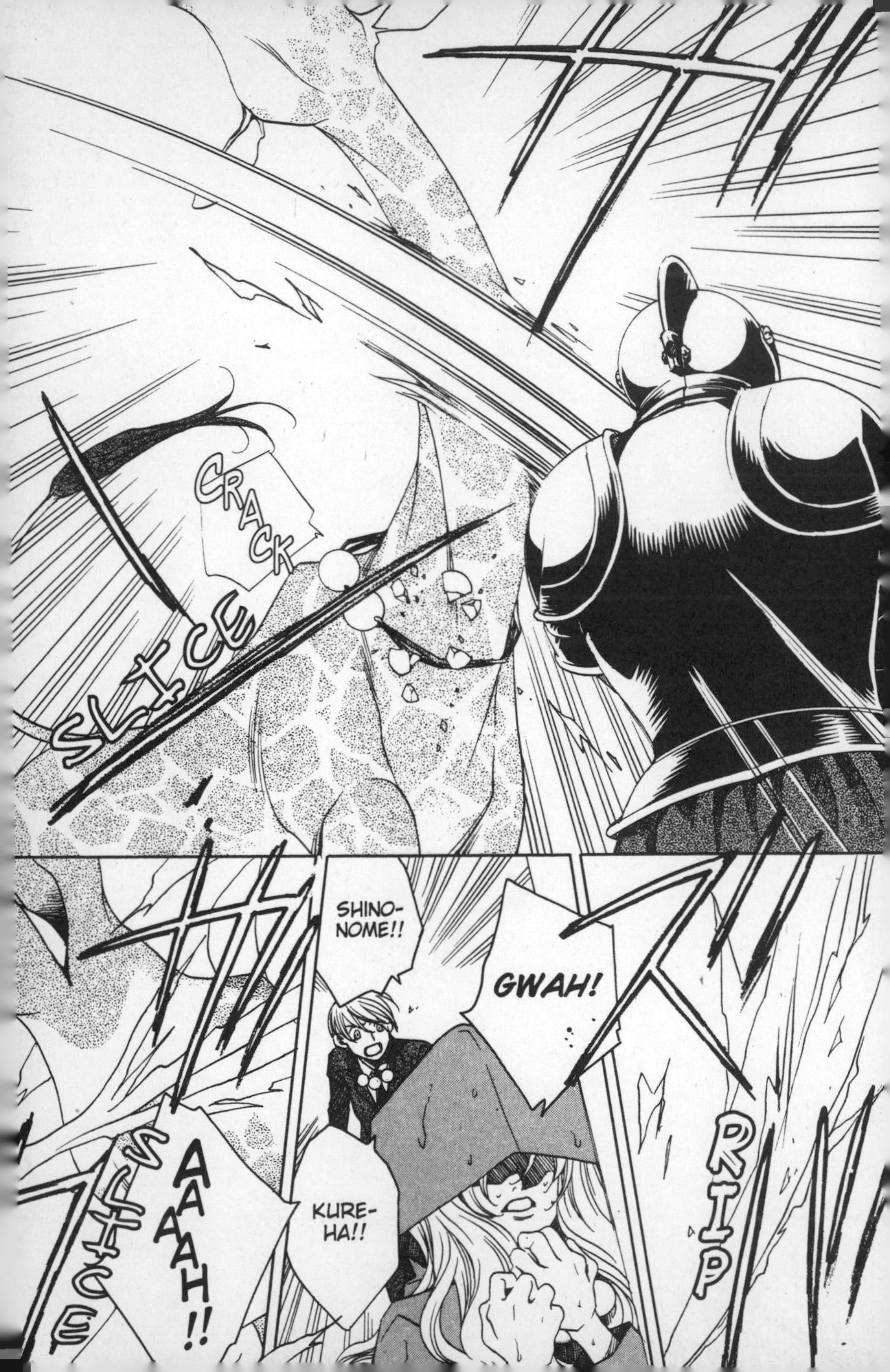
CRACK
SLICE
RIP
GWAH!
SHINO-NOME!!
KURE-HA!!
AAAAH!!
SLICE

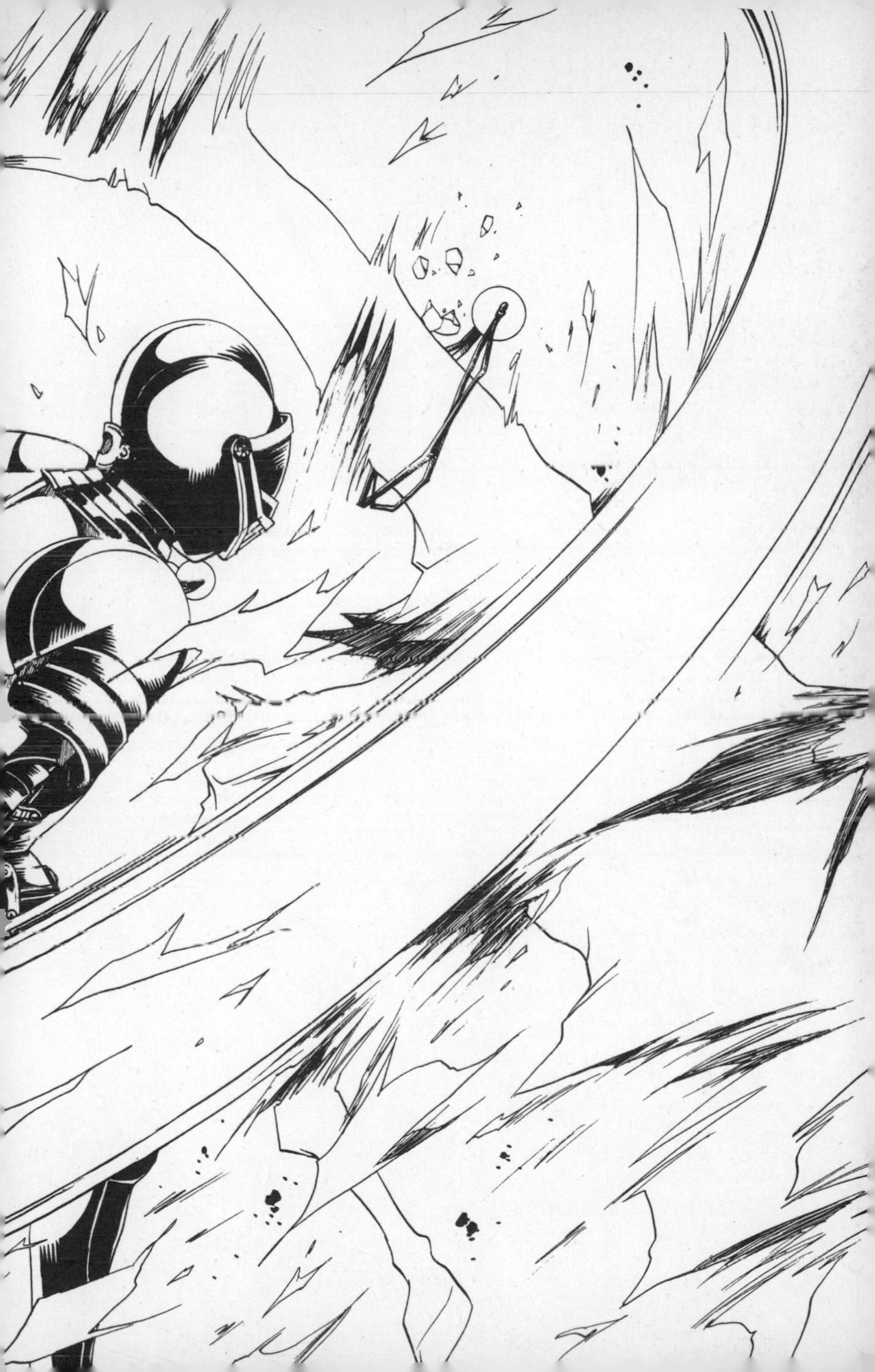

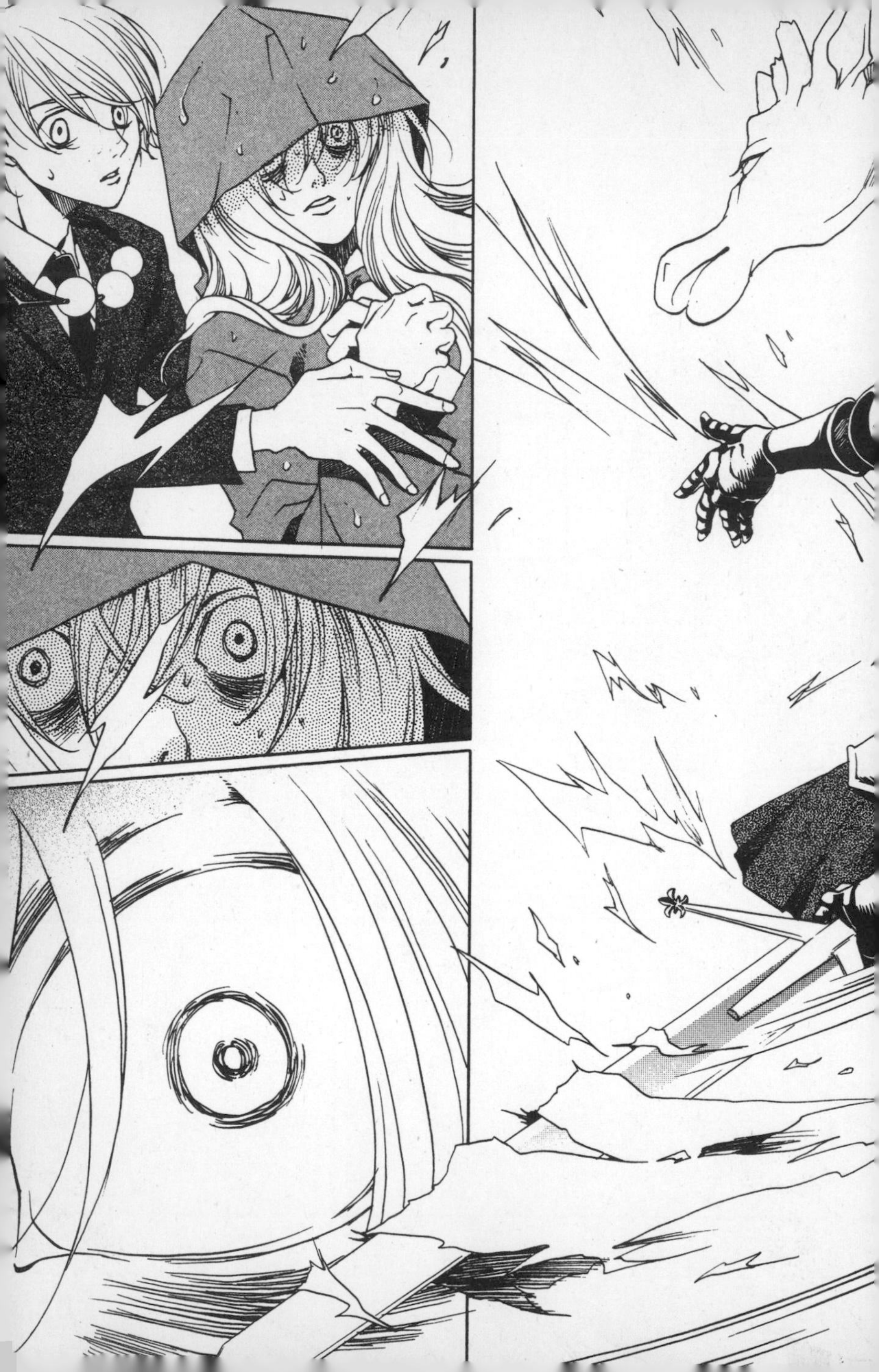

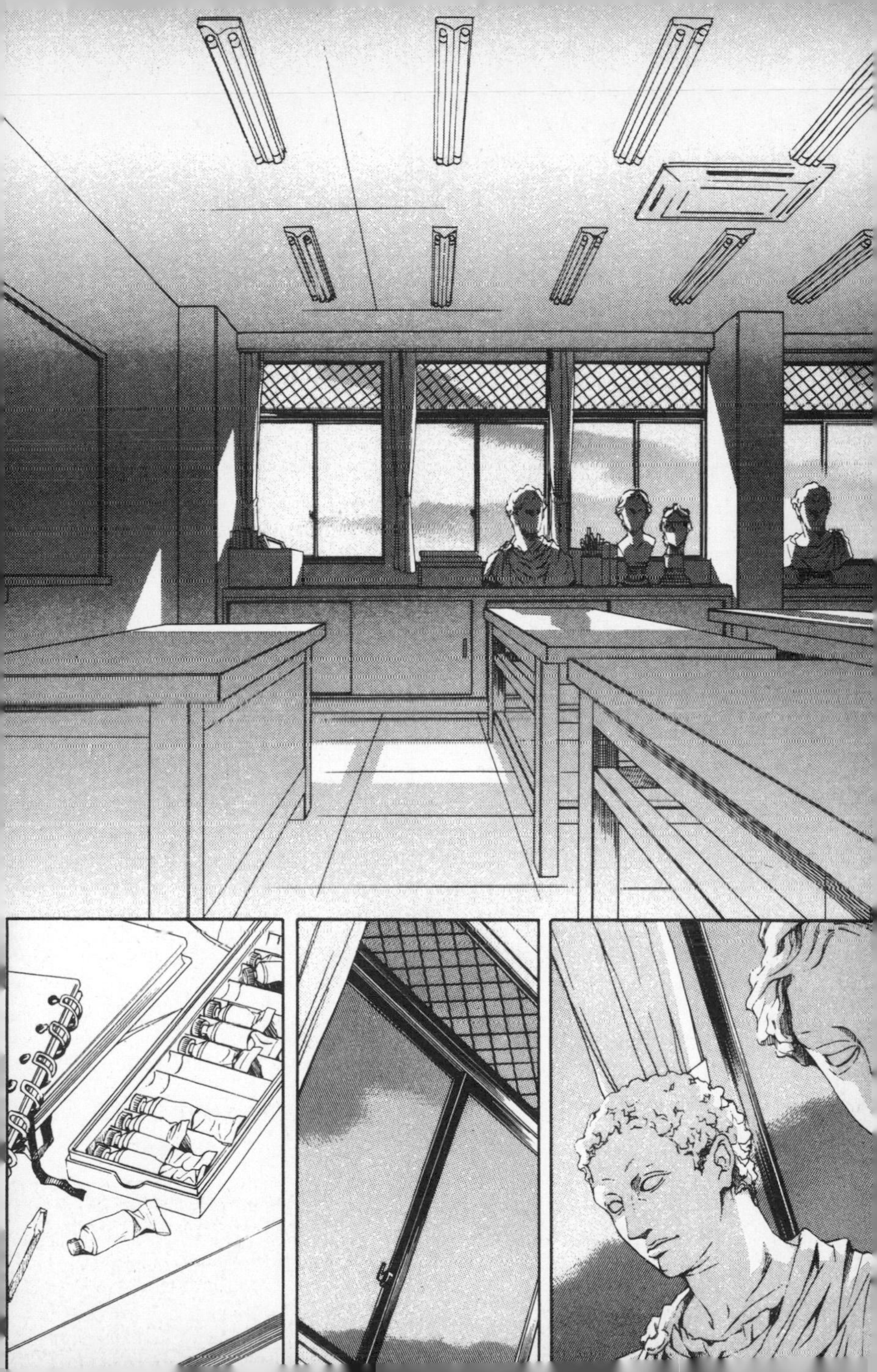

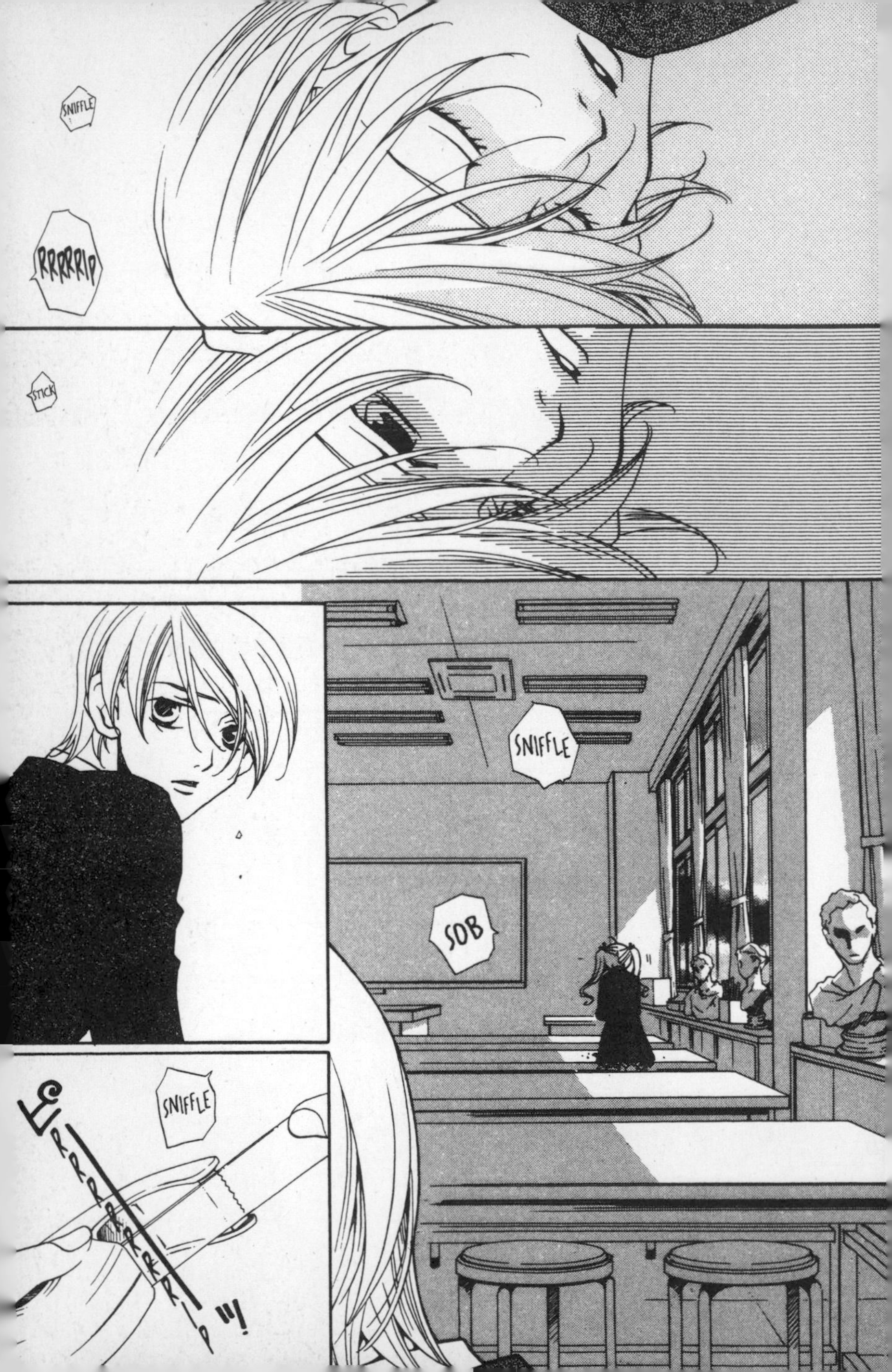
SNIFFLE
RRRRRIP
STICK
SNIFFLE
SOB
SNIFFLE
RRRRRRRRRIP!!

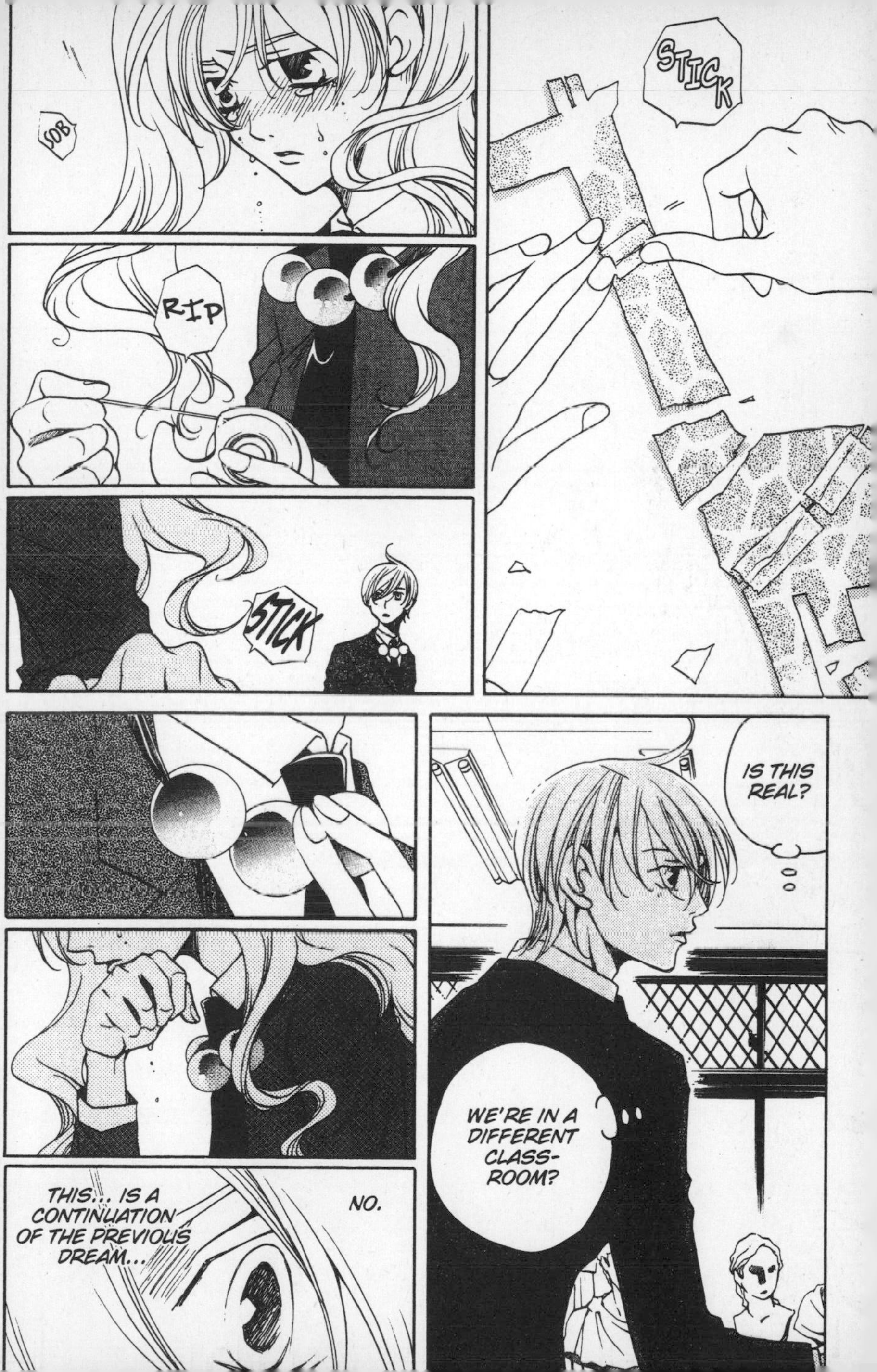
STICK
SOB
RIP
STICK
IS THIS REAL?
WE'RE IN A DIFFERENT CLASS-ROOM?
NO.
THIS... IS A CONTINUATION OF THE PREVIOUS DREAM...

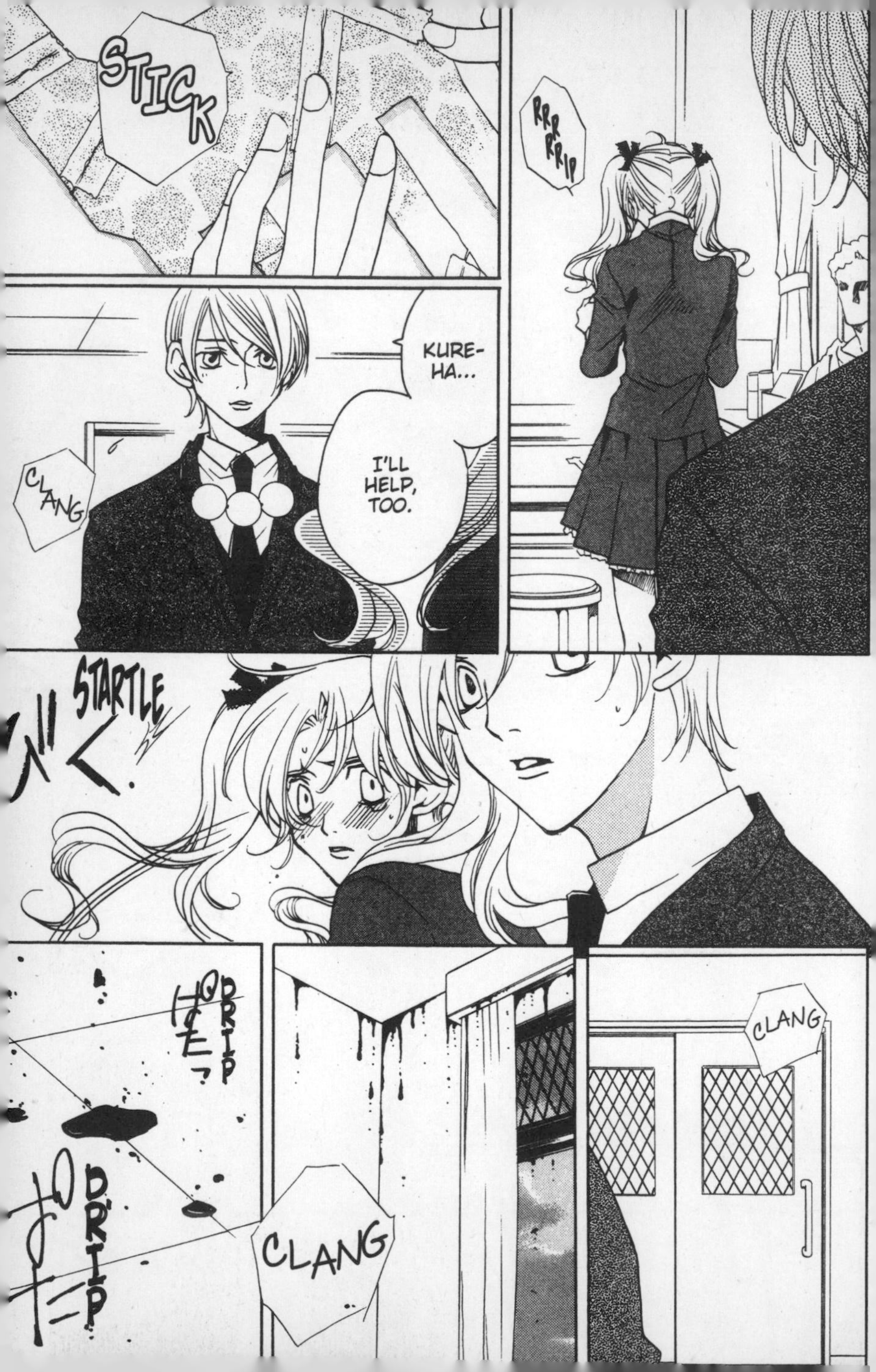
RRRRRIP
STICK
KURE-HA...
I'LL HELP, TOO.
CLANG
STARTLE
CLANG
CLANG
DRIP
DRIP

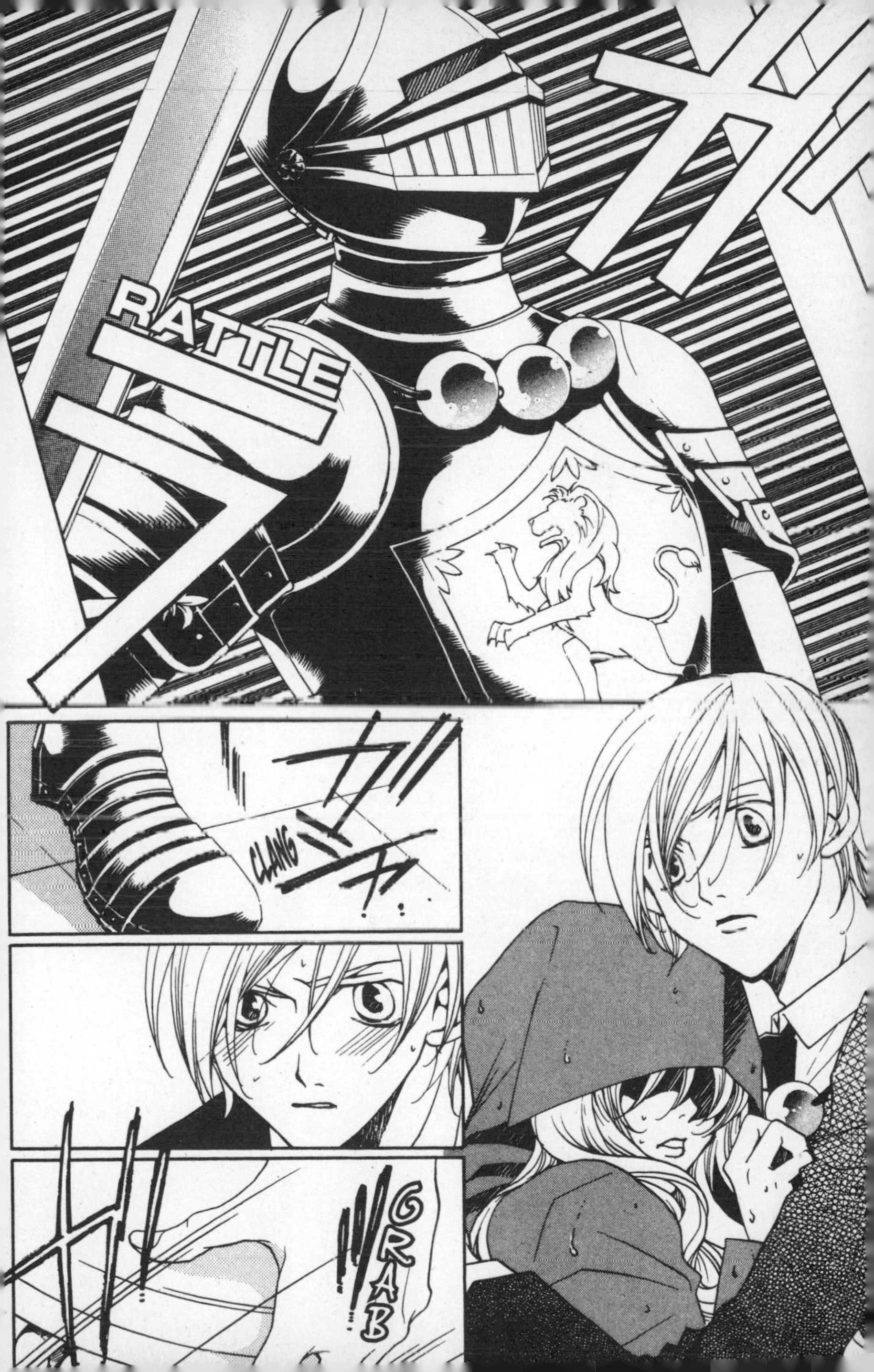
RATTLE
CLANG
GRAB

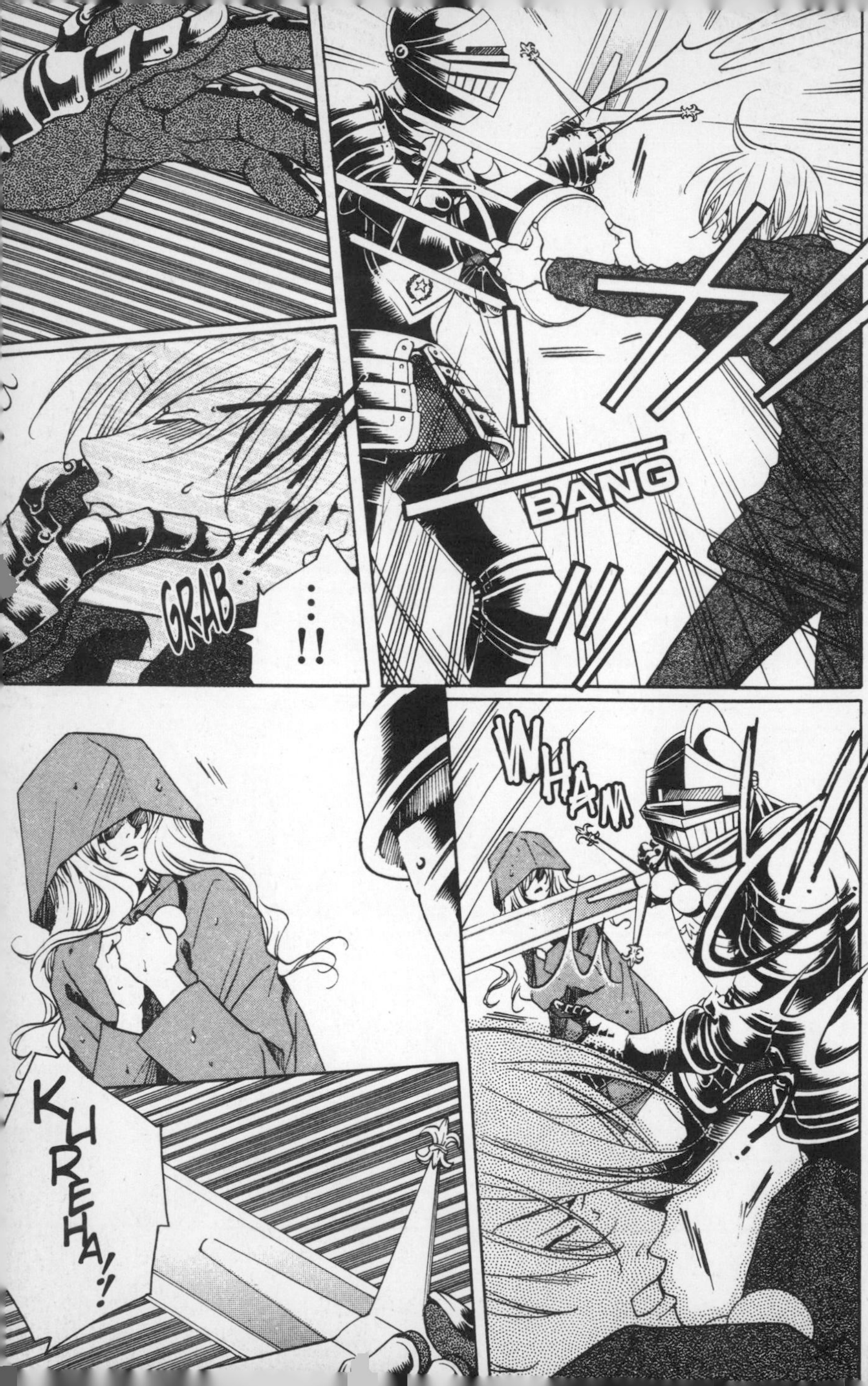
BANG
GRAB
...!!
WHAM
KUREHA!!

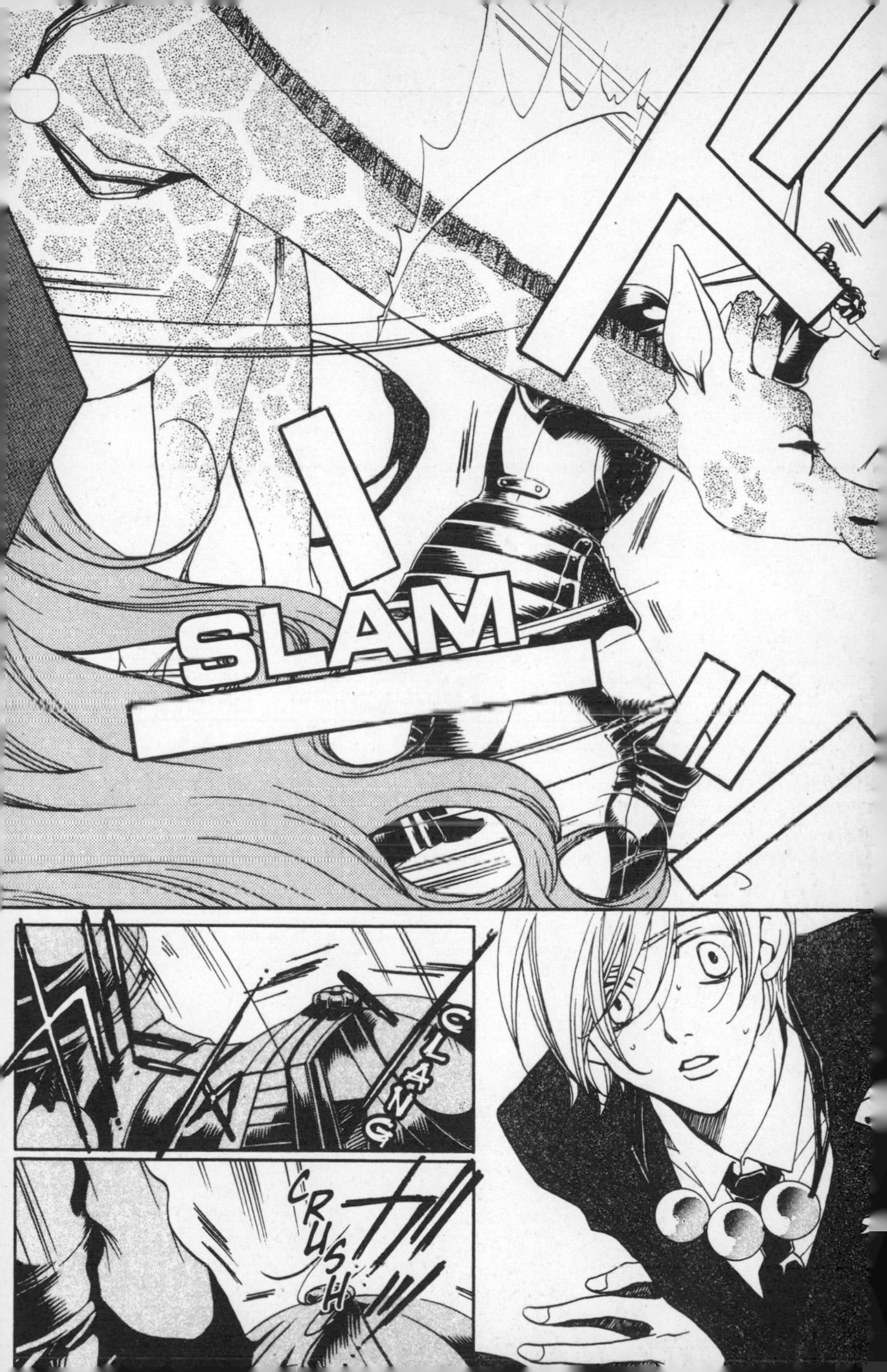
SLAM
CLANG
CRUSH

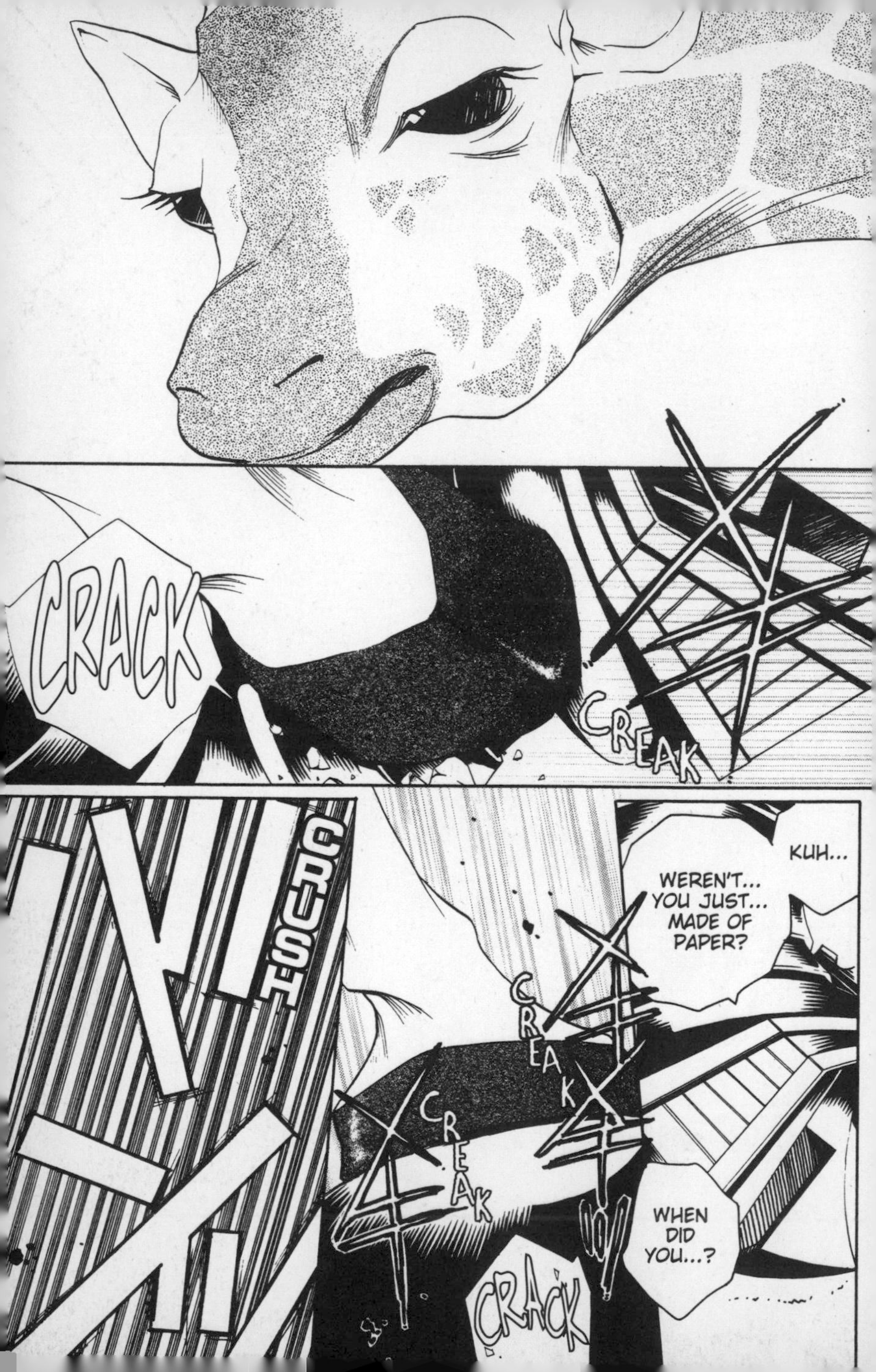
CREAK
CRACK
KUH...
WEREN'T... YOU JUST... MADE OF PAPER?
CREAK
CREAK
WHEN DID YOU...?
CRACK
CRUSH

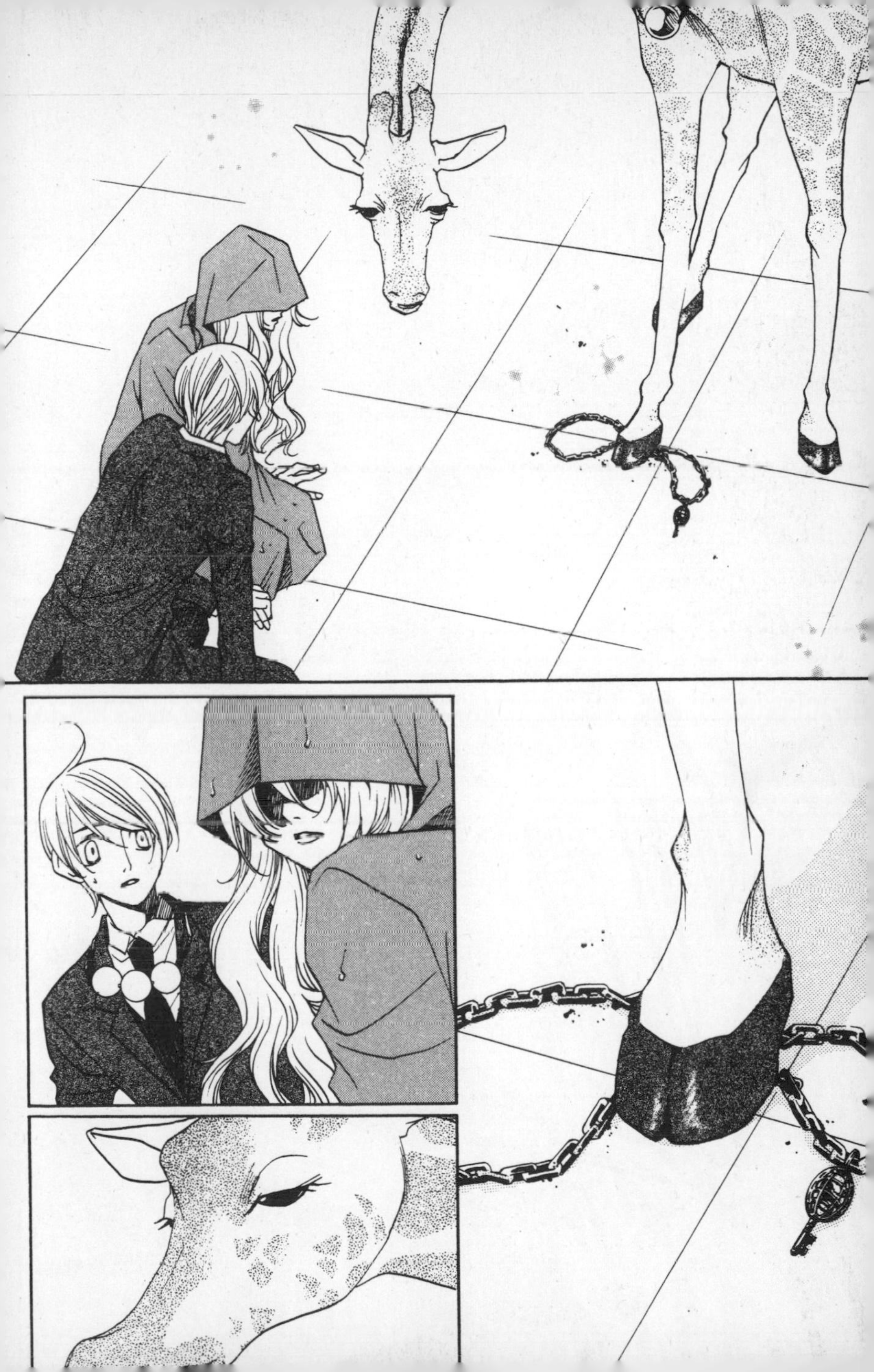

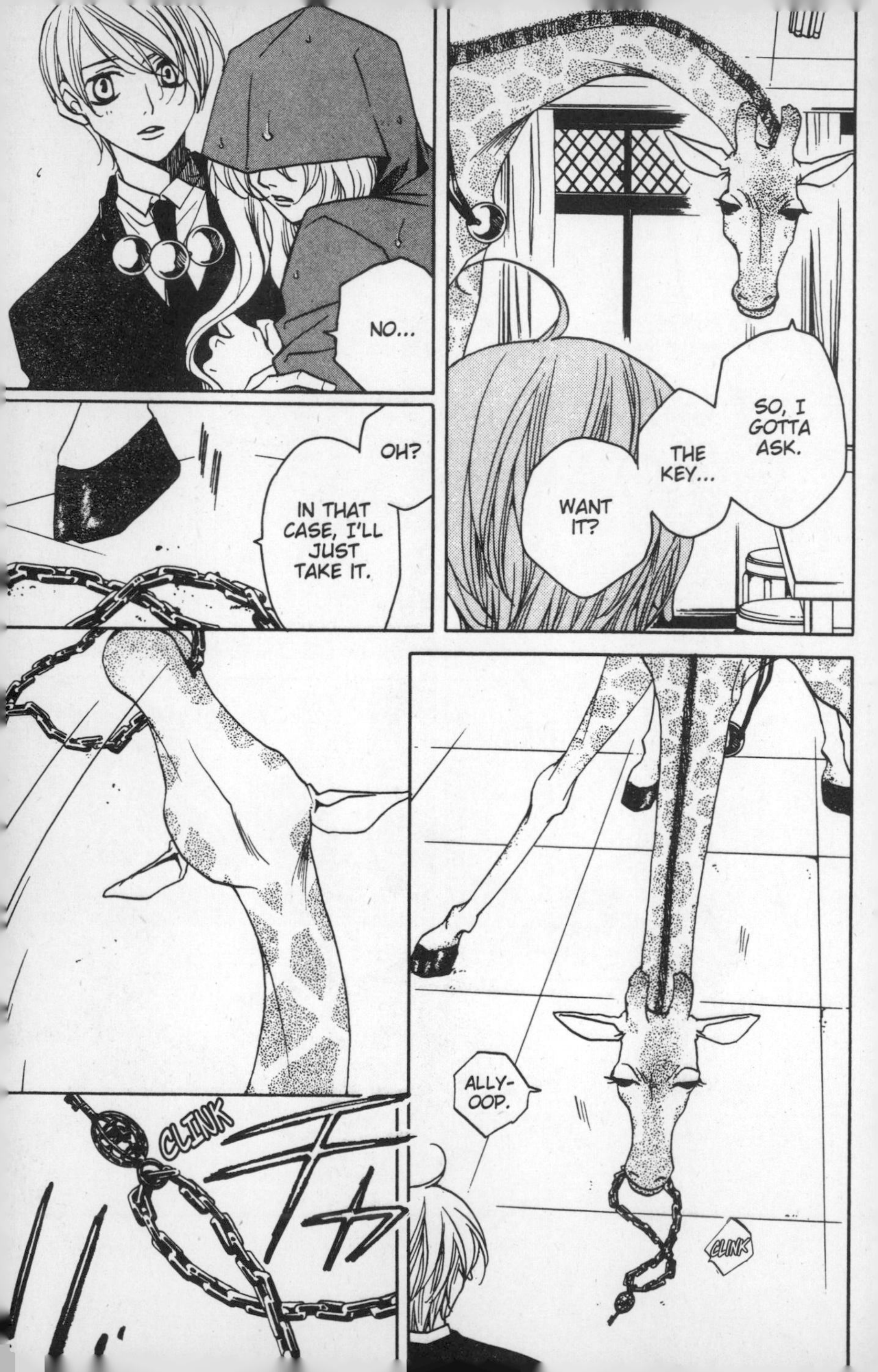
SO, I GOTTA ASK.
THE KEY...
WANT IT?
NO...
OH?
IN THAT CASE, I'LL JUST TAKE IT.
ALLY-OOP.
CLINK
CLINK

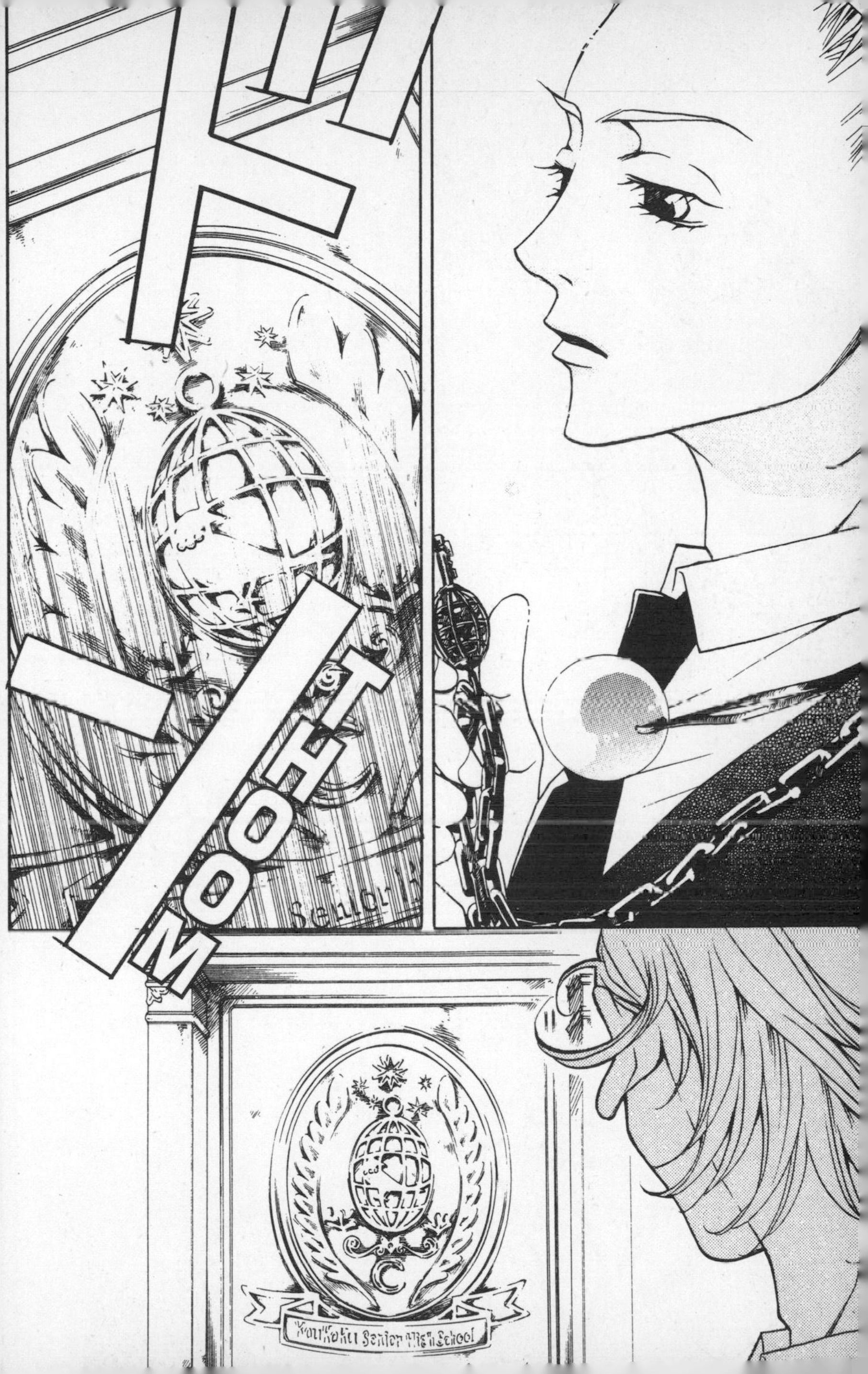
ドーン
THOOM

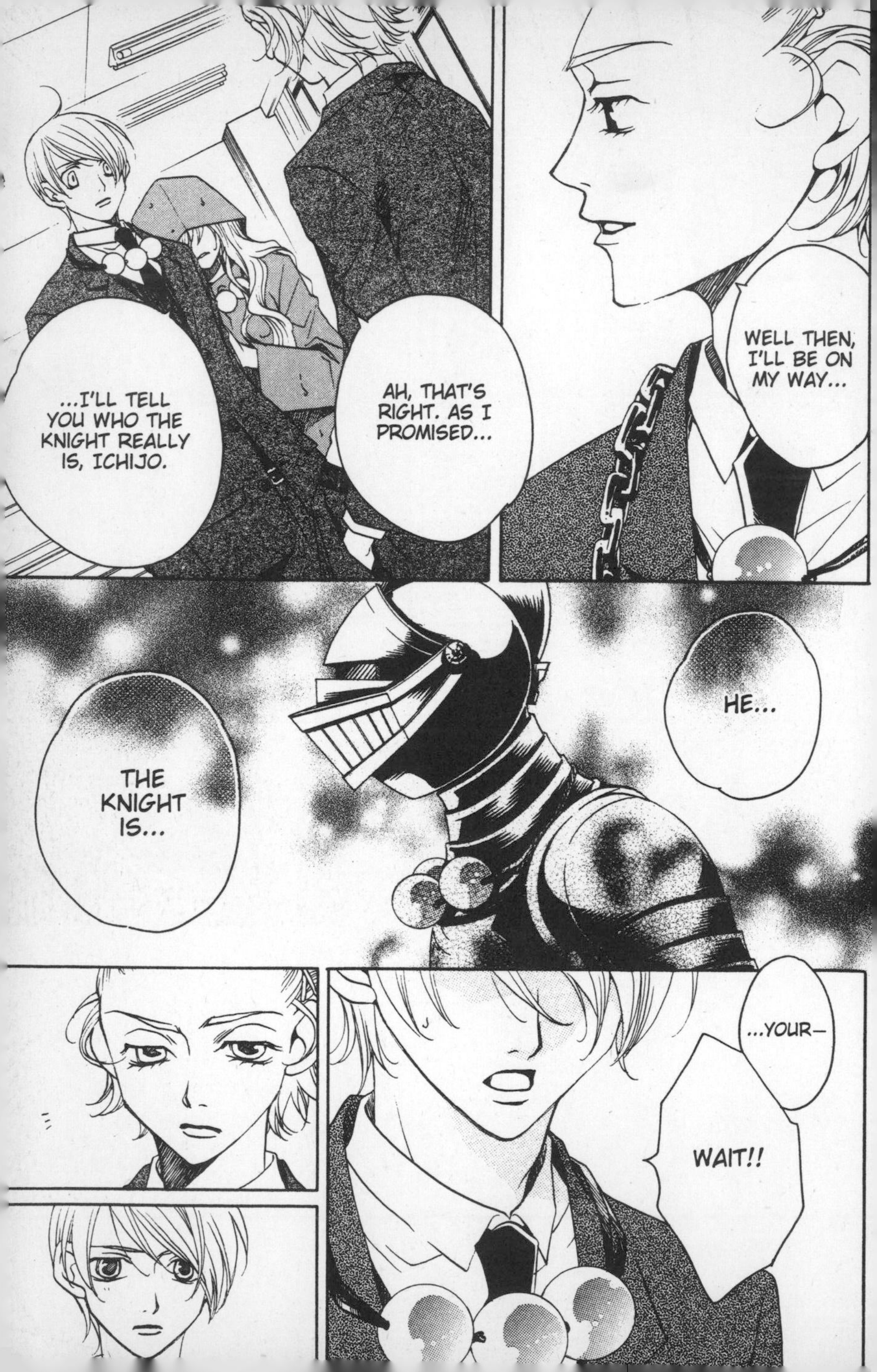
WELL THEN, I'LL BE ON MY WAY...
AH, THAT'S RIGHT. AS I PROMISED...
...I'LL TELL YOU WHO THE KNIGHT REALLY IS, ICHIJO.
HE...
THE KNIGHT IS...
...YOUR—
WAIT!!

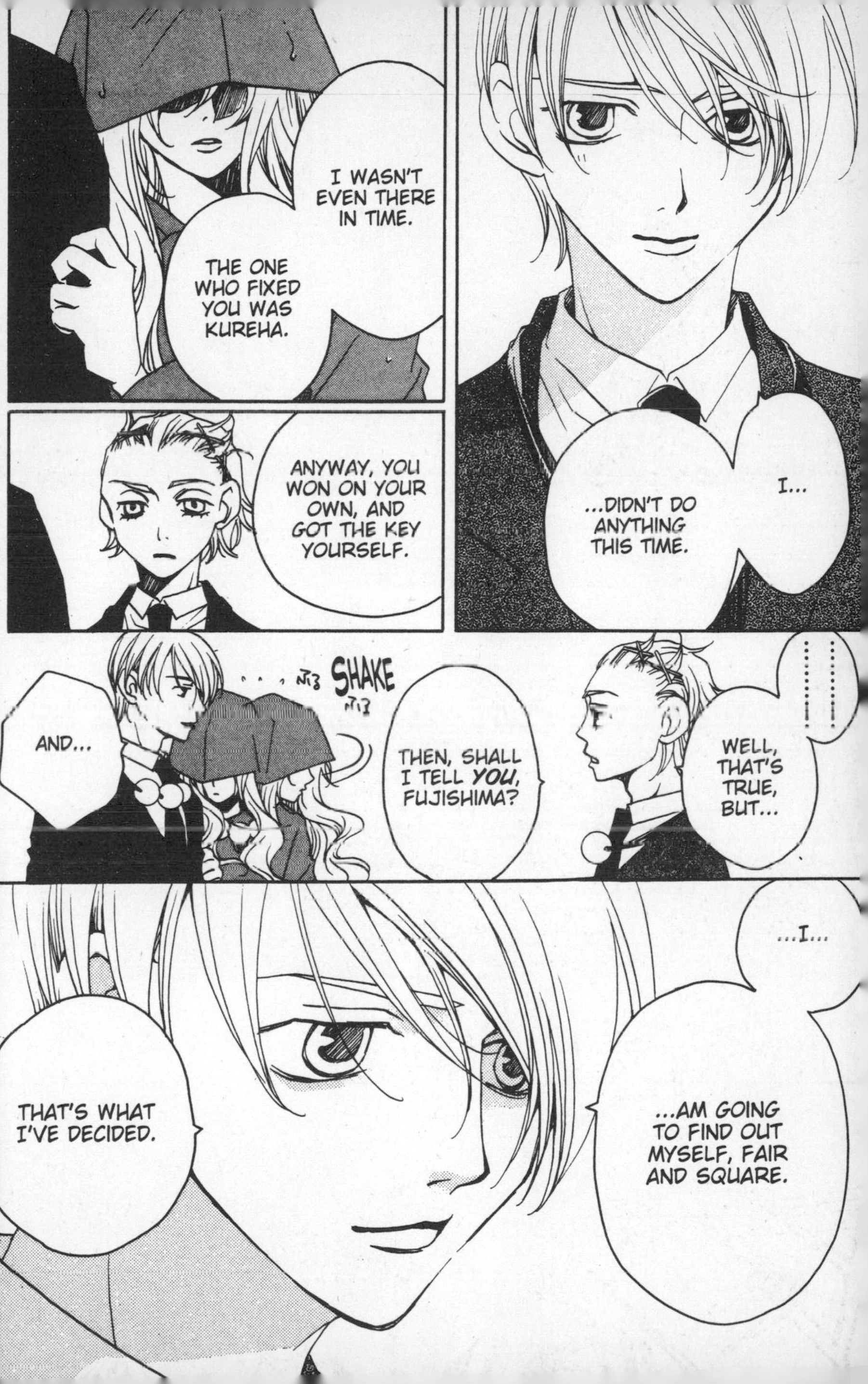
I...
...DIDN'T DO ANYTHING THIS TIME.
I WASN'T EVEN THERE IN TIME.
THE ONE WHO FIXED YOU WAS KUREHA.
ANYWAY, YOU WON ON YOUR OWN, AND GOT THE KEY YOURSELF.
!!
WELL, THAT'S TRUE, BUT...
THEN, SHALL I TELL *YOU*, FUJISHIMA?
SHAKE
AND...
...I...
...AM GOING TO FIND OUT MYSELF, FAIR AND SQUARE.
THAT'S WHAT I'VE DECIDED.

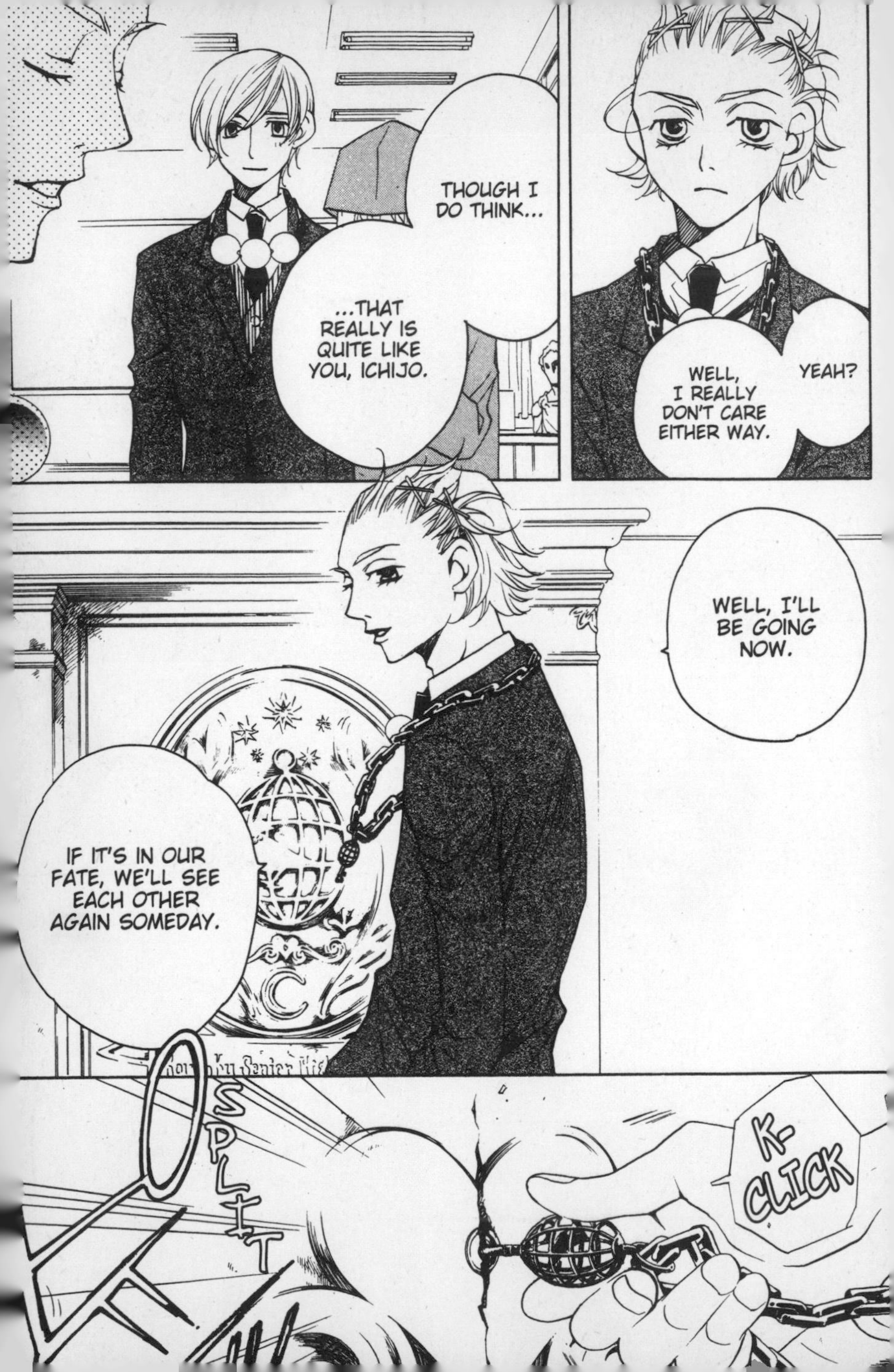
YEAH?
WELL, I REALLY DON'T CARE EITHER WAY.
THOUGH I DO THINK...
...THAT REALLY IS QUITE LIKE YOU, ICHIJO.
WELL, I'LL BE GOING NOW.
IF IT'S IN OUR FATE, WE'LL SEE EACH OTHER AGAIN SOMEDAY.
K-CLICK
SPLIT

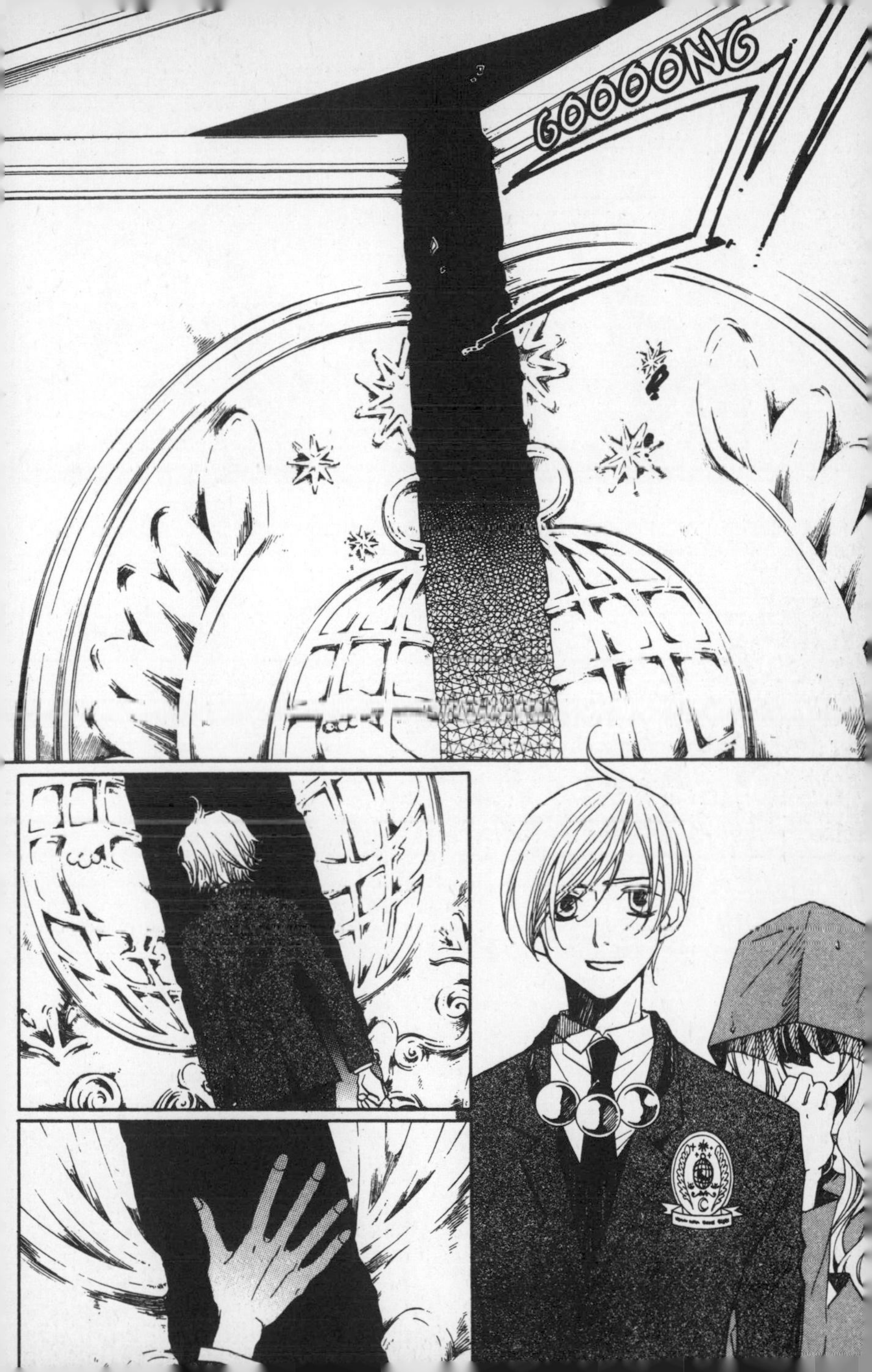
GOOOOONG

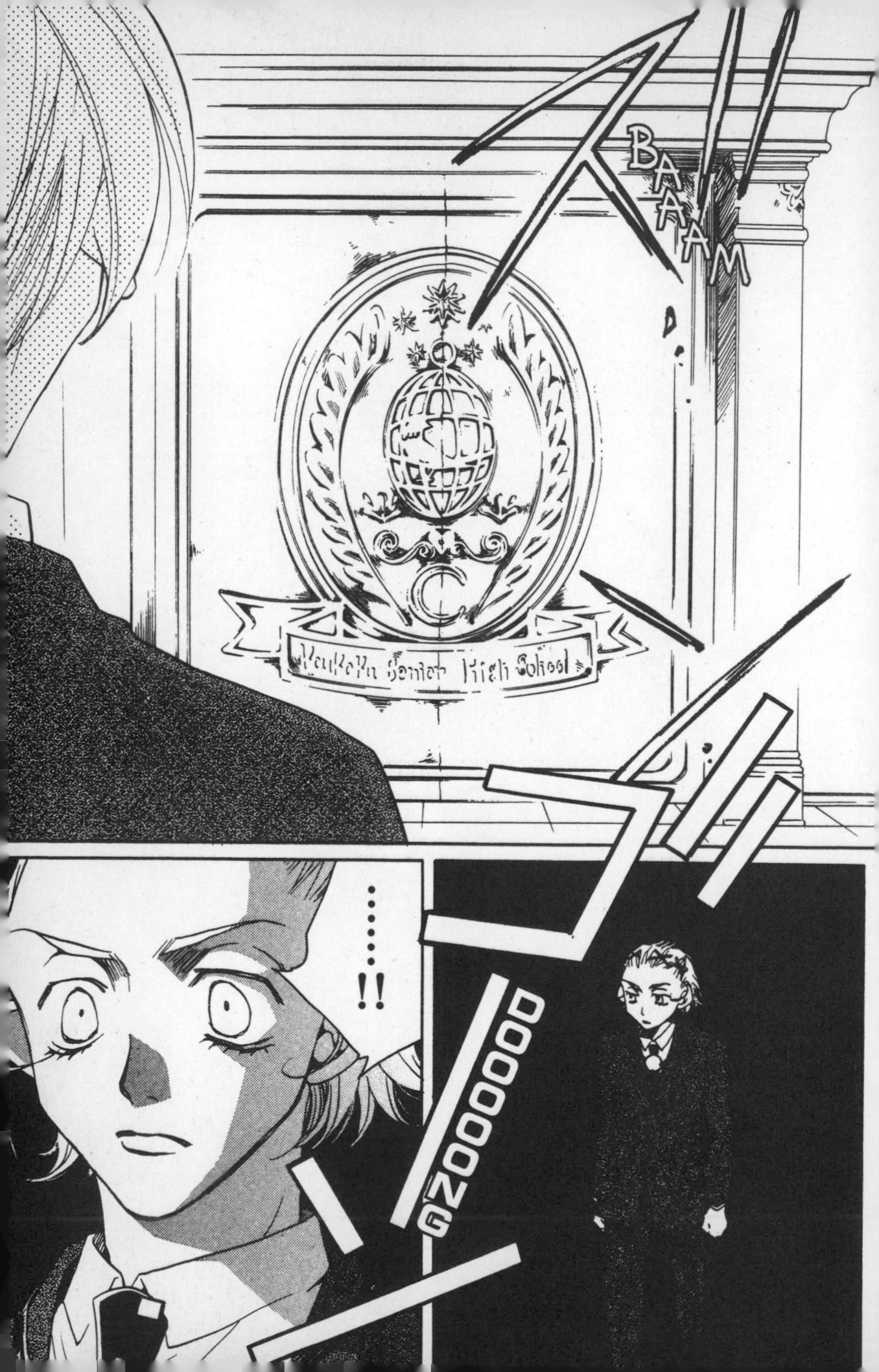
BAAAAM
Senior High School
DOOOOOOONG
......!!

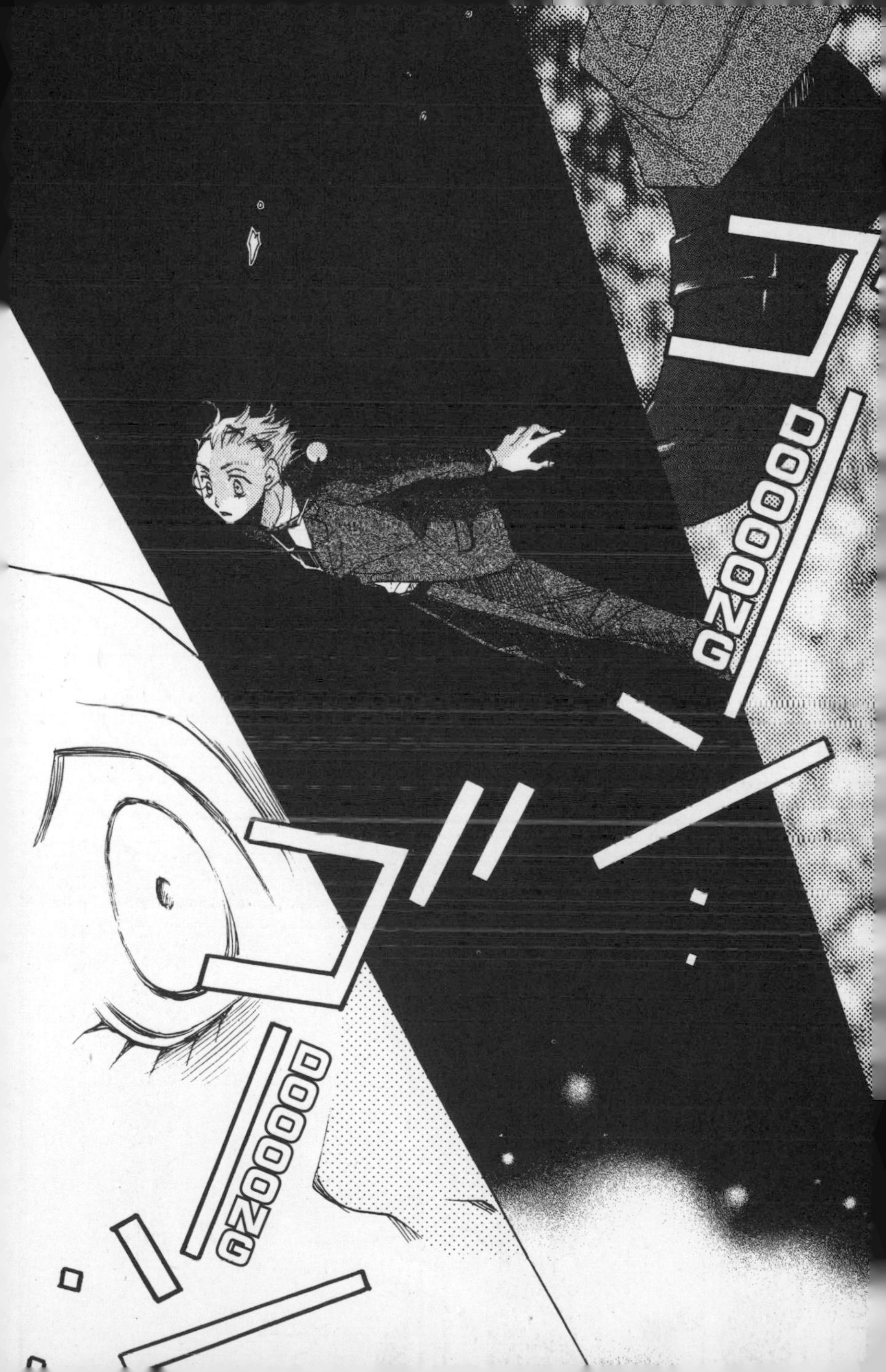
DOOOOONG
DOOOOONG

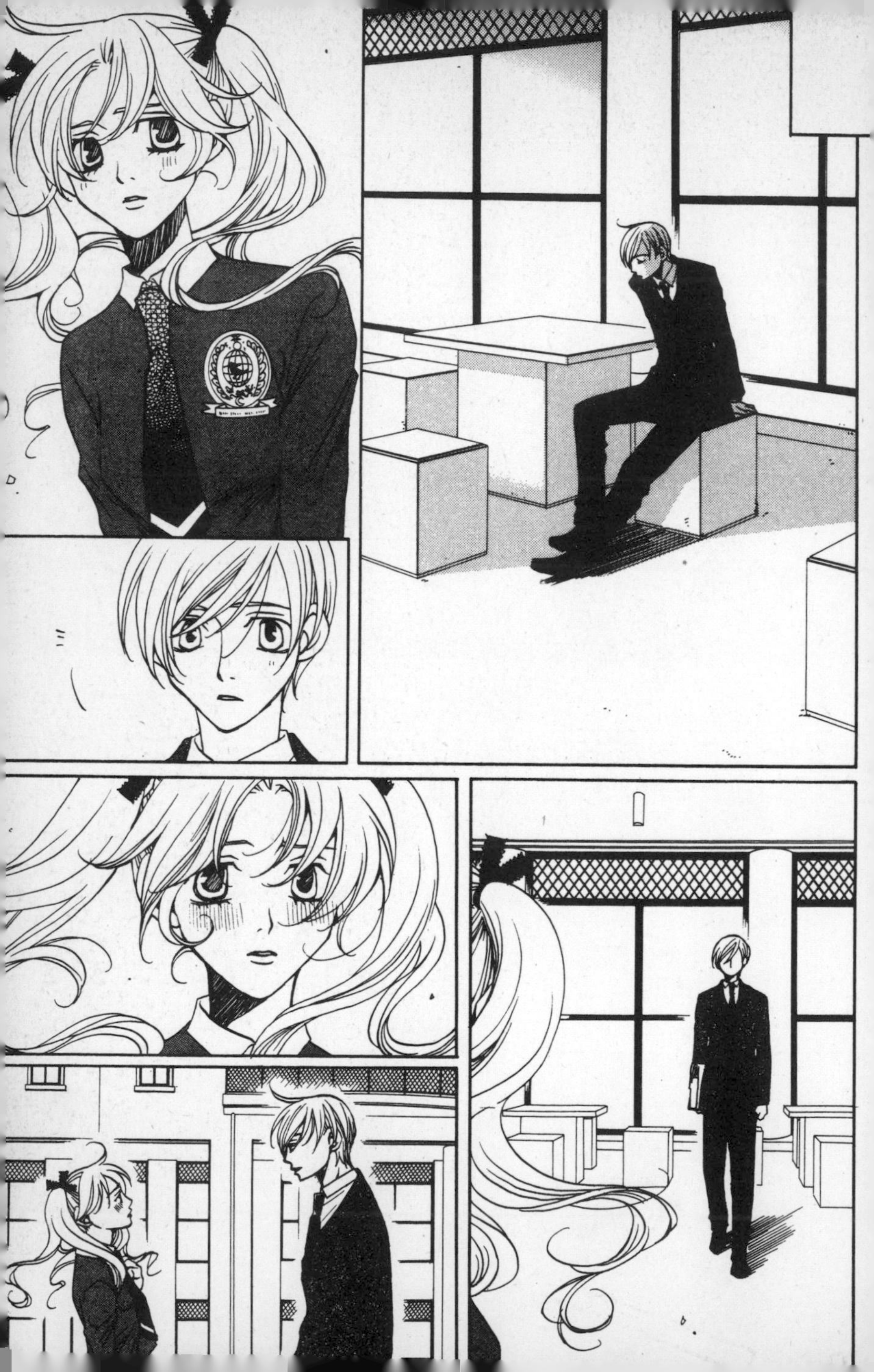

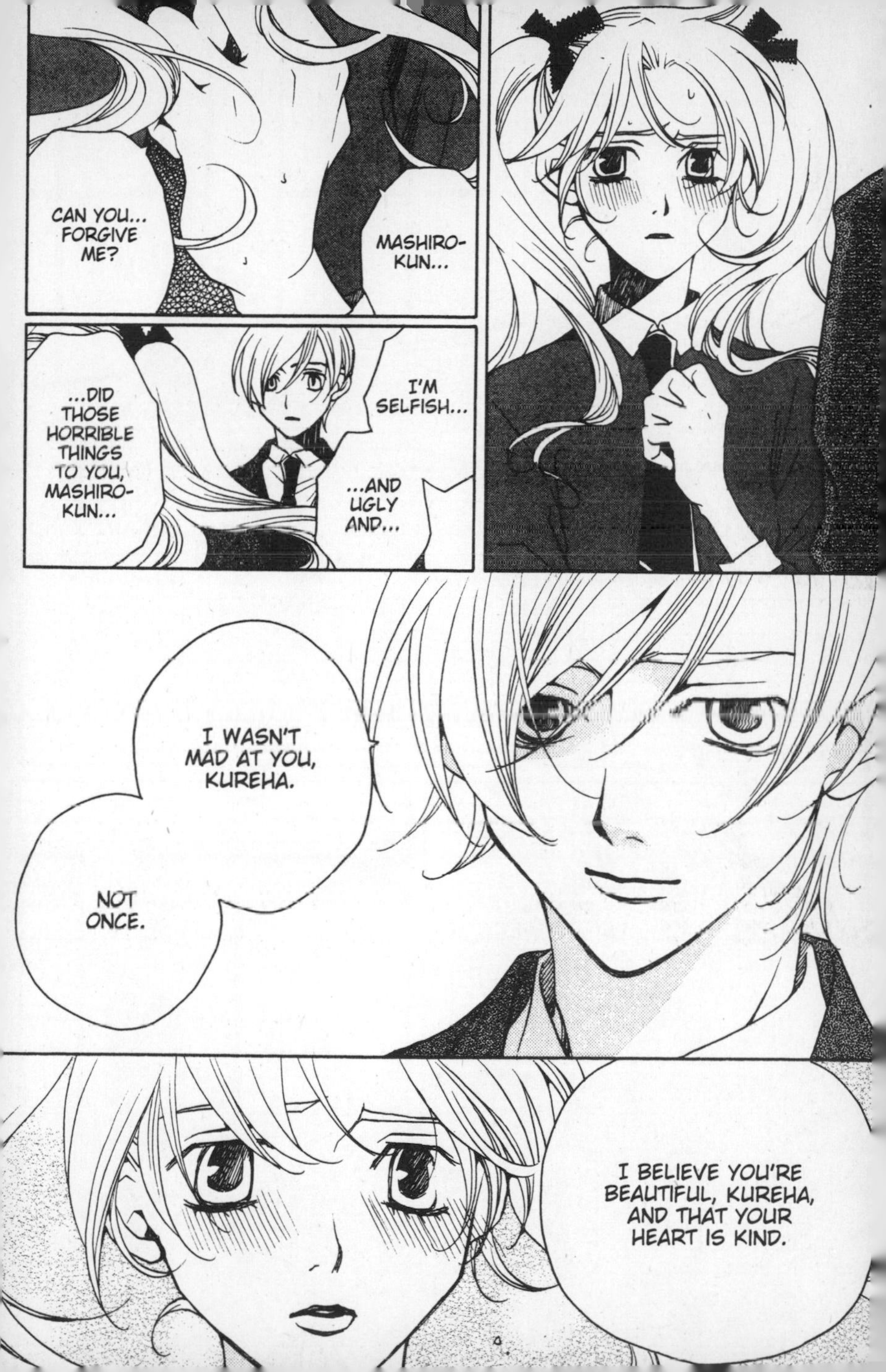
MASHIRO-KUN...
CAN YOU... FORGIVE ME?
I'M SELFISH...
...AND UGLY AND...
...DID THOSE HORRIBLE THINGS TO YOU, MASHIRO-KUN...
I WASN'T MAD AT YOU, KUREHA.
NOT ONCE.
I BELIEVE YOU'RE BEAUTIFUL, KUREHA, AND THAT YOUR HEART IS KIND.

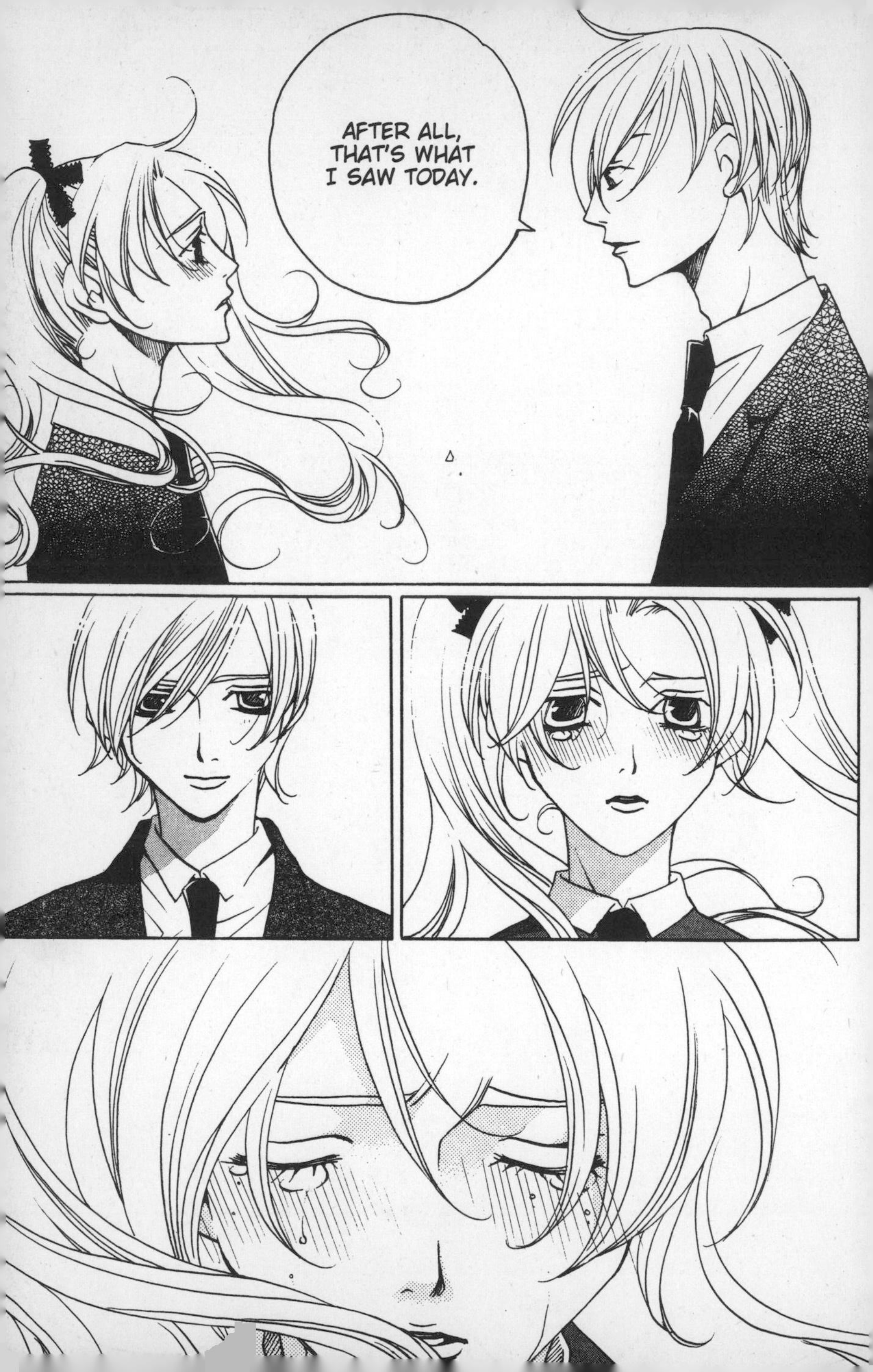
AFTER ALL, THAT'S WHAT I SAW TODAY.

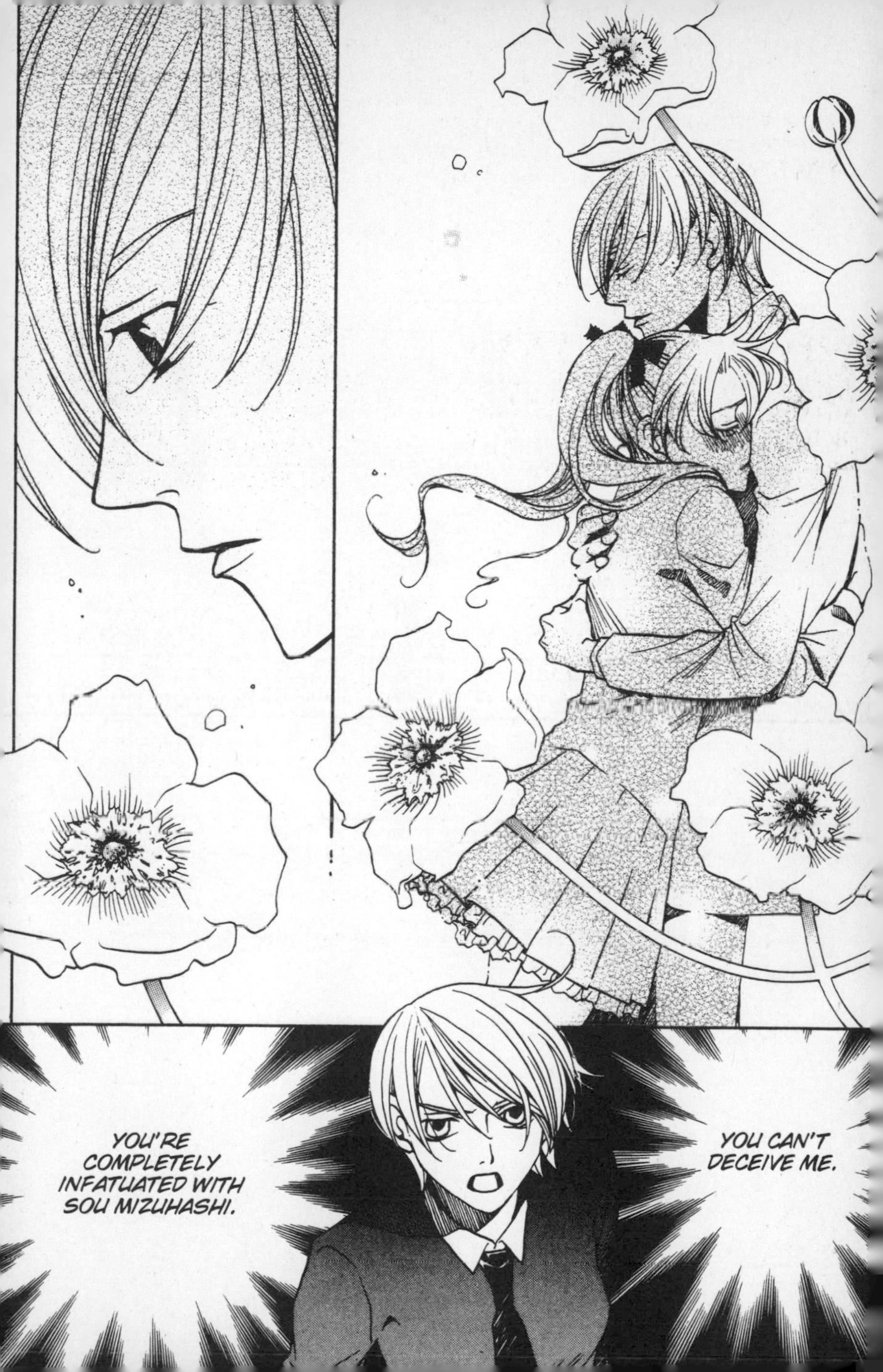
YOU CAN'T DECEIVE ME.
YOU'RE COMPLETELY INFATUATED WITH SOU MIZUHASHI.

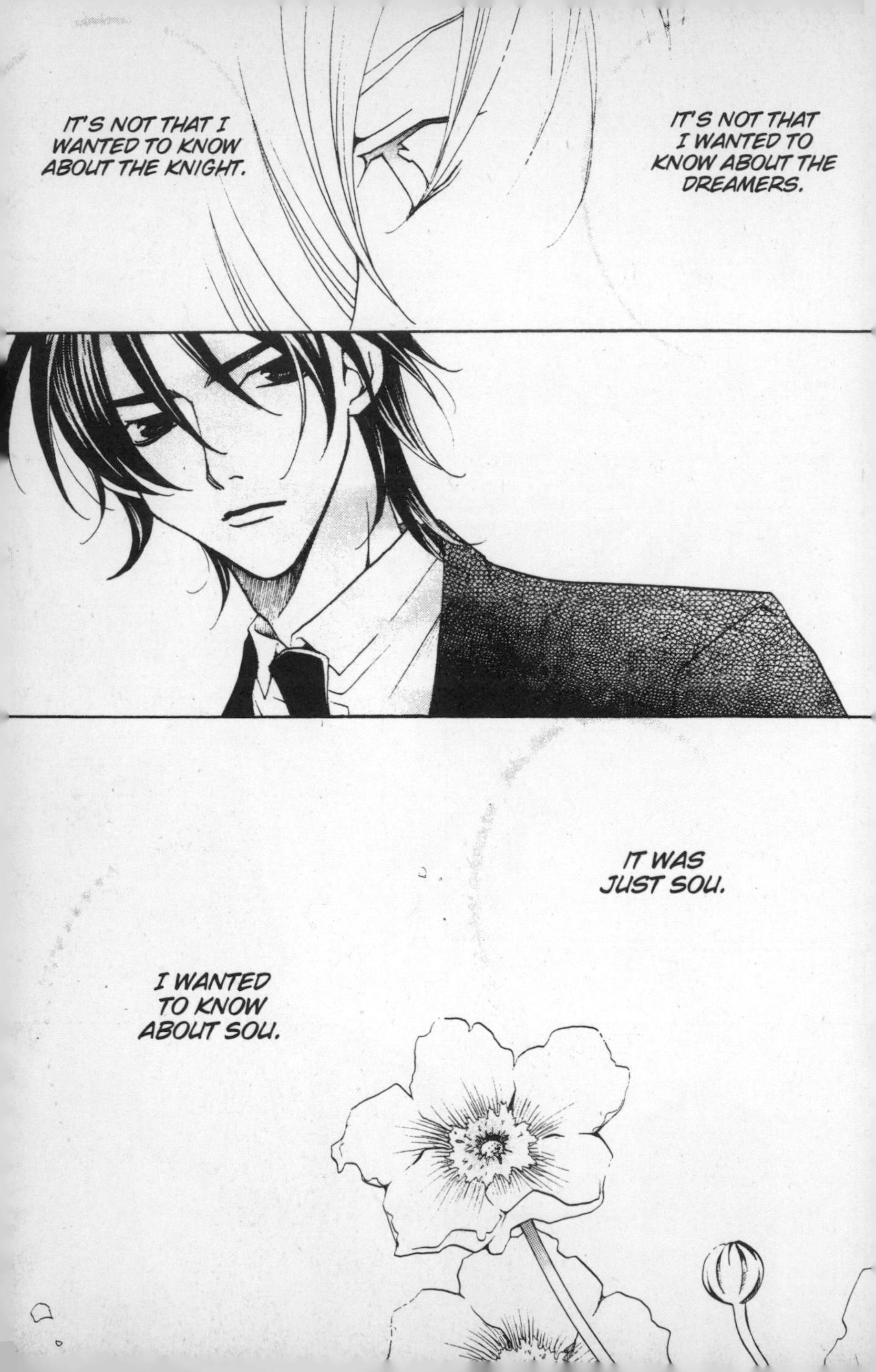
IT'S NOT THAT I WANTED TO KNOW ABOUT THE DREAMERS.
IT'S NOT THAT I WANTED TO KNOW ABOUT THE KNIGHT.
IT WAS JUST SOU.
I WANTED TO KNOW ABOUT SOU.

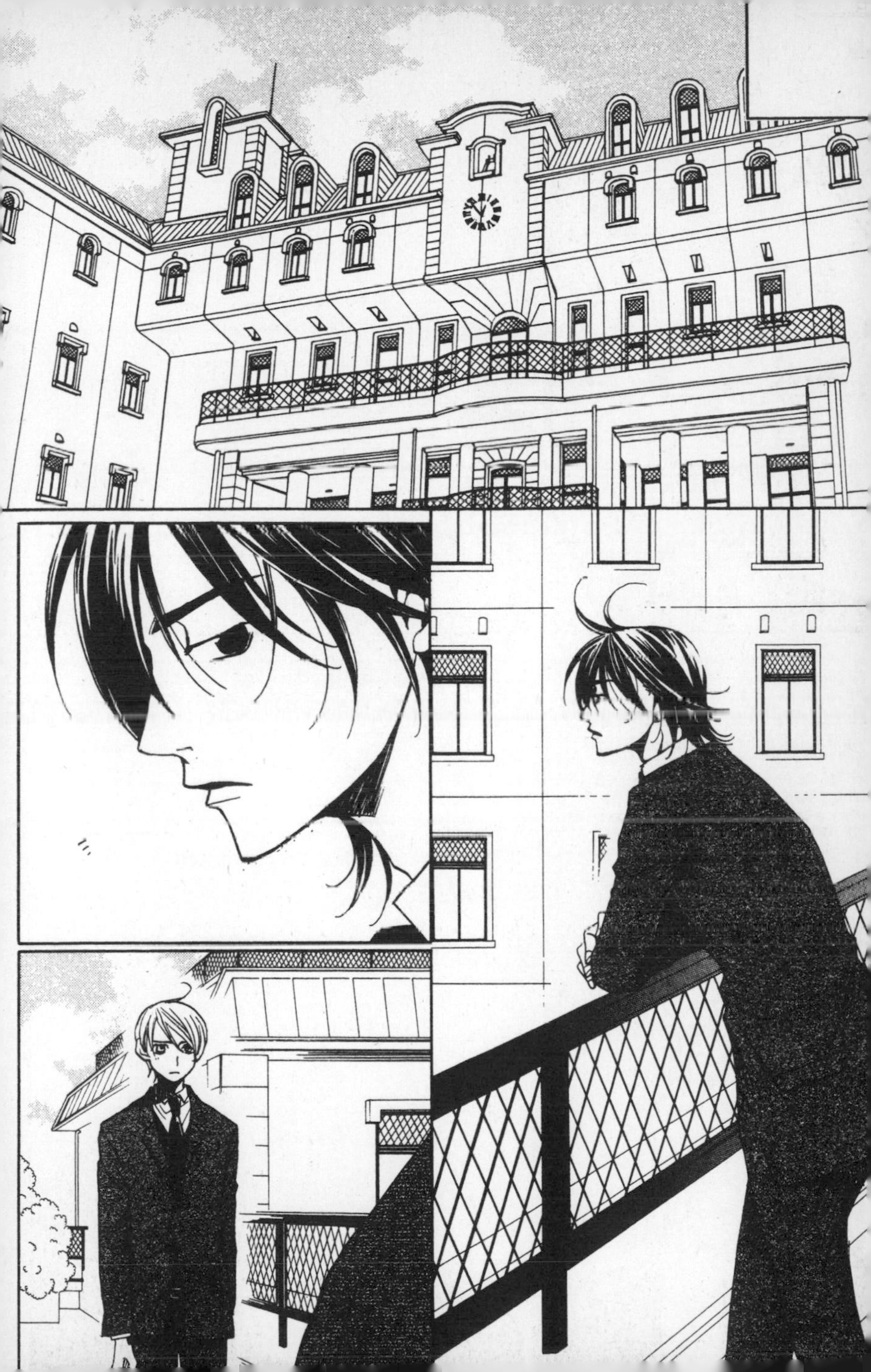

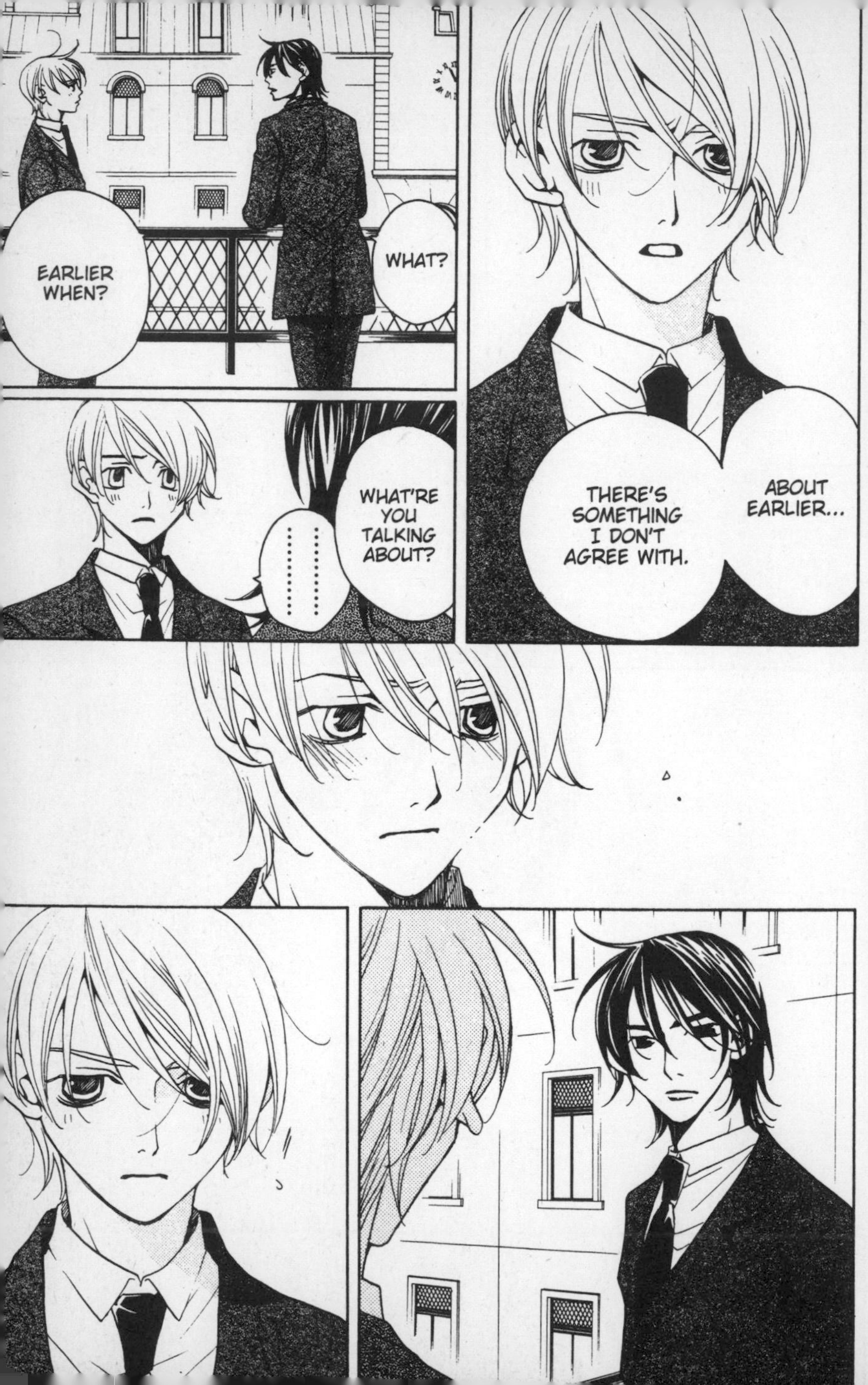
ABOUT EARLIER...
THERE'S SOMETHING I DON'T AGREE WITH.
WHAT?
EARLIER WHEN?
WHAT'RE YOU TALKING ABOUT?
......

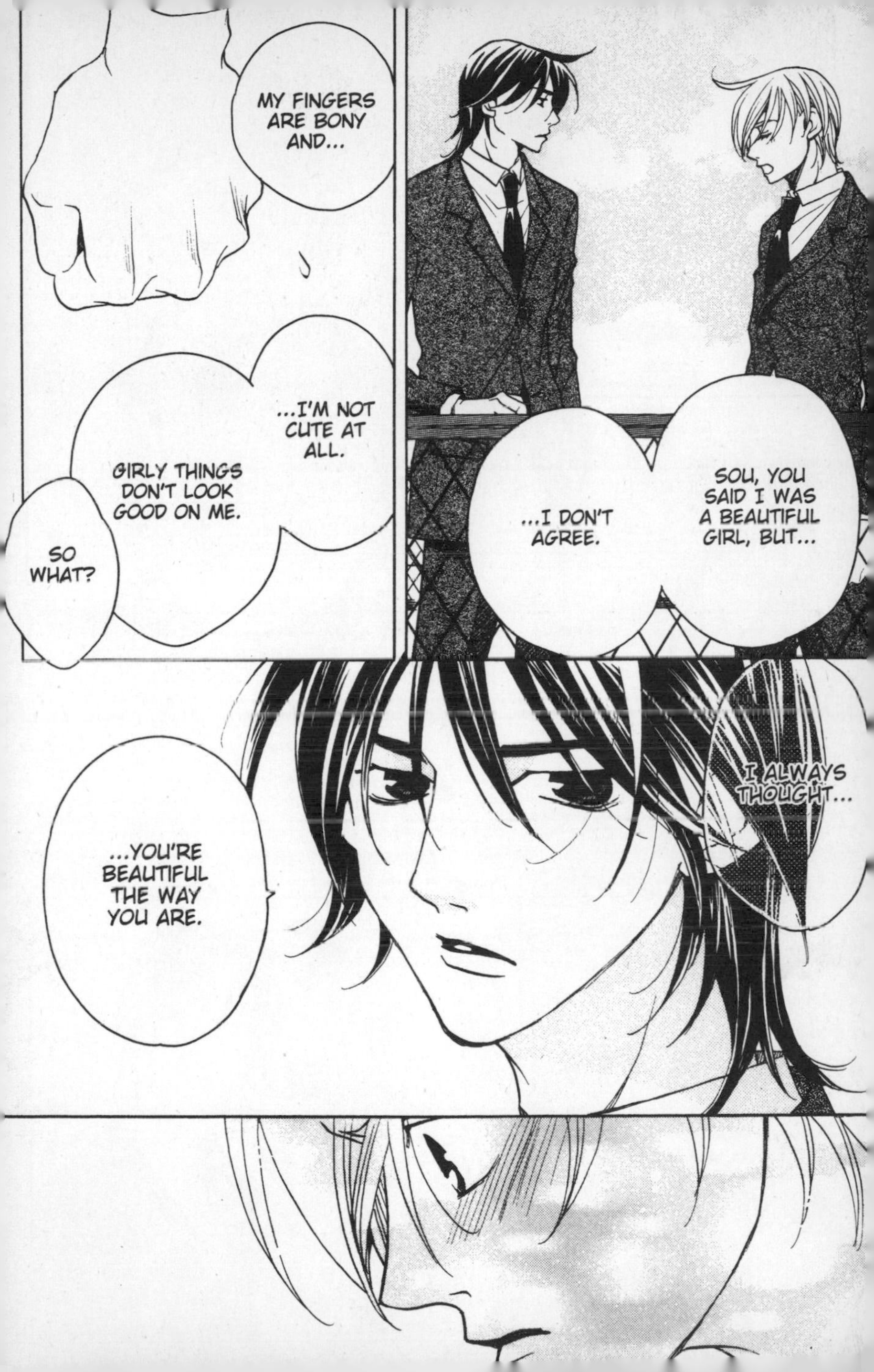
SOU, YOU SAID I WAS A BEAUTIFUL GIRL, BUT...
...I DON'T AGREE.
MY FINGERS ARE BONY AND...
...I'M NOT CUTE AT ALL.
GIRLY THINGS DON'T LOOK GOOD ON ME.
SO WHAT?
I ALWAYS THOUGHT...
...YOU'RE BEAUTIFUL THE WAY YOU ARE.

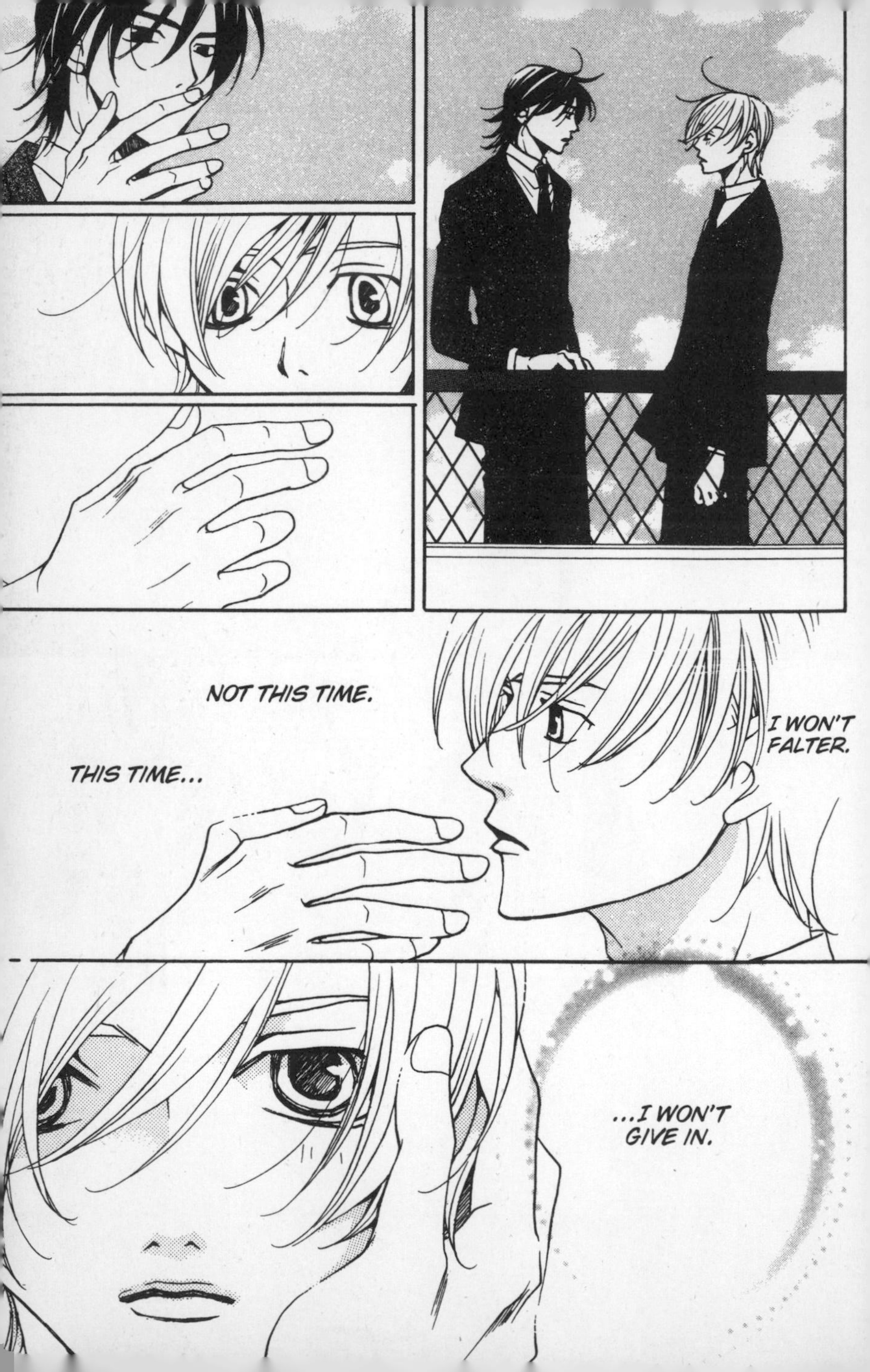
I WON'T FALTER.
NOT THIS TIME.
THIS TIME...
...I WON'T GIVE IN.

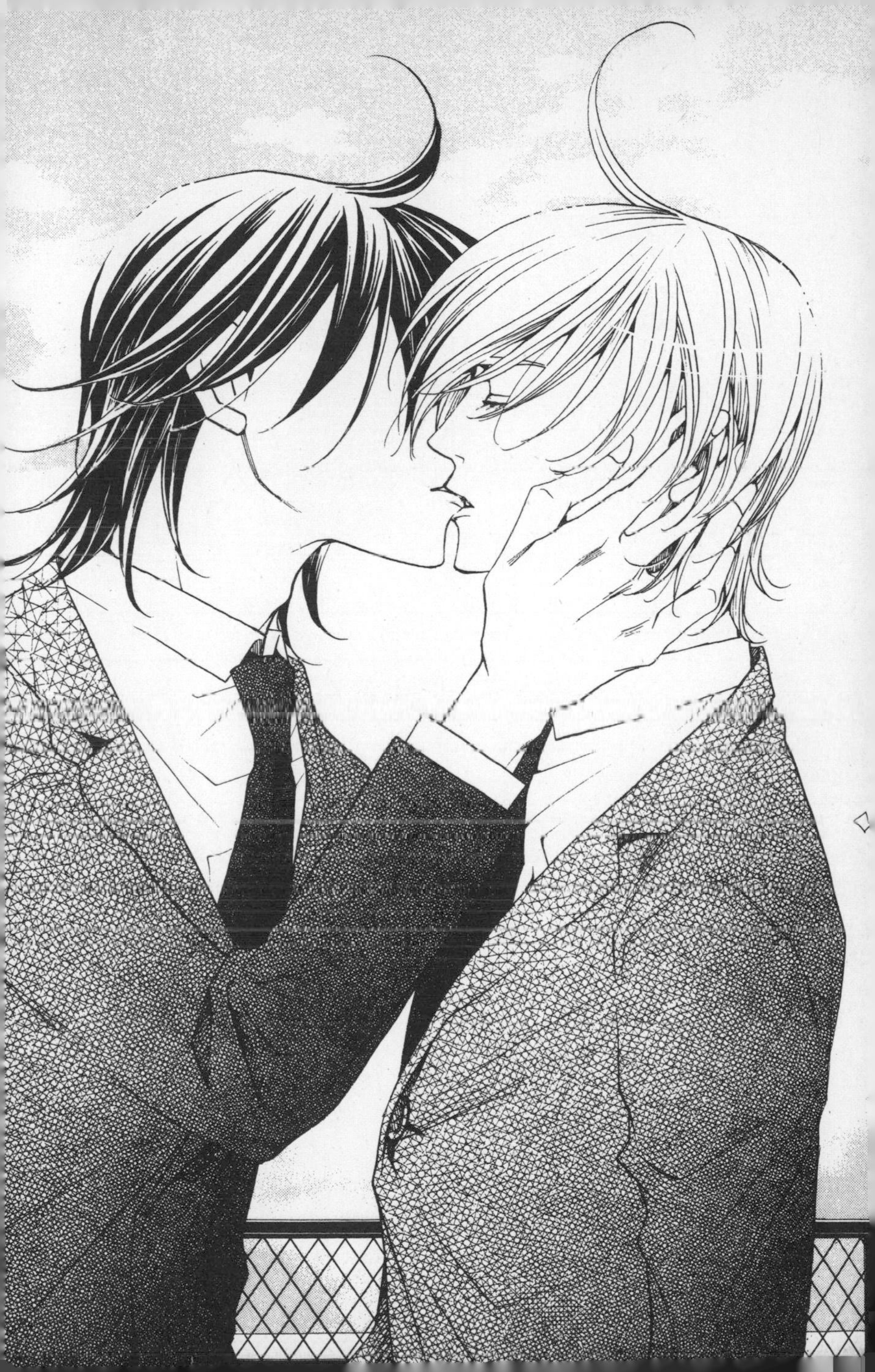

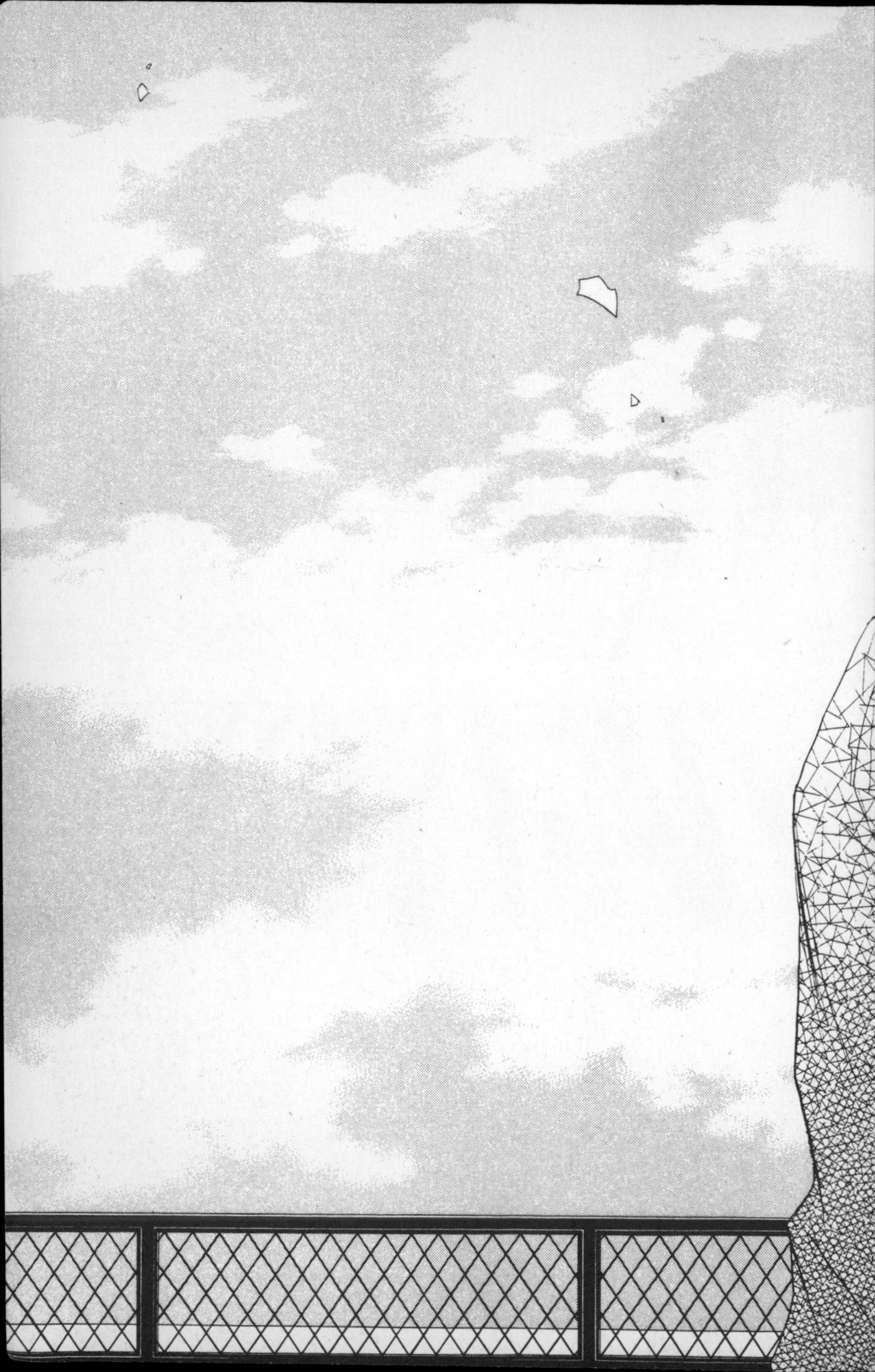

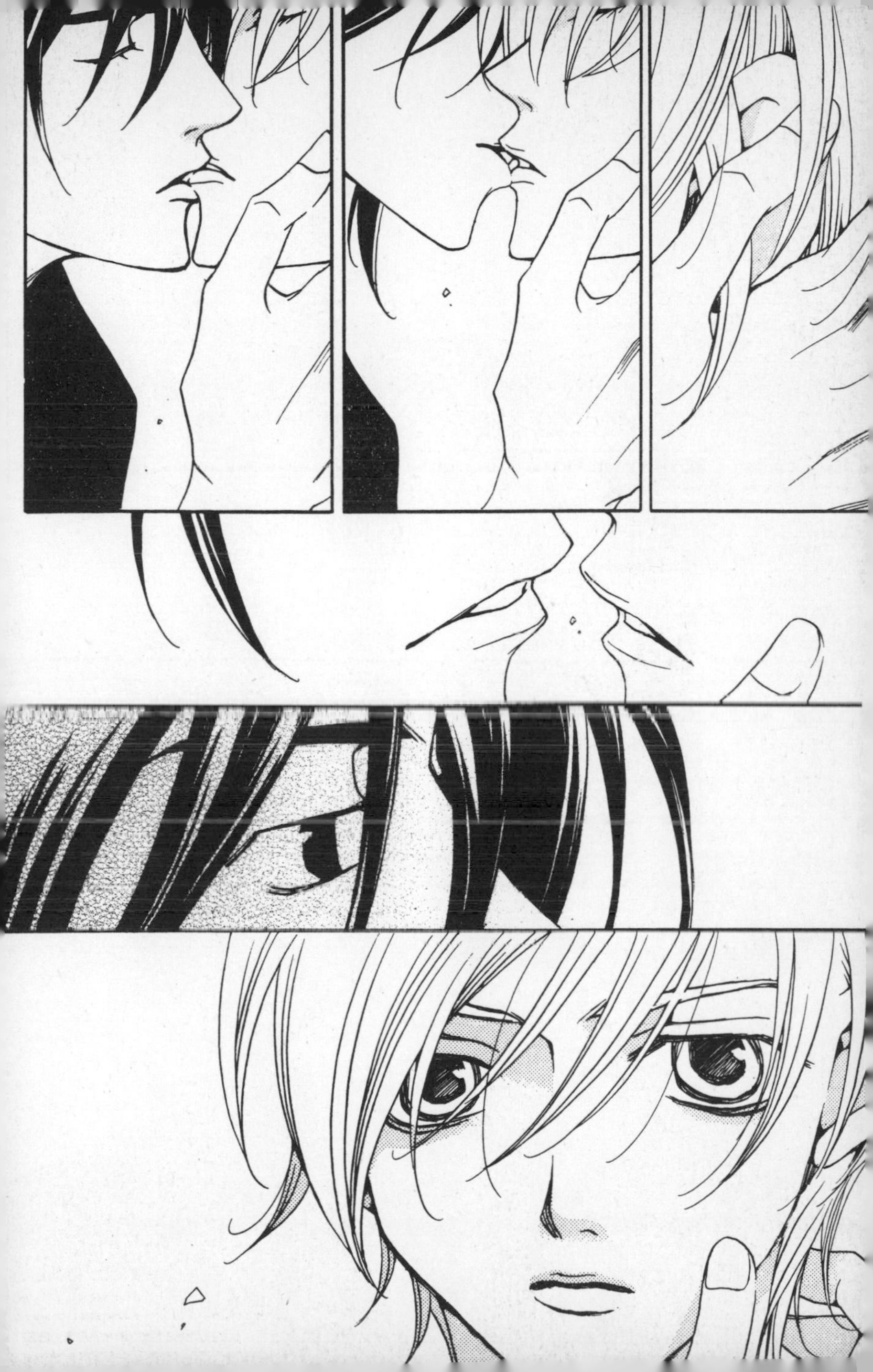

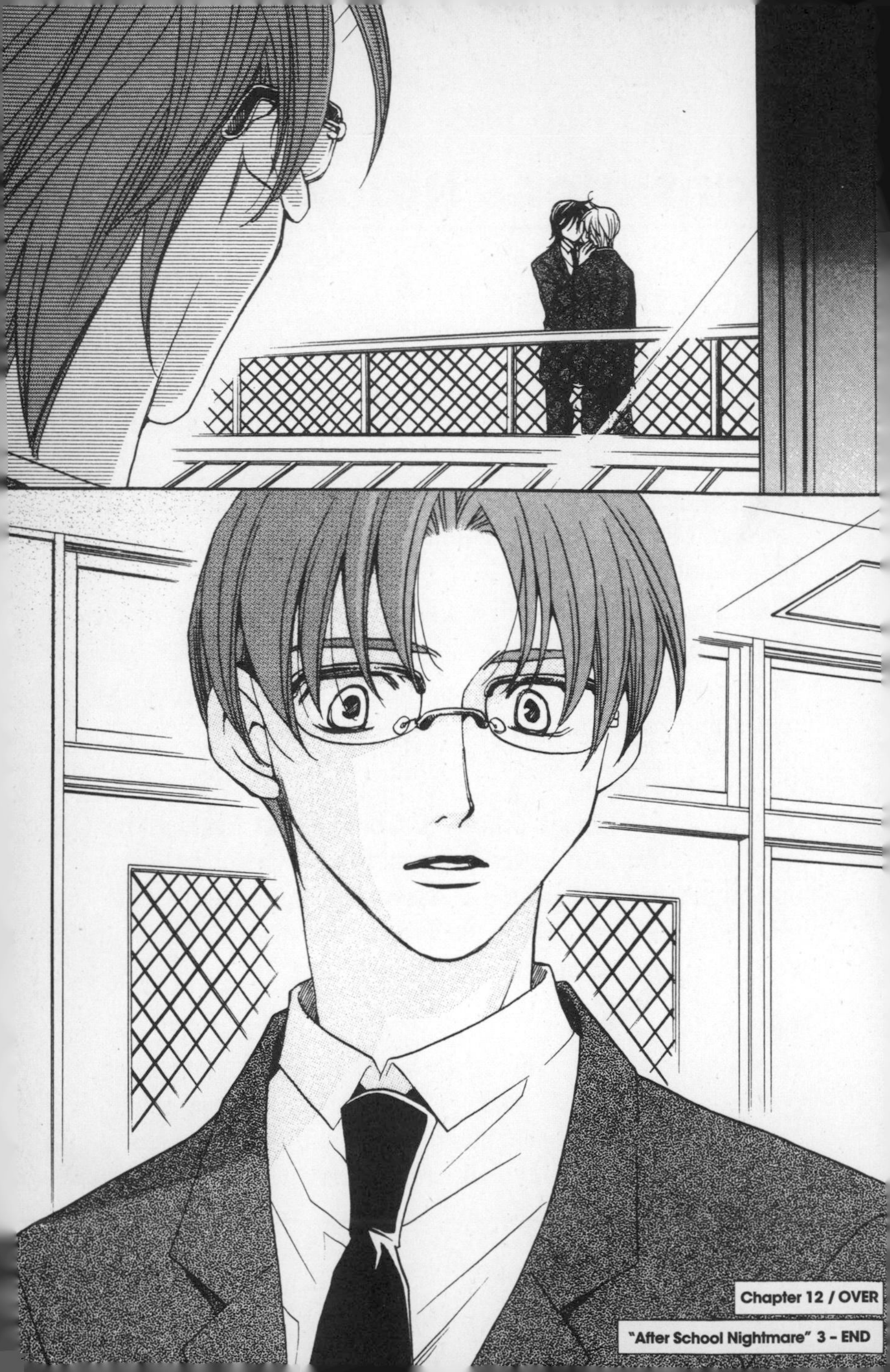
Chapter 12 / OVER
"After School Nightmare" 3 - END

Translator's Notes:

CHARACTER NAMES:
Many character names in this manga have a color-full significance!

新橋 **Shinbashi** - a traditional color in Japan that means a dark/medium turquoise.

東雲 **Shinonome** - the two kanji in this last name mean "eastern clouds" and are associated with the dawn. It is a light salmon color.

黒崎 **Kurosaki** - the first kanji in Sempai's last name means "black."

黄川田 **Kikawada** - this female student was only mentioned in passing, but the first kanji in her last name means "yellow."

Pg. 88 – Kokoku
The name of Mashiro's school, Kokoku, means "large swan" in Japanese, but also serves as a way to call someone a "great and mighty person." Besides his school being obviously elite, this name will hold deeper meaning as the story unfolds and you learn more about this eerie school!

Pg. 106 – *obento*
A boxed meal quite similar to a boxed lunch, only more common in Japanese society for old and young alike. It usually consists of rice, fish or meat, and some pickled or cooked vegetables. They make for an easy picnic, anytime!

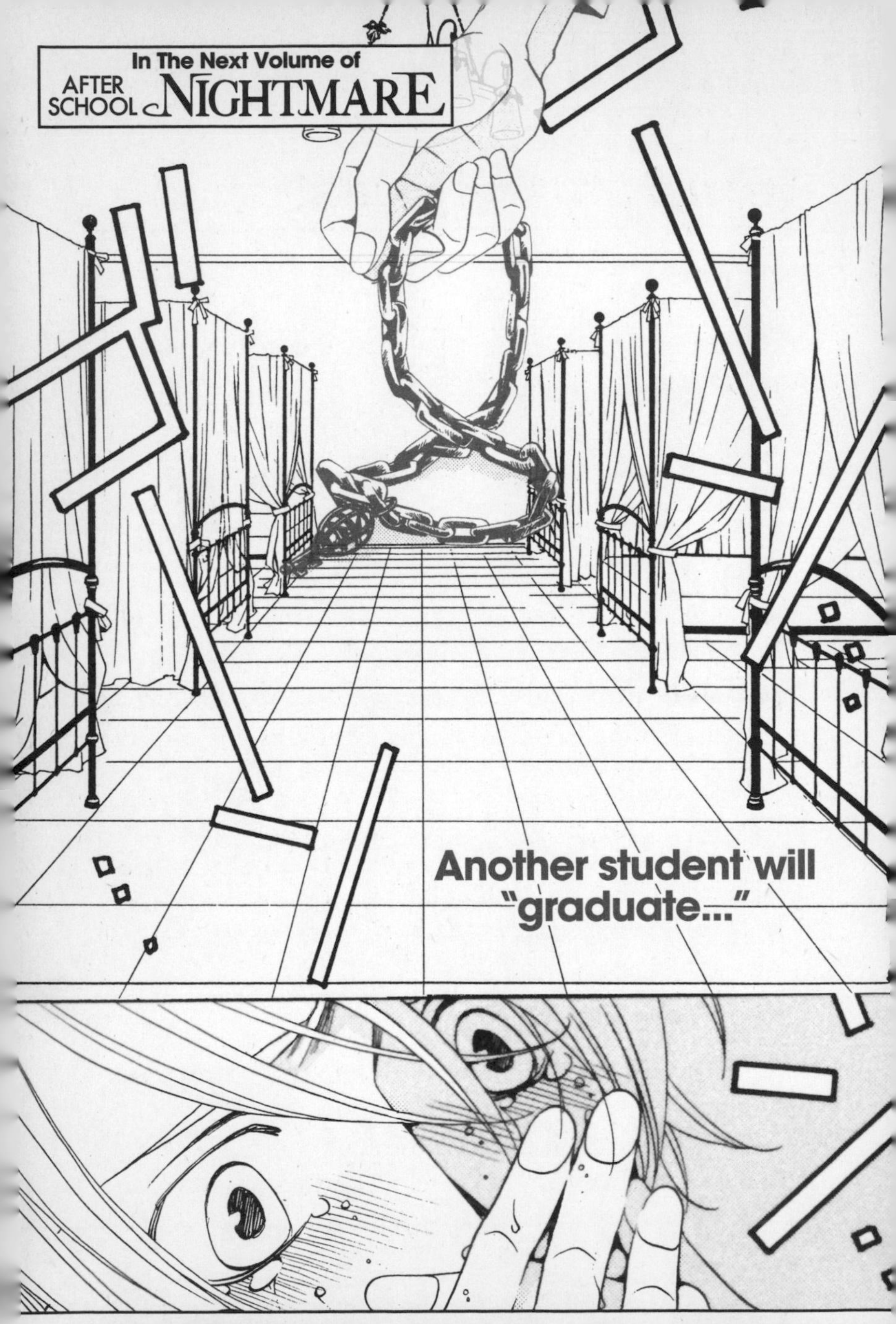
In The Next Volume of
AFTER SCHOOL NIGHTMARE
Another student will "graduate..."

...leaving not even a memory behind.

BLACK SUN ● SILVER MOON

SAVING THE WORLD... ONE ZOMBIE AT A TIME.

go!comi
THE SOUL OF MANGA

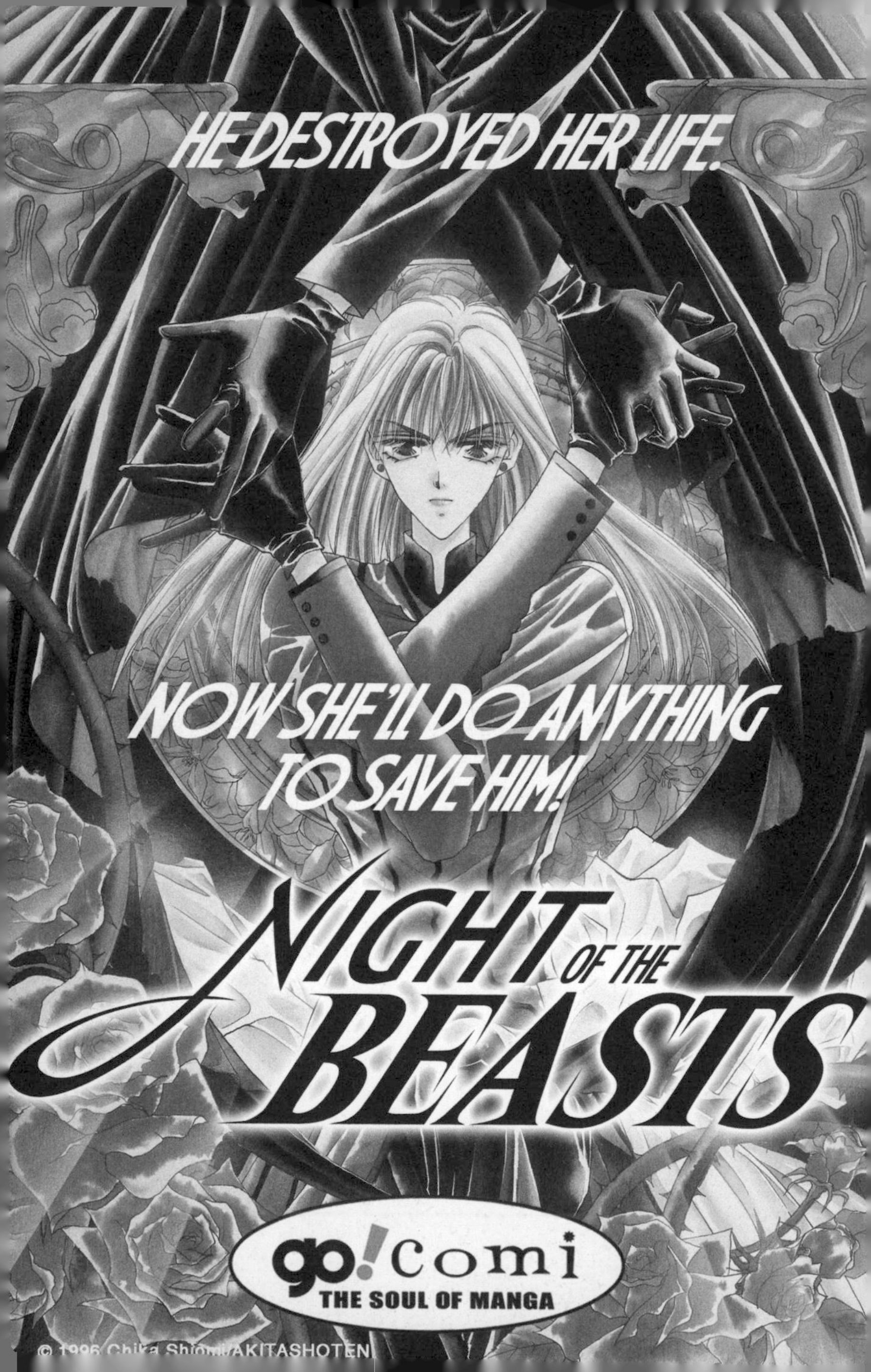
HE DESTROYED HER LIFE.
NOW SHE'LL DO ANYTHING TO SAVE HIM!
NIGHT OF THE BEASTS
go!comi
THE SOUL OF MANGA
© 1996 Chika Shiomi/AKITASHOTEN

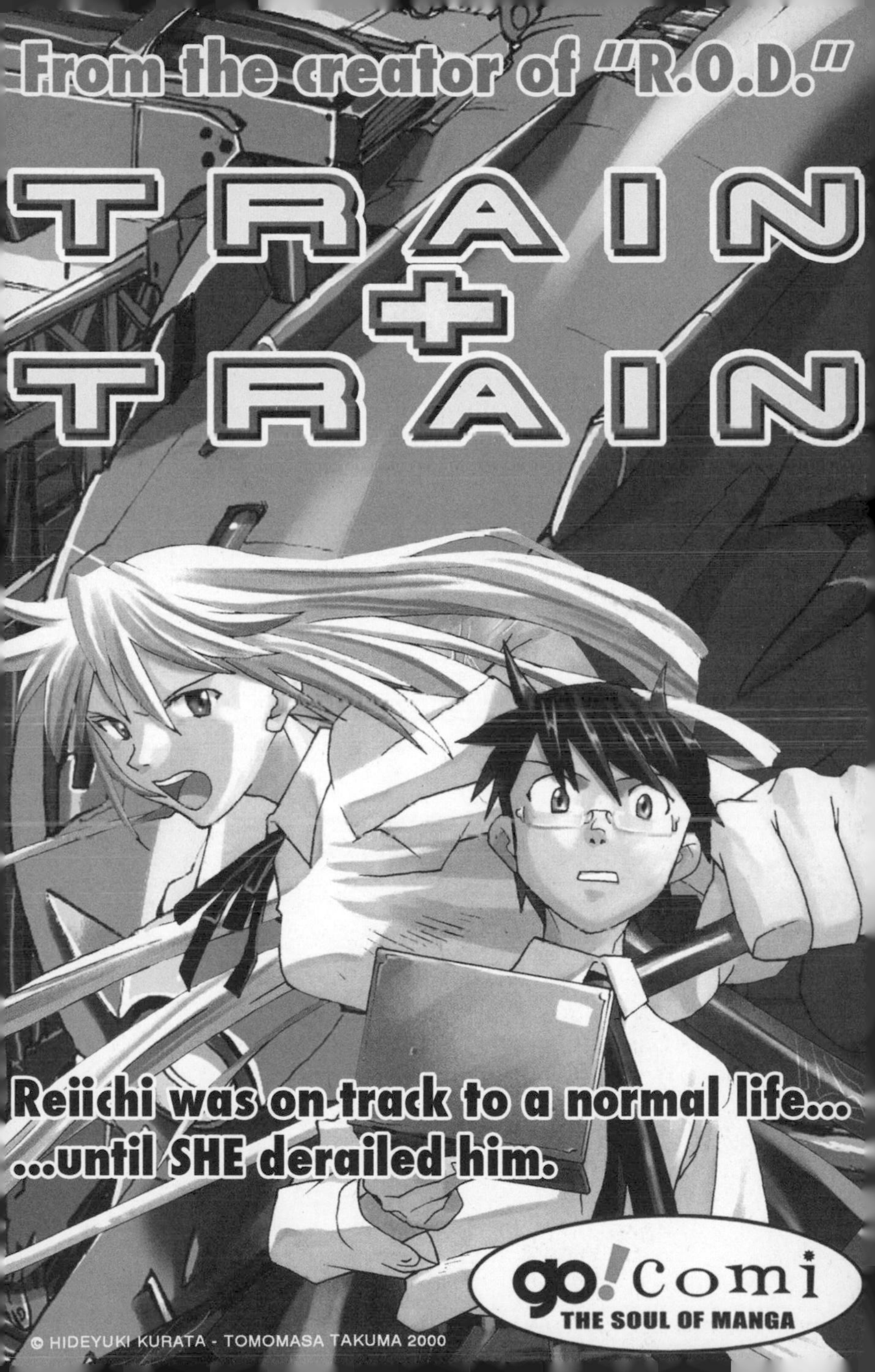

From the creator of "R.O.D."
TRAIN + TRAIN
Reiichi was on track to a normal life...
...until SHE derailed him.
go! comi
THE SOUL OF MANGA
© HIDEYUKI KURATA - TOMOMASA TAKUMA 2000

AFTER SCHOOL
NIGHTMARE

This dream draws blood.

"Enthralling!" – Library Journal

"An absolute must-buy! I haven't been this blown away by a first volume of a series in a long time."
– Anime on DVD

go! comi
THE SOUL OF MANGA

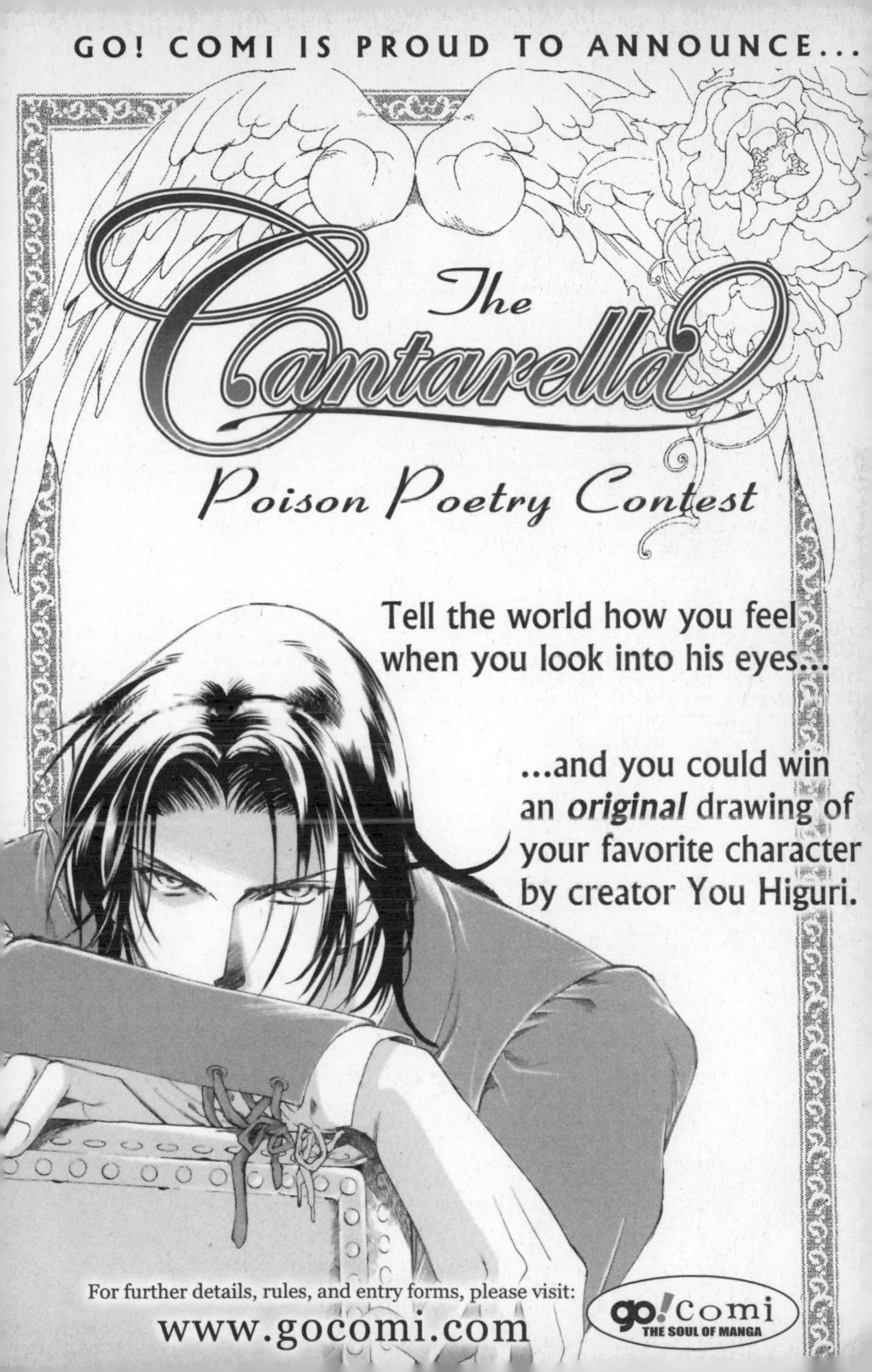
GO! COMI IS PROUD TO ANNOUNCE...
The Cantarella
Poison Poetry Contest
Tell the world how you feel when you look into his eyes...
...and you could win an *original* drawing of your favorite character by creator You Higuri.
For further details, rules, and entry forms, please visit:
www.gocomi.com
go! comi
THE SOUL OF MANGA

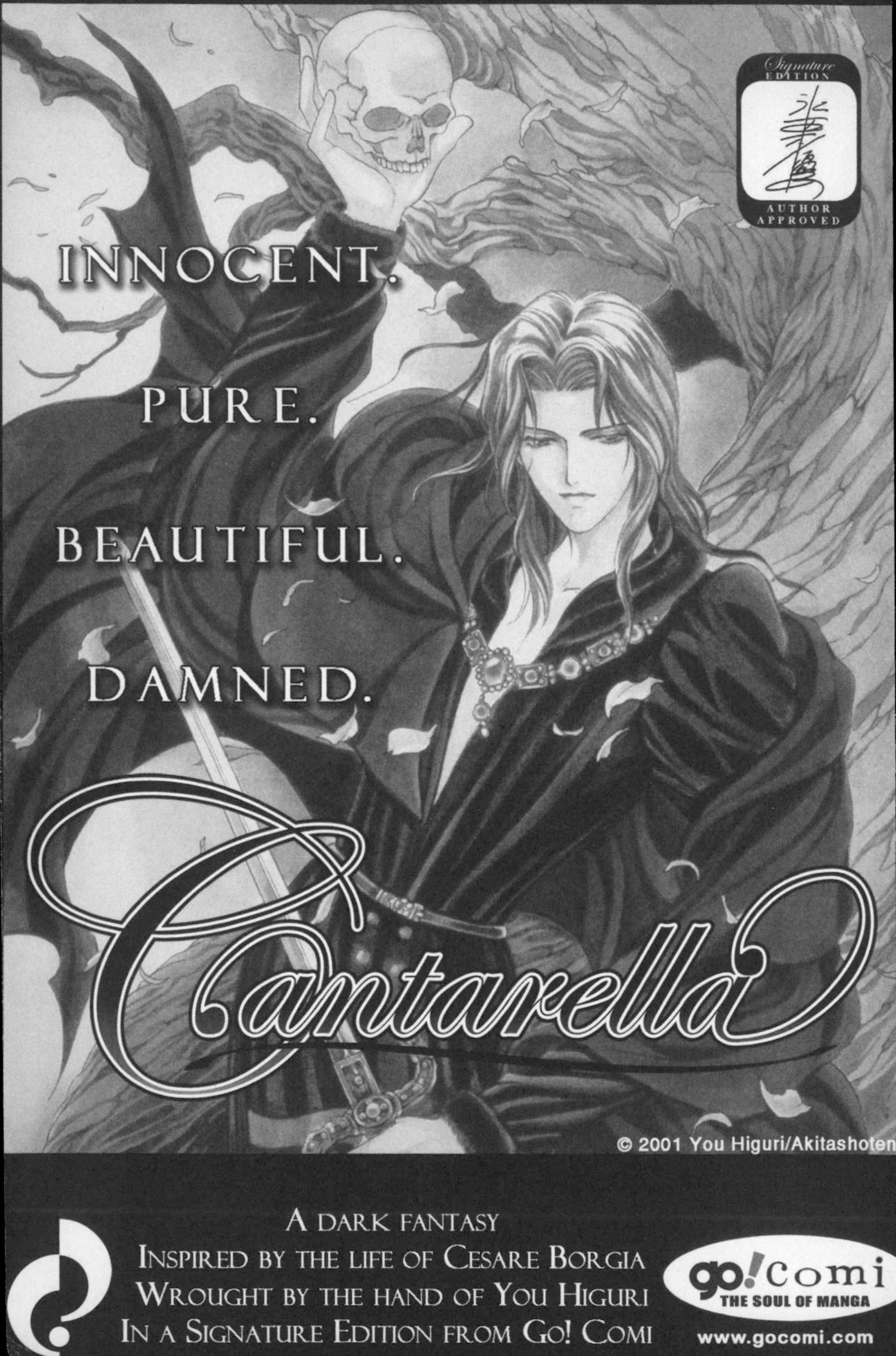
Signature EDITION
AUTHOR APPROVED
INNOCENT.
PURE.
BEAUTIFUL.
DAMNED.
Cantarella
© 2001 You Higuri/Akitashoten
A DARK FANTASY
INSPIRED BY THE LIFE OF CESARE BORGIA
WROUGHT BY THE HAND OF YOU HIGURI
IN A SIGNATURE EDITION FROM GO! COMI
go!comi
THE SOUL OF MANGA
www.gocomi.com

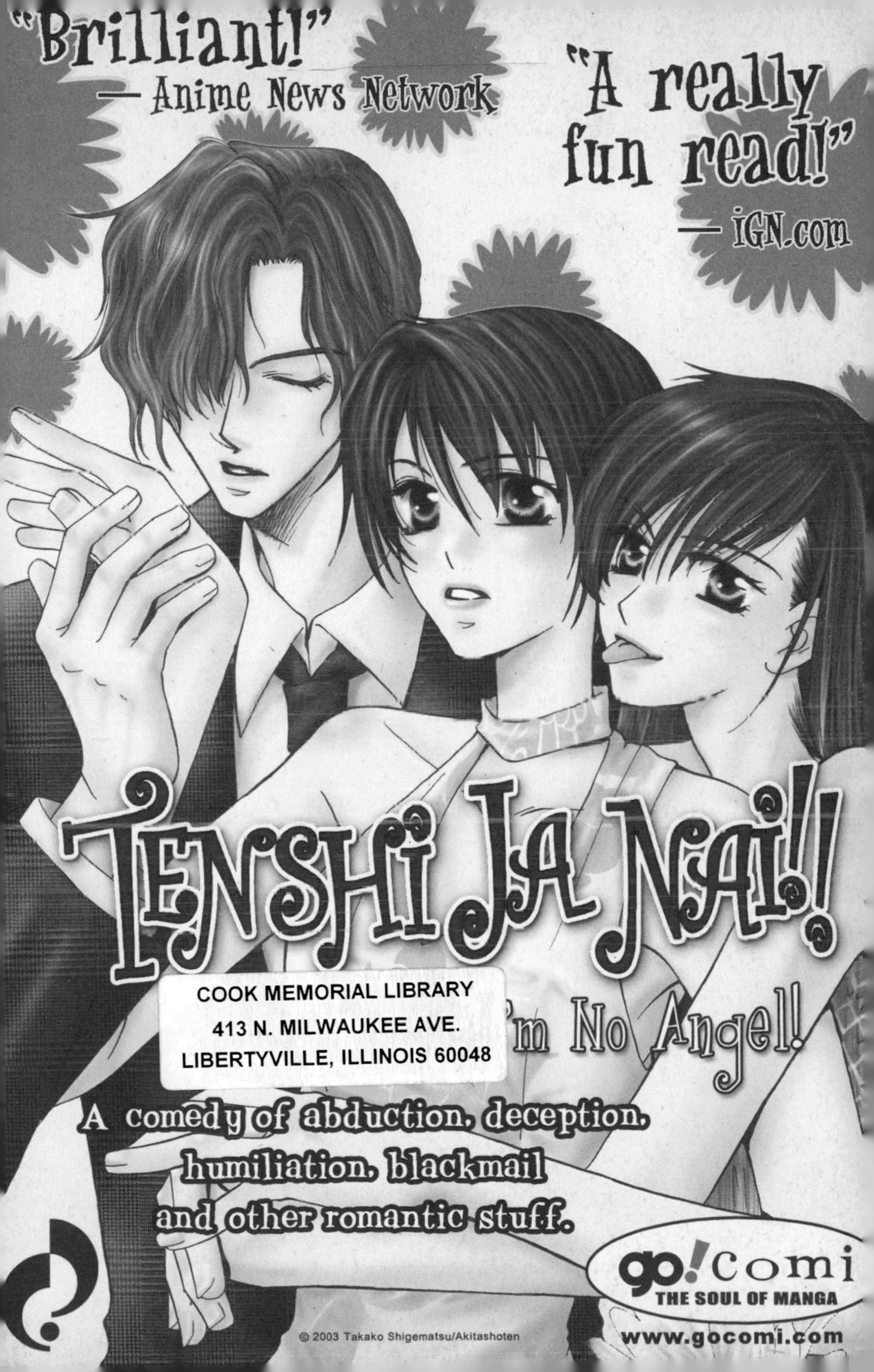
"Brilliant!"
— Anime News Network
"A really fun read!"
— IGN.com
TENSHI JA NAI!!
’m No Angel!
A comedy of abduction, deception, humiliation, blackmail and other romantic stuff.
go!comi
THE SOUL OF MANGA
www.gocomi.com
© 2003 Takako Shigematsu/Akitashoten

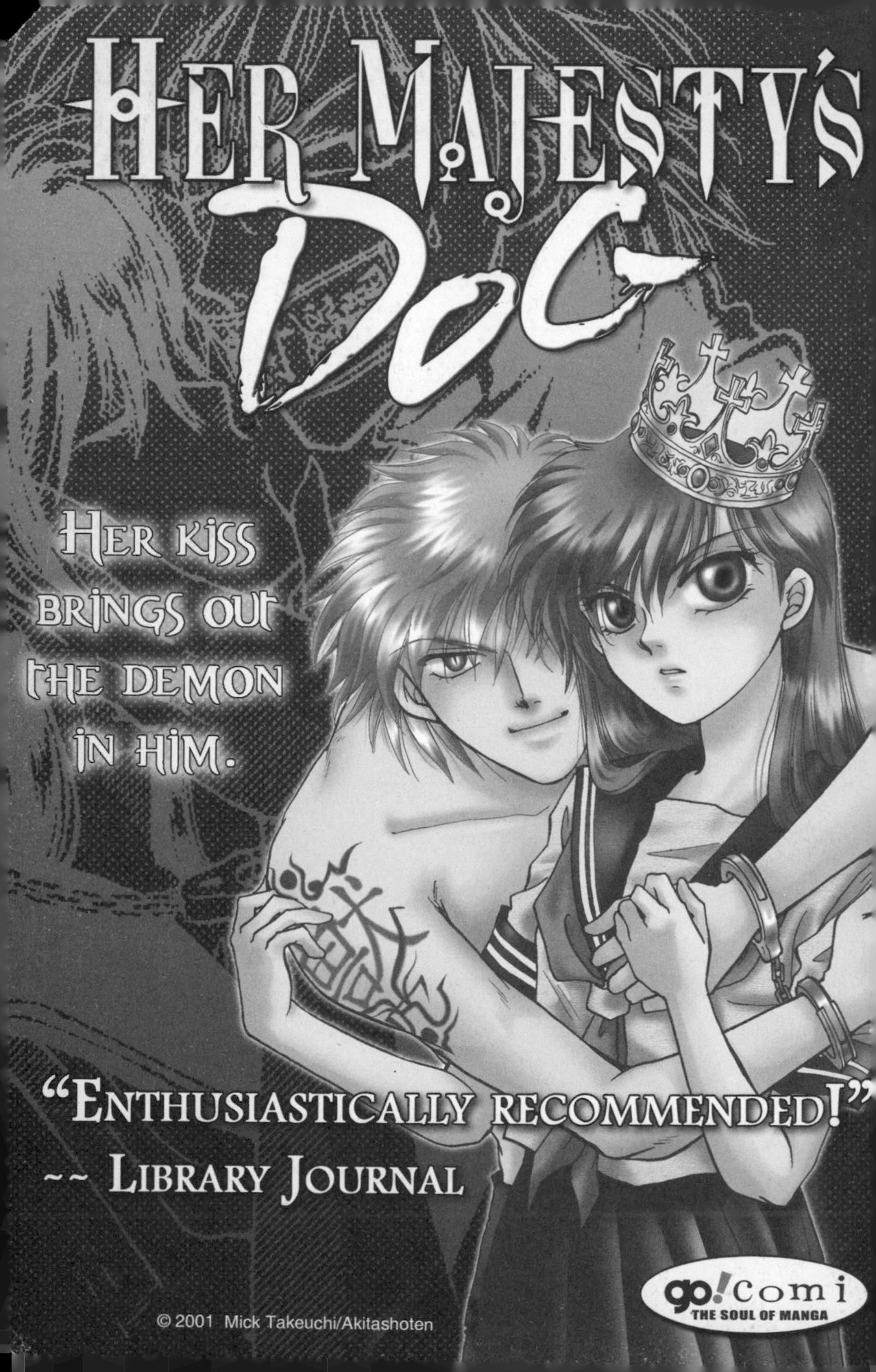
HER MAJESTY'S
DOG
HER KISS BRINGS OUT THE DEMON IN HIM.
"ENTHUSIASTICALLY RECOMMENDED!"
~~ LIBRARY JOURNAL
go!comi
THE SOUL OF MANGA
© 2001 Mick Takeuchi/Akitashoten

SETONA MIZUSHIRO

Since I had to write Shinonome's story, I went to the zoo for the first time in ten years to look at giraffes. I took photos from every angle, and drew Shinonome from the mountain of pictures I took... but... giraffe heads make for some really strange expressions! I mean, their faces are so bizarre, it's enough to make you tilt your head and wonder "Is this thing really a creature of Earth!?" (Even though that's kind of what makes them so cute.)

So, I'm sure there are a lot of you who'll read this and think "What is with that giraffe? Boy, Mizushiro did a horrible job!" when they see Shinonome's dream form. Well, I won't deny that I did a bad job... but I swear giraffes really do just have strange faces like that!

Please believe me...

ABOUT THE MANGA-KA

Setona Mizushiro's first real dabble in the world of creating manga was in 1985 when she participated in the publication of a dojinshi (amateur manga). She remained active in the dojinshi world until she debuted in April of 1993 with her short single *Fuyu ga Owarou Toshiteita* (Winter Was Ending) that ran in Shogakukan's *Puchi Comic* magazine. Mizushiro-sensei is well-known for her series *X-Day* in which she exhibits an outstanding ability to delve into psychological issues of every nature. Besides manga, Mizushiro-sensei has an affinity for chocolate, her two cats (Jam and Nene), and round sparkly objects.